www.transworldbooks.co.uk

CORGI BOOKS

TRANSWORLD PUBLISHERS
61–63 Uxbridge Road, London W5 5SA
A Random House Group Company
www.transworldbooks.co.uk

MADELEINE
A CORGI BOOK: 9780552165150

First published in Great Britain
in 2011 by Bantam Press
an imprint of Transworld Publishers
Corgi edition published 2012

Addresses for Random House Group Ltd companies outside the UK
can be found at: www.randomhouse.co.uk
The Random House Group Ltd Reg. No. 954009

Penguin Random House is committed to a sustainable future for
our business, our readers and our planet. This book is made from
Forest Stewardship Council® certified paper.

Typeset in 11/14pt Minion by Falcon Oast Graphic Art Ltd.

Printed and bound in Great Britain by Clays Ltd, Elcograf S.p.A.

8 10 9

To our three beautiful children,
Madeleine, Sean and Amelie,
for enriching our lives and making us very
proud and happy parents.

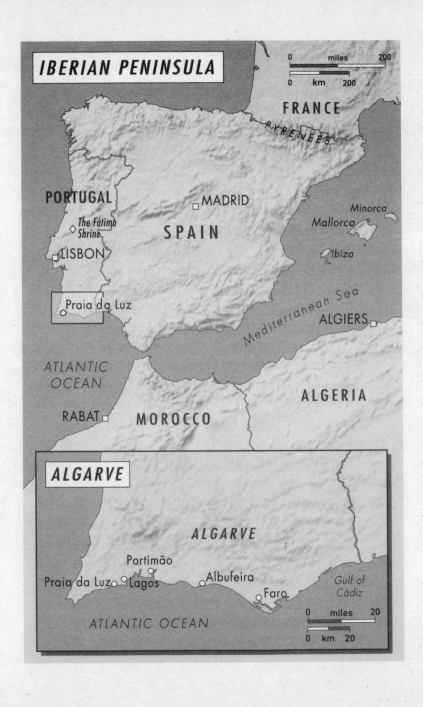

IBERIAN PENINSULA

0 miles 200
0 km 200

FRANCE

PYRENEES

PORTUGAL

♢ The Fátima Shrine

□ MADRID

SPAIN

Minorca

Mallorca

Ibiza

□ LISBON

○ Praia da Luz

Mediterranean Sea

ALGIERS □

ATLANTIC OCEAN

ALGERIA

RABAT □ MOROCCO

ALGARVE

ALGARVE

Portimão ○

Praia da Luz ○ ○ Lagos

Albufeira ○

Faro ○

Gulf of Cádiz

ATLANTIC OCEAN

0 miles 20
0 km 20

CONTENTS

FOREWORD

The decision to publish this book has been very difficult, and taken with heavy hearts. Before making up our minds to tell our story, my husband Gerry and I have had to give very careful consideration to a number of issues, not least its impact on the lives of our three children.

My reason for writing it is simple: to give an account of the truth. It has always been my intention to set down a complete record of what happened to our family, for our children, Madeleine, Sean and Amelie, so that, when they are ready, the facts will be there for them to read. I wanted to make sure they would always have access to a written chronicle of what really happened, no matter how many years have passed. They have already been through too much, and there will be further challenges ahead. Understanding our ordeal will give them the best chance of dealing with whatever life throws at them.

Choosing to share this personal account with the world has been much harder. Of course we want the truth to be told. For the past five years it has been excruciating to stand

9

by as all kinds of tales have circulated about Madeleine's disappearance and about Gerry, me and our family. The press have published a mountain of stories, often without knowing, and perhaps caring, whether or not there was any substance to them, causing great distress to our family and, more importantly, hindering the search for Madeleine. Others have seized the opportunity to profit from our agony by writing books about our daughter, several of them claiming to reveal 'what really happened'. Which is extraordinary, given that the only person who knows this is the person who abducted her on 3 May 2007. Many of these authors have no first-hand knowledge of the case and have based their theories on the half-truths, speculation and full-blown lies appearing in the media and on the internet.

Dealing with Madeleine's disappearance has been almost all-consuming, leaving us little time or strength to address these further crimes against our family. The appalling loss of our daughter has been too much to bear. Everything else, however huge, has had to take second place. There is only so much pain human beings can stand at once. It doesn't mean the injustices hurt any less. On the whole Gerry and I have managed to dig deep and remain focused, although the temptation to shout the truth from the rooftops has always been there. There have been many times when I have struggled to keep myself together and to understand how such injustices have been allowed to go unchallenged over and over again. I have had to keep saying to myself: I know the truth, we know the truth and God knows the truth. And one day, the truth will out.

Yet publishing the truth is fraught with risks for our

family. It lays us open to more criticism, for a start. We have discovered that there are those in society who will always criticize. It doesn't matter who you are, what you do or why you are doing it. We don't know what motivates these people (although I have a few theories). In the early months, I found such censure incredibly upsetting and sometimes over-whelming. Our beloved daughter had been stolen from us, we were suffering terribly and I could not begin to compre-hend why anyone would want to add to that pain. As time went on, I was able to shoulder it a little better, either by try-ing to understand why people did it (unfair as it was) or by simply trying to ignore it. These detractors didn't care about Madeleine, so why torture myself by even listening to them? We've met many wise people along the way who have stressed the importance of not being derailed by those with their own agenda. It has proved to be good advice.

We realize that Madeleine's abduction has been hard for every parent to bear. It has brought home to everyone how vulnerable our children are and how fragile our lives. I have come to understand that some of these critics have been act-ing out of self-preservation. Holding us culpable in some way makes them feel their own children are safer. Who knows how we might have reacted if this had happened to another family and we had been the ones watching from the sidelines? Whatever lies at the root of these negative reactions, they have never stopped us doing what we think is best for Madeleine, and they won't do so now. As long as we are acting in her interests, we will withstand whatever slings and arrows we must face.

The sacrifice of our privacy has been another concern.

Given the choice, we would prefer to try to sink back into the anonymity we took for granted before 3 May 2007. But our anonymity has gone now anyway, and we constantly have to weigh our desire for privacy against the need to keep our search for Madeleine in the public eye. I have wondered whether we haven't already given too much of ourselves and our family to the world. It is not something with which we are comfortable but often the considerations involved in such decisions seem irreconcilable. Writing this memoir has entailed recording some very personal, intimate and emotional aspects of our lives. Sharing these with strangers does not come easily to me, but if I hadn't done so I would not have felt the book gave as full a picture as it is possible for me to give. As with every action we have taken over the last five years, it ultimately boils down to whether what we are doing could help us to find Madeleine. When the answer to that question is yes, or even possibly, our family can cope with anything.

My biggest worry has undoubtedly been invading the privacy of our children. My account obviously exposes them, to a certain extent, as well as Gerry and myself. Later in their lives they may feel I have made public information they would prefer had been kept private. My instinct tells me, however, that it will be far more important to Sean and Amelie to know that their mum and dad have left no stone unturned in their efforts to find their big sister, and if that has included publishing a book, I'm sure they will understand and accept that necessity. And I have no doubt that Madeleine, too, would feel the same way.

What tipped the balance in our decision is the continuing

need to fund the search for Madeleine. While she remains missing, the onus has been on us to keep looking for her, since after July 2008 there was no longer any law-enforcement agency *at all* actively looking into her disappearance. Investigations and campaigns cost money, which we have had to raise. It is still a struggle for me to see beyond tomorrow. Every day I wake up hoping this will be the day we find Madeleine. But having lived through five painful years without my dear daughter, I have reluctantly been forced to acknowledge that our quest could take weeks, months or yet more years, and the reality is we have to ensure we have adequate funding for the long term. Every penny we raise through the sales of this book will be spent on our search for Madeleine. Nothing is more important to us than finding our little girl.

We are also hopeful that this book may help the investigation in other ways. Perhaps it might prompt someone who has relevant information (maybe without even knowing it) to come forward and share it.

Somebody holds that key piece of the jigsaw. Indirectly, it may boost our search simply by enlightening those who, for whatever reason, believe Madeleine is no longer alive, or that there is nothing else that can be done to find her. We trust it will put to rest some of the myths that have sprung up around her abduction. As will become clear in the following pages, while we still do not know what happened to Madeleine, there remains no evidence whatsoever to suggest that she has come to serious harm.

Although writing this book has been a time-consuming and, at times, heartbreaking experience, it has been made a little easier by the fact that I have kept a daily journal since towards the end of May 2007. This is something that would not have occurred to me. It was suggested by a man I met in the course of the innumerable meetings Gerry and I had that month with experts helping us to negotiate the emotional and practical minefield in which we found ourselves. I am for ever in his debt for this advice. Initially, it seemed a good way of keeping a record for Madeleine of what happened in the days she was away from us, but writing everything down turned out to be immensely therapeutic for me. It provided me with a release valve for my thoughts and extreme feelings. It was a place where I could shout what I was unable to shout from the rooftops. And it gave me a means of communicating with Madeleine.

My journal was also to prove invaluable when Gerry and I later felt it necessary to quash claims made about where we were and what we were doing at various times. Now it has been pressed into service once more as the basis for much of this book. It has enabled me to recall with clarity my innermost reflections at periods when my whole life was clouded by despair, and it is the reason why I have been able, four years down the line, to be so precise about the timings of particular events.

What follows is an intensely personal account, and I make no apology for that. Since 3 May 2007, there has undoubtedly been much going on behind the scenes we haven't known about and perhaps never will. I have been as open as possible about everyone involved in the story. As our investigation is still ongoing, and for legal reasons, some opinions or episodes cannot be shared until Madeleine is found. I hope readers will understand this and not judge this record harshly because of it.

Thank you for buying and reading this book. In doing so you are supporting the search for our daughter.

1

GERRY

Before 3 May 2007, I was Kate Healy, a GP married to a consultant cardiologist and the mother of three children. We were a perfectly ordinary family. Boring, even. Since settling down to bring up our longed-for babies, Gerry and I had become such strangers to the fast lane that we were often the butt of good-natured teasing from our friends. We'd give anything to have that boring life back now.

It began for me in Liverpool, where I was born in 1968 – on the first day of an eleven-week bus strike, according to my mum. My parents, too, were Liverpool born and bred, though my dad's family were originally from Ireland and my mum's mum from County Durham. My dad, Brian Healy, was a joiner, and served his time initially at Cammell Laird shipbuilders. My mum, Susan, trained as a teacher when I was small – which can't have been an easy juggling act – but eventually ended up working for the Civil Service. I was an only child, which prompts many people to assume, quite wrongly, that I must have grown up either spoiled or introverted, or both. I certainly never went without food, or clothes, or love, but I was not spoiled in material terms, and if I was a little shy, I don't remember ever being lonely.

Until I was nearly five, home was a cul-de-sac in Huyton, in the east of the city. It was also home to several big families, and my earliest memories are of fun-filled days playing outside with the neighbours' kids. After we left Huyton I returned often to join my friends for games of Kerby and Kick the Can in the street. I'm sure the residents didn't enjoy that as much as we did, and if there is anyone out there who still remembers it less than fondly, I apologize. Better late than never.

A couple of years after my maternal grandmother died, still only in her fifties, we moved in with my grandad in Anfield. Now retired, he had been chief clerk for a firm importing nuts and dried fruits. He had excellent accounting skills but, like many men of his generation, he hadn't a clue about housework or cooking, and he was struggling without my nana. Yet I remember him always being very smartly turned out, appearing in shirt, tie and waistcoat for church every day. I went regularly, too. I was baptized and brought up in the Roman Catholic faith, I attended Catholic schools and went to Mass on Sundays. It was expected of me, it was what I was used to and I didn't question it.

So my Catholicism and my belief in God were part of the foundations of my life and I didn't question them, either, or at least, not to any great extent. There were momentary blips when I wrestled with life's big issues quietly in my mind – God, the universe, my own existence – but for the most part I was satisfied with what I'd come to believe and what I'd been told by the people who mattered to me. I might not have acknowledged my faith on a daily basis – and there were certainly times when church took a back seat, especially in my university days – but it was always there in the background, a source of comfort, refuge and support.

Perhaps because I didn't have brothers or sisters, I have always been very close to my cousins, and I had plenty of mates, many of whom remain dear to me to this day – one of them, Lynda, a neighbour in Huyton, has known me since I was born. Our mothers were friends then and still are. As well as being shy I was quite sensitive, which aren't qualities to be envied, as I have discovered, but I loved company and wasn't one to sit around quietly on my own.

Michelle and Nicky have been my friends since primary school. I met Michelle on our first day at All Saints in Anfield, and we were inseparable from that moment onwards. At the time my parents were planning a family trip to Canada to visit Auntie Norah, my dad's sister, who had emigrated there, and I was very excited about it. Michelle must have been an immediate hit with me because I asked her on that first day at school if she'd like to come with us. Naturally, she said yes, and she was rather upset when she got home and her mum put paid to that idea. Michelle and I both passed the Eleven-Plus and went on together to Everton Valley (Notre Dame Collegiate School), followed the next year by her sister Lynne, who is ten months younger. They came from a big Catholic family and I spent every Tuesday evening at their house. They came to mine every Friday. In the holidays we were rarely apart, either. I even used to go to the Liverpool FC parties in their street (well, this was the 1970s), which, given that the Healys were dyed-in-the-wool Blues, speaks volumes for my love for Michelle.

Nicky was another All Saints pupil. Although our educational paths diverged when I went on to Everton Valley, she lived very close to me and we remained firm friends. If you asked my mum for her abiding memory of Nicky when we were kids, she'd instantly say, 'Pickled onion crisps.' We used to have midnight feasts when Nicky stayed overnight and leave the evidence under the bed. They didn't all involve pickled onion crisps, but apparently it is that unmistakable aroma that sticks in my mum's mind from those innocent days. Nicky has always been happy-go-lucky and full of energy. She was a great singer and dancer – she grew up to become a fitness instructor – and we spent many days together making up little dance routines to 1970s disco hits like Baccara's 'Yes Sir, I Can Boogie'. I'd like to say we were good but I have a feeling only one of us was. She was a real tonic, Nic. She still is.

At school I was hardworking and conscientious and did well academically. I think the fact that I was sporty, too, and was always picked for the school team – I was netball captain for a while, and played rounders in the summer – was what saved me from being branded a swot. At that stage I didn't have a particular career in mind. My decision to opt for a degree in medicine emerged gradually from the choices I made after my O-levels. So it wasn't a lifelong vocation. In my early teens I wanted to become a haematologist and find a cure for leukaemia (God knows where that came from, or how I even had a clue what a haematologist was). I'd also toyed with the idea of training as a vet. When choosing my A-level subjects I wasn't sure initially whether to go with three sciences or maths, economics and French, and then, when looking ahead to university, whether to aim for medicine or engineering. At both crossroads I could have gone either way.

Although I wanted a fulfilling and worthwhile career I have never been overly ambitious, except in one respect: it was no secret to anyone who knew me that my main goal in life was to be a mother, and preferably a mother to many. I certainly wasn't one of those girls prepared to devote everything I had to climbing to the pinnacle of my profession if it meant sacrificing relationships and babies along the way. That might be viewed as lame by some, though not, I suspect, by most mothers. When I graduated from Dundee University in 1992 my entry in the university yearbook concluded with the line: 'Prognosis: mathematician and mother of six.' I achieved neither of these predictions, but I was extremely happy and proud to end up with the best prize imaginable: my three beautiful children.

Dundee University might seem a surprising choice for a Scouse girl with no particular Scottish connections. But back then it was almost a rite of passage for students from English schools to choose a university a decent distance from home, and Dundee came into the equation when it was recommended to me by a good friend who knew somebody studying there. I went up to have a look at the university and was shown round by a very amiable bunch of fourth-year students. It was Guy Fawkes night, I remember, they were all going on to a party afterwards and they invited me to go along with them. There were so many student parties and other social events happening over the next few days that I wound up staying there rather longer than I'd planned. I had a ball and was made to feel really welcome.

So Dundee it was for me. The social scene lived up to its initial promise (partying is practically obligatory for medical students, after all) and I made lots of friends. I had a fantastic time at university and did my best to achieve a balance between work and play, not always successfully. I kept myself fit by playing for the university netball team. After qualifying in 1992, the next step was to complete two six-month stints as a junior house officer, one in general medicine and one in general surgery or orthopaedics (I opted for the latter). On finishing my first six-month post, at King's Cross Hospital in Dundee, I felt I was ready for a change of scene, and the bright lights of the big city – Glasgow – beckoned.

It was in Glasgow in 1993 that I remember first meeting Gerry McCann. He says that we actually met in 1992, when we were both interviewed for the same job (neither of us got it), but I have no recollection of that. Sorry, Ger. He had qualified in medicine in the same year as me from Glasgow University (Scotland has a much stronger tradition of students going to local universities). Although we didn't work together early in our careers we moved in the same circles and our paths often crossed in the course of the many social events so beloved of junior doctors, including the infamous doctors' and nurses' 'pay night' extravaganza at Cleopatra's nightclub, affectionately known as Clatty Pats.

Gerry was good-looking, confident and outgoing. He also had a reputation as a bit of a lad. But as I got to know him I discovered a natural warmth and honesty, especially when he talked about his family, that revealed an endearing sweetness and vulnerability beneath the potentially intimidating façade.

We had quite a lot in common apart from our profession. We both came from ordinary, working-class Catholic families with Irish roots. Like me, Gerry had attended Catholic schools and gone to Mass on Sundays. Of course, when we first met we didn't know this about each other and it wouldn't have entered either of our heads to ask, though our names would have been a pretty strong clue if we'd thought about it. And Gerry's dad was a joiner, like mine. His mum, Eileen, had been born in Glasgow to Irish parents. She had been sent to live with her grandmother in Donegal shortly after the outbreak of the Second World War, returning to Glasgow when it was over. Gerry's father, Johnny, was from St Johnston in County Donegal, just over the border with Northern Ireland.

Johnny had had a tough start in life. He'd lost his mother, his elder brother and his father before he was sixteen. After spending some time with an uncle in Sligo, Johnny found himself responsible for his father's pub and a small brother. Having been forced to give up his own education at a Jesuit college, Johnny wanted better for his own children and insisted that they all worked hard to gain the grades to get to university.

Unlike my own family, Gerry's was large and boisterous. Born in the same year as I was, 1968, he was the youngest of Johnny and Eileen's five children. He has an elder brother, also Johnny, and there are three sisters in between them –

Trisha, Jackie and Phil. From Gerry's stories it sounds as if it was a fun, loud and colourful household, quite mad at times. It must have been hard, too: seven people living in a one-bedroom place in a Glasgow tenement – and that was without the occasional 'lodger' with nowhere else to go who'd be offered a berth on the floor. Johnny senior was away working for long periods, and Eileen also worked intermittently, as a shop assistant and later as a cleaner, so 'wee Gerry' was often entrusted to the care of his elder siblings. But life in a tenement full of Catholic families and hordes of other kids had more advantages than dis-advantages. Everyone was in the same boat, so to the McCann children and those of their neighbours, this was perfectly normal, and nobody felt deprived.

Like me, Gerry did well academically in school. By the time he came along, the family work ethic was well established, his goals had been set for him and he followed in the high-achieving footsteps of his brother and sisters, com-peting with them and always determined to do even better. 'Shy' and 'Gerry' are words that would never occur in the same sentence. All the McCann children are very sociable and self-assured – and McCann confidence is of the kind that would make you a fortune if you could bottle it and sell it. My dad often cheekily remarks that they were born with silver microphones in their mouths.

Gerry was good at sport, too, and being Gerry he was hugely competitive. Middle-distance running was his forte and at seventeen he was the fastest in Scotland in his age group over 800 metres. At Glasgow University he ran with the Hares and Hounds club, whose team strip was a hideous bright yellow. Fine for sports kit, but he was so attached to his running shirt that he insisted on wearing it out socially as well. You could see him coming from a mile away.

To me, the contrasting strands of Gerry's personality – the confidence and ebullience interwoven with that honesty and openness – combined to produce a very engaging and attractive man. He was a lot of fun on one hand and kind, serious and loving on the other. And yet I kept my distance and tried to play it cool. It was his jack-the-lad image that held me back, I suppose. I was hesitant to plunge into a relationship in which I might end up getting hurt and I guess there was an element of pride to it, too. I didn't want to be just one of a succession of girlfriends. It all seems a bit silly now, after Gerry's wonderful qualities have been confirmed to me so many times over the years. I'm not suggesting that his reputation as a ladies' man was completely without foundation – it wasn't – but there is no doubt that it was unfairly exaggerated, as these things often are, and that I paid too much attention to gossip. And believe me, I know now how damaging that can be. As things turned out, it took both of us moving to the other side of the world to finally bring us together as a couple.

I was keen to travel, and I knew if that was going be anything more than a pipe dream I needed to do it sooner rather than later. The further my career progressed, the more committed I was likely to become at work and the more difficult it would be to break away. After completing my 'house jobs' (as they were known then – basically a doctor's first year post-qualification), I'd found myself embarking on a career in obstetrics and gynaecology. While that hadn't been my intention – I'd planned simply to gain the experience I needed for general practice – I really enjoyed O&G. Looking back, I have to admit that the departmental social scene was great, too, and this might well have added to its appeal. But it was an incredibly busy and competitive area, with many apparently dissatisfied and overworked doctors, mostly women, stuck on middle grades, and I wasn't completely sure it was for me.

Early in 1995, during an oncology posting I'd taken up to enhance my O&G training, I started to apply for jobs in Australia via an organized scheme. I also sent one letter on spec to a hospital in New Zealand at the suggestion of a Kiwi colleague. I was expecting a formal response by post in due course, so I was somewhat taken aback when I was called to the phone one day at work and found myself being offered a job by a neo-natal consultant in Auckland. I said yes.

While I'd been making these applications, at the back of my mind there was always the lurking regret that if I went away, the chances were I'd lose touch with Gerry. We hadn't talked about our respective plans, and what I didn't know was that he, too, was seeking to work abroad, in either the US or New Zealand. Later, the unfair, if not entirely serious, story doing the rounds of the Glasgow hospitals grapevine had it that as soon as Gerry found out I was going to Auckland, he decided to chase me across the world and immediately started applying for jobs himself in the Land of the Long White Cloud. Flattering though this version of events may be from my point of view, the truth was that he was already waiting to hear back from several hospitals in both New Zealand and America. What I would like to think, however, is that the news that I would be in Auckland made the decision between the two countries a bit easier for him!

I was the first to leave, in July 1995, and I arrived in New Zealand not knowing a soul. On my first day in my new job a friend of a friend with whom I'd been put in touch rang me to see how I'd got on and asked casually, 'Want to come for a run tonight?' in the way that at home we'd say, 'Fancy a beer after work?' Although I was sporty, running was not part of my repertoire – that was Gerry's province. But as this guy was the only person I knew in Auckland, I agreed.

That evening I found myself squelching and puffing across a muddy field. Every step involved trying to yank your foot out of the clinging mire. My new Kiwi mate pointed to a hill up ahead. 'One Tree Hill?' he suggested. I nodded confidently. All the way up he was making conversation, asking questions to which I barely had the breath to give one-word answers. Honest to God, I thought I was going to die. When, mercifully, we reached the summit he stretched out his arm to show me the view spread out beneath and around us. From this 182-metre volcanic peak, a famous Auckland landmark, you can see the whole city. 'Look at that!' he enthused. 'And look at those amazing clouds!' All I could think was, sod the clouds – I'm going to be sick.

But I wasn't about to be beaten by One Tree Hill. The next evening, I went out to do the run on my own and I did it again and again until I'd conquered it. That's me. I might not be the most ambitious woman in the world, but what I do have, in abundance, is determination and doggedness. After that I became a bit of a convert and, as well as playing mixed netball in New Zealand, I began to run regularly. Given Gerry's devotion to the sport, it was probably just as well I enjoyed it too.

I loved my job in the neo-natal unit, and I loved working with babies, but it was something of a baptism of fire. I was classed as a registrar even though I had no neo-natal experience and had junior doctors working under me who did. I was going to be putting big, fancy lines into tiny, twenty-four-week-old babies on my own. 'Just give us a ring and we'll come in for the first few, then you'll be fine,' the consultant said. And I was. I just needed to get used to the laid-back Kiwi way of doing things. Once I had, I found New Zealanders to be lovely, capable, easygoing people who worked to live rather than the other way round.

Gerry arrived in the country two months after I did but he wasn't exactly round the corner. His post, in general medicine and cardiology, was in Napier – a flight or over five hours by road from Auckland. But in spite of the distances involved we saw as much of one another as we could. Away from home, and from everyone else we knew, we focused on each other at last and our relationship immediately moved up a notch to the romantic level. In some ways the fact that we'd been friendly for over two years made that transition easier. We already knew quite a lot about each other, after all. Initially, though, adjusting to this new footing was a bit strange and awkward, and we were both very nervous, like teenagers going on their first few dates. Thankfully, that stage soon passed.

After my stint at the neo-natal unit, I took a six-month job in O&G in Wellington (which is about the same distance from Napier as Auckland). We were in New Zealand for a year altogether. It was an amazing time and we were so happy. We both loved the country and our lives there. I think Gerry would seriously have considered staying on for good but, sad as I was to leave, for me it was just too far away from my family and friends, particularly my parents. And now there was no question that wherever we went, it would be as a couple. Having finally found each other, we felt we were the luckiest people on the planet.

So in September 1996 we returned to Glasgow, Gerry to the Western Infirmary and to begin his research for an MD in exercise physiology, while I worked initially at the maternity unit at the Queen Mother's Hospital before transferring to anaesthetics at the Western Infirmary in 1997. We rented a flat together to start with and then bought our own terraced house very close to Gerry's brother Johnny and his family. We were married in Liverpool in December 1998 by our good friend Father Paul Seddon. We chose the weekend before Christmas for the wedding: with our friends and extended families scattered all over the place, taking advantage of the holiday period was the best way of making sure as many of them as possible could be there. Added to that, I had always loved Christmastime. It was a wonderful day, and we looked forward eagerly to our future as a married couple and to the children who would make our lives complete.

2

MADELEINE

Gerry and I were keen to start a family as soon as possible, but after a couple of years with no sign of a pregnancy, it became clear that it wasn't going to be as easy as we'd assumed. Those who have been lucky enough to conceive effortlessly often fail to appreciate how heartbreaking and testing trying fruitlessly for a baby can be: month after month of aching disappointment, punctuated by a mid-cycle urgency to have sex at the crucial time, which removes all the spontaneity, and much of the fun, from making love. Sex becomes a clinical requirement rather than an enjoyable and intimate experience. And as time drags by, you find yourself having to force a joyful smile and congratulate your friends as they become pregnant, apparently without the slightest difficulty.

We were now living in Leicestershire, having taken the decision to move south in 2000 to enable Gerry to take up a training post in cardiology, positions that were very hard to come by. Even then, he had to complete the first part of his rotation in Boston in Lincolnshire, a two-hour, cross-country drive away. By this time I had been promoted to a registrar post in anaesthetics in Glasgow and was working hard towards completing my postgraduate exams or 'fellowship'. Within six months, I'd been able to transfer to the registrar rotation in Leicester and we had settled in Queniborough, a picture-postcard village with a couple of pubs, a general store and an excellent butcher.

By coincidence my mum's brother, Brian Kennedy, lived in Rothley, just ten minutes along the road. Now retired, he had been headmaster of a school in Loughborough. I was close to Uncle Brian and Auntie Janet – when I was a child we'd spent every Christmas and Easter with them – and their children, Aileen and James, were like a little sister and brother to me. It was a great bonus to have family nearby. Leicester wasn't Liverpool or Glasgow, and I found people more reserved than I was used to, but our neighbours, a mix of young professionals and retired people, were all new, too (our mews home was part of the recent conversion of an old country house, so everyone there was new), and that helped.

Shortly after we moved to Queniborough I decided to leave anaesthetics and train for general practice. It wasn't an easy decision to make – I was happy in anaesthetics, and it meant that my fellowship would be redundant in terms of furthering my career – but just as Gerry was finishing his stint in Boston I was due to begin six months there. I felt that if we both continued to work as hospital specialists, on call at different times and in different places, it would not only be our quality of life that suffered but also our chances of conceiving a child.

With the variety of hospital posts I already had under my

belt, all I needed was a six-month position in psychiatry to gain the breadth of experience required for GP training. However, I still wanted to finish my anaesthetics fellowship. It entailed loads of work and everybody told me I was crazy to carry on with it. But I had started it, I wanted to complete it, and I did. Deep down, Gerry understood. We are both 'finishers', Gerry and I. Neither of us gives up anything easily.

I did my GP training at a surgery in Melton Mowbray, one of the first specialist GP practices in the country, which is among the largest in the UK. It boasts a number of GPs with specialist interests, including cardiology, ophthalmology, dermatology, sports medicine and ENT, as well as a sizeable team of nurses, receptionists and so on, and operates an internal referral system, whereby one GP can refer a patient to the appropriately qualified colleague. This system greatly reduces the number of patients having to be sent to hospital with conditions that can be treated in the surgery by a GP with expertise in the relevant field.

When I'd finished my training I secured a locum post at the surgery. I enjoyed the job, particularly attending and chatting to the old folk, though I found it much harder in many respects than working in a hospital. In general practice you are right at the coalface, with no idea what you are going to be presented with next. Although you have the support of your colleagues, you are working much more independently, making quick decisions on your own all day long about a limitless array of problems without lab tests and X-rays on hand to guide you. Both jobs can be stressful, of course, in their different ways, but I think general practice is especially hard to do well: you need the skill and aptitude to spot the unusual amid the ordinary, not to mention the ability and compassion to deal with emotional and social issues in a very short space of time.

In spite of the big changes in our home and working environments, we had soon made friends, two of the closest being Fiona Webster and her partner David Payne. I had first met Fiona in December 2000 in the staff coffee room at the Leicester General Intensive Care Unit, where we were both anaesthetic registrars. It was the day after I passed my anaesthetics fellowship, so I'd been in an upbeat mood. It didn't take me long to discover that she was my kind of person. We became such great mates that one of our consultant colleagues rather cheekily used to refer to us as Charlie's Angels.

In our spare time Gerry and I would go out for meals with friends or run in the fields around Queniborough. Gerry played the occasional game of squash and joined Rothley Park Golf Club. Life, then, was full and busy, and good, apart from the dark shadow cast over everything by the absence of any developments on the pregnancy front. I tried not to talk too much about how hard all this was for me, even to Gerry. I didn't want to come across as mad or obsessed. In reality, though, I think most women probably become a bit fixated once they have made the all-important decision to have a baby. And in my case, of course, there had never been the slightest doubt about whether motherhood was for me. It had only ever been a question of when.

Eventually I saw a doctor, underwent tests and was diagnosed with endometriosis – a common condition in which cells similar to those lining the womb grow in areas outside it, and which can sometimes cause fertility problems. I embarked on over a year of surgery with laser treatment and hormonal injections, all to no avail. When we still failed to conceive naturally the only option open to us was assisted conception.

As a senior house officer in gynaecology, I'd seen the sadness and desperation etched on the faces of women coming up to the ward to undergo fertility treatment and declared that, in their position, I'd accept what was meant to be rather than put myself through in-vitro fertilization. The whole process seemed too traumatic and fraught with disappointment. Oh, the certainties of youth. I never dreamed then that the same thing might happen to me. And as is the case with so many aspects of life, it is impossible to predict how you will feel or react in a certain situation until you actually experience it for yourself. When it came to it, I didn't think twice. Having never for a moment questioned that I wanted to be a mother, to share my life and my love with a brood of children, I reasoned that if accomplishing my goal meant subjecting myself to IVF, so be it.

In a strange way, even taking that decision gave me a huge sense of relief. Suddenly, it seemed, the responsibility for conceiving had been lifted from our shoulders and the pressure on Gerry and me was eased. Our first attempt at IVF went smoothly and the invasive nature of the treatment – the injections, scans and subsequent procedures – didn't upset or worry me at all. Everything was going marvellously: I was responding very well to the drugs, I produced plenty of eggs and an excellent percentage of those, once fertilized by Gerry's sperm, resulted in embryos. Not all embryos survive beyond the first few days and opinions on the optimum time to transfer them into the womb were divided. Some clinicians favoured implanting them early, on day two or three, on the grounds that they were 'better inside than out'. Others felt that the embryos that had made it to the blastocyst stage (five days) outside the womb would be the strongest, and therefore the ones most likely to flourish in the long run. We had thirteen fertilized eggs. We decided to have some of them frozen and to have two blastocysts implanted.

Encouraged by the textbook progress of the treatment and the optimism of the IVF team ('It's as perfect a cycle as you can get!'), both Gerry and I were naively confident that it was going to work. Even so, we weren't prepared to run any risks, no matter how small, and I took every possible precaution. I completely avoided alcohol, exercise and sex. I had showers rather than baths, as if it were somehow possible for the embryos to float off into the bath water. I lived my life wrapped in enough cotton wool to fill an aircraft hangar.

I remember going into the hospital after two weeks for a pregnancy test, very calm on the outside, but very excited. An even more vivid memory is the physical pain of the blow that followed. The test was negative. I simply couldn't believe it. Back then I couldn't imagine there could be any pain worse than this. To this day, I cannot understand how I allowed myself to be so certain, especially as I knew, not only as a would-be mother but also as a doctor, how emotionally devastating the peaks and troughs associated with IVF can be. My baseless optimism only made the crash to earth that much harder. I cried and cried and cried.

After breaking the news to Gerry, who was almost as crushed as I was, and my mum, I went for a hard, fast run to try to expel some of my distress, pain and anger. It helped a little. A day or two later, I was back on the bus, as Auntie Norah would say, in control and geared up for the wait until we could try again.

Two months later we were ready for a second shot, using two of the embryos we'd had frozen. This time all I needed to do was to go into the hospital at the right time of the month and have the embryos transferred into my uterus. I was at work when I took the call I'd been expecting from the hospital. But instead of being asked to come in there and then, as I was anticipating, I was told, in very matter-of-fact tones, that unfortunately the defrosted embryos hadn't survived and we therefore couldn't go ahead with the procedure. And that, it seemed, was that. Another pallet of bricks dropped on my chest. That night, after the inevitable deluge of tears, Gerry and I went out for a consoling curry and a few beers. At least we had each other, we said. Then we picked ourselves up and prepared to start all over again.

Although the IVF team's plan was for us to return in six weeks to discuss the next step, after thinking it through, I could see no reason why, provided the facilities were available, we couldn't start a new cycle at the end of that week. The timing was right and I hadn't been taking any fertility medication which could potentially interfere with the procedure. It's baffling to anyone undergoing fertility treatment how casually everybody else can talk about weeks and months, as if you can just go away, forget about it and concentrate on something else. A month is a lifetime to a woman who has already spent years trying to get pregnant. Once you're on the bus, the last thing you want to do is get off.

We were so pleased when the IVF team agreed. But then a practical obstacle arose: we discovered that at the point when Gerry would need to produce his sperm sample for fertilization he was due to be in Berlin. He had been invited to the biggest cardiology conference in Europe to give a presentation about his research. It was an important stepping-stone in his career, and he was thrilled. My heart sank. It would mean more months of waiting, but how could he miss this conference? That evening, as I was cooking dinner, Gerry came into the kitchen, gave me a hug and told me he'd decided not to go to Berlin. The IVF, he told me, was far more important. I was very relieved and very grateful to him.

This time the cycle didn't go quite as smoothly. Once again I responded well to the drugs – maybe a little too well, because my ovaries became over-stimulated. I'd swear they were the size of melons. At any rate, I was very uncomfortable. It was agreed with the team that we would go for a day-three embryo transfer. On day two, however, we received an urgent call from the embryologist, who told us the embryos weren't looking as good as before. He recommended that I come into the hospital for the transfer immediately. Suddenly, we both felt very despondent. If a 'perfect' cycle hadn't worked, what were the chances of this one being successful? Two embryos were placed inside my uterus but this time we did not allow ourselves to get even slightly excited and the cotton-wool coddling went out of the window. I arrived home from the hospital and headed straight into the garden to do some planting. If this was going to work, it would, I told myself. But I wasn't holding my breath.

Given what had happened after our first attempt, we decided to do a pregnancy test at home the night before I was due to have the hospital test, so that if it was negative we could shed all our tears in private. A faint blue line appeared on the indicator. Gerry and I looked at each other. 'It's not dark enough,' I said, although I knew the instructions advised that any line should be interpreted as a positive result. I just didn't dare trust it.

I finally fell asleep that night in a strange state of controlled emotion. The next morning at the hospital the positive pregnancy test was confirmed. Everyone was ecstatic but no one, of course, more so than Gerry and me. Inevitably there were more tears, but this time they were happy tears. I felt like a different woman: taller, buoyant, instantly radiant. I could not stop smiling. I thanked God every hour. We didn't tell anyone, family or friends, for a couple of weeks – we were too concerned about tempting fate and somehow, at that early stage, it just didn't feel real. For days on end I would repeat to myself, 'I have a positive pregnancy test, I have a positive pregnancy test,' rather than acknowledging, 'I'm pregnant.' It wasn't until I had an ultrasound scan at six weeks and we saw a little beating heart that I allowed myself to believe it.

And that was the first time we saw our little Madeleine. Even then she was beautiful.

I remember how lovely it felt telling my mum and dad that they were going to be grandparents. Of course, they were overjoyed. I'm sure the heartache over the problems we'd had conceiving, added to the fact that, as an only child, I was their only chance of grandchildren, made this baby especially precious to them.

My pregnancy was totally without complication. No sickness, no back pain, no bleeding, no swelling. I felt great. I swam at least every other day, right up to the day before I went into labour. And I absolutely loved being pregnant. Rubbing body lotion over my bump was such a beautiful feeling, like touching my baby. In common with most mothers, I'm sure, I will remember for ever the amazing sensation, the pure intimacy, of my baby moving around inside me. Neither Gerry nor I wanted to know whether we were expecting a boy or a girl. I'm well known for liking surprises – one of those people who refuses to open even a single present before Christmas Day. For some reason I always thought of the baby as a boy. I've no idea why – perhaps simply because I'd visualized myself in many a dreamy moment with a little boy – who knows? We'd settled on the name Aidan, and although we had tossed around a few options for a girl, there wasn't one in particular we agreed on.

On 12 May 2003, at a routine antenatal appointment nine days before my due date, I was found to be already in labour. Like many first-time mothers, I'd had it all planned out – the music I wanted to play, the snacks I'd have to hand, the cooling mist spray for my face – but in the event I was whisked straight into the maternity unit and until Gerry was summoned I didn't even have the customary pre-packed overnight bag. When it came to it, though, I wasn't interested in any distractions, just completely focused on the job I had to do. As Gerry offered words of encouragement, I rocked from side to side, biting down on the gas-and-air mouthpiece. It occurred to me that I must look like Stevie Wonder. It's strange the things that go through your head when you're in extremis.

There's no escaping the fact that giving birth is bloody painful, but I was a very calm, quiet 'labourer', oblivious to everyone and everything around me. Fortunately, it was uncomplicated and pretty quick, as labours go. I remember finally feeling the head crowning and saying something pathetic to the midwife –'It's stingy,' if memory serves. *Stingy?* I never was one to make a fuss, I suppose! And then out popped our baby.

After years of longing for this day, here we were: parents. There can surely be no greater moment in anyone's life. And here she was: not our little boy, but our little girl. I'm not sure quite why this came as such a big surprise to us – after all, there are only two flavours – but because it was a surprise, the moment was extra special. Our daughter was perfect. A beautiful round head, no marks, and not at all squashed. Big, big eyes and a lovely, compact little body. The most wonderful thing I had ever set eyes on. I loved her instantly. Of course, Aidan was out of the frame now. Of the girls' names we had in mind Madeleine was my favourite, and Madeleine she became. Madeleine Beth McCann. She screamed straight away (something we'd get used to over the next six months). Gerry's sister Trish called while we were still in the delivery suite. 'Is that your wean?' she asked, with a hint of amusement, on hearing the 200-decibel screeching in the background. 'Jesus!'

I couldn't take my eyes off Madeleine. I thanked God over and over again for bringing her into our lives. Every time she looked even vaguely in my direction, the tears welled up. I'd never known before that it was possible to love someone so much – and I love Gerry a lot, believe me. My Madeleine.

I didn't sleep at all during my first night as a mother. I still couldn't stop looking at my beautiful daughter. Admittedly, the fact that Madeleine was testing the extremities of her vocal range for a large part of it might have been another factor. I remember one of the midwives coming into my room a couple of times and asking if I would like her to take Madeleine away for a while so that I could get some rest. Take her away? That was the last thing I wanted. I didn't care about sleep. All I cared about was being with Madeleine.

The next evening, my mum and dad, and my old friend Nicky, arrived to meet our daughter. My dad confessed to pushing a hundred on the motorway to make it down from Liverpool before the end of visiting time – but you didn't hear that from me. He was an old hand at childbirth, having been one of the first-ever fathers at Oxford Street Maternity Hospital, where I was born, allowed to stay with his wife throughout her labour instead of being ejected from the ward to pace the corridor outside. By all accounts, Granny Healy was shocked at this outrageous newfangled idea.

The new grandparents were besotted with Madeleine from the beginning. Having lost her own mother so early, I think my mum missed having her support when I was small and it had always been a sadness to her that I hadn't known my nana better. So having the chance to take care of her own granddaughter, and to be there for me, meant a great deal to her. As for my dad, he once told me that if he were able to design his own granddaughter and have her knitted for him, Madeleine would be it. 'I think I might love her even more than I love you,' he added. I wasn't too sure whether that was intended as a compliment but, knowing how much he loved me, I gave him the benefit of the doubt. Gerry's parents, and his brother and sisters, came hot on the heels of mine, all of them thrilled to bits.

The dramatic impact that one small person can have on your life never ceases to amaze me. Suddenly, your whole world revolves around this little bundle, and you don't mind in the slightest. The overwhelming love and protectiveness you feel towards your child makes you incredibly vulnerable – probably as vulnerable as you have ever been since you were a baby yourself. Now, however, you understand that this is a vulnerability that will never leave you.

3

A FAMILY OF FIVE

Madeleine suffered from colic. She cried for the best part of each day for the first four months of her life. When she had one of her screaming episodes her little fists would clench tightly and her face would turn purple with discomfort. Gerry and I spent hours running through our checklist – Is she too cold? Is she too hot? Is she hungry? Does she need her nappy changing? – before we were able to accept that this was colic, and this was what happened with colic. Unfortunately for Madeleine, it could strike at any time, not just in the early evening, as is typically the case. I remember feeling so helpless as I tried everything I could think of to ease her pain: this position, that position; feed, don't feed; rub her tummy; gripe water, Infracol; maybe a dummy? Needless to say, those early days could be very long and she was constantly in my arms. 'If you pick her up all the time, she'll never go to anyone else, you know,' people would remark.

It's hard to remember how I managed when I look back and picture myself buttering a piece of toast with one hand

43

(I am very bad at going without food), holding Madeleine in the other arm and never being able to answer the phone or even go to the toilet unaccompanied. Madeleine and I spent endless days dancing around our living room to the sounds of MTV. Beyoncé's 'Crazy in Love' and Justin Timberlake's 'Rock Your Body' were our favourites, along with a sub-consciously choreographed routine to Mummy's own rendition of 'She'll Be Coming Round the Mountain'.

Poor Gerry would arrive home from work and would hardly have a foot over the threshold before he was handed a roaring bundle while I went upstairs for a loo break, a scream-free moment and a chance to regain the use of my arms. There were several occasions when the three of us would be huddled together in the kitchen, crying – Madeleine with her colic and Gerry and I at the futility of our attempts to take away her pain.

I was always terrified that Madeleine would hurt herself. I remember once, when she was about four weeks old, refusing to make a car journey with her because the baby seat appeared to be wobbling very, very slightly. I know Gerry felt I was a bit over the top sometimes. But babies seem so fragile and with your first it's hard to get the balance right. I always erred on the side of caution.

Quite apart from the colic, Madeleine seemed to have an aversion to sleep at the best of times. It still astonishes us that she could survive on so little. There she'd be, surveying her surroundings with those great big peepers, studying anyone who came into her orbit, just taking it all in. Perhaps her curiosity and capacity for observation might explain why she always seemed so far ahead of the game and became such a knowing and endearing little girl at such an early stage. 'Auntie Michelle', my great friend, bought her a Blossom Farm baby gym from the Early Learning Centre, which had detachable soft toys. When you pressed the lamb's head, the tune of 'You Are My Sunshine' would play. I remember singing those words to Madeleine so often, with a few key personalized alterations:

> You are my Madeleine,
> My only Madeleine.
> You make me happy when skies are grey.
> You'll never know, dear, how much I love you.
> Please don't take my Madeleine away.

The terrible irony of those words brings bittersweet tears to my eyes when I think of them now. They have taken on a dark undertone, like the tinkling notes of a nursery rhyme in a horror film.

Happily, Madeleine grew out of her sleeplessness. When it came, the breakthrough was sudden. We all went to Italy in September for David and Fiona's wedding and one night, for no obvious reason, we put Madeleine down and she slept for a solid six hours. That was a real red-letter day.

Those first few months were quite an isolating time for me on the whole. While almost all my friends in Liverpool and Glasgow had children, my Leicester friends did not, which meant they were working and not around during the day. Mostly, then, it was just me and my special little buddy. Although Queniborough was a lovely village, our walks there tended to be rather aimless as there was no café or anything to walk to. And the fields where Gerry and I went running were impossible with a buggy.

So in some ways returning to work part-time in November 2003, while Madeleine started at a nursery near our home, was not such a bad thing. Although I hated the thought of being apart from her, I felt I needed to keep my hand in at the surgery: professionally, it's not a great idea to drop out for long periods. I also knew that nursery would bring a little more variety into Madeleine's world. Leaving her was an incredible wrench at first, but as we settled into our new routine I found it gave me a break of sorts, in terms of doing something different, at least, and mixing with people. And it helped get my spongy brain back into gear.

As it turned out, this arrangement didn't last long: in January 2004, when Madeleine was seven months old, we rented out our house and moved for a year to Amsterdam, where Gerry had a fellowship to study cardiac magnetic resonance imaging (MRI). The use of this specialized imaging technique in cardiology was at that time relatively new in the UK, and the posting was a big success. Gerry's great new colleagues soon became firm friends and what he learned in Amsterdam advanced his career on our return.

Since it wasn't going to be feasible for me to work in Amsterdam, I had Madeleine all to myself again. I've always considered myself very lucky to have been given this opportunity to spend quality time with her. We joined two mums-and-toddlers groups and a swimming club, where we quickly made friends; we would go to the park, drop into a café or just enjoy a lazy girls' afternoon in our apartment, treating ourselves to a movie and a slice of cake. It was a little piece of heaven.

As special as Madeleine was to us, and as fortunate as we felt to have her, both Gerry and I were keen to expand our family. Given our fertility problems, this was going to mean another attempt at IVF. We had no way of knowing if it was likely to work again and, even if it did, how long it might take. As a first step, in the spring I went along to see a GP. Not being Dutch citizens, we weren't sure if we would be entitled to any treatment at all, so we were surprised and delighted when, just a month later, we had an appointment with a specialist and within only six more weeks we found ourselves starting another cycle of IVF in Amsterdam.

For the most part, everything was far easier psychologically this time round. Much as I wanted another baby, Madeleine had lifted me from the despair of childlessness, thank God, and I was now able to approach the IVF a little more philosophically. If it succeeded, brilliant; if it didn't, then we only needed to look at what we had already to be content. It was a weird period emotionally, though. I couldn't help feeling a little guilty, as if we were somehow overlooking Madeleine, not focusing on her 100 per cent, in our haste to move on to 'the next one'. I loved her so much but I also knew that a little brother or sister would enhance her life, too.

The treatment cycle did the trick and I was pregnant again. We were overjoyed. This time, however, the scan revealed two little beating hearts. Twins. Wow! We were thrilled but also a little apprehensive. Having worked in obstetrics and anaesthetics, I was only too aware of the increased risks and complications associated with carrying twins. I wondered if my skinny body would be able to accommodate two babies. Our worries were completely brushed aside by two of Gerry's Dutch colleagues. As Gerry was voicing his concerns, he was interrupted by young Robin enthusiastically chipping in: 'Fantastic! Two for the price of one!' The lovely Aernout just looked at Gerry and revealed, 'I'm a twin,' in a 'so-what's-the-problem?' kind of way. Suddenly our concerns seemed, if not misplaced, at least excessive.

All the same, my second pregnancy was nothing like the first. Obviously, with Madeleine to look after and entertain, there was definitely no sneaking off for a little rest, for a start. More significantly, I felt very different physically, even in the early weeks. During the second month, I craved high-fat foods. I don't know how many text messages Gerry received begging him to get me some chips on his way home. The thought of so much fat is quite repulsive to me normally but at the time my body was telling me I needed it. Gerry and my friends will testify that any combination of the words 'Kate' and 'hunger' represents a kind of emergency at the best of times, but at this stage of my pregnancy there seemed no limit to the amount of chips, sausage rolls, pizzas and Mars bars my body cried out for.

It was just as well, as things turned out, because for the next five or six weeks I was completely poleaxed by nausea. I can remember doubting I'd ever be able to go through this again, which, given my overwhelming desire for a big family, is a measure of just how awful I felt. I couldn't eat and even swallowing a sip of water was a struggle. The smell of food – even the very mention of food – provoked a strong physical reaction. I would hear Gerry calling to Madeleine, 'Would you like some potatoes and broccoli?' and I'd roll into a ball with my hands over my ears.

Consciously or not, we all feel better when we can see those close to us being properly nourished. I know how satisfied I feel when my children scrape their bowls clean. Gerry found my problem very difficult to ignore. He was worried about me and about the babies and I'm sure he missed the three of us sitting down together and sharing a meal. But there was nothing I could do about it: my body simply wanted to be still and to be left alone.

Another concern was a persistent lower pelvic pressure and discomfort that came on only sixteen weeks into my pregnancy. I remember walking around Amsterdam for the next eight weeks with my hands cupped under my bump like a truss, trying to alleviate some of the weight, while at the same time occupying a very energetic toddler. Considering how normal I'd felt during my first pregnancy, I was a little worried, but only a little: the end result was going to make these trials more than worthwhile, after all.

However, it was not long before things took a more dramatic turn. At twenty-four weeks, a transvaginal ultra-sound scan to measure the cervix (the shorter it is, the greater the risk of the mother going into premature labour) revealed that mine had pretty much reduced to nothing. I was immediately put on to a trolley and admitted to a ward, where I was to remain on bed rest to reduce the gravitational pressure. The tears flowed, initially not so much because of the risk to my pregnancy but because I was distraught at the prospect of being parted from Madeleine.

'If your babies come now,' the specialist told me bluntly, 'they die.' Perhaps his English did not stretch to the expression of empathy or tact; perhaps the Dutch bedside manner is just to tell it like it is. Either way, once the seriousness of the situation sank in, so did the fear, and my prayers increased in frequency. Thankfully, my dad was staying with us at the time and was there to give Gerry a hand taking care of Madeleine. After five days of immobility, my condition improved and I was allowed home on the proviso that I did no more than I'd been doing in hospital. Nothing, in short. So from then until the babies were born we needed help, and when my dad left he was replaced by my mum, Gerry's mum and a relay of friends and relatives who came out from the UK over the next six weeks to stay with us in our one-and-a-half-bedroom apartment. It was hard for me not being able to pick Madeleine up or play with her properly. All we could do, really, was cuddle on the bed. Still, I was grateful that at least I hadn't had to remain in hospital.

My difficult pregnancy wasn't the only upsetting and stressful event that year. Gerry's dad had been diagnosed with cancer of the oesophagus in 2003 and was becoming more and more frail. It was terrible for poor Eileen to watch her husband of over forty years shrinking before her eyes. Eileen had not been well herself, either, undergoing surgery and radiotherapy for a salivary gland tumour as well as a hysterectomy. Then the marriage of two very good friends of ours broke down unexpectedly, just before their daughter's first birthday, and a distressed mother and child came out to stay with us straight afterwards. At the time Gerry described 2004 as our *annus horribilis*, but if we thought that year was bad, it would pale into insignificance compared with what lay in the future.

At twenty-seven weeks I began to bleed and had to go back into hospital. We were worried about the babies being born prematurely in the Netherlands. If that happened we would have to stay on after Gerry's fellowship had ended, with no family support and no income, so it was imperative to get me back home as soon as possible – provided, of course, our specialist felt it was safe enough for me to travel. He did, and on 1 December, a month ahead of schedule, we departed for the UK. On the advice of my consultant I flew, accompanied by my Auntie Janet, with Gerry, Madeleine and most of our belongings following by car and ferry. Gerry then had to return to Holland to complete the final two weeks of his post while a new stream of willing relatives arrived in Queniborough to help Madeleine and me. Another advantage of our early return was that it enabled me to get Madeleine re-established at nursery for a few mornings each week before the babies came rather than afterwards. The last thing I wanted was for her to feel side-lined once the new arrivals made their entrance.

In those final weeks I cut a bizarre figure, much to the amusement of my friends. I'd be the first to admit that my legs, though they serve their purpose perfectly well, have never been what you might call sturdy (pathetic might be a better word), and they looked even sadder poking out beneath the huge protuberance on top of them. An Easter egg on legs doesn't do it justice. But I was very proud of my body and its achievements and, once again, in spite of all the tribulations and worries, I'd loved being pregnant. As with

Madeleine, we'd asked not to be told the sex of the twins, but having had so many ultrasound scans we'd collected a lot of pictures of them which we couldn't help poring over. To Gerry and me the evidence seemed clear: two more girls.

At thirty-nine weeks, the twins were induced, which brought a wry smile to my face, given that I'd just spent three anxious months trying to prevent them from arriving too soon. All the same, I wouldn't have wanted to put their staying power to the test. If lying on my back for fifteen weeks meant our babies would be safer and stronger, every second was worth it.

Three days before I went into hospital, Gerry's Uncle Pat and Aunt Alexis came up from Essex to see us – and within an hour of their arrival, Uncle Pat, an ex-professional footballer, collapsed with a heart attack. When he slumped on Alexis's shoulder we thought at first he was just messing about. We soon realized he wasn't. As Gerry phoned for an ambulance and I worried that I was going to need to begin CPR – which would have been pretty difficult given that my belly was the size of a small barn and I could hardly move – a delivery man came to the door with a Chinese takeaway we'd ordered. Amid the pandemonium, Madeleine appeared, pushing her Early Learning Centre medical trolley, placed her toy stethoscope on Uncle Pat's chest and said, 'Boom, boom!' Talk about surreal.

Gerry was able to get hold of some of his on-call colleagues and explain the situation, so in spite of a slight delay with the ambulance, Uncle Pat was rushed straight through when he got to the hospital and the problem artery was unblocked. Thankfully, he was soon on the road to recovery. If you're going to have a heart attack, perhaps a cardiologist's house is not a bad place to have it.

On the afternoon of 1 February 2005, Sean and Amelie made their appearance in the world. I was lucky enough to be able to have a 'normal' delivery. Sean led the way with his head and his sister followed, preferring to flash her bottom first to all and sundry. We were totally taken aback to discover we had a boy, having fully expected two girls. How rubbish were we? Needless to say, neither of us have any plans to become obstetric ultrasonographers. Once again, being caught out made the birth a lovely surprise, and Gerry's delight at having a son was clear from the big, cheesy grin he could do nothing to disguise. For my part, I was a little shocked initially by this boy of mine lying on my tummy. He wasn't the prettiest, God bless him: he was squashed from the birth and his head was lopsided. But I loved him regardless and I'm glad to say he's a really handsome chap these days, just gorgeous. Amelie was beautiful from the start – petite with a little rosebud mouth. Suddenly we were a family of five. How lucky we felt.

A few hours later, Gerry brought Madeleine in to meet her little brother and sister. Just twenty months old herself at the time, in she came in her cute lilac pyjamas and puppy-dog slippers. When she saw Sean and Amelie her eyes lit up, her mouth opened wide in astonishment and wonder and she lifted her arms in the air, her fingers splayed like little starfish. My heart was ready to explode at her excitement. After inspecting her two new prospective playmates, she joined me on my bed and together we were wheeled off to the postnatal ward. It was such a special moment, one of my fondest memories of Madeleine, and I cannot think of it now without breaking down.

Happily, Sean and Amelie were very easy babies, as babies go. They fed and slept, fed and slept. Madeleine adapted to the changes incredibly well, especially considering how young she still was herself. Obviously ours was a very busy household, but it was full of love and laughter. On weekdays my friend Amanda would come in for a few hours every day, which freed me up to get some of the household chores done and to collect Madeleine from nursery. It mattered to me that I was the one to pick her up. I wanted her to feel as important and as loved as she always had.

I breastfed Sean and Amelie, as I had Madeleine, so there were spells when I wished I had a few extra arms, usually mid to late afternoon when I was alone with the children and Madeleine would be getting tired. I would have to feed the twins one at a time when I was on my own, which meant that as I was feeding the first, the other one would not only be getting hungry and grumpy but would also be vulnerable to attack from a big sister needing attention. Sometimes I'd be feeding one baby and pushing the other's rocker with my foot while a small girl clambered across my shoulders.

Overnight feeds were easier as then I could feed both babies at once, which cut the time it took by half. But I only managed that because my husband was an absolute star. He would get up with me, help latch the second twin on to my breast and then make me tea and toast while unloading the dishwasher. It was great teamwork, although thinking about it now, I wonder whether I had the better deal.

Only six weeks after Sean and Amelie were born, Gerry's

dad passed away. When Gerry's sister Trish rang to tell us that Johnny was approaching the end, we threw what we needed into the car, gathered up the children and drove to Glasgow as quickly as we could, arriving at the hospital in the early evening. By the next morning, Johnny had gone. We'll always regret that he never had the chance to see the twins, but it gives us some comfort that he was able to spend time with 'baby Madeleine' in his last few years, forging a bond that will doubtless have enriched both their lives.

The following two years were very happy ones. Gerry was appointed consultant cardiologist at Glenfield Hospital in Leicester soon after Sean and Amelie were born, and once they'd passed their first birthday I returned to work part-time, as a GP and also as a clinical tutor to medical students for a half-day every week. Gerry and I didn't have much time to ourselves: the days of Friday nights in the pub with our colleagues were long gone – we couldn't even manage to go for a run together now and had to take it in turns – but we didn't mind at all. We were living the family life we'd always wanted and it was everything we'd dreamed it would be. On the rare occasion when we went out for a meal on our own or with friends, Uncle Brian and Auntie Janet would babysit.

The mews house in Queniborough was a bit cramped for five of us, especially as we often had family and friends to stay, and in the spring of 2006 we moved to a larger home in a quiet cul-de-sac in Rothley, the village where Uncle Brian and Auntie Janet lived. Here we had a post office and general store, a café, several good pubs and interesting shops, which gave my afternoon walks with the children more of a sense of purpose.

The most exciting destination by far for the children, though, was a farm in the neighbouring village that was open to the public, offering all sorts of treats like tractor rides and buckets of feed for the children to give to the animals. At Stonehurst Farm Madeleine loved feeding the sheep, talking to the donkeys and swinging on the rope in the hay barn. She would chat away to Farmer John all the while. She was intrigued by the fact that his wife had the same name as hers but – as Madeleine never ceased to remind us – it was spelled differently. The highlight of the afternoon would be a thrilling ride on the trailer towed by Farmer John's tractor. He would lift Sean and Amelie in their double buggy on to the trailer, Madeleine and I would clamber aboard alongside the other visitors, and off we would go.

I have such wonderful memories of our first summer in Rothley. The new house really felt like home and the five of us spent many sunny, fun-filled days in the garden, on the swings and slide, blowing bubbles, painting 'in the skud', as Auntie Trisha would put it (that was just the kids, I hasten to add), or chatting in the paddling pool together.

It was fascinating watching how the children interacted with one another as they developed and how different their personalities were. When they were small, Sean and Madeleine were the closest in nature, and early on they formed a natural alliance, although later, Madeleine and Amelie began to do lots of girly things together. Amelie was confident, brave and a bit mad, and initially the one in whom I saw myself least but always admired. In the garden she would run up the steps of the slide and hurl herself down the chute with a crazed cry of exhilaration: 'Ha, ha, *ha*!' Sean – Cautious George to Amelie's Fearless Fred – would often climb the steps carefully, then, on reaching the top, have second thoughts, turn round and come back down the same way. When they did jigsaws, Amelie would use brute force to wedge any old pieces together. Sean would meticulously study all the pieces before completing the puzzle unaided. He is probably the more academic and methodical of the twins; Amelie the more intuitive and artistic. They've changed a little now, of course. Sean has grown in confidence – the Gerry genes coming to the fore! – and his obsessive need for order has receded. Amelie has lost her mad edge (much to my relief) although she's still adventurous. She has also grown into the most loving, sensitive and caring seven-year-old I know. And they remain the best of friends.

Madeleine has always been confident and independent. Like 'shy' and 'Gerry', 'shy' and 'Madeleine' are not words you would readily associate with one another. At three she was incredibly bright and extremely perceptive. As her mother I would say that, but many far more objective observers than I commented on it. She was always very aware of her surroundings, just as she had been as a baby. Entering a roomful of people, she wouldn't just rush in obliviously, as toddlers tend to do, and make a beeline for me or Gerry. Instead she would be weighing up what was going on, apparently analysing everything and everyone, before asking intelligent and sometimes very pointed questions.

Madeleine loved Harry Potter. I remember her going out into the hall one afternoon at our house in Queniborough and knocking on the living-room door. 'Hello! Come in!' I called. In she came, smiling but looking anxious and pre-occupied. She tilted her head towards her shoulder and whispered, 'Mummy, Harry Potter's next to me.'

'Oh, hello, Harry. How nice to see you. Come in and join us for a cup of tea.' A few minutes later, she went out again and returned with Hermione. And so it went on until I'd welcomed into our living room Ron Weasley, Professor Dumbledore and Professor McGonagall. Madeleine was brilliant at role play and I loved these games, too, even if whenever we played 'Mummy and baby' I was always the baby.

Gerry and I didn't like the children to have too much in the way of sweets or chocolate when they were little. Auntie Norah used to tease me because I'd give Madeleine a Rich Tea biscuit as a treat. 'Call that a treat? Big wow!' I swear Madeleine could pick up the rustle of a biscuit or sweetie wrapper at five hundred yards. Grandad Brian is well known for being very partial to a chocolate biscuit. I don't think he could manage a cup of tea or coffee without one. There have been many occasions when we've found him hiding behind a cupboard door, shoving a few biscuits into his mouth. But at the faintest fluttering sound coming from my dad's direction Madeleine, the treat detective, would be on to him: 'What have you got there, Grandad?' Once he'd stopped laughing at her grave, suspicious expression he'd be obliged to share his booty.

It was on New Year's Day 2007 that the idea of a spring holiday in Portugal was first raised. Fiona and David Payne, who had come with their children Lily and Scarlett to spend the day with us, were planning a week's break at a Mark

Warner resort in the Algarve, probably with two other couples and their families, and they asked us if we'd like to join them.

We'd been away with Fiona and David on several occasions and we'd always enjoyed ourselves. They favoured the same kind of holidays we did – we've never been interested in swanky hotels, preferring a reputable resort with good sports facilities and, since the arrival of the children, plenty for them to do, too. Gerry and I took the kids everywhere – in fact I'd only ever been apart from them for one night – so they were used to travelling. They had been on lots of trips, to Glasgow, Liverpool, Stratford, Skipton and Crieff, Donegal, Guernsey and Spain, and they loved their 'mini-holidays', as we called them, to visit friends and family.

The other couples pencilled in for this trip were Russell O'Brien and Jane Tanner and Matt and Rachael Oldfield. Russell and Matt were also doctors. Jane, a marketing manager, was taking a break from work to be a full-time mum for a while. Rachael, a lawyer by profession, was working in recruitment. Although they were all originally friends of David and Fiona's, we knew them quite well, too – in fact Gerry had worked in the past with both Russell and Matt – so we had no concerns about whether we'd all get along.

I'd never been to Portugal, although Gerry had been there on a couple of golfing trips a few years before. From people who had taken holidays in the Algarve I gathered that it was a quite upmarket, family-friendly destination. We had never been on a Mark Warner holiday, either, but the others had, to Sardinia and Greece. Everybody had been very impressed by the locations, accommodation and amenities.

Gerry was quite keen on the Portugal idea, attracted by the sporting facilities, children's clubs and activities on offer. I was more reluctant. It wasn't that I didn't fancy the resort – and it certainly wasn't that I had some kind of premonition, because I didn't. My reservations were more practical. The holiday was quite pricey, and although Madeleine, Sean and Amelie were good travellers, I just wasn't sure that it was worth all the packing and hassle involved in flying three children under the age of four to Portugal when there were plenty of alternatives in the UK. We'd had two great breaks at Center Parcs the previous year and I was sorely tempted to stick with something similar this time.

The others all confirmed that they were on for it and in the end I was persuaded by the enthusiasm of Gerry and our friends that it would be fun (at least, it would be once we got there). The party would consist of David, Fiona, Lily, who was two, and Scarlett, nearly a year old; Matt and Rachael and their toddler, Grace; Jane and Russell with Ella who, coming up to four, was almost exactly the same age as Madeleine, and Evie, another toddler; the five of us, and Fi's mum, Dianne. As all the children except Sean were girls, he was going to be a bit outnumbered, but at least they would keep him in touch with his feminine side!

Madeleine was so excited about going on a plane, and about going on holiday with her buddies. At nursery she was full of it. When I went to pick her up the girls who looked after her there would comment, 'I hear you're going to Portugal!' or 'Someone can't wait for her holiday!'

It was the first in a series of apparently minor decisions I'd give anything to change now.

4

THE HOLIDAY

On Saturday, 28 April 2007, Fiona, David, Dianne and the girls arrived at our house before 7am (the others, who were based down south, were flying separately from Gatwick). As soon as the kids wiped the sleep from their eyes they were giddy with excitement. In the people carrier we'd pre-booked to take us to East Midlands airport the chatter and laughter escalated and by this stage even I was feeling quite up for it. We all had breakfast together at the airport, everybody in high spirits.

Boarding the aircraft, Madeleine, her princess trolley-bag gripped tightly in one hand, perhaps over-ambitiously took hold of Lily's hand with the other and tripped, clattering her shin on the sharp front edge of one of the metal steps. Even that wasn't enough to spoil her holiday mood. She handled it so bravely, letting out only a momentary whimper in spite of the large bruise that appeared almost immediately. The flight was otherwise unremarkable. With each other for company, the children were easily entertained. At the risk of sounding totally biased, I must say that Madeleine behaved perfectly. Her sore leg forgotten, she spent the flight chatting away happily, reading and colouring, as she'd spent many previous journeys.

We found the people carrier plus driver we'd pre-booked to meet us at Faro airport and arrived at the Ocean Club resort in the village of Praia da Luz at around three. After checking in we were driven over to our accommodation in a minibus by a Mark Warner rep. Our apartments were in a five-storey block accessed from the front by a road, Rua Dr Agostinho da Silva. There was a car park outside. At the rear, a veranda overlooked a garden, pool area and tennis courts. All of us except David, Fiona and Dianne, who were on the first floor, had ground-floor flats. Matt and Rachael were next door to us in 5B, and Jane and Russell in 5D. Ours, 5A, was on the corner of the block. It was lovely: much nicer and larger, in fact, than we had expected, and well equipped. Though I envied David and Fiona their sea view, being on the ground floor meant we didn't have to worry about the children's safety on a balcony.

Later, we were told by the British police that the ground-floor location, access to roads front and side, secluded entrance and partial tree cover made our apartment a prime target for burglars and other criminals. Never once did this occur to us when we arrived. As far as we were concerned, we were in a safe, family-oriented holiday resort.

From the front door of the apartment, there was a kitchen to the left with a hallway leading into a sitting room at the back. On the right-hand side were two bedrooms, separated by a bathroom. The sitting-room area was furnished with two blue sofas, coffee table, TV and dining table and chairs.

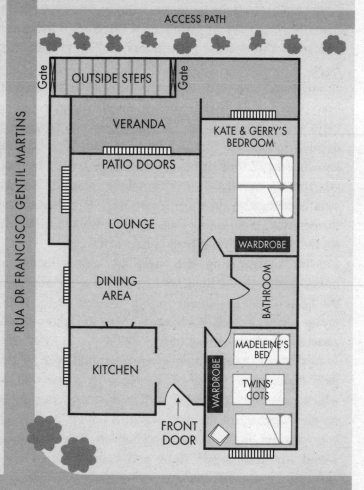

TAPAS and
POOL AREA

ACCESS PATH

RUA DR FRANCISCO GENTIL MARTINS

Gate

OUTSIDE STEPS

Gate

VERANDA

KATE & GERRY'S
BEDROOM

PATIO DOORS

LOUNGE

WARDROBE

DINING
AREA

BATHROOM

KITCHEN

MADELEINE'S
BED

TWINS'
COTS

WARDROBE

FRONT
DOOR

RUA DR AGOSTINHO DA SILVA

Glass sliding patio doors gave out on to a veranda, with a flight of steps down to a little gate at the side of the building. At the top of the stairs there was a child safety gate. After the first couple of days we barely used the front door, coming and going through the patio doors and up and down the steps.

The travel cots we'd requested for Sean and Amelie had been placed in the back bedroom. As there were full-length patio doors here, too, and it was bigger and brighter, we decided to put the three children in the front bedroom, knowing they'd only be using their room to sleep in, and to take this one ourselves. We removed the cots and shoved the twin beds together. In the other room, we pushed the beds further apart, positioning each against a wall, to make room for the cots, which we placed in between them.

After reorganizing the sleeping arrangements and unpacking some essentials, we went down to the pool area at the back of the apartment to join the rest of the holiday group – Jane, Russell, Rachael and Matt and their kids had arrived a few hours ahead of us.

At the back the apartments were separated from an access path that ran the length of the block by a low wall, into which gates to the ground-floor flats were set. The pool area on the other side of the path was also walled, so to reach it you went out on to the road to your left, Rua Dr Francisco Gentil Martins, turned right and came back in via an entrance a few yards along. As we were on the corner of the block, our gate led directly on to Rua Dr Gentil Martins.

The weather was pleasant enough, although there was a cool breeze. It was still April, after all. As I am one of those people who really feel the cold ('Get a bit of meat on yerself!' my hardy Scottish in-laws are always telling me), when Madeleine immediately wanted me to go swimming with her, I was not exactly keen. But she was so excited about the pool. I took one look at her eager little face and went off to put on my costume. The water was absolutely freezing, but Madeleine was straight in there, even if her voice disappeared for a second or two with the shock of it. 'Come on, Mummy!' she called when she'd got her breath back. I tentatively inched my way in. 'The things you do for your kids!' I remember commenting to a dad lying on a sun-lounger with his two sons nearby, watching us. I told Madeleine to count to three and steeled myself. It was worth it – it will always be worth it – just to see her delight. Even if it did take us both the best part of three hours to warm up afterwards.

We were still shivering when we went off to a 'welcome' meeting with the Mark Warner team, who outlined the facilities and events on offer. We booked the children into the kids' clubs, starting the next day. These provided a wide range of activities, both indoor and outdoor, that varied from day to day: swimming at the indoor pool, 'ice-cream' trips, boat rides at the beach, sandcastle-building, games like mini-tennis and the usual arts and crafts, singing and stories.

Afterwards we strolled over to the Millennium restaurant for dinner. The Mark Warner resorts the others had visited before had been quite compact. The apartments and facilities in Praia da Luz were spread out around the village, which meant some of them were ten minutes' walk away. The restaurant turned out to be nearly half a mile from our base – a bit too far, really, certainly for a gaggle of weary toddlers. As we were only going to be away for a week, we'd decided not to bring Sean and Amelie's double buggy with us, preferring to travel light and thinking we wouldn't be doing much walking, given that everything we needed was on-site. So there were many stops and negotiations about whose turn it was to be carried by whom. At the restaurant the staff were very kind and obliging, pushing up several tables so that we could all sit together.

Once we'd eaten everyone was feeling pretty tired, and by the time we got back to the apartment the children's night-time routine – bath, pyjamas, milk, stories and bed – was an hour behind the normal schedule. Madeleine was very taken with the novelty of sharing a room with Sean and Amelie – at home she has her own – and it was nice to have them all together. She had the bed nearest the door, leaving the one by the window empty. On our arrival we had lowered the blind-style shutters on the outside of the windows, which were controlled from the inside, and closed the curtains. We left them that way all week. This early in the season, the nights were not that warm, there was no need to open a window and we reasoned that having the shutters down and the curtains drawn would keep it cool during the day. Although it meant the room was very dark, the children weren't going to be in there in the daytime, and at night we always left the door ajar to let in a little light.

With Madeleine and the twins settled, Gerry and I chatted and read for a while before going to sleep ourselves. The holiday had got off to a good start, and we felt mellow and content.

* * *

Everyone had a good night's sleep and the next morning, Sunday 29 April, we woke up bright and early and feeling refreshed. After a quick wash, we returned to the Millennium restaurant, where we joined our friends for breakfast, and then took the children to their kids' clubs. While our three were having fun elsewhere with their buddies, there would be a rare chance for Gerry and me to spend time together playing tennis, going for a run or just relaxing. It seemed to us an ideal way for everyone to get the most out of the holiday.

We wanted to balance these activities with enjoying our break as a family, and we made it clear to Madeleine that she didn't have to go to the club if she didn't feel like it. We wouldn't have minded if she'd asked to stay with us as we loved her company, but she was far less concerned about being apart from Gerry and me than the other way round. The main thing was that everyone was happy.

Sean and Amelie were enrolled in the Toddler Club for two-year-olds in a building adjacent to a bar and the open-air Tapas restaurant, just across from our apartment on the other side of the main pool. The nanny who was to take care of them there seemed very pleasant and capable. Amelie, true to form, was completely unfazed; sensitive Sean, when it came to it, was initially a bit upset, all of which was situation normal with the twins. The staff had our telephone numbers and we left details of our whereabouts, as we would do for the rest of the week, in case there were any problems or in the unlikely event that Sean failed to settle.

Madeleine's group, the Mini Club for three-to-fives, was based in a light, airy room above the twenty-four-hour reception. This was slightly further away and it was a few

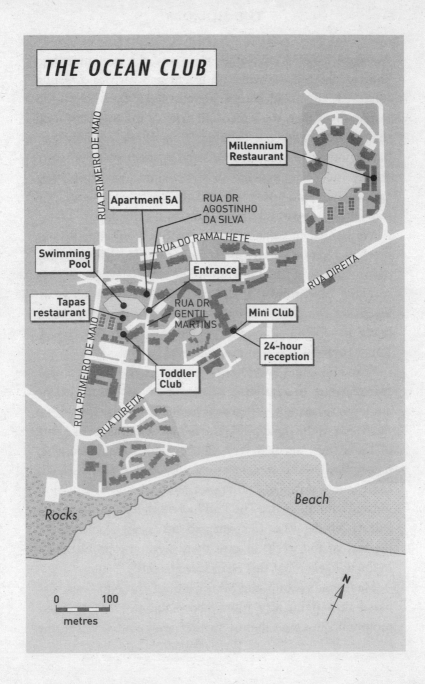

THE OCEAN CLUB

Millennium Restaurant

Apartment 5A

RUA DR AGOSTINHO DA SILVA

RUA DO RAMALHETE

RUA PRIMEIRO DE MAIO

Swimming Pool

Entrance

RUA DIREITA

Tapas restaurant

RUA DR GENTIL MARTINS

Mini Club

24-hour reception

Toddler Club

RUA PRIMEIRO DE MAIO

RUA DIREITA

Beach

Rocks

0   100

metres

N

mornings before we got our bearings and found a quicker route there. Ella went too and although until the previous day the two girls hadn't seen each other for several months, they soon became great pals. Madeleine's nanny, Cat, I warmed to straight away, as did Madeleine. She was bubbly, smiley, kind and bursting with enthusiasm. It was obvious that she was doing the job because she loved children, not simply as a way of spending a few months in the sun.

After dropping off the children we went along to a 'tennis coffee morning'. Neither of us is a regular tennis player but before we'd had the kids we'd spent many holidays knocking a few balls around. Perhaps that's a bit of a casual way of putting it: we're both pretty competitive so there have been some fierce matches over the years, thankfully all ending amicably with a hug over the net and a post-match beer. So we were keen to get in some tennis on this break and maybe improve our technique a little. We played a few games and signed up for group lessons for the rest of the week, me at level 1 and Gerry level 2 (I must grudgingly concede that he is better than I am).

Soon after midday we collected the children. I loved going to pick up the kids when they were little. The moment when your child spots you and rushes over to throw a pair of tiny arms around you makes your heart sing. It doesn't happen every time, of course, but I have many special memories of meeting Madeleine at nursery at home. Hurtling across the classroom and into my embrace, she would shout, '*My* mummy!', as if establishing ownership of me in front of the other children. What I'd give to have that again.

Gerry had made a trip to Baptista, a supermarket a short

distance from the Ocean Club on Rua Dr Gentil Martins, to get in a few bits and pieces for lunch, plus some cereal, to save us making the trek to the Millennium restaurant for breakfast each morning. We all had lunch on the balcony of the apartment Fi and Dave were sharing with Dianne. Today we'd been able to make a dinner reservation for the adult contingent at the poolside Tapas restaurant. Apparently, this restaurant, a canopied outdoor addition to the bar, catered for only up to fifteen diners in the evenings, and reservations could not be made until the morning of the day in question. Being so close, it was far more convenient than the Millennium. The children could have their tea together earlier, play for a while and then go to bed at their usual time, which meant they wouldn't get overtired and out of sorts, and we could eat later on.

In the afternoon the children went back to their clubs and, after a leisurely hour by the pool with Fiona, David and Dianne, Gerry and I took a run along the beach. Being able to play tennis and run together for the first time in ages was a real treat.

Just before 5pm, the arrangement was that the nannies would bring all the children to a raised area next to the Tapas restaurant to meet their parents and have their 'high tea', as they called it. Madeleine's Mini Club arrived walking in single file clutching Sammy Snake, a long rope with coloured rings fastened to it at regular intervals for the children to hold on to. Very cute. The nearby play area had several small slides and a little playhouse, which our team of kids adored, and after tea we all spent half an hour or so there.

We headed back to our apartments, the kids all tired but

happy after their busy day. At home, the twins were usually asleep soon after seven, while Madeleine enjoyed the big sister's privilege of an extra half-hour with Gerry and me. Sean and Amelie had always been perfect sleepers, and Madeleine had outgrown the restlessness of her babyhood, so, barring illness and the odd instance of playing up at bedtime, ours was normally a relatively quiet household by 8pm. If Madeleine ever woke during the night it was always in the small hours, practically never earlier than two or three in the morning.

In Portugal the only difference was that all three children went down around seven, seven-fifteen. None of them had been taking daytime naps for quite a few months before the holiday, and after the activities and excitement of each day, they were all ready for their beds by then. Familiar with their bedtime ritual, they accepted it as a prelude to sleep and, after milk and stories, settled very quickly. It's a time-honoured routine viewed as the norm by the vast majority of British parents and children, and we were dumbfounded when, in the months to come, it provoked sceptical comments in Portugal.

After putting the children to bed, Gerry and I showered, dressed and sat down with a glass of wine before heading over to the Tapas restaurant, booked for eight-thirty. At that time, most Mark Warner resorts provided a baby-listening service – basically, members of staff listening at regular intervals at the doors of the apartments and villas to check that none of the children inside had woken up. This service was not offered by the Ocean Club, presumably because it was less of a 'campus' resort than others, with apartments scattered over a greater area. Instead there was a crèche, where children could be looked after from about 7.30pm to 11pm. Given that our children needed to be in their beds by the time it opened, the crèche wasn't really workable for us. We both felt it would be too unsettling for them and would disrupt their sleep.

As the restaurant was so near, we collectively decided to do our own child-checking service. This decision, one that we all made, has naturally been questioned time and again, not least by us. It goes without saying that we now bitterly regret it, and will do so until the end of our days. But it is easy to be wise after the event. Speaking for myself, I can say, hand on heart, that it never once crossed my mind that this might not be a safe option. If I'd had any doubts whatsoever, I would simply never have entertained it. I love my three children above everything. They are more precious and special to me than life itself. And I would never knowingly place them at risk, no matter how small a risk it might seem to be.

If we'd had any concerns we could have hired a babysitter. I could argue that leaving my children alone with someone neither we nor they knew would have been unwise, and it's certainly not something we'd do at home, but in fact we didn't even consider it. We felt so secure we simply didn't think it was necessary. Our own apartment was only thirty to forty-five seconds away, and although there were some bushes in between it was largely visible from the Tapas restaurant. We were sitting outside and could just as easily have been eating on a fine spring evening in a friend's garden, with the kids asleep upstairs in the house.

As it was, we were in an apparently safe, child-friendly holiday complex full of families just like ours. The children were fast asleep and being checked every thirty minutes. Even if there had been a baby-listening service it would not have given our kids as much attention as our own visits did. We were going into the apartments and looking as well as listening. We later heard it was an option that had been chosen by many other parents at similar resorts before us. But I'm willing to bet not many since.

Bringing up children – like all aspects of life – involves making hundreds of tiny and seemingly minor decisions every single day, balancing the temptation to mollycoddle them with the danger of being too laissez-faire. Sometimes, with hindsight, our judgement proves to have been right, sometimes wrong. Mostly when you make the wrong call you can just chalk it up to experience and do it differently next time. It is our family's tragedy that this particular decision would have such catastrophic consequences.

That Sunday night we headed over to the restaurant. We were all there except Matt, who had a bit of a dodgy stomach, which he attributed to something he'd eaten en route to Portugal. The rest of us enjoyed our meal. The food was good and it was nice to have a little adult time. There weren't many other diners and, since we were such a large group, we were focused on chatting to and bantering with each other and not taking much notice of anyone else. It was, I remember, very cold and windy and I discovered that five layers of clothing were required to keep me comfortable. We nipped back to our respective apartments every half-hour to check on the children – apart from Rachael, since Matt had stayed behind, and Dave and Fiona, who had a state-of-the-art baby monitor with them. Our visits also gave us a convenient opportunity to pop to the loo or, in my case, to pick up an extra cardigan.

Gerry and I were back in our apartment by 11pm. Mind you, back then we considered ten-thirty a late night. As I've said, we didn't exactly live life on the edge, and David and Fiona in particular seemed to find our early bedtimes highly amusing. Who cared? We were happy – and well rested. From some of the things that would be written about us in the coming months, you'd think we and our friends had been partying wildly every night in Portugal. We may have been noisier than other tables at dinner – there were up to nine of us talking across each other, after all – but we didn't linger late and our alcohol consumption could hardly be described as excessive. We all had young children (which, as any parent knows, makes it impossible to burn the candle at both ends) and we were all up at seven, seven-thirty every morning.

The following days settled into a similar pattern: we'd have breakfast in the apartment, drop Madeleine, Sean and Amelie at their clubs and head to the courts, behind the Tapas bar building, for our hour-long group tennis lessons (mine was at nine-fifteen, Gerry's at ten-fifteen). We'd collect the children between twelve and twelve-thirty and return to the flat for lunch and tales from the kids' clubs. Afterwards we would often call in on the others at David and Fiona's apartment or pop down to the play area for a while. Most afternoons the children went back to their clubs, while we played tennis, went for a run or read and chatted by the pool. We'd usually meet up with the children and nannies for tea, along with the rest of our friends, and then it was off to the play area again for some fun and a good run-around before the kids' bedtime. Sometimes in the early evening there would be a light-hearted tennis event: Monday was 'ladies night', for example, and on Tuesday there was 'object tennis', which involved the guests providing the coaches with various objects they had to use instead of a racquet.

Gerry and I have always quite liked having a routine, though I wouldn't say we were obsessed by it, and our children, like most children, seemed to like it, too. This holiday was no exception. It's hard to accept that living our lives in such an ordinary way might have been our downfall. Was someone watching us that week? Watching Madeleine? Taking note of the pattern of our days?

In spite of what we'd been told about booking the Tapas restaurant, Rachael managed to get a table for nine at 8.30pm pencilled in for the rest of the week after having a word with the receptionist at the pool and Tapas area.

It wasn't until a year later, when I was combing through the Portuguese police files, that I discovered that the note requesting our block booking was written in a staff message book, which sat on a desk at the pool reception for most of the day. This book was by definition accessible to all staff and, albeit unintentionally, probably to guests and visitors, too. To my horror, I saw that, no doubt in all innocence and simply to explain why she was bending the rules a bit, the receptionist had added the reason for our request: we wanted to eat close to our apartments as we were leaving our young children alone there and checking on them intermittently.

On the evening of Monday 30 April, I made my first foray to Baptista with Jane. We wanted to stock up on a few essentials as the next day was a public holiday. We all managed to make it for dinner at the Tapas restaurant that evening. Again, there was quite a cold wind, but there were plenty of amusing stories and mickey-taking to keep us cheerful.

Our apartment was cleaned on the Monday and Wednesday (another perk) by a middle-aged Portuguese lady. On Tuesday 1 May, after my tennis lesson, two maintenance workers came to have a look at our washing machine, which I couldn't get to operate. Gerry had also managed to break the window shutter mechanism in our bedroom shortly after we'd arrived, in spite of the sign asking guests to be gentle with it. What can I say? It's the Gerry touch . . . The two men looked at the washing machine first. Once they'd established that the problem was something simple – not quite as simple as me not having pressed the 'on' button, but not much more complicated than that – I went to meet Gerry, whose lesson had started at ten-fifteen, leaving them to fix the shutter.

During Gerry's tennis lesson, Madeleine and Ella came to the adjoining court with their Mini Club for a mini-tennis session. Jane and I stayed to watch them. It chokes me remembering how my heart soared with pride in Madeleine that morning. She was so happy and obviously enjoying herself. Standing there listening intently to Cat's instructions, she looked so gorgeous in her little T-shirt and shorts, pink hat, ankle socks and new holiday sandals that I ran back to our apartment for my camera to record the occasion. One of my photographs is known around the world now: a smiling Madeleine clutching armfuls of tennis balls. At the end of their session, the children had been asked to run around the court and pick up as many balls as they could. Madeleine had done really well and was very pleased with herself. Gerry loves that picture.

In the afternoon Gerry and I decided to take the children down to the beach. To be honest, I think they'd have been just as happy to go back to their clubs, but we wanted to do something slightly different with them, just the five of us. We borrowed a double buggy from Mark Warner to make the walk easier for Sean and Amelie. The weather wasn't great: in fact, on the beach it started to rain. A bit of rain is not something that bothers a Scotsman like Gerry, but Sean and Amelie didn't like the feel of the wet sand and insisted, in the way two-year-olds do, on being carried.

Our trip to the beach wasn't exactly a roaring success and the kids certainly weren't thanking us for it. Still, we made the best of it, and the suggestion of ice-creams soon brought smiles to three little faces. The children and I sat down on a bench and Gerry went off to fetch them. The shop was only about 25 feet away, yet when he called to me asking me to give him a hand with the five ice-creams he was paying for, I was momentarily torn. Would the children be OK on the bench while I nipped over? I hurried across, watching them all the time.

How could I balk at leaving the kids to run a few yards for ice-creams and feel comfortable with the child-checking arrangement we had at dinner? I haven't ever been able to rationalize this discrepancy in judgement to my own satisfaction. Perhaps in my subconscious the prospect of three active children squabbling, hurting themselves or being hurt by somebody else in a public place in the middle of the afternoon rang more alarm bells than three sleeping children, safely tucked up in bed, being checked on regularly. If the fear of abduction had ever entered my head it would have been in the former situation.

Having polished off her ice-cream, Madeleine asked if she could go back to Mini Club now, please. So much for extra family time! Before heading up the road, we stopped at a shop on the corner of Rua da Praia and Avenida dos Pescadores, one of several open-air, market-style stalls, as Gerry needed a pair of sunglasses. A couple of the women who worked there were sitting by the stall, admiring and making a fuss of the children, who responded quite happily. These ladies were warm and friendly, this is the kind of thing that occurs every day, especially in southern European countries, and I only remember it at all because of what subsequently happened.

You may be wondering not only what relevance all these minute details might have to anything, but also how I can recall them so distinctly and how accurate my recollections can possibly be. The answer is that, within a couple of days, every single apparently inconsequential thing that took place on that holiday would become vitally important, and Gerry and I would soon be painstakingly trying to extract from our brains every tiny incident, no matter how small, that might have been significant. Armed with notebook, pen and dated photographs, I would be challenging myself to piece together as comprehensive an outline of the sequence of events as I could. The regular routines of the week helped to make any deviations from them stand out and undoubtedly made this easier.

We dropped the kids off at their clubs for the last hour and a half, meeting up with them as usual for tea. Only two minor aspects of that evening stand out as differing from the norm. The first was that Russell didn't join us for dinner. Evie wasn't well so he stayed with their girls in the apartment and Jane took his meal to him there. The second was that some time in the early hours Madeleine came through to our bedroom, complaining that Amelie was crying and had woken her up. Gerry checked on Amelie, who settled quickly, and we let Madeleine jump into bed with us.

Wednesday, 2 May 2007. Our last completely happy day. Our last, to date, as a family of five. If only it was possible to rewind. Even for an hour.

Today it rained. The children went to their clubs, but our tennis lessons were postponed. Instead we joined Fiona, David and Dianne at the Millennium restaurant for coffee. We then returned to our apartment and a little while later I left again, to go for a run with Matt. I'd bought a new pair of running shoes a few days before we'd left for Portugal and they were certainly getting a good initiation. They were pink, which I wasn't quite sure about – I wondered how seriously a runner in pink trainers could be taken – but after a few outings in the sand they weren't looking quite so glaring and girly. As we ran along the promenade, a small dog jumped out from under a bench and attacked my right calf. It was pretty sore and I was a bit shaken, but I carried on as coolly as I could manage. Maybe he just didn't like those pink trainers.

Gerry and I picked up the children, had lunch in the apartment and then took them to the play area for an hour before walking them to their clubs. The tennis group lessons were rescheduled for the afternoon: Gerry's group first, followed by mine. After that it was the usual routine: tea with the children, playtime, bathtime, milk, stories, kids' bedtime, get ready, Tapas at 8.30pm.

Tonight it was Rachael's turn to be feeling a bit under the weather and she gave dinner a miss, remaining in her apartment next door to ours. The only other difference was that after dinner we ventured into the enclosed bar area – where it was, to my relief, warmer – for a liqueur. As a result we went back to our apartments a little later than normal. It also meant that the time between our last check of the children and our return was longer, closer to forty-five minutes.

At about 11.50pm, Gerry abruptly announced, 'Right, I'm off to bed. Goodnight.' As he turned to leave, Dave said jokingly, 'She's not *that* bad, Gerry!' I must admit I was slightly hurt that Gerry should just go off without me, as if I was unimportant – irrelevant, even – and Dave's remark was an indication that it wasn't just me being over-sensitive. Let me tell you something about Gerry. His honesty and openness make him very direct, often to the point of bluntness, and he's not a touchy-feely guy. Like many men, he assumes I take his feelings as read and doesn't see any need to express them with soft-soaping, flowers or cards. And although, like most women, I would appreciate the odd romantic gesture, the fact that he has always been loyal, solid and loving deep down, where it really matters, is far more important. It's just Gerry, I'm used to his foibles and generally any deficiencies in gallantry simply go over my head.

As far as Gerry was concerned, it was late, he was tired, and he was going to bed. End of story. I am not sure why I was miffed by his lack of social graces that particular evening. Perhaps because the other guys in the group were all attentive 'new men', compared with Gerry, at least, and I was a bit embarrassed. Anyway, I followed him a few minutes later. He certainly was tired, because by the time I got into the apartment, he was asleep – snoring, in fact. Still feeling a bit offended, I decided to go and sleep with the children. This was highly unusual; unprecedented, even: the only occasions when we ever slept apart were when our jobs and on-call duties dictated it. I wasn't the type to flounce off to the spare room and never would have done so at home.

I suppose it was because there was a bed made up and ready in the other bedroom and at that moment my peaceful, slumbering babies were more attractive room-mates than my snoring husband. It was a storm in a teacup, and I'm loath even to mention it as it was such an isolated incident and not at all representative of our relationship. However, since every scrap of information was shortly to become potentially crucial, I feel it is necessary to state for the record that I was in that room that night.

Though it can have no bearing that I can imagine on subsequent events, the thought of Gerry and me sleeping alone on this of all nights still makes me feel sad.

5

MISSING

On Thursday 3 May I awoke in the children's bedroom. I can't remember who was up first but I know we had all surfaced by about 7.30am. I'm not even sure whether Gerry had actually noticed I'd slept in the other room and I chose not to mention it. At breakfast time, Madeleine had a question for us. 'Why didn't you come when Sean and I cried last night?'

We were puzzled. Did she mean when they were having their bath? we asked her. Or just after they'd gone to bed? Children often get a bit fractious around bedtime, though I had no recollection of any tears from either Madeleine or Sean before they settled the previous evening. And it certainly hadn't been in the early hours, because I'd been in the room with them, even closer than usual.

Madeleine didn't answer or elaborate. Instead she moved on to some other topic that had popped into her head, apparently unconcerned. She certainly didn't seem to be at all anxious or upset. Madeleine is bright, articulate and has never been backwards in coming forwards. If something had happened to make her cry, it was pretty unlikely that she wouldn't tell us about it, assuming she remembered what it was.

Gerry and I were disconcerted. Could Madeleine and Sean have woken up while we were at dinner? If so, it was worrying, obviously, but it didn't seem very probable. As I've said, not only did they rarely stir at all at night, but if they did it was hardly ever, and I mean ever, before the early hours. If they had done so on this occasion, it would mean they'd woken up, cried for a while, calmed themselves down and fallen asleep again – all within the space of half an hour. Or forty-five minutes, if it had been after our last check. Children usually need some soothing back to sleep once they've woken, especially if two of them are awake and upset at the same time, and it seemed highly unlikely they'd have gone through all these stages without one of them over-lapping with one of our checks. It wasn't impossible, but it seemed implausible.

Not for a moment did we think there might be some sinister reason for this occurrence, if indeed anything had occurred. If only foresight came as easily to us as hindsight. Within hours, the explanation for this would seem hugely important, and so haunted have I been ever since by Madeleine's words that morning that I've continued to blame myself for not sitting down and making completely certain there was no more information I could draw out of her.

Why hadn't this rung any alarm bells with me? How did I manage to conclude, subconsciously or otherwise, that if she had woken it was simply a rare aberration with a benign cause: a bad dream, perhaps? If in fact I ever did come to any

real conclusion. It was more a case of her question just hanging there quietly, unanswered. This could have been my one
chance to prevent what was about to happen, and I blew it. In
the infrequent moments when I'm able to be kinder to myself,
I can acknowledge, if only temporarily, that there was absolutely nothing to give me any reason for suspicion and that we can
all be clever after the event. But it is my belief there was somebody either in or trying to get into the children's bedroom that
night, and that is what disturbed them.

The only other unexplained detail I remember from that
morning was a large, brown stain I noticed on Madeleine's
pink Eeyore pyjama top. I couldn't recall seeing it the night
before and I had no idea how it might have got there. It
looked like a tea stain. Gerry and I do drink quite a bit of tea,
and Madeleine, too, would have the odd small cup. So at the
time I just assumed it was a drink spillage that had escaped
our attention, and that might well be all it was. But now, of
course, we can no longer make assumptions about anything
that can't be accounted for.

The morning continued like the others with kids' clubs
and tennis. After my lesson, I hung around on the grassy play
area, watching Gerry on the court and chatting to Russell,
who I'd found there. Another guest appeared with a video
camera to record his three-year-old daughter playing mini-
tennis. He looked a little embarrassed and laughingly
remarked to us that filming in this way made him feel like a
dirty old man. It led to a conversation between the three of
us about paedophiles. I remember Russell talking about how
everything had got a bit out of hand, that these days people
were so untrusting you hardly dared speak to children you

didn't know. What he was effectively saying was that the world had become paranoid; that he wanted his daughters to grow up with confidence and a sense of freedom. The other dad and I chipped in with our views – I mentioned not being allowed to take photographs of your own kids in swimming pools any longer – and we agreed that it was a shame things had come to this, especially for the children. It would be some days before Russell and I were able to acknowledge to each other the horrible irony of this conversation.

A little later, near the sun-loungers at the Tapas end of the swimming pool, some of our group were discussing whether to cancel our dinner booking in the evening and take the kids to the Millennium instead. We'd heard that another couple we'd met had tried unsuccessfully to book a table at the Tapas restaurant and we wondered whether it was fair of us to be taking over the place. Although the restaurant was accepting other reservations, our party of nine occupied most of the available places and I, for one, felt rather guilty about that. However, when someone pointed out that we'd be gone by Saturday whereas this family was staying on for another week, it didn't seem quite so unreasonable, and we decided to stick with our original plan. Another of those apparently trivial decisions . . .

I returned to our apartment before Gerry had finished his tennis lesson and washed and hung out Madeleine's pyjama top on the veranda. After preparing some lunch, I went with Fiona to pick up Madeleine and Scarlett, who was in the adjoining Baby Club, taking her on the quicker route through the grounds of the Ocean Club, which she hadn't yet discovered. Fiona and Dave had been windsurfing that morning and had seen Madeleine's group, who had gone down to the beach for their 'mini-sail' activity. We heard later that they'd been on a speedboat as well as a dinghy. Fiona told me she'd spotted Ella there but not Madeleine.

Some images are etched for all time on my brain. Madeleine that lunchtime is one of them. She was wearing an outfit I'd bought especially for her holiday: a peach-coloured smock top from Gap and some white broderie-anglaise shorts from Monsoon – a small extravagance, perhaps, but I'd pictured how lovely she would look in them and I'd been right. She was striding ahead of Fiona and me, swinging her bare arms to and fro. The weather was a little on the cool side and I remember think-ing I should have brought a cardigan for her, although she seemed oblivious of the temperature, just happy and care-free. I was following her with my eyes, admiring her. I wonder now, the nausea rising in my throat, if someone else was doing the same.

At the Toddler Club near the Tapas restaurant Fiona collected Lily and headed back to her flat. Madeleine and I met up with Sean, Amelie and Gerry and returned to ours for lunch. As the children were getting quite restless in the apartment we decided to get them out in the fresh air before the afternoon's activities. We went to the play area, which was such a hit with our three that they never seemed to get fed up with it. We then sat round the toddler pool for a while, dipping our feet in, and I took what has turned out to be my last photograph to date of Madeleine. Heartbreaking as it is for me to look at it now, it encapsulates the essence of Madeleine: so beautiful and so happy.

Together we took Sean and Amelie back to the Toddler Club at around 2.40pm and dropped Madeleine off with the Minis ten minutes later. Ella was already there. Gerry and I had booked an hour-long couples' tennis lesson with the professional coach at three-thirty, and as the courts were unoccupied, we decided to have a knock-up for half an hour first. Near the end of our lesson, as I strove desperately to improve my substandard backhand, another guest appeared, and he and Gerry decided to have a game together.

Having arranged for Gerry to meet the children, I opted to go for a run along the beach, where I spotted the rest of our holiday group. They saw me and shouted some words of encouragement. At least, I think that's what they were shouting! I remember feeling fleetingly disappointed that we hadn't known they were all heading for the beach, as it might have been nice to have joined them, especially for the kids. I wondered whether Madeleine had been OK about staying behind at Mini Club when Russ or Jane had collected Ella. I wasn't to know at that stage that in fact they had only just arrived when I ran by. It's hard work being a mum sometimes, fretting about the possible effects of the smallest of incidents on your children. I'm sure a lot of these worries are unfounded but it doesn't stop us having them, and we'll probably go on having them for the rest of our lives.

I had finished my run by five-thirty at the Tapas area, where I found Madeleine and the twins already having their tea with Gerry. The others had decided to feed their kids at the beachside restaurant, the Paraíso. Madeleine was sitting on the Tapas terrace, eating. She looked so pale and worn out, I went straight up to her and asked if she was all right.

Had she been OK at the club when Ella left to go to the beach? Yes, she said, but now she was really tired and wanted me to pick her up, which I did. Ten minutes later, the five of us went back to our apartment. I was carrying Madeleine. Because she was so exhausted we skipped play-time that evening.

Gerry was meeting Dave, Matt and Russell at 6pm for the men's social tennis night. We decided we'd bath the children early, especially as they were all tired, and then I might take them down to the play area in their pyjamas for a little while, if they weren't quite ready for their beds. Gerry left just before six, as I was drying the kids and putting on the twins' nappies. When they were all in their PJs, we went through to the sitting room and I brought them some milk and a biscuit. (Actually, as a very special treat, tonight they had a few crisps as well.) While they were looking at their books and playing with their games, I took a quick shower. Every other evening I'd waited until the children were asleep before showering, but as we were ahead of schedule, and I wanted to freshen up after my run, I thought I'd take advantage of these quiet few minutes. At around six-forty, as I was drying myself off, there was a knock on the patio doors and I heard David's voice calling me. Swiftly wrapping my towel around me, I stepped into the sitting room.

David had popped his head round the patio door, looking for me. The others had met up with Gerry at the tennis courts and he'd mentioned we were thinking of bringing the kids to the play area. Dave had nipped up to see if he could give me a hand taking them down. As they were all ready for bed and seemed content with their books, I decided they were probably past the stage of needing any more activity. So he went back to the tennis while I quickly dressed and sat down on the couch with the children.

Here is another of those vivid, now cherished memories: Madeleine, in her Eeyore pyjamas, sitting on my lap and cuddling in – something of which she was especially fond when she was tired. We were on one of the two blue sofas, the one facing the patio doors, with Sean and Amelie to our right. I read them a Mog story by Judith Kerr. Auntie Ail – my cousin Aileen – and Uncle Andy had bought this for Madeleine on her third birthday and it remained one of her favourites. She asked if she could wear my engagement ring, which she often liked to do. I took it off and she put it on her middle finger for a few minutes. Gerry arrived back promptly at 7pm, sat down on the other couch and we all chatted for a while. Then we shepherded our three weary little ones through to the bathroom to brush their teeth and for Madeleine to do her bedtime 'wee-wee'.

I took them all into their bedroom. Madeleine got into her bed and then Amelie, Sean and I settled ourselves on top of it, with our backs against the wall, for our final story, *If you're happy and you know it!*, another present to Madeleine, this one from Great-Auntie Janet and Great-Uncle Brian. If you're happy and you know it, clap your hands! says the monkey. Stamp your feet! says the elephant.

If you're happy and you know it . . . It seemed so fitting at the time. Madeleine was obviously exhausted and her head sank down on her pillow intermittently, although she did join in with the babbled responses of her little brother and sister. It's strange the things you remember. Two pages at the end of the book are divided up into squares, most of them containing one of the animals featured earlier. Madeleine started to count these. She included a couple of the blank squares and I was about to point this out to her when I checked myself, realizing that she was counting the squares regardless of whether or not there was an animal inside. What did it matter, anyway? I felt a surge of pride in her. A boring and redundant detail, you may think, but now *any* memory of my baby is to be treasured, especially one of the last to date I have to cling on to.

Gerry came through to say goodnight. We helped Sean and Amelie give their big sister a 'night-night' kiss before laying them in their adjacent travel cots. Then we kissed the twins, and kissed Madeleine, already snuggled down with her 'princess' blanket and Cuddle Cat – a soft toy she'd been given soon after she was born and never went to bed without. We were in no doubt that all three would be asleep in an instant. As always, we left the door a few inches open to allow a glimmer of light into the room.

Between 7.15 and 7.30pm Gerry took his shower and I went to blow-dry my wayward fringe and put on a bit of make-up. We then sat down together in the sitting room for three-quarters of an hour or so and relaxed with a drink. We talked about the holiday and whether we'd do anything differently if we were to come again, which we had been considering. We both thought that another time we'd quite like to stay in the apartment on our own some evenings (the other couples probably felt that way, too), have a leisurely dinner in the sitting room or on the veranda, and enjoy one of our famous early nights. In fact, we'd wondered about doing that tonight, but as it was such a short holiday, and almost over, it seemed a bit unsociable not to join in with everyone else. Another decision that could have gone either way.

Just after 8.30pm, Gerry checked on the children and then we left for the Tapas restaurant. We exited via the patio doors at the back, facing the restaurant and pool area, just as we had done the previous three nights. There was a lamp on in the sitting room. The long curtains on the inside of the glass doors were drawn and the doors themselves closed but not locked. We shut behind us both the child safety gate at the top of the short flight of steps and the gate at the bottom, as we always did. We headed straight to the restaurant without seeing anyone else. We were the first of our party to arrive. Catching sight of Steve and Carolyn Carpenter, a couple from Gerry's tennis group, at a small table near the one reserved for us, we stood talking to them for five minutes or so. As we chatted, our friends began to appear. Jane arrived first, at about eight-forty, followed a few minutes later by Rachael and Matt. Next came Russell, and finally Fiona, David and Dianne. Jane reported that Evie was still a little off her food, despite being her usual cheery self. By 9pm we were all seated and had begun ordering drinks, starters and main meals.

We mentioned to the others what Madeleine had said that morning. Obviously, we didn't want any of our children waking and wondering where we were even for a few minutes, and if the chances of that happening seemed remote, it was enough of a concern to make us absolutely prompt with our checks on the kids. That is why Gerry and

I were subsequently able to be so accurate about timings.

After ordering his food, Gerry left to do the first check just before 9.05 by his watch. He entered the apartment via the patio doors and noticed almost immediately that the children's bedroom door was further ajar than it had been. He glanced into our room to make sure Madeleine hadn't wandered in there, as she was prone to do if ever she woke in the small hours. Seeing no little body curled up in our bed, he went over to look in on the children.

Madeleine was lying there, on her left-hand side, her legs under the covers, in exactly the same position as we'd left her. For Gerry, this became one of those images I described earlier, pictures that fix themselves indelibly, almost photo-graphically, in the memory. He paused for a couple of seconds to look at Madeleine and thought to himself, She's so beautiful. After pulling the bedroom door to, restoring it to its original angle, he went to the bathroom before leaving the apartment.

As he closed the gate to the street behind him, Gerry saw Jes – Jeremy Wilkins, a guy from his tennis group – walking towards him on the other side of Rua Dr Francisco Gentil Martins, pushing his younger child in a buggy. With his meal already ordered, Gerry hesitated about pausing to speak to Jes and took a few strides before making up his mind and crossing over to say hello. Jes explained that he was pushing his baby around in the buggy to try to get him off to sleep, and Gerry told him about our own childcare arrangement. The conversation probably lasted only a few minutes but it was long enough for me to wonder where Gerry had got to. On his return he mentioned he'd met Jes. By this time Jane had left to make sure her daughters were OK. En route to her apartment, we learned later, she had seen Gerry and Jes on the street.

For the record, there was subsequently some uncertainty about which side of the road Jes and Gerry were actually on. Jane and Jes remember it as the same side as the Tapas entrance, whereas Gerry is sure he crossed the street. Either way, exactly where they were standing is not crucial. What may be important is that all three of them were there.

At 9.30pm I stood up to go and make our second check. Almost simultaneously, Matt got to his feet to see to Grace. As his apartment was right next door, he offered to look in on our three while he was there. I hesitated. I was quite happy to go myself but it seemed a bit silly to insist when Matt was going anyway. 'Oh, OK, then. My turn next.' When Matt returned he reassured us, 'All quiet!'

At 10pm I went back to the apartment myself. I entered the sitting room via the patio doors, as Gerry and Matt had done, and stood there, listening, for a few seconds. All was silent. Then I noticed that the door to the children's bedroom was open quite wide, not how we had left it. At first I assumed that Matt must have moved it. I walked over and gently began to pull it to. Suddenly it slammed shut, as if caught by a draught.

A little surprised, I turned to see if I'd left the patio doors open and let in the breeze. Retracing my steps, I confirmed that I hadn't. Returning to the children's room, I opened the door a little, and as I did so I glanced over at Madeleine's bed. I couldn't quite make her out in the dark. I remember looking at it and looking at it for what was probably only a few seconds, though it felt like much longer. It seems so daft now, but I didn't switch on the light straight away. Force of habit, I suppose: taking care to avoid waking the children at all costs.

When I realized Madeleine wasn't actually there, I went through to our bedroom to see if she'd got into our bed. That would explain the open door. On the discovery of another empty bed, the first wave of panic hit me. As I ran back into the children's room the closed curtains flew up in a gust of wind. My heart lurched as I saw now that, behind them, the window was wide open and the shutters on the outside raised all the way up. Nausea, terror, disbelief, fear. Icy fear. Dear God, no! *Please, no!*

On Madeleine's bed, the top right-hand corners of the covers were still turned over, forming a triangle. Cuddle Cat and her pink princess blanket were lying where they'd been when we'd kissed her goodnight. I dashed over to the second bed, on the other side of the travel cots where the twins slept on, oblivious, and looked out through the window. I've no idea what I expected to see there.

Refusing to acknowledge what I already knew, and perhaps automatically going into a well-practised medical-emergency mode, I quickly scoured the apartment to exclude all other possibilities, mentally ticking boxes that I knew, deep down, were already ticked. I checked the wardrobe in the children's room. I ran into the kitchen, throwing open all the cupboard doors, into our bedroom, searching the wardrobes, in and out of the bathroom, all within about fifteen seconds, before hurtling out through the patio doors and down towards Gerry and our friends. As soon as our table was in sight I started screaming. 'Madeleine's gone! *Someone's taken her!*' Everyone seemed frozen for a split second, perhaps unable, as I'd been, to process this information. Then they all jumped up from their chairs and ran towards me. I remember Gerry saying, 'She must be there!' By now, I was hysterical. 'She's not! She's *gone!*'

Everybody sprinted back to our apartment, except for Dianne, who remained in the Tapas area, and Jane, who was away from the table seeing to her kids. I remember feeling frustrated when David said, 'Let's just check the apartment.' I'd done that, and I knew, *I knew*, that Madeleine had been abducted. I ran out into the car park, flying from end to end, yelling desperately, 'Madeleine! Madeleine!' It was so cold and so windy. I kept picturing her in her short-sleeved Marks and Spencer Eeyore pyjamas and feeling how chilled she would be. Bizarrely, I found myself thinking it would have been better if she'd been wearing her long-sleeved Barbie ones. Fear was shearing through my body.

In the children's room, Gerry lowered the shutter at the open window. Rushing outside, he made the sickening discovery that it could be raised from this side, too, not just from inside as we'd thought. Gerry, David, Russell and Matt split into pairs and dashed around the adjacent apartment blocks, meeting back at our flat within a couple of minutes. Just after ten past ten, Gerry asked Matt to run to the Ocean Club's twenty-four-hour reception to get the staff to call the police. All the screaming and shouting had now alerted other guests and staff that something was amiss and various people were beginning to appear outside the apartment, front and back. I vividly recall sobbing, 'Not Madeleine, not

Madeleine, not Madeleine.' I was trying so hard to suppress the negative voice in my head tormenting me with the words, 'She's gone. She's gone.' Even now, when the dark clouds close in on me, I find myself shaking my head manically and repeating over and over again, 'Not Madeleine, not Madeleine. Please God, not my Madeleine.'

Gerry and I were standing in the living room clutching each other, utterly distraught. I couldn't help myself, let alone try to soothe Gerry, who was in a state too harrowing for me to bear, howling for his precious little girl. I kept blaming myself – 'We've let her down! We've failed her!' – which increased Fiona's own distress. 'You haven't, Kate. You haven't,' she insisted.

By this time the Mark Warner people had rounded up as many of their colleagues as they could, off-duty staff as well as those just finishing their shifts, rousing some of them from their beds. Close to ten-thirty they activated the company's 'missing child search protocol' and mobilized people to comb the complex and its environs. At 10.35 the police had still not arrived, so Gerry asked Matt if he would go back down to the twenty-four-hour reception and find out what was happening. John Hill, the Mark Warner resort manager, came up to the veranda behind our apartment. I remember screaming at him to do something. 'Where are the police?' I yelled at him. He tried to reassure me they'd be with us soon but I could tell that he, too, was finding the waiting difficult. Minutes felt like hours.

I was just so overwhelmed by fear, helplessness and frustration, I was hitting out at things, banging my fists on the metal railing of the veranda, trying to expel the intolerable pain inside me. Gerry had been over to the Mini Club above the twenty-four-hour reception, thinking that if Madeleine had been left somewhere, she might possibly make her way back to any place that was familiar to her. Our friends were running to and from the Tapas area, pleading with people to ring the police again from there.

Despite the horror of the situation, some sense of the necessity to approach the crisis calmly and methodically appeared to kick in among our friends as they tried to exert a modicum of control over the chaos. What could be done? What should be done? Aware that we were only an hour and a quarter's drive from southern Spain, and beyond that lay the borderless continent of Europe – not to mention the short hop across the Strait of Gibraltar to north Africa – David was saying, 'We need roadblocks set up. The borders to Spain, Morocco and Algiers need to be alerted.' Russell later asked us for our digital photos of Madeleine and went off somewhere with our camera.

Gerry, meanwhile, was running from pillar to post, urging me to remain in the apartment with the twins so that I'd be on hand if Madeleine was found and brought back there. He'd asked Fiona to stay with me. I was in our bedroom, on my knees beside the bed, just praying and praying and praying, begging God and Our Lady to protect Madeleine and help us find her. They had heard many a supplication from me in the past but none so intense, nor so important, as these.

At some point, Emma Knights, the Mark Warner customer-care manager, came in and sat on the bed near me. She was very nice and tried her best to comfort me, but my grief was so agonizing and so personal that I wasn't sure whether I wanted her there or not. I didn't really want anyone around me but people I knew well. Another British woman, in her late forties or early fifties, turned up on our veranda at one point and kept trying to put her arm round me. She was quite drunk and smelled of cigarettes and I remember willing her to go away.

Then a lady appeared on a balcony – I'm fairly certain this was about 11pm, before the police arrived – and, in a plummy voice, inquired, 'Can someone tell me what all the noise is about?' I explained as clearly as I was able, given the state I was in, that my little girl had been stolen from her bed, to which she casually responded, 'Oh, I see,' almost as if she'd just been told that a can of beans had fallen off a kitchen shelf. I remember feeling both shocked and angry at this woefully inadequate and apparently unconcerned reaction. I recollect that in our outrage, Fiona and I shouted back something rather short and to the point.

I wandered into the children's bedroom several times to check on Sean and Amelie. They were both lying on their fronts in a kind of crouch, with their heads turned sideways and their knees tucked under their tummies. In spite of the noise and lights and general pandemonium, they hadn't stirred. They'd always been sound sleepers, but this seemed unnatural. Scared for them, too, I placed the palms of my hands on their backs to check for chest movement, basically, for some sign of life. Had Madeleine been given some kind of sedative to keep her quiet? Had the twins, too?

It was not until about 11.10pm that two policemen arrived from the nearest town, Lagos, about five miles away.

To me they seemed bewildered and out of their depth, and I couldn't shake the images of Tweedledum and Tweedledee out of my head. I realize how unfair this might sound, but with communication hampered by the language barrier and precious time passing, their presence did not fill me with confidence at all.

We did not appreciate until later that these two officers were from the Guarda Nacional Republicana, or GNR, who are essentially military police, like the Gendarmes in France or Guardia Civil in Spain, run by the Interior Ministry. They deal with matters like highway patrol and crowd control, and are also responsible for law enforcement in more rural areas like the Algarve, but they do not handle criminal investigations. At that stage, of course, we weren't familiar with the various tiers of the Portuguese police system. As far as we were concerned, they were simply 'the police'.

We tried to explain what had happened. David reiterated his concerns about roadblocks and border notification and I reported my fears that all three children could have been sedated. A lady called Sílvia, who worked at the Ocean Club, had arrived to help out with translation. We learned later that she was the maintenance and services manager. I remember her telling me that she had two grown-up daughters herself. She was very kind and I was glad of her help and support.

I didn't yet know that at around 9.15pm Jane had seen a man on Rua Dr Agostinho da Silva carrying a child who appeared to be asleep. When I'd discovered that Madeleine was missing she had been in her apartment three doors along. Hearing the commotion, she had come out and discovered what was going on. Taking Fiona to one side, she told her how, after leaving the restaurant to make her first check on her children, and having passed Gerry and Jes talking on Rua Dr Gentil Martins, she had seen this man crossing the junction with Rua Dr Agostinho da Silva, ten or fifteen feet in front of her, walking from left to right. Obviously, at the time she had thought little of it: as far as any of us knew, Madeleine was asleep in her bed, and, having just seen Gerry, Jane was well aware that he had been in our apartment only a few minutes before. Quite naturally, she'd assumed the man was a father with his child, perhaps on their way home from a crèche. As soon as she heard about Madeleine's disappearance, everything fell into place and she felt sick. She immediately reported this sighting to the police. Gerry was informed but, given the condition I was in, he did not share this development with me until the morning.

While the officers looked around, Gerry called his sister, Trisha. As difficult as it was to tell our family, we knew we needed help from home, and quickly. Trisha, who is a nurse, and her husband, Sandy, are Madeleine's godparents and two of life's copers. Gerry was a mess – 'roaring like a bull', as Trish put it – and sobbing down the phone. She could barely make out what he was saying. It was painful for me to see my strong, assertive husband unravelling, and frightening for her to hear her 'wee bro' in this state. I could hear him crying over and over again, 'She's gone, Trisha. She's gone.'

After Gerry rang off, Trisha and Sandy called the Foreign Office in London, the British Consulate in the Algarve and the British Embassy in Lisbon, requesting assistance. It was also left to them to tell the rest of Gerry's family. Trish drove over to their mum's. This was not news that could be broken to her over the phone.

At 11.52pm, Gerry spoke to my Uncle Brian and Auntie Janet in Rothley, at my request. Janet is a woman of strong faith and I wanted her to start praying for Madeleine as soon as possible. Brian then got in touch with the duty officer at the Foreign Office in London.

The call I'd been putting off now had to be made. My mum and dad completely adore Madeleine and I just couldn't bring myself to shatter their world. I dreaded to think what this would do to them. So, just after midnight, it was Gerry who had to tell them. Distraught, they rang friends and family who immediately rallied to their support.

I'm pretty sure that initially the GNR officers assumed Madeleine had simply wandered off by herself. By midnight, however, evidently they were concerned enough to inform the Polícia Judiciária (PJ), the main force that actually investigates crimes, under the aegis of the Ministry of Justice. The PJ were based in the larger town of Portimão, twenty miles or so from Praia da Luz, and took over an hour to arrive. It felt more like a day to Gerry and me. Eventually, shortly after 1am, two officers walked in. Once again, the events of the evening were relayed to them and brief statements taken from us. Dave asked whether we should get the media involved to increase awareness and recruit more help. The reply was swift and unambiguous. 'No media! *No media!*'

People had been in and out of the apartment for the last three hours, and until one of the PJ officers stuck a piece of police tape across the doorway of the children's room, it was

Gerry who tried to make sure everyone kept clear of it. Now one of the PJ men (I remember him very distinctly: he was quite young and, I assumed, probably quite junior) entered the room, where the twins were still asleep, with a brush and a pair of latex gloves. He also tried to take fingerprints from Gerry and me. Unsuccessfully, as it turned out: we had to provide them again the next day at the police station. Then they asked for our passports, including Madeleine's.

Meanwhile, desperate for God's intervention, for ourselves and for Madeleine, I asked the resort staff if they might be able to find a priest to come and pray with us and support us. I think they tried, but either they couldn't contact anyone or there was no priest available, so I carried on praying on my own. The pain, terror and the suffocating helplessness I felt are indescribable. There just aren't the words to adequately convey such torment. Just after 2am, I spoke to my friend Father Paul Seddon, the priest who had married Gerry and me and baptized Madeleine. He offered me words of comfort and then prayed for our little girl.

Next I called my best mate, Michelle. I needed her to get her large Catholic family praying, too. Perhaps not surprisingly, given the hour, nobody answered the home phone. Eventually, at about 3am, I managed to get hold of Michelle's partner, Jon Corner, on his mobile. When I told him what had happened, I don't think he believed me at first. He even said, 'You're joking, aren't you?' He'd undoubtedly been asleep, I wasn't at my most coherent and what I was trying to tell him was just so far off most people's radar it was hard to grasp. Poor Jon – I don't think he could quite get his brain in gear for a moment or two. He said that Michelle was asleep, implying that it wasn't a good moment, as if I'd phoned for a desultory chat at an inconvenient time. I urged him to wake her up. 'No one's listening!' I wept. 'Nothing's *happening*!'

The next thing I knew, the PJ officers were heading for the front door. I felt another surge of panic. When I asked them anxiously where they were going, they said they had finished for tonight. They told us we could take whatever we needed for the twins from the children's room. Rather more frantically, I tried to establish what would be happening next and for the remainder of the hours of darkness. The only answer the officers gave us was that they would come back in the morning. Pressed as to when, they said it would be after nine. And with that they were gone, leaving us to our own devices. It was incomprehensible. Surely that couldn't be it for the night? The sense of helplessness and agitation just kept intensifying.

Dave, seeing Gerry's anguish and frustration at how little was being done, knew Madeleine needed more help than she was getting. At some point before the PJ left, a retired British couple in a nearby apartment lent him their computer and he sent an email to Sky News alerting them to the abduction of our daughter, using an address listed on their website.

Evidently this wasn't the best way of contacting Sky, because, as it turned out, Dave's email remained buried in some inbox. Despite the fabricated tales that later emerged in certain quarters, suggesting that we had contacted the media before we'd even called the police, apparently the first Sky heard of Madeleine's disappearance was from the Press Association, and from seeing one of our friends on GMTV, later that morning. Though we knew little of what was going on at the time, it is true that the news filtered through overnight. Rachael had contacted a friend of hers at the BBC seeking help and advice and several friends in the UK informed the press some time after 7am.

We probably could have stayed in our apartment, but who would have wanted to? Looking back, it's inexplicable, of course, that we should ever have been left in what was now a crime scene. We shouldn't even have been allowed to take things out of the children's bedroom. Mark Warner had prepared another flat for us on the first floor of an adjacent block, but Gerry and I were in no condition to be on our own. We couldn't look after ourselves, let alone the twins. So the staff put up two extra cots in Fiona and David's apartment and we carried a sleepy Sean and Amelie into their sitting room. But I needed to keep them close to me. I lowered myself down on to the couch with Fiona. She took a twin from me and we both sat there hugging my children. Holding one of my babies provided me with some much-needed comfort, albeit fleetingly.

On my insistence, Gerry and Dave went out again to look for some sign of Madeleine. They went up and down the beach in the dark, running, shouting, desperate to find something; please God, to find Madeleine herself. It was only much later that Gerry told me he'd already started remembering cases of other missing children and acknowledging the horrific possibility that Madeleine might not be found. It was a possibility I could not have begun to contemplate.

I don't know whether the Mark Warner staff were still searching. I couldn't see anyone about by this time, except for a couple of GNR police cars in the road outside and a handful of officers hanging around. None of them appeared to be doing very much. I couldn't stand the thought of nothing happening while time marched inexorably onward. Madeleine could be miles away by now. At one point I went out to speak to the police, needing some reassurance. It was difficult and exasperating as communication was so limited, and there was no reassurance to be had. I walked briskly up and down Rua Dr Agostinho da Silva, sometimes breaking into a jog, clinging to the hope that I'd spot something in the dark. The fear of Madeleine being dumped somewhere and dying of hypothermia started to hijack my thoughts.

Back in the apartment the cold, black night enveloped us all for what seemed like an eternity. Dianne and I sat there just staring at each other, still as statues. 'It's so dark,' she said again and again. 'I want the light to come.' I felt exactly the same way. Gerry was stretched out on a camp bed with Amelie asleep on his chest. He kept saying, 'Kate, we need to rest.' He managed to drift off but only briefly, certainly for less than an hour. I didn't even try. I couldn't have allowed myself to entertain sleep. I felt Madeleine's terror, and I had to keep vigil with her. I needed to be doing *something*, but I didn't know where to put myself. I wandered restlessly in and out of the room and on to the balcony.

At long last, dawn broke.

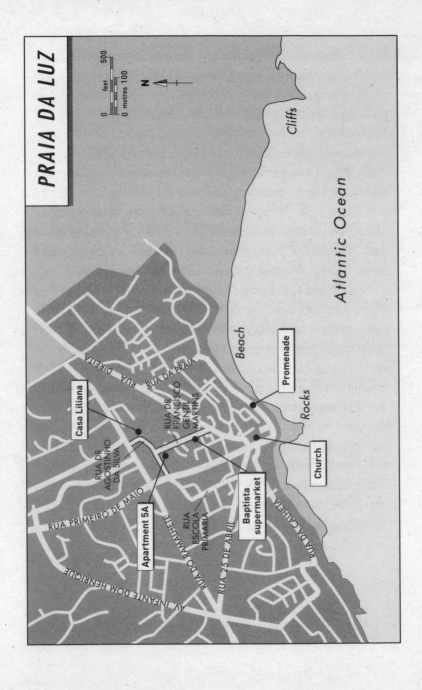

PRAIA DA LUZ

feet 0 500
0 metres 100

N

Atlantic Ocean

Cliffs

Beach

Rocks

Promenade

Church

Casa Liliana

RUA DA PRAIA

RUA DIRETA

RUA DR FRANCISCO GENTIL MARTINS

RUA DR AGOSTINHO DA SILVA

RUA PRIMEIRO DE MAIO

AV INFANTE DOM HENRIQUE

RUA DO RAMALHETE

Apartment 5A

RUA ESCOLA PRIMARIA

RUA 25 DE ABRIL

RUA DA CALHETA

Baptista supermarket

6

FRIDAY 4 MAY

Friday 4 May. Our first day without Madeleine. As soon as it was light Gerry and I resumed our search. We went up and down roads we'd never seen before, having barely left the Ocean Club complex all week. We jumped over walls and raked through undergrowth. We looked in ditches and holes. All was quiet apart from the sound of barking dogs, which added to the eeriness of the atmosphere. I remember opening a big dumpster-type bin and saying to myself, please God, don't let her be in here. The most striking and horrific thing about all this was that we were completely alone. Nobody else, it seemed, was out looking for Madeleine. Just us, her parents.

We must have been out for at least an hour before returning to David and Fiona's apartment, where Sean and Amelie were now up and about. The twins, distracted by having Lily and Scarlett to play with, didn't mention Madeleine, mercifully. Russell, Jane, Matt, Rachael and their children began to arrive. People kept telling me to have some breakfast but I couldn't eat. I had no appetite and my throat was constricted with anxiety. In any case, how could I think about eating now? There wasn't time to eat. Someone had Madeleine and we had to find her.

That morning I learned of the man Jane had seen in the street. Although Gerry and our friends had been trying to protect me from further distress by not telling me about this sooner, when they did I was strangely relieved. Madeleine hadn't just disappeared off the face of the earth. There was *something* to work on.

This man was around thirty-five, forty years old, dark-haired and of southern European or Mediterranean appearance. His everyday clothes – beige or gold-coloured trousers and a dark jacket – gave Jane the impression he was not a tourist. He was carrying the sleeping child horizontally across his arms, the child's legs dangling. Though she had no reason, at that point, to be at all suspicious of him, clearly there was something odd enough about what she saw for her to register the image. While he had been dressed for the cold evening, the child was barefoot and not covered by a blanket. Although Jane had never seen or known about Madeleine's Eeyore pyjamas, her description of this child's night clothes – light-coloured pink or white pyjamas with a 'trailing' or floral pattern and turn-ups on the bottoms – matched Madeleine's almost exactly. From the style of these pyjamas, she had also assumed the child was a girl.

There was little doubt in my mind then, nor is there now, that what Jane saw was Madeleine's abductor taking her away. But in spite of the fact that she'd reported this to both the GNR and PJ straight away, it would be 25 May before her description of the man and child was released to the press.

I have never felt any anger or disappointment whatsoever towards Jane. On the contrary, I was grateful someone had seen something. I'm sure this experience has been a terrible burden for her to carry around with her every day since and I do feel for her. There have been many occasions when I have visualized myself walking up that road instead of Jane. Would I even have noticed the man and child? Seen that it was my daughter? Would it have dawned on me, out of the blue, what was happening? If not, after going into the apartment and finding Madeleine missing, would I instantly have made the connection and been able to chase after him? I've even pictured myself catching up with him and grabbing him by the shoulder. Saving Madeleine.

Around 8am, I started to receive text messages and calls from friends back in the UK who were seeing and hearing news bulletins – messages like: 'Please tell me it's not *your* Madeleine.'

At about nine o'clock we all went out on to Rua Dr Agostinho da Silva to find out what was going on and to look out for the PJ. The GNR patrol was still in evidence, although again, there didn't seem to be much sense of urgency. So what had the police been doing? It was hard to tell. According to the PJ files, to which we did not have access until August 2008, two patrol dogs were brought to Praia da Luz at 2am on 4 May and four search-and-rescue dogs at 8am. I don't remember seeing any police dogs until the morning, and if there were any specific police searches overnight, they were not apparent. The only searches I was aware of were those carried out by ourselves, fellow guests and the Mark Warner staff.

According to the files, the tracker dogs did not go out until 11pm on 4 May. At some point in the first twenty-four hours (I could not say when exactly, but probably that morning) I recall one of the GNR patrol officers asking us for some of Madeleine's clothing or belongings to enable these dogs to identify her scent. I fetched the pink princess blanket she took to bed with her every night, which they took, and some of her clothes, which they didn't.

Several people I recognized as other Mark Warner guests were milling around and a few of the men offered to help. Steve Carpenter told us that he had approached John Hill, the resort manager, insisting that all the apartments, occupied or not (and as it was the low season, many were empty), should be opened up and searched. There had been no house-to-house inquiries at all and there wouldn't be for some hours to come. To this day, I don't know that this task has been completed.

A lady from an apartment across Rua Dr Gentil Martins, overlooking our little side gate, came over to speak to us. She said that the previous night she had seen a car going up the Rocha Negra – the black, volcanic cliff that dominates the village. There was a track leading to the Rocha Negra but nobody remembered ever having noticed any vehicle that far up in the daytime, let alone at night. This immediately conjured visions of Madeleine being disposed of somewhere on the overhanging cliff. I went to tell one of the police officers who was able to speak a little English. He was quite dismissive. It would have been one of the GNR men checking the area, he said.

The texts and phone calls kept coming. By this time our

friend Jon Corner, a creative director in media production in Liverpool, was circulating photographs and video footage of Madeleine to the police, Interpol and broadcasting and newspaper news desks. This was in accordance with the standard advice of the National Center for Missing and Exploited Children in the US, which advocates getting an image of a missing child into the public domain as soon as possible. A colleague from the surgery in Melton Mowbray suggested enlisting the help of a private investigator and offered to look into the possibility. I was bemused. Back then, I thought of private investigators – if I thought of them at all – as lone mavericks like Jim Rockford in *The Rockford Files*. And at that stage I honestly didn't know what we needed, though it certainly felt like more than we had. Had I known what I know now, perhaps I would have taken her advice.

A forensic team also arrived from Lisbon that Friday. Having moved out of apartment 5A, we weren't aware of exactly when, but presumably it was some time in the morning. All we saw of them were TV images of a woman in her street clothes dusting the shutters outside the children's room. Her shoulder-length hair was blowing free and I seem to recall that in some shots she wasn't wearing any gloves, either.

Not having slept for some twenty-six hours I was starting to feel quite jaded but my mind was teeming with horrific images. A middle-aged British lady suddenly materialized beside me and introduced herself. She announced that she was, or had been, a social worker or child protection officer and insisted on showing me her professional papers, including, I think, her Criminal Records Bureau certificate. She asked me to sit down on a low wall, plonked herself next to me and told me she wanted me to go through everything that had happened the previous night. She was quite pushy and her manner, her very presence, were making me feel uncomfortable and adding to my distress.

David was standing nearby. Concerned, he took me aside and pointed out that we didn't know who this woman was or what she was doing there. He reassured me that I wasn't obliged to speak to her if I didn't want to. And I didn't want to. Whoever she was, and whatever her credentials were, it was an inappropriate intrusion. And something about it, something about her, just didn't feel right. I was glad I extricated myself. This woman would pop up several times in the days and months to come and I still don't really know who she is or what she was trying to achieve.

Steve Carpenter returned with a man who had offered his assistance. He was, he'd told Steve, bilingual in English and Portuguese and could maybe assist with interpreting. I was grateful for any help we could get. This man was in his thirties, wore glasses and there was something unusual about one of his eyes – a squint, I thought at the time (I have since been told he is blind in one eye). He seemed very personable and was happy to be of service. When one of the GNR officers came over to request more details about Madeleine and any distinguishing features she had, this man stepped in to translate.

I was holding a photograph of Madeleine, which he asked to see. As he studied it, he told me about his daughter back in England who was the same age, and who, he said, looked

just like Madeleine. I was a little irked by this. In the circumstances, it seemed rather tactless, even if he was simply trying
to empathize. I didn't think his daughter could possibly be as
beautiful as Madeleine – though of course, as her mum, I
didn't think any other little girl could be as beautiful as
Madeleine. When he had finished translating, he turned and
began to walk briskly away. Realizing I didn't know his name,
I caught up with him and asked.

'Robert,' he said.

'Thank you, Robert,' I said.

It was about 10am by the time a couple of PJ officers
turned up. (One of them, in his thirties, tall and well built, I
thought of for ages simply as John. I'm not sure he ever gave
us his name, but later – much later – we found out that it was
João Carlos.) They told us they had to take us and our
friends to the police station in Portimão. We couldn't all go
at once as somebody needed to look after the children. After
some discussion, it was agreed that Gerry and I, Jane, David
and Matt would be interviewed first and the PJ would come
back for the others later in the day. Fiona and Dianne took
Sean and Amelie to their club along with the other children.
While our world was falling apart, the best way of trying to
keep theirs together seemed to be to stick with what they
were used to.

Gerry and I travelled in one police car with the others
following in a second vehicle. It was an awful journey. It took
twenty, twenty-five minutes, but it felt much longer. On the
way I rang a colleague – another lady of strong faith.
She prayed over the phone for most of the trip, while I
listened and wept at the other end. I will for ever be indebted

to her for her help and support at that agonizing time.

Our first impressions of the police station were not encouraging. Basic and shabby, it didn't seem conducive to efficiency and order. We were shown to a small waiting area separated from the control room – where calls and faxes came in – only by windows and a glass door, which was left ajar. In the control room, officers in jeans and T-shirts smoked and engaged in what sounded more like light-hearted banter than serious discussion.

I know as well as anybody that one shouldn't judge people – or perhaps places, either – on appearances, but it all made me immensely nervous. I was appalled by the treat-ment we received at the police station that day. Officers walked past us as if we weren't there. Nobody asked how we were doing, whether we were OK or needed anything to eat or drink or to use the bathroom. Our child had been stolen and I felt as if I didn't exist. I've tried to rationalize it since: maybe they just couldn't imagine how it felt to be a parent in such circumstances, or maybe they couldn't speak English and it seemed better or easier simply to avoid us. Whatever the case, it was a horribly isolating experience.

At some point that morning we'd become aware that friends and family were appearing on television expressing our concern about the lack of police activity overnight. I think I'd registered Trisha and a good friend in Glasgow popping up on the TV in the apartment. Gerry has a memory of seeing some familiar faces on the set in the police control room. We were quite surprised that people were giving interviews but it was understandable. After all, we'd been on the phone half the night to our friends and relatives, sobbing that nothing was being done and begging for their help. And we appreciated the swift response. We were just worried that any criticism of the police might not do us or, more to the point, Madeleine, any favours.

We were grateful for the support of the British consul for the Algarve, Bill Henderson, and the proconsul, Angela Morado, who met us at the police station. Although there was little anyone could say or do to ease our pain, they were both warm and extremely sympathetic. I especially appreciated Angela's reassuring presence – she was roughly the same age as me, a mother herself and, most importantly, strong, and I felt those common factors would help her to understand a little of what I was going through. At one point, the British ambassador, John Buck, came down from Lisbon to see us. He was pleasant and obviously concerned.

I recall Bill Henderson telling me there had been several recent cases of men getting into bed with children, but no known abductions. I'm not sure why this didn't ring a million alarm bells or sicken me to the core. As it was, it remained locked away in the dungeons of my mind for many months. At the time my brain simply couldn't connect such cases with Madeleine's disappearance. These were abuse victims, and as awful as such crimes were, Madeleine's situation was much worse. Our child had been stolen. We didn't know where or how she was.

After an hour or so, Gerry, Matt and Jane were taken off for questioning. I remember constantly looking at the clock, counting the hours since we'd last seen Madeleine, my terror mounting with every five minutes that passed. My body, as well as my mind, appeared to have locked down. Bill and

Angela went out for food and water for us but I had no interest in eating.

Gerry told us afterwards that when he'd asked about deploying helicopters and heat-detecting equipment in the search, the police officer interviewing him had replied, 'This is not the UK.' There were no helicopters and no infra-red cameras, he was told. Gerry was also insisting that they speak to Jes Wilkins, in case he had seen the man and child reported by Jane. In fact, we found out later, an officer with a translator – Robert Murat, the man who had interpreted for me that morning – visited Jes and his partner, Bridget O'Donnell, in their apartment some time the same afternoon.

In a newspaper article by Bridget published several months down the line, she describes how the officer wrote down their answers to his questions on a loose piece of paper rather than in a notebook. Of greater concern was his reaction to a photocopied picture of a little girl he noticed lying on their table. He asked them if she was their daughter. Bridget explained that this was Madeleine, the little girl they were supposed to be looking for. 'My heart sank for the McCanns,' she remembered.

Back at the police station in Portimão, it was gone two o'clock before I was interviewed. As João Carlos led me up the stairs, I inquired whether he had any children. He told me he hadn't. 'But don't worry. We will find your daughter.' It was exactly what I was yearning to hear.

I was taken into a large room containing several desks. Gerry had asked João Carlos if he could be allowed to stay with me while I was questioned because he was extremely worried about my psychological state. I was grateful to João Carlos for agreeing, with the proviso that Gerry remained seated behind me. I appreciate now that this would not be acceptable practice in most police investigations. João Carlos interviewed me, assisted by a young female interpreter. He put his questions in Portuguese, the interpreter relayed them to me in English and then she translated my answers into Portuguese. The interview was neither videoed nor audio-taped. Instead João Carlos tapped my answers, as given to him in Portuguese by the interpreter, into his computer. As you can imagine, it was an incredibly laborious process. My eyes were still continually drawn towards the clock, or my watch, and as the minutes and then the hours ticked by my body became more and more tense.

The officer began with how we came to be in Portugal and then concentrated on the point at which I discovered Madeleine was missing. When he asked me if it was the first time I had been to Portugal I said, 'Yes. Never again!' The interpreter turned to me and said, 'Mrs McCann, this could have happened anywhere.' She was right, of course, and I was a bit ashamed of that remark, but in the circumstances it was hardly surprising I felt that way at that moment. As I recounted how I'd found Madeleine's bedclothes neatly folded back my voice faltered. Every now and then Gerry would put a hand on my shoulder or give me a reassuring squeeze.

The interview lasted four long hours. Afterwards, we met Guilhermino Encarnação, the director of the Algarve Polícia Judiciária, based in Faro, who was overseeing the investigation. He told us that somebody would be in touch with us later that night with an update and gave us a telephone number to call if we had any questions. I'm fairly certain this was the number of an officer at Portimão called Tavares de Almeida. In addition, he said, Portimão would be able to get hold of him via his mobile phone at any time if we needed to speak to him.

Meanwhile, Fiona, Russell, Rachael and Dianne had been brought to the police station for their interviews, which stretched from late afternoon into the evening.

It was seven-thirty by the time one of the PJ officers drove us away from the police station. Angela Morado came with us. Ten or fifteen minutes into our journey, the police officer had a call from his station. He said something to Angela, who explained that he'd been ordered to return us to the police station straight away. He wasn't allowed to tell us why. Already driving at quite a scary speed, he suddenly swung the car into a U-turn, floored the accelerator and drove us at a life-threatening 120mph plus back towards Portimão. I cannot overstate how terrifying this was. Had Madeleine been found? Please God. Was she alive? Was she dead? Gerry and I clung on to each other for dear life. I was crying hysterically and praying for all I was worth.

Back at the police station we endured at least another ten minutes of torture in the waiting area before somebody showed us a photograph, clearly taken from CCTV, of a blonde child with a woman in a petrol-station shop. We weren't told anything about this, just asked whether the little girl was Madeleine. She wasn't. And that was that. Again we were sent on our way, utterly devastated.

We were completely unprepared for what we found when we drove back into Praia da Luz some time after 8.30pm. The road outside our apartment block was lined with what seemed like hundreds of press and TV crews, five or six deep all the way.

Although he didn't say anything to me then, as soon as he saw all this Gerry knew it was likely to lead to a terrible invasion of our privacy at the most difficult time of our lives. We'd never been exposed to the glare of the media ourselves, but we were aware to some extent from what had happened to other people how intrusive the press, and in particular the tabloid newspapers, could be. No such implications registered with me at that stage. I was only able to think about anything for a second at a time.

We stepped out of the police car amid clicking, whirring cameras and dazzling lights. To suddenly become the focus of such attention – fiercely acute, and yet at the same time disconnected, impersonal, as if we were some rare species in a zoo – was bewildering, and it certainly increased my already rocketing stress levels. But in some ways this was just another bizarre scene in a bad dream from which I couldn't seem to wake myself up.

Upstairs our new apartment, 4G, was heaving with people. Among them were my mum, dad and Auntie Norah, who had arrived from the UK. Norah, on a visit from Canada, had been booked to return today but had immediately cancelled her flight home and had come with my parents to support us instead. As we embraced them one by one we found ourselves unable to let go. We were all sobbing. It was so hard seeing each other like this. It was all such a blur I can't be absolutely certain who else was there that night, but I think I remember John Hill, Emma Knights and

Craig Mayhew from Mark Warner, and Ambassador John Buck, British consul Bill Henderson and Angela Morado, who had accompanied us back from Portimão. There were some new faces, too: Liz Dow, the British consul for Lisbon, British Embassy press officer Andy Bowes and Alex Woolfall, a PR crisis-management specialist from Bell Pottinger in the UK, who had been drafted in by Mark Warner, as had a trauma psychologist from the Centre for Crisis Psychology (CCP) in north Yorkshire, who had now also arrived in Luz.

Mark Warner had arranged for the Ocean Club staff to bring food for us up to the apartment, but I still couldn't manage anything. All I wanted at that moment was to see Sean and Amelie. Emma had been looking after them and had not long before put them into their cots, but I went in to see them anyway. My need to be with them outweighed any concerns about disrupting their sleep.

For the first time I noticed the ugly purple, blue and black bruises on the sides of my hands, wrists and forearms. I was shocked. Gerry reminded me of how I'd been banging my clenched fists on the veranda railing and the apartment walls the night before. I could only vaguely remember it.

In spite of his misgivings about the media, Gerry decided that he wanted to make a statement to them. He knew we had to try to reach anyone who might know something. My stomach knotted at the mere thought of it. I've never been one for speaking in front of an audience, and I certainly couldn't imagine doing so now, when our daughter had just been abducted. Gerry told the people assembled in the apartment what he was intending to do. Nobody objected or advised him against it – but then, there was no one taking overall control of

FRIDAY 4 MAY

the situation, other than Alex Woolfall, whose primary role was to act for Mark Warner. So Gerry sat down and drafted a statement on a piece of scrap paper. It took him only a few minutes.

I accompanied him downstairs. As we left I grabbed Madeleine's Cuddle Cat. Keeping her beloved toy close was the nearest I could be to her. I was very troubled that she didn't have Cuddle Cat with her. Just being able to hold something familiar might have given her a crumb of comfort. It was 10pm, it was dark and I found the huge crowd and incessant flashbulbs incredibly intimidating. I was only grateful that at least Gerry was used to public speaking and I wouldn't have to say anything, though it wasn't easy for him, either. This was hardly the same as addressing a conference and he was completely traumatized. His voice cracked with emotion as he read out his statement by torchlight.

Words cannot describe the anguish and despair that we are feeling as the parents of our beautiful daughter Madeleine.

We request that anyone who may have information relating to Madeleine's disappearance, no matter how trivial, contact the Portuguese police and help us get her back safely.

Please, if you have Madeleine, let her come home to her mummy, daddy, brother and sister.

As everyone can understand how distressing the current situation is, we ask that our privacy is respected to allow us to continue assisting the police in their current investigation.

Please God, this appeal would reach somebody who knew something.

I'm not entirely sure how Gerry managed to deliver a

statement on that first day, or exactly what made him feel that he must. Obviously he believed that begging the abductor to give Madeleine back, and urging anyone who might have seen or know anything to come forward, could only help. He was also aware that in the UK it would probably be expected of parents in our situation to make some kind of statement or appeal – though that was not, as we would learn, the case in Portugal.

Later that evening, we were visited by the Anglican minister and his wife who were temporarily serving the Church of England community in Luz until the arrival at the weekend of a new minister from Canada. As the Catholic priest was away on retreat, they had come to offer their support to Gerry, me and our family, which we greatly appreciated. They said some prayers with us and I remember the minister reading out the passage in St Mark's gospel which begins: 'Suffer the little children to come unto me, and forbid them not: for of such is the kingdom of God,' which took me back to my own childhood.

By midnight we'd had no more word from the police about what, if anything, was happening. More than twenty-four hours had elapsed since Madeleine had been snatched. The pain, dread and sense of powerlessness were tearing me apart. I rang the telephone number given to me by Guilhermino Encarnação and got through to the PJ at Portimão, although it wasn't at all clear to whom I was actually speaking. I tried to convey just how traumatic the lack of communication was for us, but I didn't seem to be getting anywhere. I explained that Dr Encarnação had invited us to call at any time if we had any concerns and asked to be put through to him. I was told it wasn't possible. All I was told was that 'everything that can be done is being done'. It was a line we were to hear many more times in the next twenty-four hours. How hollow it seems now. Gerry took the phone to see if he would fare any better. He didn't.

The frustration and anger were reaching boiling point. I felt like a caged, demented animal. This was, without doubt, torture of the cruellest kind. Finally, I erupted. I began to scream, swear and lash out. I kicked an extra bed that had been brought into the apartment and smashed the end right off it. Then came the inevitable tears. Prostrate on the floor, sobbing like a baby, I felt utterly defeated and broken.

After making several calls seeking help from Liz Dow, around two in the morning we both went to lie down for a while. I had not slept in over forty-two hours. I was completely exhausted and my whole body was racked with pain. But I was unable to lie quietly. I felt very cold and restless. My limbs writhed and jerked continually, as if I were compelled to keep moving them to shake off the agony that held me in its grip. This restlessness was something I was going to get used to in the months to come.

Still in the dark as to what was being done to help find our daughter – if anything was being done to find her – Gerry and I prayed together and eventually drifted into a brief and fitful sleep.

7

AFTERMATH

At the police station that first afternoon, Guilhermino Encarnação had briefly mentioned three potential explanations for Madeleine's disappearance: a burglary that had 'changed direction', abduction and the possibility that she had wandered off by herself.

In the coming months we would learn that burglaries were rife on that stretch of the Algarve coast (in Praia da Luz, burglars were 'like mice', according to one resident), and although it is difficult to imagine how a burglary could escalate into an abduction, we now know that this is not unheard of.

However, I have always found the third suggestion insulting to our intelligence, frankly. Obviously, the police are obliged to consider all possible scenarios but there was no doubt in our minds that Madeleine had not left that apartment of her own accord. For a start there was Jane's sighting of what was, in all likelihood, Madeleine being carried off. Even if you set that aside, there was no way a three-year-old would have been able to raise the shutters and open the window in the children's room. To give any credence what-soever to the idea that Madeleine could have walked out on her own you would have to accept that she had gone out the back way, pulling aside the sitting-room curtains and draw-ing them again, then opening the patio door, the child-safety gate at the top of the stairs on the veranda and the little gate to the road – and carefully *closing all three behind her*. What three-year-old do you know who would do that? And we knew our Madeleine. She simply would not wander off like this.

This theory was not only insulting, it was, much more importantly, frighteningly damaging to the chances of find-ing Madeleine quickly. If the police were wasting precious time pursuing it they were not going to be looking in the right places, or taking the appropriate type of action. In the first few days we gained the impression that this was exactly what was happening. Certainly their initial searches were all geared to looking for a stray child who had become lost in or around Luz. We would later hear from the British police that it took until 10am on Friday, almost twelve hours after the alarm was raised, for roadblocks and checks to be put in place. And it would be five more days before Interpol circulated a 'yellow notice' (global alert) to each of its member countries.

We subsequently learned that less than fifty minutes after Jane's sighting – when I had still to discover that Madeleine was missing – a family of nine from Ireland had also seen a man carrying a child, this time on Rua da Escola Primária, a few minutes' walk from apartment 5A, heading towards Rua 25 de Abril. Their description was remarkably similar to

Jane's. The man was in his mid thirties, 1.75 to 1.8 metres tall and of slim to normal build. These witnesses, too, said this person didn't look like a tourist. They couldn't quite put their finger on why, but again they felt it might have been because of what he was wearing. They also mentioned cream or beige trousers. The child, a little girl of about four with medium-blonde hair, was lying with her head towards the man's left shoulder. She was wearing light-coloured pyjamas, had nothing on her feet and there was no blanket over her. Although, like Jane, this family had taken this man and child for father and daughter, they commented that the man did not look comfortable carrying the child, as if he wasn't used to it.

Saturday 5 May was the day we should have been going home, as many other Mark Warner guests were doing. The police would just allow all these people to leave the country without delaying any departures to interview potential witnesses – or even, perhaps, potential suspects. Our own friends remained at the Ocean Club. They took it as read that they ought to stay around to be available to the police, but in any case, I'm sure they wouldn't have dreamed of flying back to the UK without us in these awful circumstances.

Gerry and I awoke at four o'clock that morning, having slept for barely a couple of hours, still feeling wretched and utterly abandoned by the PJ in Portimão. Both verging on hysteria, we were incapable of comforting each other. It was clear we were struggling to keep our heads above water.

Having been so late back from the police station the previous evening, we'd decided to wait until morning to meet the trauma psychologist, Alan Pike. But by this point we realized that we needed help urgently. Just before 5am Gerry rang Craig Mayhew, the Mark Warner overseas manager, and asked if Alan would be able to come and see us. He was at the door of our apartment by 6am.

Alan is a clinical partner at the Centre for Crisis Psychology, pioneers in psychological trauma aftercare following disasters at home and abroad. They have worked with the families and survivors of the Bradford fire, the sinking of the *Herald of Free Enterprise*, the World Trade Center terrorist attacks and the 2004 tsunami, to name just a few. Alan himself, we would learn, had been involved in the aftermath of, among other horrors, coach crashes in Gran Canaria, Cuba and South Africa, three hurricanes and the terrorist bombing at Sharm el Sheikh two years earlier.

Alan must be used to seeing people in states of profound distress, and he certainly found two in apartment 4G at the Ocean Club. By this stage I was beginning to feel that there just wasn't any way up. He started by asking us about our home, our family and our normal lives. He told us we seemed like model parents. I cannot overstate how much such kind reassurance meant to us at that moment. We were both feeling so desperately guilty. Whatever we had or had not done right, we were Madeleine's parents and in our own eyes we had failed to keep her safe. We struggled to bear that sense of guilt and we always will.

Alan got us talking, encouraging us to try to think rationally about what we were saying, and we talked a lot, for several hours. We faced our biggest fear: that Madeleine had been taken by a paedophile and killed. This was the only scenario occupying our minds just then. Alan pointed out to us that these thoughts could be no more than speculation. We didn't *know* what had happened. We needed to avoid focusing on the negative and channel everything into looking forwards. 'Madeleine might walk through that door at any minute,' he said. 'You need to be ready for that.' He discussed with us the importance of taking control of things, little by little, starting with tiny actions as simple as making ourselves a cup of tea. The effect our conversation with Alan had on us that morning was truly amazing. To say it helped would be a gross understatement. Any scepticism we might have had before about how a psychologist could possibly benefit us personally has long gone. Alan was, and remains, a saviour.

My mum, dad and Auntie Norah were all staying in our apartment with us. Once they were awake and on the go, following Alan's advice about making tea for ourselves was easier said than done as Auntie Norah had the kettle on endlessly. Poor Norah, she didn't know what else to do but supply tea for everybody. The Mark Warner staff opened up the Toddler Club – it was usually closed on a Saturday, 'changeover day' – so that Sean and Amelie and our friends' children could be looked after and entertained. That was a huge help, not only in keeping their daily routine on an even keel but also from a practical point of view: it turned out to be a bewilderingly busy day for Gerry and me and, given our fragility, we were far from being in the best state to take care of them.

Neither Amelie nor Sean had yet mentioned Madeleine, or at least, not that we had heard. It was a relief in many ways as I'm really not sure how we could or would have handled any questions at that point. With their friends around them and their grandparents there, perhaps they didn't have much of a chance to fully register her absence. There were few blessings to be counted in these terrible circumstances but perhaps one was the fact that they were too young to be properly aware of what was happening. I think it was the next day before Sean first asked me, 'Where's Madeleine, Mummy?'

Oh, God, oh, God . . . I answered him as calmly as I could, and my reply soon became our stock response to this question. 'We don't know, honey. She's missing but we're all looking for her.' In some ways explaining the situation to the children in these simple terms may have helped us, too: Madeleine is missing and we just have to find her. Put like that, it feels achievable.

The twins would continue to go to Toddler Club in the mornings (and on the odd afternoon, too, in those early days). While we wanted to keep life as 'normal' as possible for them we were well aware, of course, that it wasn't normal, and neither could it be. Gerry and I saw much less of them than would normally have been the case. When we did, we tried to make it up to them by giving them proper quality time with lots of cuddles. For a while we were in too much of a mess to cook their meals or even to bath them. Every minute of every day would be eaten up by anxiety about Madeleine and our efforts to find her. Fortunately, Sean and Amelie were always surrounded by close family and friends they'd known all their lives who loved them dearly.

Now there was a visible police presence in and around

Praia da Luz, even if it seemed to consist largely of GNR officers marshalling the media. Later we were aware of searches being undertaken – I have a memory of television images of police on horseback riding across the rugged Portuguese countryside.

All the same, we were reassured to see some UK police that day in the shape of three family liaison officers (FLOs) from the Leicestershire force, which had also officially logged Madeleine as missing. They came to introduce themselves and to outline their dual role: supporting us and our family and acting as a conduit for the flow of information between us and the PJ. After the trouble we'd had getting anyone in the PJ to talk to us, that was a relief, although the FLOs would soon find themselves almost as frustrated as we were in this regard.

The police and judiciary in the country where a crime has been committed have primacy in any investigation. If interviews need to be conducted or lines of inquiry followed in another country, they request such help under mutual legal assistance treaties and protocols, and results are sent back to them. The Portuguese police were apparently reluctant early on to accept any help beyond this from their counterparts in the UK. However, in addition to the Leicestershire FLOs, they did permit forensic psychologists from CEOP, the Child Exploitation and Online Protection Centre, and an analyst from the National Policing Improvements Agency to come to Praia da Luz the following week. Even that may have been unprecedented: we understood this was the first time the Portuguese authorities had ever allowed any foreign force into the country to assist in an investigation. In such a situation, an element of pride is bound to come into play, and the relationship always seemed quite tricky. It never amounted to an effective pooling of information, ideas or intelligence.

It appeared that the British officers were told very little about what was going on and that their role was essentially confined to making suggestions or volunteering resources. The local police, not used to disclosing the details of an investigation, were clearly wary of answering all the questions they were being asked. According to what we would hear a few weeks down the line, the Leicestershire officers were told in no uncertain terms that if the PJ declined any ideas they proposed or refused offers of additional expertise they must accept this. If they didn't, they would be excluded from the investigation completely.

Still, we were very grateful for their involvement, which would substantially improve communications. In the coming weeks we would meet DCS Bob Small, who we found straight-talking and honest. A lot of hard work went on at home as well, where DS Stuart Prior, the senior investigating officer, was kind enough to show our relatives round the incident room – and Gerry, too, later on.

As more TV and press turned up in Luz, Alex Woolfall gave us helpful pointers on handling the media. We came to rely on Alex as our de facto media liaison officer. It was he who guided us early on, giving us simple advice that has stood us in good stead since. He told us to ask ourselves the following two questions before giving anything to anyone in the press: what was our objective, and how was it going to help? We've always tried to remember those basic principles in all our interactions with the media. Alex explained the rather Pavlovian responses of the media pack. If we began to give daily statements, for example, they would expect one at the same time every day. Sometimes, he said, all they needed was to be fed something to keep them happy, and if that was the case, this might be our only objective in speaking to them.

We learned very quickly that we had to take the utmost care with anything we said in public. Not only was it likely that the abductor would be listening, but we had to make sure there was no suggestion of criticism of the PJ, while at the same time, as the days passed, maintaining the pressure on them to keep investigating.

We had so many meetings that day, and in the days to follow, with people who were trying to help us that it is hard to remember what was suggested, advised or discussed when. Neither Gerry nor I was functioning remotely properly. We were just surviving somehow, swept along by all this activity.

At lunchtime, over by the Tapas area, Gerry saw a crowd of departing guests waiting with their suitcases for the coach to take them to the airport. Among them was a guy with whom he had played tennis several times that week, accompanied by his wife and child. They still had another week of their holiday to go but had decided to return home because, as he explained to Gerry, it was just 'too painful' for them to stay any longer. Gerry felt sick. It was at this moment that it dawned on him just how many people would be leaving the resort that day without being interviewed. It would run into the hundreds. How much potentially valuable information was going to be lost for ever as a result?

With the new batch of incoming holidaymakers more of our relatives appeared: Gerry's mum, Eileen, his brother John and sister Trisha, with her husband Sandy, plus Michael, my cousin Anne-Marie's husband. Gerry had asked his youngest sister, Phil, to stay in Glasgow to be the focus in the UK for the family and inquiries from the media, who were already approaching friends, relations and more or less anyone to whom we'd ever said hello in the street for information and opinions.

Mark Warner had put two more apartments at our disposal to accommodate everyone who wanted to be there, and it felt good to be wrapped in this familiar blanket of support, although inevitably, the arrival of more family members unleashed a fresh wave of tears. It was particularly hard to bear the distress of our parents. Witnessing our mums being torn apart was absolutely heartbreaking, as was the sight of my dad, who suffers from Parkinson's disease, sobbing profusely, shaking violently, his condition exacerbated by his state of mind, and virtually collapsing on to the couch beside me. 'I'm so sorry. I've let you down. I'm so sorry, so sorry,' he kept repeating. Of course he hadn't let me down. He just felt utterly helpless, like the rest of us. The fact that our parents have had to endure such an ordeal at this stage of their lives is a crime in itself.

I remember slumping on one of the dining chairs in the apartment, looking out through the window over the sea. I had an overwhelming urge to swim out across the ocean, as hard and as fast as I could; to swim and swim and swim until I was so far out and so exhausted I could just allow the water to pull me under and relieve me of this torment. I wasn't keeping that desire to myself, either. I was shouting it out to anyone who happened to be in the room. Both this urge and the expression of it were, I suppose, an outlet for the crucifying anguish.

I also felt a compulsion to run up to the top of the Rocha Negra. Somehow, inflicting physical pain on myself seemed to be the only possible way of escaping my internal pain. The other truly awful manifestation of what I was feeling was a macabre slideshow of vivid pictures in my brain that taunted me relentlessly. I was crying out that I could see Madeleine lying, cold and mottled, on a big grey stone slab. Looking back, seeing me like this must have been terrible for my friends and relatives, and particularly my parents, but I couldn't help myself. And all this needed to come out. I dread to think what it might have done to me if it hadn't.

As the sun set on another day and still there was no news, Gerry gave a further statement to the waiting press. Again I went outside and stood with him, my arm linked through his, but left him to read out our message. There wasn't a great deal we could say: we thanked everyone in Portugal and the UK, said we were pleased that the FLOs were now working with the Portuguese police, appealed for any information that might lead to Madeleine's safe return and thanked the media for respecting our privacy, especially Sean and Amelie's.

That evening the local Catholic priest, Father José Manuel Pacheco, who had returned to Luz, came across to our apartment to introduce himself and offer his support. My first impression was of a very cheery chap. Nothing wrong with that, but at the time his smiling face seemed out of place in the grief-laden atmosphere of our apartment.

The next day, 6 May, was Sunday, and despite my fragility I was determined to go to Mass. The discovery that it was also Mothers' Day in Portugal made it even more relevant and important. From the moment Madeleine had gone, I'd turned instinctively to God and to Mary, feeling a deep need to pray, and to get as many other people as possible to pray, too. I believed it would make a difference. Although in the early days I struggled to comprehend what had happened to Madeleine, and to us, I've never believed it was God's fault, or that He 'allowed' it to happen. I was just confused that He had apparently not heeded the prayer I'd offered every night for my family: 'Thank you God for bringing Gerry, Madeleine, Sean and Amelie into my life. Please keep them all safe, healthy and happy. Amen.' *Please keep them all safe.* It must be said that when I'd prayed for their safety I'd been thinking: please don't let them fall off something and bang their heads, or please don't let them be involved in a car accident. I'd never considered anything as horrific as my child being *stolen*. But I had kind of assumed my prayer would cover every eventuality. Now, in spite of not knowing where Madeleine was or who she was with, I tried to reassure myself that God was still keeping her safe.

We all, family and friends, went to Mass at the local church, Nossa Senhora da Luz, in the centre of the village. Given the state we were in, and with the waiting press primed to follow our every move, on this occasion we were taken down by car. Alex Woolfall, well aware that we were not going to be able to go anywhere without a huge media entourage, had decided he had better accompany us, too.

I felt desensitized to everything around me. Nothing except Madeleine seemed to matter any more. I could see, in an abstract way, that the simple church, painted yellow and white, was beautiful. That first Sunday its beauty didn't reach my heart, but in the following weeks I would grow to love Nossa Senhora da Luz and it would become a precious sanctuary for me.

The little church was very full that day. Even though we were sitting at the front when Father José – or Padre Zé, as he was known locally – appeared, it took us a while to work out at which point the Mass actually started. One of the local ladies got up and adjusted his robes, giving him a bit of a dust-down, almost as if he was an untidy schoolboy. It was all quite different from Mass at home. I heard Michael comment, 'This is pleasantly chaotic!' There was something very human and loving about the lack of formality. Padre Zé, whose jolly demeanour had seemed so at odds with our distress the previous evening, was in his element here. He was certainly a character, full of life and passion. Recollections of Kenny Everett in the guise of his singing pastor, Brother Lee Love, would often spring to mind in the coming weeks.

Everybody prayed for Madeleine. A young Portuguese girl presented me with some flowers, as did many of the mums in the congregation. At the end of the Mass, every mother and child came to the front of the church to hug and kiss us. 'She will be back,' they told us. Three words were whispered to us over and over again and have remained with us to this day: *esperança, força, coragem*. Hope, strength, courage. It was incredibly emotional but so, so lovely. We felt totally enfolded and buoyed up by the warm and protective embrace of Nossa Senhora da Luz and her congregation.

Alex was keen for us to leave the church by the side door, where we could be escorted out quickly, past the media and the gathering crowd, but we were so overcome by the warmth shown to us by these people that we didn't want to run away from them. Alex was to give us so much invaluable guidance, but on that occasion, I think we were probably right to walk out of the main door along with everybody else. At that moment I suddenly felt I wanted to speak to everyone, to thank them for what they had done for us, and as we approached the few steps leading down into the street, that's exactly what I did. It's all a bit hazy now – it was then, for that matter. I know I was crying. The fact that I said anything at all, especially given my antipathy to speaking in public, is a measure of how important it felt to me to do so, and every word came from the heart.

Gerry and I would just like to express our sincere gratitude and thanks to everybody but particularly the local community here who have offered so much support. We couldn't have asked for more. I just want to say thank you.

Please continue to pray for Madeleine. She's lovely.

Within a very short space of time, the local people would sweep Gerry and me under their wing and welcome us into their community. We will always be grateful to them for their extraordinary kindness and compassion. They will probably never know just how much they bolstered us during those desperate early days. We continued to attend the Sunday Mass at Nossa Senhora da Luz and the empathy and support we found there never wavered. The words of solace and inspiration, the embraces, prayers, flowers and pictures from the children kept coming, week in, week out. Madeleine was never forgotten and neither were we.

The following Friday, on the eve of Madeleine's birthday, a youth vigil would be held at the church. Many people wore green, the colour of hope in Portugal, or carried olive branches. There was also plenty of yellow, the colour that has come to symbolize hope for the safe return of a loved one in the US and latterly in Britain, too. It was an amazingly uplifting experience. Towards the end of the service, we all took hold of two lengths of yarn, one yellow, one green, which bound us together as we sang a Taizé chant: 'Nada nos separará . . . do amor de Deus' – 'Nothing will separate us . . . from God's love.' Once again it felt as if the whole congregation was underpinning us, sharing our burden. On that occasion we came out of the church actually smiling. Thankfully, we hadn't quite forgotten how! We would soon adopt those two colours in our campaign to find our daughter.

That first Sunday saw two further arrivals in Luz: my childhood friends Michelle and Nicky. Both wanted to be with me, and both were naturally very upset, for Madeleine and for me. Michelle, seeing my pain, struggled to contain her own emotions and needed support herself. Nicky's empathy manifested itself in more practical ways – she was more likely to jump up and ask what she could do. Perhaps that was her way of coping. It was good to have them both there, even if it was just to hold them, or be held by them, when I needed it.

So grateful were we to have our nearest and dearest around us, we failed to notice that our ballooning party of supporters was becoming unwieldy. It took Alan Pike, who was keeping a watchful eye on us and our family and friends, to gently draw our attention to this situation. Alan was great at seeing and anticipating difficulties and at tackling them before they got out of hand. Everyone had felt helpless at home and had rushed out to Portugal to take care of us and to do what they could to find Madeleine. When they arrived, to their dismay they felt just as helpless – perhaps more so, having made the trip in the hope of achieving something only to discover it was not within their power in Luz any more than it had been in the UK. They wanted to be with us, and we wanted them with us, but the presence of so many loved ones, some of them in almost as bad a state as we were, was proving counter-productive.

Alan pointed out that all our family and friends had their own needs but that ours, Gerry's and mine, had to be para-mount. And we scarcely had the emotional resources to prop ourselves up, let alone anyone else. He planted in our minds the idea of reducing the size of our support group. Some people would be better off at home, he said, in their own surroundings and with their own support networks, and would also be better equipped to assist us from there. He felt, too, that we would function better ourselves within a more streamlined, focused team of helpers.

Listening to Alan, it all seemed so obvious. But of course, it left us with the problem of deciding who should go and who should remain, not to mention telling them. It was clear that our parents were struggling to cope and would have more help at home. Johnny, too, seemed like a fish out of water in Praia da Luz. Michelle was very distressed and had two babies in Liverpool who needed her. After giving the matter some thought, we agreed we would ask Trisha, Sandy, Michael and Nicky to stay on. But I was dreading raising the issue for fear of offending anyone.

When it came to talking about it, however, we discovered that Alan, who had spent time with our friends and family as well as with us, had already broached this subject with them, which made it all much easier. Having said that, we ended up getting down to the nitty-gritty rather earlier than antici-pated – that Sunday evening, in fact – and not in the way we had planned, either. Gerry had gone round to one of the other apartments our party was occupying, where apparently something was said that annoyed him, precipitat-ing the discussion we'd intended to hold in a rather calmer atmosphere.

We can laugh about it now, but at the time, Gerry and I couldn't laugh at anything. After the bombshell had been dropped, Gerry's mum had turned to my mum and said, 'Well, Sue – it looks as if we're on the "Granny Express" home!' We also heard that after Gerry left, there had been a few cracks about 'Big Brother evictions'. However bleak the situation, whenever a roomful of Glaswegians and Liverpudlians is gathered together, you can guarantee some gallows humour will break through. Still, a decision had to be made and, as it turned out, it was the right one for everybody.

As some of our family and friends prepared to return to the UK in a day or so, we were beginning to become aware of the help being offered locally. We had that Sunday morning experienced the warmth and sympathy of the Portuguese community and soon we would find supporters among the British expatriates living permanently in Praia da Luz, who organized a search of the area around Luz the next morning, Monday 7 May. The volunteers were joined by most of our family and friends, keen to do something practical to help while Gerry and I were tied up with Andy Bowes and Alex Woolfall.

The remainder of our party – namely my mum and dad, Gerry's mum and Auntie Norah (I'm probably best not describing them as 'the oldies') – walked down to a café near the beach. This day provided us with a good example of one of the disadvantages of a large group: unless it is coordinated with military precision, people do not always know who is doing what and tasks can slip through the net. When lunchtime came, Gerry and I were in the middle of another meeting when we discovered there was no one around to collect Sean and Amelie. We had to interrupt proceedings and go to the Toddler Club ourselves, phoning round our friends and family en route to try to get somebody who wasn't too far away to come back and give them their lunch. A classic case of too many cooks. Or in this instance, not enough!

Once we were left with our leaner support group, we allocated general roles: Trisha and Nicky took over the childcare, while Sandy and Michael dealt with mail, admin and finances. Trish and Sandy ended up staying with us for three solid months. I don't know what we'd have done without them.

It had been suggested that I should record a televised appeal aimed at Madeleine's abductor, and this is what we had been discussing that morning with Andy and Alex. I was concerned about how I might come over on film as I was beginning to feel numb, almost detached, from everything that was happening. Since this seemed worryingly unnatural, both Gerry and I had talked it over with Alan Pike. He told us it was a perfectly normal reaction at this stage. It was physically impossible, after all, for me to keep on crying twenty-four hours a day. I was simply physically and emotionally drained. We both were.

In fact I would soon be advised by British police experts to try to stay as calm as possible and not to show any emotion in public, so it was probably no bad thing that my feelings seemed to be temporarily on holiday that day. The thinking behind this advice was that Madeleine's abductor might get some kind of perverted kick out of my distress and perhaps change his behaviour in some way. Of course we were terrified by the implications of this theory. It meant that quite natural actions or expressions of emotion caught on camera could potentially jeopardize Madeleine's safety.

Alex and Andy had arranged for the appeal to be handled on a 'pooled' basis, which meant that one company, in this instance the BBC, would be chosen to record it and they would then distribute the film to all the other media outlets. This was a system we would use often, because as well as significantly reducing the time we would otherwise have spent recording separate statements and interviews, or facing a barrage of cameras and microphones, it involved dealing with only one reporter and one cameraman, which made the whole experience less intimidating. Nevertheless, shooting the appeal was totally unfamiliar territory for me. I was very anxious, mainly because I was so aware of how important the way I delivered my message could be, but also because I found it difficult and unnatural to talk into a camera lens as if it were a person.

Andy Bowes had proposed delivering part of my appeal in Portuguese, which I did. Gerry sat beside me with a reassuring arm around me.

Madeleine is a beautiful, bright, funny and caring little girl. She is so special.

Please, please do not hurt her. Please don't scare her. Please tell us where to find her or put her in a place of safety and let somebody know where she is.

We beg you to let Madeleine come home. We need our Madeleine, Sean and Amelie need Madeleine and Madeleine needs us. Please give our little girl back.

Por favor devolva a nossa menina.

I was hugely relieved when it was over. My numbness was evidently visible to my closest friends: one later commented that she wondered if I'd been given something to sedate me. I hadn't. In fact I hadn't taken anything to help me through my ordeal since Madeleine had gone missing. I didn't want to. I felt I needed to be constantly alert, sharp and focused, though initially, God knows, I was nothing of the kind, drugs or no drugs. In any case, there was no magic pill that could dull pain like this.

Around teatime, Father Zé turned up with twenty or more local people to say a decade of the rosary with us and our family (a decade is one 'Our Father' followed by ten 'Hail Marys' and a 'Glory be to the Father'). At Mass the day before, we had been aware of him announcing a possible gathering for the rosary but the details had been a little confusing. So their arrival at our apartment was a pleasant surprise. It was an amazing experience. Mothers and their children hugged and held us, placed rosary beads in our hands and spontaneously offered prayers out loud for Madeleine and for us. There were many tears but the warmth of our new friends helped to sustain us. They left giving us heart with those three increasingly familiar words – *esperança, força, coragem*. Father Zé's mother, now in her eighties, took my hands, looked into my eyes and said simply, 'Be patient.'

British consul Bill Henderson and Ambassador John Buck were visiting us on a fairly regular basis and we were seeing the Leicestershire FLOs every day. The flow of information, however, was slow and limited. The Portuguese police were divulging very little to the British police and vetoing many of their suggestions – bringing out specialist dogs, for example, or staging a reconstruction. What was forthcoming, particularly in terms of the quality and depth of the investigation, would become increasingly concerning to us. Grounds for elimination, for instance, often seemed very

Carefree days in Devon, New Zealand, at our wedding in Liverpool and on honeymoon in Lake Tahoe and Maui. Gerry and I felt like the happiest couple on the planet.

The arrival of Madeleine, followed by Sean and Amelie (**below left**), made our lives complete.

Our wonderful family and friends have supported us through the best and the worst of times. Madeleine with 'Granda' Johnny (**left**), Auntie Trisha, Granny McCann, Sean and Amelie (**centre**), and Grandad and Grandma Healy (**below**).

With Michelle in 1997 and Fiona (**below**), on her wedding day in Umbria in 2003.

Our family of five. Life doesn't get any better than this.

April 2007: the week before we left for Portugal. This is how I remember our Madeleine. Happy and enjoying life – and especially ice-cream!

flimsy. I remember Gerry and me exchanging quizzical looks after the FLOs tried to explain how one couple had been ruled out of the inquiry. When we asked them if they were comfortable with this decision, there was an awkward pause before they replied, 'No, not really.'

That Monday evening, completely exasperated, we lost it with the liaison officers. Within a few seconds of arriving they were telling us, 'We've had a very frustrating day today.' It transpired that they'd had to spend the whole day without an interpreter. In other words, it had been a complete waste of time. We were raging. '*Why* did you have to spend the whole day without an interpreter? If you haven't got one, then get one! This is our daughter's life, for Christ's sake. We don't have days to waste and she certainly doesn't. And if you can't get one, then let us know and we will.' I couldn't believe it.

A couple of days later, the FLOs' efforts were bolstered by the arrival from the UK of the specialists from the Child Exploitation and Online Protection Centre (CEOP). The director of the forensic psychology unit, who was a detective superintendent, and a social worker came to see us to outline their current lines of inquiry. In the weeks ahead the input of the UK experts would encourage us to feel more optimistic that the investigation was gaining momentum. This initial discussion, though, was unsettling, focused as it was on the typical profile of a paedophile. All I could think was, not Madeleine. Please, *not Madeleine*!

8

THE BIRTH OF OUR
CAMPAIGN

We were existing in an information vacuum. A big part of
the problem was the fact that in Portugal all criminal cases
are governed by the law of judicial secrecy, which means that
once an investigation is under way, neither the police nor
anyone else is allowed to reveal anything about it, including
details of potential suspects, on the basis that this could
jeopardize a trial. Even the statements and appeals we made,
quite usual in the UK, were not something the PJ advocated.

Of course, this was torture for us. The British media were
not accustomed to it, either. For those familiar with police
and court reporting in the UK, the Portuguese system is a
'hall of mirrors', as one reporter described it. Because
nothing can be confirmed on the record, and the police often
don't bother to contradict false reports, rumours proliferate.

Although it wasn't apparent to us at the time, because the
PJ were not guiding the press, particularly the international
press, no agenda was being set. This left the media with a free
rein and would soon lead to speculation on a massive scale

and the broadcasting and printing of erroneous 'facts' in the interests of filling column inches and airtime. It is incredible, looking back, how so much could be said with so little hard information available.

In the first few days after Madeleine's abduction, the media in general were very respectful and their coverage was largely sympathetic. Aside from when we were delivering a pre-arranged statement, we were pretty much left alone. Yet although there didn't seem to be very much happening in terms of the investigation, the media presence grew. This was very surprising to us and we've always been at a loss to understand why our 'story' attracted quite such unprecedented attention. Obviously the circumstances were extremely rare: a British child being abducted on holiday. The only other such case we knew of was that of Ben Needham, who had been snatched sixteen years earlier from a Greek island at the age of twenty-one months, and who still hasn't been found. The world had changed dramatically since then, particularly in terms of communications. In 1991 the internet and mobile phones had been in their infancy, and there were no twenty-four-hour news channels to be fuelled. The fact that Gerry and I were both doctors seemed to make the story more newsworthy, as, no doubt, did the fact that Madeleine is such a beautiful little girl.

We came in for some criticism, of course, for leaving the children in the apartment while we had dinner. Some initial reports were very misleading, suggesting that we had been sitting several hundred metres away. Journalists who were actually in Praia da Luz and saw the proximity of the Tapas restaurant to the apartment (as the crow flies, just under fifty metres; a little further walking round 'the road way') were clearly shocked that Madeleine had been grabbed at such close quarters, and we were given the definite impression that they wanted to help. This also went for their bosses, the TV executives and newspaper editors. There was unquestionably a sense of 'There but for the grace of God go I.' I looked on them as allies in the search for Madeleine. And although I don't doubt that many of them did genuinely want to help, it was a while before I realized that finding our child came some way down their list of priorities and learned the hard lesson that the media are not about spreading news but selling products. Their overriding concern was not us or, sadly, Madeleine, it was someone shouting down the phone that the editor needed eight hundred words by ten o'clock.

For the first few days after Madeleine was taken, with the apartment full of people, the English-language news from Sky or the BBC was on pretty consistently in the background. We saw quite a bit of the coverage ourselves but once the speculation mushroomed it crucified us. Gerry said to me, 'We have to stop watching this.' We also began to avoid the English newspapers, readily available from Baptista on the same day as they were published at home.

In the village, drivers had to find alternative routes and parking places because of the roadblock outside our apartments and the satellite trucks stationed permanently nearby. Reporters hung out in Baptista and the Hugo Beaty bar, or trawled the beaches, assailing locals and holidaymakers alike for quotes and soundbites.

On the plus side, it became apparent very quickly that

Madeleine's plight had struck a chord with huge numbers of the British public. Messages of support, sympathy and empathy came flooding in. Mark Warner's email was bombarded soon after the news broke and hundreds of letters were arriving on a daily basis.

That first gruelling week was so hectic and seemed so long. The unrelenting agony made every minute feel like an hour, but for us the days literally were long, as we slept so little. By midweek we were starting to manage, through sheer exhaustion, a few hours' sleep every night, though if I happened to wake up, that would be it until morning. The moment I opened my eyes, Madeleine was the first thing on my mind and I would be instantly aware of a painful heaviness in my chest and an unsettling dread. I was always awake by 6am and usually I would get up, go out on to the veranda and make a few phone calls – nobody at home was sleeping well, either. I had begun to eat a little, too, though nowhere near enough. (Reports of my weight loss were greatly exaggerated: in the first week I did lose about 4½lbs, which I could ill afford, and which it took me months to regain, but nowhere near the stone removed from me by some of the press. I have always been thin. It's the way I'm made.) There were days when I would say to myself, 'How can I sit here and eat breakfast when Madeleine is missing?' or 'How can I possibly take a shower?', but somehow I did. As Gerry kept telling me, 'Crumbling into a heap and doing nothing will *not* bring Madeleine back.' He was right, of course, but there would be many crumbles along the way.

We spent so much time closeted with various advisers that we didn't see much of our holiday friends, except for

Fiona. She knew us and our children so well: she understood, as far as anyone else could understand, and that made her support very important to me. I bumped into the others at the Tapas area one day. They were standing there helplessly and Jane and Russ were crying. Soon we were *all* crying and hugging each other. It was just so awful.

On Tuesday 8 May, we said an emotional goodbye to the family and friends who were leaving us, including my parents and Gerry's mum. It was so sad, but we all knew it was for the best. Later, I went down to sit on the beach for a while with Fiona. I still felt oblivious to everything around me; nothing whatsoever mattered except Madeleine. We talked and cried and held on to each other. It was like a horror movie that refused to end. But this was my life now, until Madeleine was found.

As we were walking up from the beach at about 5pm, I had a call from Cherie Blair, in her final days as wife of the prime minister (her husband Tony would announce his resignation two days later and leave office the following month). She was kind and helpful. She told me it was amazing but encouraging that Madeleine was still the first topic on the news every night. This was only five days after the abduction: as it turned out, our poor daughter would continue to headline the bulletins for some time to come. Cherie also warned me, 'Whatever happens, your life will never be the same again.' She mentioned that a friend of hers, Catherine Meyer, was the founder of PACT – Parents and Abducted Children Together – and said she would get in touch with her on my behalf. Doubtless I asked Cherie if there was anything the British government could offer the Portuguese in the way of resources to assist or expedite the search for Madeleine. It wasn't my intention to make her feel uncomfortable by asking this, and I'm sure I didn't. We were just so desperate I couldn't let the opportunity go by.

We had been given a key to the church so that we could go there and pray whenever we wished. We cherished these little oases of relative peace and solitude. One night early in the week – I think it was that Tuesday evening – while we were praying privately at Nossa Senhora da Luz, Gerry had an extraordinary spiritual experience. He suddenly became aware of a long tunnel with light at the far end of it. He felt himself enter the tunnel and, as he went deeper and deeper inside, it became wider and wider and brighter and brighter. He had never known anything like this before and he immediately interpreted it as a sign urging us to do absolutely everything within our power to find Madeleine ourselves. From that moment he was convinced that we did not have to sit back passively, issuing statements and waiting for others to bring her home. We needed to take the initiative. Straight away he shared this revelation with me and tried to explain what it meant to him. We had to start right now to mobilize all the resources available to us.

His 'vision' – I don't know what else to call it – in that beautiful little church had a huge impact on Gerry. It was this experience that laid the foundations of our organized campaign to find our daughter.

From the minute he got up the next morning, Gerry was on a mission. Among the first people he spoke to was the ambassador, John Buck. The foreign secretary, Margaret

Beckett, also happened to call him. He pleaded with them both to try to improve the way the investigation and the search were being handled. We needed it to be far better than this, he told them. They knew that, too, I'm sure. Many friends and colleagues also heard from Gerry that day, asking them to think hard. *What* could help us to find Madeleine? *Who* could help? 'Think about your contacts, then think about the contacts of your contacts. Can they help?'

Gerry's mobile phone appeared to be permanently attached to his ear the whole day long. I can remember even feeling slightly irritated that he was able to function in this way and to be so busy. Why was his pain for Madeleine not crippling him, as mine was me? He was simply responding to the challenge he'd set himself the evening before to leave no stone unturned – a phrase that became a rallying cry after he used it in a statement to the press at the end of that week. I will for ever be immensely proud of him and thankful for his determination, effort and sheer hard work so early on, when we were both still raw and reeling. Although the ultimate goal of all this work hasn't so far been achieved, there is no doubt that we (and Madeleine) would have been in a much worse place without it, and who knows what it might yet yield?

There were so many people, our family and friends in particular, who desperately wanted to help. Gerry's call to arms spurred them into action and gradually they began to pursue their own avenues. The very next evening Gerry's sister Phil sent a chain email round the world asking every recipient to help find our little girl. It came with a downloadable poster featuring a photograph of Madeleine, the one of her holding the tennis balls, taken two days before she vanished. This led the following day to the first conversation, between Phil, a teacher, and Calum Macrae, a former pupil of hers and an IT whizzkid, about establishing a website for Madeleine. Jon Corner had opened up the file transfer protocol he'd set up on 4 May to circulate Madeleine's image to family, friends and other supporters. No, I didn't know what one of those was, either: basically, it provided access via a password to a repository for photographs and other material, allowing people to share their resources. Helpers could post their material on a dedicated server via the FTP and use that supplied by others to create flyers, posters and so on. The press already had the password, which gave them access to pictures and video footage.

Already there were people and organizations coming forward with offers of a reward for information leading to Madeleine's safe return. We heard that a colleague of mine in general practice had, amazingly, pledged £100,000. A good friend in Liverpool, a police officer, warned us that we would need a great deal more than this to tempt anybody connected with the crime to give Madeleine up. It seemed a huge sum of money to us but, being a policeman, he was more used to dealing with criminals than we were.

Alex Woolfall told us that the *News of the World*, spearheading a group of other benefactors – including Bill Kenwright, the theatre impresario and chairman of Everton FC, businessmen Sir Richard Branson and Sir Philip Green and Harry Potter author J. K. Rowling – was prepared to put up a reward 'package' totalling £1.5 million. It would involve companies such as British Airways and Vodafone helping with publicity and awareness initiatives. They needed to know by the following day whether we would like them to proceed. This may sound like a no-brainer, but we had to be careful. We hadn't a clue how such rewards worked. Would the police be involved? Who would coordinate any ransom negotiations? How would we actually get hold of all this money if necessary? And, most importantly, what were the potential pitfalls? Surely it could lead to fraudulent claims that might waste valuable time and resources. We had no idea, either, what implications this might have for Madeleine's safety.

Under pressure to make a decision, we solicited advice from various quarters, which confirmed that this kind of thing could indeed be a bit of a double-edged sword. We felt that, on balance, the pros outweighed the cons, thanked all the participants and accepted the offer, as much because we did not want to turn down any corporate help as anything else. With the £100,000 from my GP colleague and a stagger-ing £1 million added by Stephen Winyard – the owner of Stobo Castle spa in the Scottish Highlands and a man who had so far never even met us – the rewards promised now totalled £2.6 million.

I went with Nicky to an Anglican service at Nossa Senhora da Luz, which the Catholic and Anglican communities shared for their services and celebrations. I remember that there was a film crew inside the church. How this came to be allowed I have no idea – I have always considered a church to be a sanctuary, a function that is especially important in times of personal difficulty – but everyone was trying their best to do the right thing and I'm sure it was with the best of intentions. Unfortunately, I wasn't holding up too well and having to put up with a giant camera lens pointing at me even here added greatly to my agitation. Around the first anniversary of Madeleine's disappearance, I saw some footage of me coming out of the church after that service and I barely recognized myself. Nic was practically having to carry me – and she's only five foot three!

By contrast, in the following weeks and months I would be subjected to cruel comments describing me as 'cold' and 'poker-faced'. Had these critics not seen the television pictures? Or is it that people have short and selective memories? It is true that as I grew a little stronger I was better able to control my grief in public. I was also terrified to show my emotions after the warnings I'd been given that this might influence Madeleine's abductor. So if I seemed 'poker-faced', is it any wonder? But that was beside the point, really. Who were these people to dictate how the mother of a missing child should appear? Judging others and expressing those opinions is part of human nature, it seems, but it's astounding how some individuals feel entitled to do so, and with such vitriol, from a position of total ignorance.

A week had now passed since Madeleine's abduction. Later that day, Thursday 10 May, the Portuguese police held a press conference, at which they released a photograph of a pair of the same Marks and Spencer pyjamas Madeleine had been wearing and confirmed that they were winding down the ground search.

Meanwhile, Gerry and I, along with a couple of our

friends, were called back to the police station in Portimão. The police were much friendlier on this occasion and the junior officers, at least, gave the impression that by this time they were working very hard. Gerry was taken in to be interviewed while I remained downstairs. I made use of the long wait I anticipated by sitting down with a notebook, pen and my camera, containing dated photographs of the holiday, and trying to write a detailed account of everything that had happened the week before.

The interview system we'd encountered on our previous visit – questions asked in Portuguese and verbally translated into English; answers given in English, translated into Portuguese and typed up by the interviewing officer – was exhausting for everyone. At the end of the interview the statement prepared by the officer would be printed out in Portuguese, verbally translated, on the spot, into English, and then signed by the interviewee. It was obvious that at every stage of the process the scope for mistakes in translation and misunderstandings was considerable.

I sat in the waiting area for eight hours before I was told that it was now too late for me to be interviewed and I should go home and come back the next day. Gerry was there for thirteen hours. When he finally returned to the apartment he related how Matt had been almost hysterical during his interview. Gerry had heard him shouting and crying. Apparently, it had been put to Matt that he'd handed Madeleine out through the window to a third party. It was like something out of *Life on Mars*.

Alan Pike was concerned about my wellbeing and asked for my rescheduled interview to be postponed for a few days.

The PJ couldn't have considered it all that important: it was 6 September before I was interviewed again.

One of the offers of help we'd received came from a para-legal based in Leicester, via a colleague of Gerry's. He worked for a firm specializing in family law, the International Family Law Group (IFLG). It was difficult to know what this company could do but we decided it would be worth meeting them to discuss the possibilities. So on the afternoon of Friday 11 May, the paralegal, accompanied by a barrister, flew out to Portugal. We'd warned them to keep their arrival at our apartment low-key, so as not to attract any unwanted attention from the media lying in wait outside. In they came, dressed in bow ties and braces – the barrister was even wearing a panama hat. I heaved a sigh. They might as well have had great big arrows pointing at their heads reading 'lawyer'. Not to worry: it was their presence and input that were important.

As well as this initial meeting we had two further sessions with the lawyers over the course of that weekend to explore how they might be able to assist us. There had already been some speculation in the press, based on those erroneous reports that when Madeleine was taken we were dining 'hundreds of metres away', that we could face prosecution for negligence. After examining the proximity of the Tapas restaurant to apartment 5A, the barrister first of all assured us that our behaviour could not be deemed negligent and was indeed 'well within the bounds of reasonable parenting'. This had hardly been our biggest concern, but it was reassuring to hear, all the same. The lawyers then talked to us about applying for an order to make Madeleine a ward of court.

Wardship status gives the courts certain statutory powers to act on a child's behalf in any legal disputes and to bypass some of the data-protection laws that deal with access to information (hotel guest records, for example, and airline passenger lists), when knowledge of this information is considered to be in the interests of the child in question. Such an order could be useful in acquiring records not otherwise available to us that might be relevant in our case. We decided to proceed with an application, which was granted in due course.

We also discussed the offers of help that were now pouring in, including many financial pledges. Gerry and I were at a loss to know how to handle these. One of Gerry's colleagues, for example, had called to say that the staff in his department wanted to make a donation to assist with the search for Madeleine but didn't know how or where to deposit it. IFLG told us that we needed to set up a 'fighting fund'. They would devise the objectives of the fund and instruct a leading charity law firm, Bates Wells and Braithwaite (BWB), to draw up articles of association.

At the last two meetings the barrister and legal assistant were joined by a consultant called Hugh, whose profession was not at first explained ('Just call me Hugh,' he said enigmatically). It transpired that he was a former intelligence officer, now a kidnap negotiator and counsellor. We were told that an anonymous (but evidently very generous) donor had set aside a considerable sum of money for us to put towards the cost of hiring a private-investigation company if we wished. Hugh had been brought in by a firm called Control Risks, which was primed to help.

This company is an independent specialist risk consultancy with offices and investigators on five continents and their main line of work is corporate security. It was a big gesture, we were immensely grateful and it was good to know this option was available to us.

The first session Hugh attended, which took place at night, had something of a James Bond atmosphere to it, and not in a good way. I felt as if I'd entered a whole new world, and it was an extremely mysterious and frightening one. Perhaps the worst bit was a remark Hugh made about the reward that was on offer. He told us dispassionately that such an inducement would have 'put a price on Madeleine's head'. I was very upset. The thought of anything we had done jeopardizing Madeleine's life was too much to bear.

By the Sunday evening, we found ourselves giving our statements again, this time to a couple of detectives from Control Risks. We were concerned that parts of the statements we had made to the Portuguese police, especially on that first day, might have been lost in translation. We also felt that these accounts were not sufficiently thorough and wanted to have every detail we could remember registered properly. Unfortunately, in our haste to pass the new statements on to the PJ, we made the mistake of assuming that the transcripts would be correct and discovered only many months later that these, too, contained inaccuracies. And they had been given and recorded in English! A word of advice, in case you are ever unlucky enough to find yourself involved in a criminal investigation in *any* country: always make sure that you read your statement, in your own language, after you've provided it.

It was after one of the IFLG meetings that Hugh asked me whether I was keeping a diary. Quite apart from the fact that I was an emotional wreck and hadn't had time to blink for the past week, the idea had never crossed my mind. I hadn't kept a diary since my early teens, and the accounts of my life then were mind-numbingly boring: what time I got up, what I ate for each meal and which lesson I'd enjoyed most that day.

'You should,' he said. He didn't elaborate on why. The barrister handed me a spare A4 notebook he happened to have with him.

When I thought about it, I realized it would be a good way of remembering these dark and confusing days; of filling in the gaps for Madeleine on her return. It would also be a record of our story that might help all three children to understand what had happened when they were older. Setting aside some blank pages in the notebook I'd been given for the days that had already passed, I wrote a few paragraphs on a couple of occasions the following week, though I didn't begin in earnest until 23 May, twenty days after Madeleine was taken. From then on, I kept my journal consistently, and when I had a spare moment I went back and filled in the blank pages with notes of our activities and my recollections of every day since 3 May 2007.

Though my main purpose was to keep a proper account for the children of everything that had happened, I found writing it down very therapeutic. It gave me an outlet for my thoughts and emotions, and a means of communicating with Madeleine. *I could talk to her!* I could also talk to God, and even to the abductor, if I wanted to. Whatever Hugh's intention was, I am very grateful to him for his suggestion. It might just have saved my life.

So many people were supporting us in so many different ways, from the high-profile donations of the reward consortium to the quiet prayers and unsung practical acts of friends and strangers alike. On the day of our first meeting with IFLG, I had gone over to the Tapas area to meet up with Paddy, the husband of Bridget, a good friend of mine in Leicester. Paddy is, as Bridget puts it, 'a man of God'. He's also six foot three, a big fella generally, with very dark hair and eyes – not someone you'd miss in a crowd. I was so touched that, even though we didn't know each other all that well then, he had decided, completely off his own bat, to come out to Praia da Luz and join the search parties that were being organized locally. He'd texted me to say, 'If you want me to call and see you while I'm there, I'll come. Otherwise I'll just get on with the search.'

I had asked Paddy if he had a Bible with him I could borrow. He brought me one that had been a Christmas present from him to Bridget several years earlier. That Bible is still sitting next to my bed. I must get round to returning it one day!

Saturday, 12 May 2007. Madeleine's fourth birthday. Until it was upon us, we hadn't been able to think about it: we simply couldn't countenance the idea that by the time it arrived she wouldn't be back with us to mark it. Not being with her today, loving her, pleasing her, enjoying her delight, was unbearable. We should have been at home, where we'd arranged a joint party in Leicester for Madeleine and two of her classmates at nursery, her best friend Sofia, who had been born on the same day, and a little boy called Sam whose birthday was within a few days of theirs. They had been going to have their first disco. I'd bought a couple of girl-band CDs a few weeks earlier and we'd been having singalongs in the car to warm up for it. The memory of Madeleine, sitting in the back seat, singing her heart out along with the Pussycat Dolls still makes me laugh. And cry.

John Hill had arranged for us all – Gerry, Sean, Amelie and myself, Trish and Sandy, and Fiona, David, Dianne, Jane, Russell, Matt and Rachael and their kids – to spend the day at a private villa. (Nicky left that weekend, and Michael had popped home for a couple of days.) We didn't know what to do, really. We couldn't let the occasion go unmarked and we wanted to celebrate Madeleine on her birthday whether she was with us or not, but *nothing* we did felt right. It was good to be away from the Ocean Club and the media circus, and the kids enjoyed themselves, playing in and around the pool with floats and toys. But Madeleine's absence hung heavily over everyone else.

The Mark Warner staff had brought over stacks of food for us. The men organized a barbecue and there was wine and beer. We ate mostly in silence, concentrating on the kids. I couldn't eat much, and alcohol was completely off my agenda. Fiona recalls that Gerry and I were completely shut down that day, barely able to talk, and although our friends tried to remain cheerful and behave normally to get us through it, they all felt awkward about being at this lovely villa, in the sunshine, in these circumstances. There was no cake. Gerry did attempt a toast but he was visibly upset and couldn't manage much more than 'I can't even say happy birthday to my daughter . . .' before choking up. The physical loss was more intense than ever. I ached for Madeleine.

After attending a special Mass for her at the church early in the evening we were visited in the apartment by Cat, Madeleine's nanny at Mini Club. She had some news for us: she and some of her colleagues were being sent to another Mark Warner resort in Greece. None of them wanted to leave, and to this day we do not fully understand this decision. We think it might have been made for logistical reasons – after Madeleine's abduction, guests with bookings at the Ocean Club for the next few weeks were being offered alternative destinations, and perhaps the company needed to adjust their staffing levels accordingly. But from our point of view, it meant the removal of key witnesses from Praia da Luz.

Having spent much of the previous four days cooped up, first with the police and then with the lawyers, by the Sunday afternoon Gerry and I felt the need to escape into the open air. We decided to go for a walk along the beach. Perhaps 'escape' isn't the right word, since we were soon tailed by a posse of journalists, and there could be little escape in any case from the hell engulfing us. Thankfully, we were left alone when we reached the shore, and were able to stroll along the sand in relative solitude.

I remember this walk well. It had been a chaotic and confusing ten days, shot through with unremitting cold dread and dark thoughts that were hard to push away when we had nothing else with which to replace them. That is the anguish of the 'not knowing'.

I asked Gerry apprehensively if he'd had any really horrible thoughts or visions of Madeleine. He nodded. Haltingly, I told him about the awful pictures that scrolled through my head of her body, her perfect little genitals torn apart. Although I knew I had to share this burden, just raising the subject out loud to someone else, even Gerry, was excruciating. Admitting the existence of these images somehow confirmed them as a real possibility, and with that confirmation came renewed waves of fear.

So many of the emotions and physical sensations I've experienced over the past few years will be beyond the scope of most people's comprehension, thank God. I felt as if I'd embarked on a slow, painful death. Just imagining your child, any child, like this is agonizing and unless such thoughts have any basis in reality, it is normal and understandable to banish them from your mind. Everybody has their own mechanisms for self-protection and surrounding yourself only with 'nice thoughts' is one of many. I wished I could do that. The pictures I saw of our Madeleine no sane human being would want in her head, but they were in mine. I simply couldn't rid myself of these evil scenes in the early days and weeks.

That walk with Gerry was, however, a small watershed. The mutual acknowledgement of such delicate and deeply upsetting responses drew us even closer together.

It would be some time before we could get far enough past the terrible scenes seared into our minds to think logically about that night. Once we did begin to function within what felt like an endless bad dream, we started to comb through our memories, searching for something significant.

Had Madeleine been specifically targeted, either for herself or because someone knew that apartment 5A would be a breeze to raid? Not only did its corner position allow for easy access and escape, but, unlike many other residences, it had no protective wrought-iron bars at the windows and no security light.

Could Madeleine's apparently excessive tiredness on that last Thursday afternoon have been caused by some kind of tranquillizer administered earlier in the day, or even the night before? It had been noticeable, but then we'd been approaching the end of our break and the children had all been extremely active for almost a week. It might simply have been, as we'd thought at the time, the holiday catching up with her. Inevitably, though, since we cannot yet know for sure, a little nugget of doubt remains.

For a long while we would assume that the abductor had entered and exited through the window of the children's bedroom, but it is equally possible that he used the patio doors or even had a key to the front door. Perhaps he'd either come in or gone out via the window, not both; perhaps he hadn't been through it at all, but had opened it to prepare an emergency escape route if needed, or merely to throw investigators off the scent. He could have been in and out of the apartment more than once between our visits.

That would explain the movement of the door to the children's bedroom. At 9.05pm, when Gerry had found it further ajar than it should have been, he had pulled it back to its original position. On his arrival half an hour later, Matt hadn't gone into the room, he had simply listened at the door, which he hadn't adjusted. And yet when I returned at

10pm it was open wider once again. How had that happened? Had there been somebody inside the room, behind the door, when Gerry looked in, just waiting for him to leave? Gerry feels that's unlikely, but again, we can't know for sure. What we do now believe is that the abductor had very probably been into the room before Gerry's check.

Whatever the case, it may have helped if I had made the nine-thirty visit instead of Matt. I would have noticed that the door was not how we'd left it – something that nobody could have expected to be apparent to Matt – and raised the alarm sooner. Of course, I will always feel bad that I didn't. I know it's nobody's fault that I didn't. I know nobody could have foreseen how it could possibly matter. I know that it might well not have made the slightest difference in any case. *But it might have.*

So many little things had and would continue to come to light, so many chance incidents and minor decisions made in all innocence, which on their own would not have driven events to such a disastrous conclusion. Together, though, they seem to have accumulated into a monstrous mountain of bad luck.

9

NO STONE UNTURNED

Monday 14 May. Today I went for my first run since Madeleine was taken. Anyone who doesn't run or exercise generally might wonder why, and more to the point, how I could possibly do this in the circumstances. Why is easy. Exercise, and running in particular, is good for the mind as well as the body. It can induce a sense of wellbeing, lifting your mood, and aids the relief of stress, anxiety and sleeplessness. I needed all the help I could get there. As to how, well, I suppose I made myself do it in the same mechanical way as I made myself wash my face in the morning, brush my teeth and acknowledge another day.

However, I was also driven by additional and more complicated motives. One was that somehow I knew running would help numb the torment, albeit temporarily. Even more bizarrely, I felt I needed to do it to bring Madeleine back. I can see now that this makes no rational sense, but at the time it was as if I had to push myself to the limit in every way in order to achieve my heart's desire. My child had suffered and therefore so must I.

I remember speeding along the beach, concentrating totally on Madeleine. I had a picture of her in my hand which I would squeeze when I felt tired to spur me on, especially going up the sharply rising Rua da Praia. I could not have entertained stopping. Simultaneously I was saying a decade of the rosary in my head. When I returned to the apartment block, I sat on the steps at the bottom and cried like a baby. Either the run or the crying, or both, seemed to induce a sense of calm.

That first weekend I'd felt a burning desire to run up the Rocha Negra, and Gerry and I would in fact do so many times over the next few months. In places it was just too steep and I had to slow down to walking speed, but if I dared to stop (interpreted by my brain as failure) I would mentally beat myself up. It still felt as if every challenge had to be met on Madeleine's behalf. I wouldn't recommend such mind games: they certainly don't make life any easier. But as Gerry will readily confirm, I can be quite stubborn, though I'd prefer to call it determined.

We gave another statement to the media outside the apartment that Monday and on this occasion answered a few questions. Then, early in the evening, we heard that Robert Murat, our erstwhile translator, had been taken in by the police for questioning. We had no prior warning of this from the police. The first we knew of it was when we happened to catch the 'breaking news' on television, the same as everybody else. We stood there, paralysed, watching live pictures of the police going in and out of Murat's home, removing computer equipment and boxloads of other stuff. We were terrified that the next thing we were going to see was an officer carrying out a little body bag.

Was it really too much to ask to be spared this harrowing experience? Whether the police were simply being completely thoughtless or whether this was something to do with the judicial secrecy law I cannot say. Sandy and Michael walked up to the Murat family home, Casa Liliana – which was only 100 yards from our Ocean Club apartment – to try to find out what was happening. A *Sunday Times* journalist filled them in on a few more details. A little later, one of the British FLOs popped up to our apartment to apologize for the lack of warning. It wasn't his fault, of course, but the damage had already been done.

Murat, the thirty-three-year-old son of a Portuguese father and British mother, was described in the press as a self-employed property developer. He lived at Casa Liliana with his mother. He had been reported to the police by a *Sunday Mirror* journalist, Lori Campbell, suspicious of what she felt was his odd behaviour – apparently he had been hanging around the media pack, constantly asking questions. Taking what others perceive as an unusual level of interest doesn't make you a criminal, of course, but it worried several people among the press corps.

We soon found out that Murat had been made an *arguido*. This formal status meant he would be officially treated as a suspect in the crime. It also confers various rights, such as the right to remain silent and entitlement to legal representation. For this reason it is possible and indeed not unheard of for a person being questioned as a witness, with less protection from the law, to declare himself *arguido*, for example if he feels that the line the police are taking suggests they suspect him.

We met up with Alan Pike to talk through how we were feeling. Strange, was the short answer: for a brief period I found myself feeling positive, almost excited, that we might be nearer to finding Madeleine. That evaporated when we went round to see Fiona and David. Fiona told us she'd seen Robert Murat outside apartment 5A on the night of Madeleine's disappearance. Then I began to feel panicky. It had belatedly begun to dawn on me that it probably wouldn't be good news at all if someone living as close as Robert Murat was involved. As Fiona and David speculated I became more and more anxious. I didn't want to hear it. Within the space of a couple of hours I went from feeling cautiously optimistic to very, very low. Another long, dark night followed.

It later transpired that on the evening before Murat was taken in for questioning, the police had summoned Jane to a mysterious rendezvous in the car park next to the Millennium area, refusing to say why they wanted to see her and insisting she told no one. Their behaviour seemed so sinister that she was quite scared.

Russell walked her to the car park. On the way they passed Casa Liliana, just as Murat was returning to his villa in his van. He stopped to speak to Russ, whom he must have seen around, eager to tell him what he and his mother were doing to help find Madeleine. Jane, who had never met Murat, was not taking much notice. She was just anxious to get going and for this cloak-and-dagger meeting to be over with. When Russell managed to extricate them, Murat said he needed to be off, too, mentioning that the police wanted to see him.

From the car park Jane was driven round to a nearby street, where a PJ officer asked her to get into the back of a van disguised to resemble a refrigerated delivery vehicle ('Like Sooty's van,' she told us). The police took her straight back to the Ocean Club. They had wanted to park at the point where she'd seen the man and child on 3 May but there was another car there and they had to stop further down the road. She was instructed to look out of the window and tell the police whether she could identify anyone crossing the junction of Rua Dr Gentil Martins and Rua Dr Agostinho da Silva as the person she had seen that night. Three men walked by. Two of them looked nothing like the figure she had described: one was blond and tall and the other too fat. The third could have been him, but at that distance she couldn't make him out properly and unfortunately, just as he crossed the road, he was obscured by the car in the space the police had wanted, which chose that moment to pull out.

The police moved the van to the car park opposite the Ocean Club entrance to try to give Jane a better look at the third man, but here he was walking along a path and her sightline was blocked by foliage. By now the van windows were steaming up, too. She told the police she could not be sure either way. One of the officers made a phone call to check whether she needed to sign a statement to this effect but then informed her it wouldn't be necessary.

When Murat appeared on the TV news the next day, Russell pointed him out as the man who had stopped to talk to them outside Casa Liliana the previous evening. Jane was concerned that he might have been picked up purely as a result of the amateurish identity parade in which he had unwittingly participated. Like Fiona, Russell declared he'd seen Murat outside apartment 5A on the evening of 3 May, as, they discovered, had Rachael.

Jane phoned DCS Bob Small. She told him she'd encountered Murat before her rendezvous with the PJ and mentioned that Russell and Rachael had said they'd noticed him outside our flat on the night Madeleine vanished, in case either piece of information was important. Although at that stage it didn't appear to our friends to be noteworthy for Murat to have been nearby when Madeleine was abducted – he lived just along the road, after all, and there was no reason why he shouldn't have been there – the police took further statements from Fiona, Russell and Rachael.

It was perhaps telling that Jane had not been required to sign anything, since the absence of documentary evidence to the contrary allowed claims to be made later that she had identified Murat as the man she'd seen on 3 May. This was completely untrue. Jane would've loved to have been able to make a definite identification, because it might have helped the investigation, but the fact is she couldn't. The set-up was so inadequate that she was unable even to recognize Murat as the man she had met half an hour earlier, let alone say with any certainty that he was the one she had seen ten days before.

We had pleaded for an informal meeting with the PJ to keep us abreast of what was happening. We took it as read that those in charge of the investigation would have a duty to tell us, as the parents of an abducted child, whether they were any closer to finding her. It would be standard practice, surely. No, not in Portugal. The judicial secrecy law ruled this out, we were told. An information blackout in such a painful situation is nothing short of inhumane. Not knowing where your child is, how your child is, who she's with or indeed whether you will ever see her again is a glimpse of hell. Not knowing, either, about anything that is (or worse, isn't) being done to find her, or whether those looking for her are privy to more information about her circumstances than you are, only piles on the agony.

With little chance of learning a great deal from the PJ, we tried to focus on the imminent launch of Madeleine's fund and on coming up with ways to put the accumulating donations to the most effective use. The response of prominent philanthropists and the general public alike to our daughter's plight and Gerry's call to arms had already been fantastic. That weekend, well-wishers had queued at St Andrew's Cathedral in Glasgow to join a vigil for Madeleine. Football star David Beckham had appealed for information and there had been words of support, too, from prime-minister-in-waiting Gordon Brown. In Portugal, hundreds of bikers set off to ride the length of the country with leaflets and posters.

It was an ex-colleague of Gerry's in Glasgow who had suggested the Beckham appeal. Gerry's ex-boss, who was the Scotland football team doctor, spoke to Sir Alex Ferguson on our behalf, Sir Alex got in touch with David Beckham, and he instantly agreed to do it. We are so grateful to him: he said his piece with such feeling that it couldn't fail to touch people. Sir Alex Ferguson was also behind the appeal made by Cristiano Ronaldo, the world-famous Portuguese footballer who played for him at Manchester United. There followed more spontaneous messages from other players, including Chelsea's John Terry, Ricardo Carvalho and the Ukrainian Andriy Shevchenko, who made his appeal in several languages.

BWB, the law firm drawing up the articles of association for the fighting fund, had talked to the Charity Commission about whether it would be eligible for charitable status. As its objectives were limited to the search for a single child and the beneficiaries were essentially one family, it was deemed that the 'public benefit' test would not be met. So the fund took the form of a not-for-profit, private limited company. It was set up with great care and due diligence by experts in the field. From the outset everyone agreed that, despite the costs involved, it must be run to the highest standards of transparency. There needed to be independent directors as well as family representatives, and people from a variety of professions joined my uncle Brian Kennedy and Gerry's brother Johnny on the board. At the time, though, we had little idea how important these measures would prove to be in enabling us to withstand the massive scrutiny to which the fund would be subjected, especially when the tide turned against us.

Meanwhile, Alex Woolfall had recommended that, given the high profile of our situation and the fact that he was there principally to represent Mark Warner, we really ought to engage our own family spokesperson. Gerry had contacted the Foreign Office to ask if they could help and they kindly arranged for Sheree Dodd, an independent consultant, to come to Praia da Luz for a week or so to act as our family spokesperson and assist us with our burgeoning campaign. Sheree joined us on 15 May and got down to work straight away.

By this time we were using one of the apartments loaned to us by Mark Warner as an office (immediately nicknamed 'Mission Control' by the family) and it was fast becoming a hive of activity. Also helping out at that time were my good friend Lynda, who used to keep a sisterly eye on me playing in our road in Huyton when I was four and she was ten, and Father Paul, aka Seddo, an important figure in our family life. It meant a lot to me to have him there, providing spiritual support as well as an extra pair of hands.

We realized that the extraordinary media coverage given to Madeleine's case was probably reaching saturation point in the UK and Portugal. As it was just as likely that she could have been taken out of the country, we were now thinking about ways of extending the scope of our campaign abroad.

Sheree was experienced at running campaigns – she had previously handled one for the Department of Trade and Industry – and, equally importantly, she was warm, considerate and easy to get on with. Soon she was almost one of the family, joining us for meals and always happy to muck in. She even ironed a shirt for Gerry once, which was definitely above and beyond the call of duty.

On the day after Sheree's arrival, Wednesday 16 May, Madeleine's Fund: Leaving No Stone Unturned was launched in Leicester. Rugby player Martin Johnson, the former Leicester Tigers skipper and World Cup-winning

England captain, generously agreed to front the launch. We were represented there by a large contingent of family and friends and saw it ourselves live on TV in Praia da Luz. Jon Corner had produced a DVD of photographs and video images of Madeleine to the soundtrack of the Simple Minds song 'Don't You Forget About Me'. It was a wonderful film but very difficult for Gerry and me to watch. That evening it was shown at the UEFA Cup final at Hampden Park in Glasgow, which happened to involve two Spanish teams, Sevilla and RCD Espanyol. With Spain so close and accessible from Luz, we were heartened that it would help to increase awareness there. The more people who knew Madeleine, the more eyes there would be out there looking for her and the greater our chances of finding her would be.

That day, Gerry played tennis with Seddo, David and the Mark Warner tennis coach. There was no way I could have done this. As well as being acutely aware that the last time I'd played tennis was the last day I'd seen Madeleine, I was far from ready to take part in anything that could be classified as pleasurable. Although I'd been for a run two days before, to me, as I've said, this seemed a necessity rather than a pleasure, and there is no doubt there was an element of self-punishment to it. All recreational activities seemed inappropriate, verging on disrespectful, and because they weren't yet right for me, I found it hard to understand how Gerry could enjoy them, either.

In spite of what I felt, I knew that, whatever our different ways of coping and adjusting, our common and indeed only goal was to find our daughter, and everything else was un-important. So my oversensitivity never caused any real problems between us. The last few years have been a crash course in the complete spectrum of human nature and one lesson I have learned from it is never, ever to judge. There are no 'right' or 'wrong' responses in any case. To judge in ignorance is conceited, inconsiderate at best. Gerry needed to keep active. Perhaps he needed, and was able, to briefly switch off. I know how much he loves Madeleine and I can feel how painful it is for him not to have her in his life. He is a good, strong, incredibly focused and loyal man, and to this day I feel guilty that I questioned his actions, albeit silently in my head.

As Gerry, Lynda, Paul and I headed down to the church early that evening we noticed satellite trucks pulling up and journalists gathering in Rua 25 de Abril. One or two cameramen spotted us and began to run over but we managed to get into the church before they caught up with us. Thank heaven for small mercies. Very small. We didn't find out until later the reason for all the activity, and when we did, once again it was from the television and not from the police. This street was home to Sergey Malinka, a young Russian IT expert and business associate of Robert Murat, for whom he had set up a property website. After police found a logged call to his phone from Murat's shortly before midnight on 3 May, Malinka was taken to the police station to be questioned as a witness and his flat was searched. Ultimately, the PJ were satisfied that he was not implicated in any wrongdoing.

Gerry and I spent the rest of the evening with our holiday group in Jane and Russell's apartment. It was the first time everyone had been able to get together in the past thirteen days and it would be the last: the next morning, Jane, Russell, Matt, Rachael and Dianne would be flying home. Fiona and David had decided to stay on until the following Tuesday. I'm sure this was a very difficult step for them all to take and they probably felt quite guilty about leaving us behind in Praia da Luz with Madeleine still missing, but obviously they had to return at some point. Their lives had to go on. But the terrible experience we shared would stay with us all, on one level or another, and bind us together for ever. It was, understandably, a very emotional farewell.

With three of their buddies now on the plane back to Britain, Sean and Amelie continued to attend the Toddler Club every weekday morning. With the realization that we had to be proactive in the search for Madeleine, Gerry and I had become busier and busier, but, looking back, I don't feel we could or should have done anything differently in those first few weeks, with regard to the twins or indeed anything else. We were always around somewhere and in the time we did have with the children, I'd like to think we made it clear how much we loved them and how vital they were to us. And they seemed to glide through the chaos and misery around them completely unperturbed. If they saw images of Madeleine on the television, they would wave and blow her kisses.

It is difficult to know how much they could have understood then. They were only two years and three months old. But there again, they had spent virtually every day of their lives with Madeleine and, like her, they were bright for their age. There is no doubt that twins have a special relationship, and although Sean and Amelie are like chalk and cheese in many ways, the fact that they have always had their 'other half' to cuddle, play with and talk to must have cushioned the effect on them to some degree. I'm sure the altered family dynamics and psychological consequences would have been a lot worse for one child, or even two of different ages.

Alan Pike talked to us about the twins, of course (and although we weren't aware of it at the time, he had a session with our friends, too, about what they should and shouldn't say to their kids). Alan also put us in touch with David Trickey, a chartered child psychologist specializing in traumatic bereavement, who had experience in dealing with families of abducted children. David – who had, co-incidentally, recently taken up a post in Leicester – came out to Praia da Luz the following month and spent four hours with us. We just wanted reassurance, really, that we were handling everything in the way we should.

David told us that it was important to be totally honest with children. If they asked a question it should be answered as truthfully and openly as possible. In our case, he said, there wasn't an awful lot we could tell Amelie and Sean because we didn't know ourselves what had happened to Madeleine. Obviously, as they got older they would ask more searching questions and, as we continued to respond, they would gradually build up a picture of the situation in their own heads – a kind of 'pyramid' of information. After meeting Sean and Amelie – who put on a tremendous performance for him, playing and laughing, as usual, apparently without a care in the world – David assured us that he had no concerns at all about their wellbeing. Even so, we remained in touch, just to reassure ourselves again from time to time that we were still on the right track.

On Thursday 17 May, Michael gave a statement to the media, with Sheree riding shotgun, to follow up the launch of the fund with news of our plans to widen our campaign. The Find Madeleine website was now up and running and would receive 100 million hits over the next four days. The distribution of posters was being expanded across Europe and various multinational companies supporting us had begun to include Madeleine's image on all outgoing emails. In addition several of our friends and family were photographed dealing with some of the many letters arriving in Praia da Luz.

These encounters with the press went well – all except for the introduction of two little words. Sheree had thought 'Team McCann' was quite punchy and suggested a united, determined and resourceful group, which is what we were. But there was a minor backlash, mutterings about it sounding too slick, which led to snide references in the media to the 'McCann media machine' and even the 'juggernaut'. This marked the start of a thread of criticism we would become used to in the coming months.

Taking a short walk along the promenade with Lynda and Seddo, I met up, by chance, with Fiona, David and Scarlett. We all went to a café for a drink and a snack. Never mind playing tennis, even small, 'normal' activities like this felt all wrong. Madeleine needed us and it didn't seem right to take time out, even for fifteen minutes.

I still have this feeling today, at varying levels of intensity:

a restless, anxious sense that we have to be doing something in connection with our quest in every waking moment. It remains resistant to logic or 'sensible talking' and I've just had to learn to live with it. But I am able to accept now that it is important for us to take proper breaks, even holidays, to avoid burning out. It is also important, of course, that Sean and Amelie get quality time with us. And I feel reassured that when we do pause for a rest, we have so many staunch supporters who can be relied upon to press on in the meantime. It became apparent very early on how fortunate we are to have such good and resourceful family and friends.

The following day, Friday 18 May, Lynda and Paul left us. It's so hard parting in such circumstances. We'd already had so many hellos and goodbyes and there were many more to come, but the goodbyes never got any easier.

Gerry was going home on Sunday, too – just for a couple of days. We had been in Portugal ourselves for almost three weeks. For the moment, Gerry was on paid compassionate leave. As a locum, I wasn't entitled to this but the partners at my surgery all agreed they wanted to give me two months' pay, which was greatly appreciated. The inaugural meeting of the board of Madeleine's Fund was due to take place at home and we wanted a meeting, too, with our lawyers, Control Risks and the British police. We decided that Gerry should go back to the UK to deal with these matters. Given the huge media interest, this flying visit had to be planned quite strategically. The authorities in both countries helped out, ensuring that it ran as smoothly as possible.

Saturdays had become family days: a bittersweet idea. Family without Madeleine? How could that be? We were a family of five! We felt we needed to set aside a whole day in the week, or as near to a whole day as we could manage, to spend with Sean and Amelie, and Saturdays, when they didn't go to Toddler Club, suited everyone. But these were incredibly difficult times emotionally for Gerry and me. We felt guilty about enjoying anything with the twins while Madeleine was still missing. The twins were adorable and of course they brought us such joy. Madeleine's absence, though, was crucifying. We tried our best: we have three children and they all deserve a happy and loving life with parents who are there for them.

On Saturday 19 May we all went down to the beach with Fiona, David and their kids. We built sandcastles, ran into the water with Amelie and Sean and played near the hire boats with them. It was a scene that must have seemed so ordinary to any casual observer, but underneath it ran that unshakeable unease that denies me any peace even today. I fretted, too, about what people who recognized us might be saying. 'How can they possibly be playing on the beach when their daughter is still missing? There is *no way* I would be able to do that if it were me.' A month ago, in their shoes, I would probably have been saying the same thing myself.

That afternoon, we'd agreed to see a photographer from the *Sunday Mirror* whose pictures would be put into the press pool for the other Sunday newspapers. Having our photograph taken for media purposes was and remains a difficult issue. Apart from the fact that it's uncomfortable for us and often feels staged, how are we supposed to appear and behave for the camera? Smiling seems completely inappropriate in the circumstances, and even when it isn't, for example, when we're playing with Sean and Amelie, as we were that day, it doesn't stop people criticizing us. 'Look, they're smiling – they don't seem bothered at all, do they?' Of course, if you don't smile, you are labelled 'cold' or 'stony-faced'. You can't win.

At least on this occasion the pictures were fairly natural, showing us engaged in normal activities in the apartment that we'd have been engaged in anyway, and the photographer was very nice, but, to be honest, it all felt a bit naff, for want of a better word. Reflecting on it now, I'm not sure why we agreed to things like this. I suppose it was part of keeping the papers 'on side': if we 'gave' them something, it would help maintain Madeleine's high profile. Journalists were always telling us it was important for the general public to see that we were a very ordinary family. The jury's still out on that argument, I think. What I do know is that trying to maintain the balance between our privacy and the media's appetite for the 'human-interest' angle was very tricky. We were still quite naive back then, especially me, and it would be a little while yet before I began to gain a sense of their priorities. This dilemma has always been at the heart of our difficult relationship with the media. Much as we shrank from the intrusion, we needed them to keep Madeleine in the public eye.

We had also been asked if we would be filmed watching Jon's Madeleine DVD, which was to be shown again later that day during the FA Cup final coverage. We declined. Now that definitely would have felt staged.

Two weeks into our ordeal, if anything the media attention seemed to be increasing. Apparently, Sky had three anchors in Praia da Luz. The BBC sent out Huw Edwards. ITV dispatched Sir Trevor McDonald, who did a one-hour special from the village. Everyone wanted the first interview with us – there were direct approaches from the BBC and from ITV, in the form of a handwritten note from Sir Trevor – and it seemed the broadcasters were relying on their big guns to get it. We were simply not ready at that point to do such interviews. Gerry was also worried that once we did, the interest would begin to wane and with it the spotlight on Madeleine.

10

MEETING THE PJ

On Sunday 20 May, Gerry left for the UK. It was the first time we'd been apart since coming to Portugal and it was an emotional separation for us both. Going back to Leicester alone, with Madeleine gone, made it particularly hard for Gerry. He had decided not to stay at our house. It would have been too distressing at this stage and, from a practical point of view, there is no doubt that the media would have set up shop outside. In the end he spent both nights with friends who had so far managed to steer clear of the media searchlights, which was much better for him. I was fine, too. Trish and Sandy were there and I had Amelie and Sean. And Cuddle Cat.

At Monday's meeting with the British police, Gerry was told about plans to launch an appeal in the UK aimed at holidaymakers who had been in the Algarve in the weeks leading up to Madeleine's abduction. They would be encouraged to send in to the Child Exploitation and Online Protection agency any photographs they had taken in which people they didn't recognize could be seen in the background. CEOP would use facial-recognition software to screen these pictures for known offenders who might have been in the area. To us this seemed a massive step forward, a sign that the unique collaboration between the UK and Portuguese police was beginning to bear some fruit.

It was later the same day that Gerry met Clarence Mitchell for the first time. Clarence, a former BBC news correspondent working for the Civil Service, was the director of the Media Monitoring Unit attached to 10 Downing Street. He still had many press contacts and had made it known to his Cabinet Office bosses that he missed the cut and thrust of big stories and would be interested, if an opportunity arose, in acting as a government press handler on a major event. As a result, he was seconded to the Foreign Office to come out to Portugal to handle our media liaison as part of their consular support for us.

Gerry hit it off with Clarence straight away. He was also struck very quickly by Clarence's professionalism and expertise in dealing with the media. Gerry wanted to go to Rothley to see the thousands of messages, flowers and cuddly toys that had been left for Madeleine in the centre of the village. Clarence sprang into action immediately, apparently. Within seconds he was on the phone to the police and talking to the media on the ground about how this could be arranged to give Gerry some space and at the same time allow the press access to his visit. Gerry was able to go and look at the mountain of cards, notes and gifts without intrusion. He was incredibly touched to see a message from one of Madeleine's best friends from nursery, who had recently moved to Yorkshire. I know how difficult this was for him. He told me how he had struggled to contain his emotions and had only just held it together. The tears did start to flow, however, when he bumped into the landlady of our local pub. This was par for the course: for months afterwards, whenever we met any friends for the first time since Madeleine's abduction we began to relive what had happened to us all over again and invariably broke down.

Back in Praia da Luz, that Monday evening I went round to Fiona and David's apartment. Dave fetched an Indian takeaway but I was too upset to eat much. While I was on the phone, talking – or rather crying – to Gerry in Leicestershire, there was a knock on the door. We were slightly alarmed: it was almost midnight. And when I saw Sandy standing there with two GNR officers, I began to panic.

The officers told me that outside were a lady and her husband who had travelled a long distance to give me some important information. Straight away I went with Sandy and the two officers to their mobile police unit, parked at the front of the apartments. This couple were waiting inside. Having no idea what they were going to say to me, to start with I was very anxious and at the same time trying to rein in my hopes that this might represent a breakthrough. Thirty minutes later, having had a crystal waved about in my face, I could feel the hysteria building up inside me. I could see from his expression that Sandy was sitting there thinking, What is this mumbo-jumbo? and struggling to keep a straight face. There was no way in a million years something like this was going to bring Madeleine back. How had the police allowed such a situation to arise? I was tired and I'd been frightened half to death, but, crazy as this was, these people probably meant well and I didn't want to offend them.

In the early weeks, I gave my fullest attention to all information passed on to us, including reports from every psychic, medium, dowser, diviner, visionary and dreamer, you name it, though I'd never in my life before had dealings with mystics of any description.

There were a couple of 'visionary' experiences in particular I took very seriously. One of them had come through prayer which, at the time, gave it even greater credibility in my eyes. I begged the police to look into these. They were very sceptical, to put it mildly. By now any police officer reading this will no doubt be smiling ruefully or shaking his or her head – whatever many psychics, mediums, dowsers, diviners, visionaries and dreamers tell you about helping the police with investigations, most officers won't have anything to do with them.

For several months we invested some time and even resources in following up reports from some of the thousands of psychics who have contacted us; time and resources that would, with hindsight, have been better used in more orthodox investigative work. Much of the information we received, and still receive, is extremely vague. Describing a white house near a dirt track is not helpful. There are millions of white houses in the world and millions of dirt tracks.

A few years down the line, my experience has turned me from open-minded ingénue into confirmed sceptic. Sometimes a very resentful sceptic. Well, they can't all be right, can they? Madeleine can't be in a thousand different locations. Even after Gerry and I decided enough was enough, family and friends have felt obliged to pursue information that has found its way to them, occasionally travelling overseas at their own expense, *just in case.*

Just in case. This is at the core of what I find most upsetting about the visions of the psychics et al. In our desperation to find Madeleine we are extremely vulnerable, and in our position it is very difficult to ignore any information. Even though Gerry and I are scientists by inclination and profession, we still get reeled in. In some letters, a shifting of responsibility, laced with emotional blackmail, comes into play. 'Well, it's up to you now,' psychics might write. 'I've done my bit,' thus discharging what they feel is their duty to Madeleine. Some have gone a step further and added, 'I suppose it depends how much you want to find your daughter.'

Having said all this, I don't mean to sound critical of or ungrateful to the majority of psychics who, I'm sure, pass on their reports with the best of motives. But as is the case in any group of people, there are some who perhaps do so in order to feel important or involved and others, of course, who are simply looking for publicity. What I am trying to emphasize is the emotional pressure all this information can put on the recipient. Almost invariably it isn't helpful; sometimes it saps our time and energy and leaves us feeling wretched. And that, in turn, can hamper our search for Madeleine. So over the years I have learned how to deal with it. If it doesn't have close to 100 per cent credibility, it goes into the lowest-priority action pile. We need to protect ourselves, too.

* * *

Tuesday, 22 May 2007. Fiona, Dave and the girls left Praia da Luz at 6.30am. It was hard for me and probably even harder for them. I know how badly they wanted to be there for us, helping in whatever way they could to try to make our existence a tiny bit easier. But they had jobs to go back to, and they needed to restore some normality to their lives. It was some time before the magnitude of the chasm that divided us from our holiday group became fully apparent to me. While Fiona, who was closest to me and has remained such a wonderful support, was probably the most deeply affected, like the others, she *had* to move on, whereas we would always remain in limbo until Madeleine was found, or until we learned the truth about what had happened to her. It wasn't that I ever envied our friends their contentment: it was simply a harsh fact that while they would increasingly be able, to a degree, to set this terrible event apart and carry on with their daily lives, we couldn't.

For us, there was no question of leaving Luz. Wherever Madeleine was now, this was the last place we had seen her, held her, talked to her, and it would have been tantamount to leaving her there. When we went home, we vowed, it would be as our family of five.

At lunchtime, Gerry arrived back in Praia da Luz with Clarence. My first impressions of Clarence were good. He was very friendly and knowledgeable, and, most importantly, he seemed genuinely concerned about Madeleine: it was clear that to him this was not just about a challenging secondment. He and Gerry had chatted non-stop during the two-and-a-half-hour flight to Faro. When Gerry had told

Clarence about Jane Tanner's sighting he was astounded that this still hadn't been made public. We decided we would really push the PJ to release this critical piece of information in the hope of identifying this man and child.

My cousin Anne-Marie also joined us today. It was great to have her there. She is intelligent and practical but fun and easygoing with it. As a child I'd spent every summer holiday with Anne and her brothers on the Isle of Man, and we've always been very close. She and Michael were incredible, coming and going in relays, with their spells in Portugal sometimes overlapping so that they were both with us at the same time.

Many people, especially the local Portuguese, had suggested we would benefit from visiting the shrine at Fátima, a notable place of worship for Roman Catholics that draws over 6 million pilgrims a year. Although I was aware of the shrine, and of the Marian apparitions to three shepherd children there in 1917, I didn't know a great deal about it. The more I learned, the keener I became to make the trip.

We'd arranged to go to Fátima the following day – our twentieth day without Madeleine – so part of Tuesday afternoon was spent preparing for that. In the evening, Gerry's sister Phil flew in from Glasgow. It was so good to see her. From the first hours after Madeleine's disappearance, Phil had been our linchpin at home, coordinating family, friends, other helpers and the media and campaigning tirelessly. We all had dinner together. I was struck that night by how united the two sides of our family had become in such a short space of time. They seemed to be merging into one, and what an amazingly strong and loving alliance it was. It was hard to consider myself lucky – it still is – but without doubt all of us, Gerry, myself, Madeleine, Sean and Amelie, are blessed to be part of such a family.

Wednesday 23 May was Clarence's first full day in Portugal as our media liaison and spokesperson, and it was going to be one on which his assistance would be essential. He'll kill me for mentioning this, but he managed to over-sleep. To be fair, it was a particularly early start as we had the 250-mile journey to Fátima ahead of us. When our car and driver arrived, a knock on the door summoned a somewhat dishevelled and bleary-eyed Clarence. 'Oh, right, oops!' he said. 'I'll be with you in a minute.' And he was as good as his word. In no time at all he was on parade and in fire-fighting mode, which, I have to say, he does impressively well. Clarence is a force of nature. He is always organizing some-thing, always on the phone to somebody. When he disembarked from a plane after the shortest of flights and switched on his phones he'd find fifty texts and fifty missed calls or voicemails.

My desire to go to Fátima had been increasing steadily over the preceding few days. As we neared our destination, I was filled with nervous anticipation and a peculiar excite-ment. Seconds before we arrived Gerry received a phone call from Gordon Brown. After their conversation Gerry relayed his message of support and encouragement to me, commenting on the marked empathy and sincerity in Mr Brown's voice.

At the shrine the media presence was as heavy and intense as we had known it so far. Yet somehow, on this day and in this place, I was able to ignore the huge camera lenses barely a couple of centimetres from my face as if they were not there at all. I was equally oblivious to the swarms of other pilgrims. I only remember feeling 'drawn in' and captivated by the beauty of the shrine.

Walking through the central plaza, a potent sense of calm and hope descended on me. The vast, open space triggered a feeling of freedom and a strange but pleasant temporary weightlessness. The bells in the basilica began to ring out 'Immaculate Mary'. Almost instantly a tight knot developed in my stomach, my heart began to race and I started to cry. I could see Michelle and me standing in our classroom, aged six or seven, singing all the verses of 'Immaculate Mary'. I thought of Michelle and of the long and nourishing friendship we shared. I ached for Madeleine to have a best friend like Michelle. I ached for her to be given that opportunity. Please God, let it be so.

During the couple of hours we spent at the shrine, we were able to attend one of the Masses being celebrated and were also allowed some time to pray privately in one of the small chapels. Before leaving, we lit five candles outside the Chapel of Apparitions, one for each member of our family. I kissed Madeleine's candle and prayed with all my heart that Our Lady of Fátima would keep her arms safely around our daughter.

As we made our way back to our car, many well-wishers, most of them Portuguese, embraced us and squeezed our hands tightly. The sincerity of their desire for us to be reunited with Madeleine was unquestionable. We received various gifts we still treasure, including a child's set of wooden rosary beads, which remains around Cuddle Cat's neck to this day. The strength and encouragement we drew from this incredible demonstration of solidarity and compassion was immense.

That night I wrote a few words in my journal summing up our visit to Fátima. Not a bad place to begin. From this point on I began to make regular entries at night, or in odd moments during the day.

It was with our spirits renewed, then, that we attended our first informal meeting with the Portuguese police. In response to our pleas, they had at long last agreed to see us at the British Consulate. To say that we were grateful to be given this 'special treatment' (as it would be described by the Portuguese media) is a huge understatement. It was 24 May: three whole weeks since Madeleine had been taken. And to our huge relief, the next day the PJ finally released Jane's description of the man who had in all probability carried Madeleine away.

The officers we met on that occasion, and would continue to meet regularly, were the two men ultimately in charge of the investigation. Guilhermino Encarnação, chief of the Algarve PJ, based in Faro, we had encountered at the police station in Portimão on the day after Madeleine's abduction. The other was Luís Neves, head of the DCCB (Direcção Central de Combate ao Banditismo) in Lisbon. The DCCB, the equivalent of the Serious Organised Crime Agency, dealt with gang crime. Neither man spoke English, so an interpreter was always present, usually Angela Morado, the British proconsul.

Encarnação was sixty years of age at the time. He was quiet and certainly the less forthcoming of the two. He appeared to be what you might call 'old school' (indeed, we learned later that he had joined the PJ in 1973, a year before the dictatorship was overthrown). It took us a while to warm to him. Although we did feel that our rapport with him improved slightly in the course of subsequent meetings, it's probably fair to say that neither Gerry nor I ever felt entirely comfortable with him.

Luís Neves was a totally different character. He was our age and had a son who was the same age or maybe just a little older than Madeleine. He seemed intelligent, personable and strong, open to suggestions and new ideas. My initial impressions of him were all positive. I wrote in my diary that night:

A good fella; on the ball; humanitarian, sensitive.

We felt relaxed with Neves and he and Gerry seemed to get on well. He was quite tactile and would greet us warmly, often patting Gerry on the back or giving him a brotherly hug or a little punch on the arm. As Gerry churned out suggestions and strategies, he would joke about how my husband would make a great detective.

We also became quite friendly with Ricardo Paiva, one of the detectives based at Portimão. Because he spoke good English he was drafted in as the police liaison officer for Gerry and me, and as a result we spent a fair amount of time with him. He came to our apartment at the Ocean Club on several occasions. My apologies for the mugs of instant coffee we were always handing him became a bit of a standing joke. I'm sure the Portuguese hate what the British call coffee. Ricardo was probably in his early thirties, and married with a son the same age as Sean and Amelie. Both Gerry and I thought he seemed a decent enough guy, quiet but pleasant.

I don't think I was naive in believing that we built up a good and friendly relationship with these officers over the coming months, although subsequent events have certainly made me question this judgement. We would have eight of these informal meetings, one approximately every seven to ten days, and the crumbs Encarnação and Neves gave us were meat and drink to me. They made me feel that at least something was happening, even if I cannot be sure now just how much of what we were told was true. I longed for the meeting dates to come round. They gave me something to look forward to and somehow brought me a tiny bit closer to Madeleine. But while they were better than nothing, they never repaid my hopes of them.

Luís and Guilhermino usually volunteered little but would respond quite candidly to direct questions. We were often surprised at the detail they were prepared to share with us. In fact, the British police once suggested that we might be better off putting any questions or requests directly to the PJ, as we seemed to have more influence with them than they did.

The two officers talked openly about Robert Murat, who remained an *arguido*, and drip-fed us snippets of 'evidence' linking him to Madeleine's disappearance. Not enough, apparently, to arrest and charge him. In some ways, I wish now they hadn't done this. It served only to colour my judgement of Murat. They told us, for example, about a newspaper clipping they'd seized from his house, an article entitled 'Lock up Your Daughters', which claimed that Casanova had been a paedophile. It made us shudder. Back then we feared everything and, perhaps understandably, leaped to the worst conclusions without pausing to consider innocent explanations.

Nothing we were told by the police indicated that Murat took Madeleine or was in any way involved in her abduction. We had no context for the disconnected pieces of information Neves and Encarnação did pass on to us, which we assumed were all they were allowed to reveal. In isolation these suggested it was possible Murat was linked in some way to the events of 3 May, and for a long time we didn't know what to think. Once we fell victim ourselves to the vagaries of the Portuguese police system, we soon discovered how easy it was for two and two to be put together to make five.

When I read through the PJ files in microscopic detail after their release to the public in 2008, I found nothing to implicate Murat. It is clear that the police never had any credible case against him. His *arguido* status was eventually lifted, no charges were ever brought and any apparent evidence they gathered was no more than circumstantial. Several witnesses, including Fiona, Russ and Rachael, reported seeing Murat near our apartment on the night Madeleine vanished. He has always categorically denied being there, and his mother confirmed that he was at home all evening.

On Friday 25 May, the day after our first meeting with Neves and Encarnação, we gave our first 'sit-down' interviews to

the media in response to the incessant requests for an opportunity to speak to us. Sheree and Clarence had prepared for
this event (Sheree had now had to leave us but had passed on
the baton to Clarence), along with Hannah Gardiner of the
Association of Chief Police Officers, who was helping us as a
kind of police media liaison officer. They had held the press
at bay until Gerry and I felt strong enough to handle it. The
fact that so far the public had not heard from us directly,
other than in our brief statements and appeals, together with
the massive appetite for the 'story' and the scarcity of information available from the police, made these interviews
very significant. I have to say that the prospect of doing them
filled me with dread.

Before I faced the press, Anne-Marie and I went along,
briefly, to a lunch in Lagoa to mark International Missing
Children's Day. A month before I'd never even heard of
ICMD, which encourages people around the world to
remember all missing children and their families and
to express their solidarity with them. Now, of course, the
date is engraved on my brain. We had been invited to this
lunch by Susan, the wife of Haynes Hubbard, the new
Anglican minister in Praia da Luz. The Hubbards had come
to Portugal from Canada three days after Madeleine's
abduction and this was the first time I had met Susan. She
was to become a very close friend and has been a real
support to me ever since.

I had to be back to meet Gerry for the interviews at 3pm.
When we arrived, I was asked by one of the television people
if I could change my top as the colour 'wouldn't work well on
camera'. I'd already been pretty bemused by all the

instructions I'd received beforehand. I'm sure these are very useful if you are going on TV to present a programme or take part in a chat show, but to me this seemed insensitive, almost offensive. Surely in the circumstances what Gerry and I had to say mattered more than how we dressed and the overall look of the 'media package'?

We did a whole lot of interviews, one after the other – Sky, BBC, ITV, the Press Association, Portuguese television and GMTV. In spite of my aversion to speaking in public and the anxiety it caused me, everything went much more smoothly and felt easier (or at least, less awful) than I'd expected. Each interviewer asked us about our decision to leave the children alone in our apartment while we ate. All we could do was answer this honestly, over and over again, as we have had to do on numerous occasions since. We love our children; we would never knowingly put them at risk; we were naive; it was the biggest misjudgement of our lives; we regretted it bitterly and we would have to live with the guilt we felt for ever. But at the same time, we knew that the person who had taken Madeleine was the real criminal, and he remained free and almost forgotten.

It was a huge relief when it was all over. But in truth it was just the beginning: I had no idea then of quite how many interviews we would be required to do in the weeks, months and years to come.

In the meantime, hope and comfort were at hand from an unexpected source. It was on Sunday 27 May that Clarence first mentioned the possibility that we might be invited to the Vatican (or 'accepted' there) to meet Pope Benedict XVI. The 'relevant people' in Rome, he told us, had already been making the necessary preparations. I didn't dwell on whether this was unprecedented, as it was later described, or even unusual. I just remember thinking how important and wonderful this would be for Madeleine. For a Catholic, meeting the Pope is about as close as you can get to meeting God, and we certainly needed His help. I truly believed that if I was able to speak to the Pope, my pleas for Madeleine's safe return would be channelled more efficiently and effectively to Heaven. I also believed that this meeting might lead to many more Catholics offering prayers for Madeleine. Surely if God received a bombardment like this, Madeleine would be returned to us?

Even so, I can say, hand on heart, that at that time I never thought our encounter with the Pope would be such big news. Although I was of course aware of the huge public interest Madeleine's plight continued to generate, I was still in my own little bubble, detached to some extent from the outside world, and this proposed journey to Rome felt like a necessity rather than a privilege. To me it was the Church's way of supporting a fellow child of God, a humane and compassionate gesture. Gerry, on the other hand, was able to see the wider picture, the massive global awareness it would bring, in addition to the spiritual benefits for our family.

Our audience with Pope Benedict XVI, as part of a public session at St Peter's, was confirmed the following day and scheduled for Wednesday 30 May. Sir Philip Green kindly offered us the use of his private jet. But what would people say? That we were hobnobbing with celebrities and swanning around in the lap of luxury while our daughter was suffering? The unpleasant scrutiny we were under was soon to become an integral part of our lives whether we liked it or not. In the end we accepted Sir Philip's offer for logistical and emotional reasons. The key factor was that it would dramatically reduce the period of time we'd need to spend away from Amelie and Sean.

Not for the last time, we agreed to a small group of UK and Portuguese journalists and photographers travelling with us on the plane. To this day, I wonder why on earth we did. We would have been under some gentle and well-meaning pressure from Clarence, a journalist himself until fairly recently, who was working so closely with the media that he was keen to maintain a friendly relationship with them. I know it's the way politicians do things, but our situation was rather different. Obviously, the press were going anyway, and travelling with us made their lives much easier, but it meant we couldn't relax or let our guard down for fear that something we said or did would turn up in the papers, spun to suit a particular story. From time to time, inevitably, we forgot that while on a personal level some of the journalists were lovely to us, they were there to do a job.

We were informed that we would need to wear 'dark suits' to meet the Pope. Clothes again! On the Tuesday morning Gerry and I went to a big shopping centre to buy something appropriate. As a woman who could not yet enjoy a snack in a café without feeling guilty, I could not get my head round this. My daughter was missing and here we were *shopping*! It was unthinkable. I moved randomly from rack to rack, from shop to shop, the tears rolling down my face. I longed for it all to go away.

Leaving Sean and Amelie behind in Portugal a few hours

later was even worse. I just wanted to cling to them for ever. We faced a dilemma several times as we travelled abroad in the weeks to come. Could we take them? What would be fairer on them? I have no doubt that we did the right thing. It would have been nice for us to have the twins with us, their comforting cuddles on tap, but it would have been selfish. Being shuffled from meeting to meeting, buffeted by crowds and dazzled by flashbulbs, was never going to be fun for them. In Praia da Luz they were in the care of loving family and friends and could play in comfortable surroundings to their hearts' content. There was no contest, really, not for a pair of two-year-olds.

I've never been great at take-offs and landings. In recent years I'd taken to squeezing Gerry's hand tightly until we were safely in the air or back down on the ground in one piece. Since Madeleine was taken that anxiety has given way to something else: an aching sadness. Somewhere deep down it always seems wrong to be going anywhere, or returning from anywhere, without her. It's such an awful feeling that nowadays I'd rather not fly at all unless it's absolutely unavoidable.

We were warmly welcomed at the airport in Rome by Francis Campbell, the ambassador to the Holy See, and Monsignor Charlie Burns, who, like Gerry, was from Glasgow, along with several representatives of the British Consulate. We were taken to the ambassador's residence, where we were to spend the night. That evening holds fond memories for us both. Francis, Charlie and Pat, the housekeeper and social secretary, were absolutely lovely to us and made us feel like

family. They provided a wonderful dinner and great conversation. Francis is an amazing storyteller and must be one of
the most talented impressionists I've ever come across.
Listening to him I experienced the strangest sensation. I
realized that, for the first time in nearly a month, I was
laughing – not what I'd anticipated at all. As bizarre and
inappropriate as laughter felt then, it helped both
Gerry and me to relax and gave us a boost we sorely
needed.

We couldn't face much breakfast the following morning,
however. Reality kicked in again: Madeleine was missing and
we were going to meet the Pope. I was a bag of nerves. We left
for St Peter's at around nine o'clock, picking up Charlie en
route. On arrival we were taken to our seats in the Prima Fila
by the Vatican staff. Within minutes, the black clouds that
had been looming overhead gave way to bright skies. The
heat of the sun was uplifting, a good omen, perhaps?
The only problem now was that we were sitting directly in its
blazing rays, dressed in dark suits, very stressed and anxious,
and growing hotter all the time. Charlie, sitting behind us,
very sweetly held a parasol over our heads.

Amid an almost carnival atmosphere sat Gerry and I, at
the front, vulnerable and sombre. For an hour and a half
following the Pope's arrival there were addresses in different
languages, prayers, singing and blessings. Gerry's intolerance
of heat and his building apprehension edged him to the
brink of fainting. Thankfully he just managed to hang on. It
was shortly after midday by the time Pope Benedict started
to move along the Prima Fila to greet people. He was much
smaller than I'd imagined, a quiet and gentle man. I could

feel my heart pounding. This was the moment. Madeleine's moment.

The festival going on around me suddenly receded, the sights and sounds fading away, and I was aware of nothing and nobody but myself, Gerry, Madeleine and the Pope. He seemed about to turn back when one of his aides directed him to us. His eyes widened and it was evident that he knew who we were and recognized our sorrow. It was a brief but intense encounter. I said what I had planned and needed to say. Nothing earth-shattering: I simply thanked him for allowing us to be there and asked him to pray for Madeleine's safe return. He held our hands and assured us that he would keep Madeleine, our families and ourselves in his prayers. I gave him a photograph of her. I'd intended him to keep it but instead he placed his palm softly over it and blessed Madeleine before handing it back to us. In a minute, perhaps less, it was all over and yet we felt we'd accomplished something enormous for Madeleine.

Clarence, who had been sitting behind us with Francis and Charlie, told me a little later that during the proceedings a butterfly had landed on the ribbon in my hair. It flew off, only to return a short while later, this time alighting on the lapel of my jacket. At the time we all wondered whether it was a sign, a harbinger of good news. Remembering that now makes me sad. Back then we still had so much hope, seeing omens in sunlight and butterflies. It's not that we don't have hope any more. Of course we do. We'll always have hope, as long as we remain in this limbo. It's just that it feels so far away. Everything feels far away: our last moment with Madeleine, any future moments with Madeleine. These moments are like the pot of gold at the end of a perpetually extending rainbow. They're there, but still just beyond our reach.

It was so lovely to see Sean and Amelie when we returned to Praia da Luz. True to form, they appeared quite unfazed by our absence. Sean seemed more eager to tell us about a naughty doggy who'd weed on their sandcastle than to know where we'd been.

After feast comes famine, they say, and that evening, as the euphoria subsided, my spirits took a plunge:

Low point tonight ... Despairing about the lack of information. Makes it appear like the police haven't got a clue ... Four weeks tomorrow since Madeleine was taken. Four weeks since we've seen our special little girl. Not sure we'll see her again but I'm aware that we need to stay hopeful and strong. Love you so much Madeleine. Need you back! x

11

THE EUROPEAN CAMPAIGN

On we pressed with our campaign to spread the word across
Europe. We had decided it would further our cause to visit
one or two key countries ourselves and appeal personally to
their people for help, seeking assistance and advice from
politicians and children's charities. We wanted to reach some
of the hundreds of potential witnesses from elsewhere on the
continent who had been on holiday in the Algarve around
the time of Madeleine's disappearance. Perhaps even more
importantly, it was quite possible that Madeleine was in
another country now. Had anyone noticed a little girl who
seemed out of place, or somebody behaving suspiciously?

We chose Spain first, as it is so close to Portugal. After the
British and Irish, most other visitors to the Algarve are
German or Dutch, so we added Berlin and Amsterdam to the
itinerary. Finally, we felt we needed to venture beyond
Europe, to north Africa. Morocco was so easily accessible
from Praia da Luz – ferries make the thirty-five-minute
crossing from Tarifa in Spain to Tangiers several times a day
– that there was a distinct possibility Madeleine could have

been taken there. The Foreign Office helped us by arranging consular assistance in all these countries.

Now that it looked as if we were going to be based in Praia da Luz for the long haul, with frequent journeys to airports and regular meetings set up with the police at the British Consulate in Portimão, we'd decided it would be easier if we had our own car. We'd duly taken possession of a rented Renault Scenic on 27 May.

We left for Madrid on Thursday 31 May, taking a flight from Lisbon airport. Again it was horrible leaving Sean and Amelie. As well as the huge, central agony of missing and fearing for Madeleine, there were lots of other heartaches, and I resented being put in the position of having to make choices like this. I cursed the person who had brought such pain and suffering to our family. Our only comfort was that these essential separations seemed to affect Gerry and me far more than they did the twins.

At the check-in desks at Lisbon airport I looked around for pictures of Madeleine. I couldn't see a single one. I was dismayed. I talked to one of the staff, who explained that there were some notices pinned up behind a few of the desks. The tears pricked my eyes yet again. This just wasn't enough. Lisbon turned out to be one of the few European airports we visited that wasn't plastered with Madeleine's image. Poor Phil almost got herself arrested later for trying to rectify this by putting up some of our posters. The Portuguese, it seemed, took a less liberal view of flyposting than that encountered by our supporters elsewhere.

Sitting in an airport café, I couldn't avoid casting my eyes over the people rushing for planes or pushing trolleys backwards and forwards aimlessly. Where were they all going? Did they not know a little girl had been stolen? How could they take a holiday, or a business trip to talk in meetings about projected sales figures, when Madeleine was missing? Not for the first time, and certainly not the last, I had an overwhelming urge to shout, 'Stop! *Everybody stop!*' It's so hard to accept that for everyone else life goes on, but of course it does.

We were met at Madrid airport by several British Embassy staff, a liaison officer and two press officers, as well as a crowd of journalists and photographers, and taken to the hotel where we were to spend the night. Clarence briefed Gerry and me about the meetings and press conferences arranged for the next day and then we went up to our room to get some rest.

> *A bit tearful again tonight. It's getting harder to black out the bad thoughts.*

After a troubled night, we got up, dressed and went down to breakfast. I couldn't focus on the day ahead, on what we were trying to accomplish. Every now and then, by taking a few deep breaths and giving myself a firm talking-to, I gained a little control, only to collapse minutes later into a blubbering wreck. I was so angry with myself. Stop crying. Just stop it. You have to help your daughter. You will achieve nothing if you spend the whole day crying and wallowing in your grief. But trying to 'snap out of it' when every thought, every action, every breath is polluted by anguish is easier said than done. As I continued to sniffle over my untouched cup of tea, Gerry said, 'Kate, you don't have to do this. We don't have to do any of this. These meetings can be cancelled quite easily.' I knew he meant it but I also knew that I'd persecute myself later if I pulled out.

Once we'd been introduced to the British ambassador to Spain, the British consul for Madrid and a lady from the Justice and Home Affairs Department, we were scheduled to talk to representatives of three Spanish non-governmental organizations (NGOs) working with missing and exploited children. We'd both been a little nervous about this meeting. Conscious of the fact that there were many children abducted around the world whose plight hadn't been given anything like the publicity Madeleine's had, we were concerned that this might have caused some resentment.

We couldn't have been more wrong. The reception we were given by the NGOs was nothing but appreciative. 'Thank goodness you are doing this,' they said. 'We are so grateful to you for drawing attention to the whole issue of child abduction and exploitation.' We listened for an hour while they explained to us the extent of the problem in Spain and the difficulties they faced. While the situation had improved slightly (possession of child pornography, for example, had finally been classified as a criminal offence in Spain a couple of years before – which it still has not, incidentally, in many other nations), they felt that many cases of child sexual abuse, pornography and trafficking were still being swept under the carpet. The authorities and even the general population seemed unwilling to acknowledge that this kind of thing happened in their country.

As empathetic as the NGO representatives were, with every horrendous fact and statistic they shared with us I became wobblier and wobblier. Afterwards I took refuge in the ladies' room as the next deluge of tears gushed forth. Gripping the rim of the washbasin, I glanced at the red, swollen eyes and blotchy face looking back at me in the mirror. Come on, Kate. Deep breath in, deep breath out. And again. Nice and slow. Calm. Calm. I soaked some tissues in cold water and pressed them against my eyes and cheeks, then performed a few eye-widening exercises in an attempt to look vaguely human. Taking a final deep breath, with my mind refocused, I joined Gerry and Clarence and we made our way to the press conference that had been arranged, followed by a few short interviews.

In the afternoon we met Señor Rubalcaba, the Spanish interior minister. He listened attentively and his manner was gentle and sympathetic. He showed us the case file that had already been opened for Madeleine, which instantly brought us both some reassurance. There are two things I remember Señor Rubalcaba saying to us. 'We are treating Madeleine as if she is one of our own,' and 'As time moves on, people forget. Please feel free to come and knock on my door at any point to remind me.' Of course, I have no idea how genuine either statement was, but he certainly seemed sincere and we were grateful and encouraged.

As yet another day draws to a close and you are no nearer to finding your missing child, such fleeting flashes of optimism can disappear very quickly. That evening, as we flew back to Portugal, my mood was no doubt influenced by what we'd heard from the NGOs.

Quite upset on the way home. Can't stop thinking about Madeleine again – her fear and her pain. Dark thoughts have been creeping in a lot this week. How can I carry on, knowing that her life may have ended like this?

Saturday 2 June. It wasn't unusual for investigative or campaign issues to eat into our family days, and this was one of those occasions. Before we took the children out to Praia da Rocha beach, Gerry needed to catch up with the emails that had accumulated while we'd been in Madrid and I had a letter I wanted to write to J. K. Rowling. A couple of weeks earlier, a friend had mentioned to me that the author had a new Harry Potter story coming out in July and suggested I got in touch to see whether she could do something to raise awareness around the launch of her book.

'July?' I'd said. *'July?'*

Surely Madeleine would be back by then. I was panic-stricken at the idea that she might not; that my friend could imagine she might not. I simply couldn't think this way. I needed Madeleine home tomorrow. But here I was, several weeks later, writing my letter to J. K. Rowling. How on earth had I survived this long? I wondered. It is quite staggering how much stress the human mind and body can endure and still function on some level. You simply can't see how it is possible that you are still alive, and yet there you are, still breathing, speaking, moving. I clung tightly to the hope that whatever help J. K. Rowling might be able to offer in a month's time, when it came to it, it wouldn't be needed.

It wasn't enough to prevent me from sliding down the slippery slope for the rest of the day.

Crying in bed again – can't help it ... The thought of Madeleine's fear and pain tears me apart. The thought of paedophiles makes me want to rip my skin off. Surely these people along with psychopaths are not 'normal' human beings? I've never been in favour of the death penalty but these people should be 'kept' in a secure location of some description. I don't mind if it's in nice surroundings but certainly, in the case of paedophiles, away at all times from ANY contact with children.

In the event, J. K. Rowling's support was needed, and greatly appreciated. When *Harry Potter and the Deathly Hallows* was published on 21 July, it was distributed with a new poster of Madeleine, which she asked all retailers to display.

It was the following evening, Sunday 3 June – exactly a month after Madeleine's abduction – that Gerry and I opened up a little more to each other and shared some of the thoughts and anxieties that had been quietly tormenting us both; thoughts and anxieties that perhaps we hadn't felt able or ready to voice up to now.

We'd been sitting alone at the table, working at our computers. It was quiet and the lights were low. Though I can't remember how the conversation started, I'm glad it did. We talked through the guilt we felt about not having been in that apartment with the children; about having left the patio doors unlocked. How we found it hard to comprehend that we could have been so naive. We acknowledged the possibility that Madeleine might no longer be alive; the possibility that we might never find out what had happened to her. Would we ever be able to return to our home, the home we had all shared with her? Maybe we should move elsewhere.

Where? We discussed the need we felt to do our utmost to prevent this from happening to another child; to prevent another family from having to go through what we were going through. We had to ensure that something positive for someone, even if it wasn't us, came out of this horrific experience.

For me, the honest exposure of this buried poison was like lancing a boil. Admitting these secret fears and concerns, bringing them out into the open and sharing them with the only other person who was persecuted in the same way, made them suddenly a little easier to understand and to manage. Strengthened and comforted, I fell asleep that night more peacefully than I had in many days.

At the beginning of June, Gerry had a call from the director of communications at the Foreign Office. There was concern in the government, he said, that Clarence was 'becoming the story'. I am not quite sure what he meant by this. Clarence was certainly a visible presence and perhaps his open, affable style prevented him from being quite as anonymous as the Foreign Office would have liked. Perhaps it had drawn attention to the fact that they were still providing us with a media spokesperson and questions were being asked. It had been a month since Madeleine's disappearance, so maybe they were simply trying gently to prompt us into appointing somebody of our own to help us.

Whatever the case, it was suggested to Gerry that we should use Madeleine's Fund to employ someone to replace Clarence once our campaign visits were complete. Reluctantly, Gerry agreed. We honestly hadn't bargained for having to pay a salary for media liaison out of the fund, which we'd envisaged being used primarily to meet costs related directly to the search for Madeleine. It hadn't occurred to us that we'd still be needing this kind of help a month down the line. With no way of knowing how long this would continue, we had no idea how long the money would last.

On Monday 4 June, we recorded an appeal to be screened the following evening on *Crimewatch*, the long-running BBC programme that has a good track record in helping the police to solve crimes using information supplied by the public. Our appeal was aimed in particular at any British holidaymakers who had been in the Algarve at the time of Madeleine's abduction.

Frustratingly, *Crimewatch* was not allowed to film a reconstruction of the abduction. This was something we had wanted from the beginning, in the hope that it would encourage potential witnesses to come forward. In Britain the police often broadcast reconstructions through programmes like *Crimewatch* and news channels, but we were told that this was not possible in either Portugal or Britain because of the judicial secrecy law. We were able to show a pair of pyjamas like Madeleine's on the programme, which was particularly important since at the time it had been incorrectly stated in some press reports that her pyjamas were white.

Wednesday 6 June. Today we left on our campaign visits to Berlin and Amsterdam. For this three-legged trip we'd been offered the use of a plane by one of the directors of Netjets, a company that sells fractional jet ownership (a bit like a holiday-home timeshare, only with planes), which we accepted gratefully for the same reasons as we'd decided to accept Sir Philip Green's help to get us to Rome. Again, a small press contingent travelled with us.

Our schedule in Berlin looked a bit daunting, but in the event everything ran incredibly smoothly. Admirable German efficiency! After a television interview, we were off to meet the ambassador, Peter Torry, a nice man with three daughters of his own.

Next came that infamous press conference – infamous in that it produced such outrage in the British press and public. Our reaction was far less dramatic, regardless of headlines such as 'McCANNS APPALLED BY NEWSGIRL'S SLUR' in the *Mirror*. The fuss began when Sabine Mueller from German radio asked us, 'How do you feel about the fact that more and more people seem to be pointing the finger at you, saying that the way you behave is not the way people would normally behave when their child is abducted, and they seem to imply that you might have something to do with it?' In spite of the gasps and restless shuffling around the room, at first I failed to pick up on her last eight words: I was still concentrating on the first part of her question, which related to criticism there had been of our participation in the European campaign to find our daughter.

Some commentators seemed to be very preoccupied by how it was we were able to cope with meeting and greeting politicians, NGOs and news crews without breaking down all the time, as if managing to display a modicum of calm and control in public meant there must be something wrong with us. My ability to function on any level with Madeleine missing, albeit on autopilot, is something I've always found difficult to comprehend myself, and I can completely understand why somebody who hasn't walked in our shoes might find it weird. I responded by saying I thought these critics were in a very small minority. It was only after Gerry stated firmly, 'There is absolutely no way Kate and I are involved in this abduction,' that the second part of her question caught up with me. 'I have never heard before that anyone considers us suspects in this,' he went on. 'And the Portuguese police certainly don't.'

Honest to God, I almost want to pat my lovely husband and myself sympathetically on the head or put an arm round us both when I recall how trusting we were back then. To think we could have made comments like this, in all confidence and conviction. The fact that we could and did highlights why we were so totally dumbfounded when the tide turned against us two months later. We knew we were innocent, and we believed the PJ knew that, too. And despite everything that happened, we still believe that.

Our next meeting was with the deputy justice minister, who gave us a document relating to a conference on child welfare that had been held in Berlin two days previously. Over lunch, I browsed through it. It dealt with the dramatic rise in child pornography and the way the internet had turned this hideous blight on our society into a billion-dollar industry. I couldn't eat a thing.

The final encounter of the day was with the mayor of Berlin, Klaus Wowereit. We'd heard that he was a colourful and charismatic man, well liked and something of a celebrity in the region. If his popularity and the respect in which he was held by the citizens of Berlin could benefit Madeleine, we were more than prepared to have another few hundred photographs taken standing next to him while he appealed for help.

With the completion of the formal programme of events, the plan had been to relax for an hour before our departure to Amsterdam. At 3pm, however, a message was relayed to us from the British police with instructions for us to be taken immediately to the British Embassy. 'What's happened?' We had barely got the words out before the reply came: 'I'm sorry, we don't know.'

A wave of nausea. Immediate tears. Was she dead? Had she been found? We had been here before and couldn't believe this was happening all over again, but there we were, holding on to each other in the back of a car, crying, shaking and praying. Please God, let it be good news. Please God, let Madeleine be all right.

At the Embassy, Ambassador Torry had been joined by David Connolly, an officer from SOCA (the Serious Organised Crime Agency). David told us how sorry he was we'd had to go through another twenty minutes of suffering and reassured us that nothing terrible had happened. I felt myself breathe again. He explained that the Spanish police had received a call, on an Argentinian mobile phone, from a man calling himself Walter, who told them he had information about Madeleine but would speak only to Gerry or me. The Spanish police conferred with the Portuguese police and both concluded that it might be significant. The Spanish police were going to ring Walter back and arrange for him to talk to us.

David warned us that it might be a hoax, but it was equally possible it might be genuine, perhaps a ransom demand. My heartbeat quickened. I tried to keep a lid on any optimism, knowing how bad the crash would be if this amounted to nothing, but it was incredibly hard to suppress the flicker of hope it had ignited.

David briefed Gerry on what would happen. Gerry and I would take the call at the police headquarters in Berlin. He talked Gerry through the questions he would need to ask and how he should respond. As we waited to hear from the Spanish authorities we were joined by two German specialist kidnap officers. The whole team oozed professionalism and experience, which sustained Gerry and me as the minutes ticked slowly by.

At 5pm local time, the Spanish police rang Walter. There was no answer. I was completely gutted.

We were given three options: we could return to the UK, where, it was felt, the facilities for dealing with such operations were probably the best; we could stay on in Berlin in case the authorities were able to make contact with Walter; or we could carry on to Amsterdam as planned. After some discussion, we decided that, since it now seemed that this was in all probability a crank call, we should press on to Amsterdam. The episode had caused us enough heartache already and we didn't want it to scupper this important trip as well. If there were any further developments, we could easily be contacted there.

An additional complication was that the journalists travelling with us were waiting to be told when the plane was going to leave and had already begun speculating about the reason for the delay. Clarence was being bombarded with questions and had so far managed to field them without disclosing any sensitive details, but it could only be a matter of time before the press got wind of something. The last thing we needed was another dramatic and wildly inaccurate story blowing up. In the unlikely event that Walter's call had been genuine, who knows what effect it might have had on any negotiations?

As it turned out, that was the last we ever heard of Walter. But it was a good illustration, if any were needed, of the inadvisability of allowing the media to fly with us.

The Netjets plane eventually took off shortly before 7.30pm, several hours later than planned. By then I was such a nervous wreck that I accepted a restorative gin and tonic. Come to think of it, that might well have been my first drink since Madeleine was taken. It helped me relax for a few minutes, anyway.

On our descent into Schipol airport, the sensations that were now becoming familiar returned: the tight throat, the stinging, wet eyes, the heavy, dragging feeling in my chest. Oh God, how could this be? Amsterdam held so many happy memories of the year we'd lived there with Madeleine. How could we be coming back without her? I'm so sorry, Madeleine. I'm so, so sorry.

It was late and Gerry and I were both completely drained by the stress and seesawing emotions of the afternoon. On our arrival in Amsterdam, with profuse apologies, we cancelled a broadcast interview that had been scheduled to take place two hours earlier.

Unbelievably, the producers were really quite angry. I've

learned to accept this kind of insensitive reaction, which we have encountered from time to time over the years, mainly with the international press. Some people have become pretty belligerent when they've felt we haven't given them what they wanted from us. One guy even threw his mike on the floor in a fit of pique. It's as if news, events and 'human-interest stories' exist solely to serve their programmes and publications rather than the other way around; as if we, and Madeleine's situation, are there simply as fodder for their airtime or columns. It's disappointing but we are used to it. It would be pointless to let it get to us. We move on.

We did manage a short interview that evening, in our hotel room, with a nice lady called Eleanor from *The Tablet*, the weekly Catholic newspaper. This was more like a chat than anything else and certainly more relaxing than any other media interviews we'd done so far. Afterwards, at 10pm, five of our Amsterdam friends came over to see us. I could hardly bear to let go when they hugged me. I knew the moment I stepped back to look at them their faces would instantly remind me of days spent together with Madeleine. A fresh surge of pain mingled with the comfort brought by these special friends. We had never expected to be seeing them without Madeleine. These were people who had shared her first birthday cake with her. This incomplete reunion made no sense.

The next day followed a similar tightly packed format to our visits to Madrid and Berlin. We had meetings with the ambassador, the UK police liaison officer for the KLPD (the Dutch national police), the consul general and a government policy adviser. We talked to the national police coordinator for missing persons. It became apparent very quickly just how much more advanced than many other countries the Netherlands was in dealing with missing children. The systems in place were extremely well structured and organized. The fact that they had systems at all gave them a head start on much of Europe. We were given books on what to do if your child went missing and how to deal with the media if your child went missing (unfortunately for us, in Dutch, and a little late) – vital sources of information and guidance for families thrown into this terrifying unknown territory.

We also met Charlotte from Child Focus, an NGO for missing and exploited children in Belgium. After suffering a spate of child abductions and murders in the 1990s, Belgium had set out to tackle these heinous crimes head on. The establishment of Child Focus in 1997 was a part of this strategy. Charlotte told us she was the case manager at Child Focus for Madeleine. We were speechless. We couldn't believe there was actually a lady in *Belgium* working officially on Madeleine's behalf. I was so grateful I burst into tears. I cried at sad news, I cried at heartwarming news. I did a lot of crying! Those who criticized us for appearing too controlled didn't know the half of it.

After several interviews for national television and radio, including *Opsporing Verzocht*, the Dutch equivalent of *Crimewatch*, we were back on the plane heading for the Algarve. I needed a fix of Sean and Amelie's beautiful smiles, their funny toddler chatter, their sticky fingers, their baby breath on my face. I had to drag myself away from the twins all too soon. Gerry and I had been invited to a concert, a

Music Marathon for Madeleine, in Lagos. We were both absolutely exhausted but we wanted to go to show our gratitude for this demonstration of support and solidarity. The music was fantastic and it was wonderful to see so many kids taking part, doing their bit for Madeleine. Just as we began to flag, four young rappers got up on stage. They were so entertaining and so funny that at one point I found myself laughing. It felt good and bad at the same time, prompting a confusing concoction of responses. The warmth it brought was tainted by a disgust with myself for even being able to laugh. Was this how life without Madeleine was going to be? Would I never again, until the day she came back, be able to laugh in public or feel pure, uncomplicated joy?

12

MOROCCO

Sunday 10 June. Rabat, Morocco. Shortly before leaving for the airport, I made the mistake of reading an article in a *Sunday Express* I'd found lying around – a double-page piece, I think, illustrated by a photograph of an over-crowded, chaotic market scene – about child trading in Morocco.

I can't believe our dear little Madeleine has potentially ended up with such a scary, sordid life. Please God, please, please protect her. She loves us, God. Please bring her back to us.

We were lucky we managed to get on a plane to Rabat at all. I use the word 'lucky' loosely. The jet had broken down and a pre-war propeller plane was drafted to help out. It was too small to carry all the passengers and had to make a return trip to get everyone to Morocco. Flying was hard enough for me now as it was, and this was scary. The plane, a bare metal tube, was basic. It had about twenty seats and no separate cockpit, no overhead lockers or storage racks, no in-flight service (thank goodness I'd had that butty in the airport), no life jackets. I'm probably sounding a bit precious now, but of course it wasn't the absence of small comforts that bothered me, it was the fact that I really didn't feel safe. Still, it must be said that my imagination was in overdrive to start with, and I allowed it to run away with me to the point where I was terrified we were going to die on our way to Rabat and leave all of our children orphaned. It's hard to stay level-headed when you've forgotten what it feels like to be at peace.

In the event, our journey was absolutely fine. I remember feeling reassured about the stringency of Morocco's immigration procedures when I was required at the airport to fill in a form stating the reason for my visit, among other things. In truth it didn't mean a lot, and their security system might be lousy for all I know. I think I just needed to latch on to any positives I could find.

Miss Biddy Brett-Rooks, the consul general for Casablanca, was there to meet us when we landed. She looked and sounded exactly as I'd imagined from her name: very sweet and *very* English. We went first to a hotel where we had arranged to meet an ITN crew from the UK. They wanted to show us an interview they'd recorded with a Norwegian lady called Mari Olli.

We'd heard about Mari Olli only two days earlier. On 9 May, she'd seen a little girl who looked like Madeleine at a petrol station on the outskirts of Marrakesh. While her husband filled up the tank, Mari had gone into the garage shop to buy some water. She'd noticed a man there hanging around with a blonde child of around four, who looked pale and tired. Mari heard her ask the man in English, 'Can we see

224

Mummy soon?' to which he replied, 'Soon.' It wasn't until Mari and her husband were back at their home on the Costa del Sol the next evening that they learned of Madeleine's abduction.

In ITN's interview, Mari stated that as soon as she saw Madeleine's photograph, she recognized her as the girl she'd seen in Marrakesh and rang the Spanish police straight away. Gerry and I watched the footage with heavy hearts. Not only was it upsetting, it was also deeply concerning. From what we could infer, this lead simply hadn't been adequately followed up. Indeed, a month later, Mari still hadn't been formally interviewed. It was intolerable. This was our daughter's life they were dealing with, not a stolen car radio.

It was pretty late by the time we arrived at the ambassador's residence, where we would be spending the night. In the morning, at a meeting with the consular staff, we heard from a British Metropolitan Police attaché, a counter-terrorism liaison and cooperation officer, that Morocco was a police state with excellent networks and intelligence-gathering systems. If Madeleine was here, she was sure to be found. It was something we'd be told several times during our visit.

We talked to the president of the Ligue Marocaine pour la Protection de l'Enfance, the Moroccan equivalent of the NSPCC, and visited Touche Pas à Mon Enfant, an NGO based on the upper floor of a very dark, tenement-like build- ing. Once again we were astounded and moved by the volume of work being done on Madeleine's behalf and by the kindness and advice offered by these lovely people.

That day several senior and powerful figures spent time

with us, including the minister of the interior, Mr Benmoussa, and the director general of the police, Charki Draiss. The police attaché had told us earlier that for these meetings to take place, permission must have been granted by the King himself. Both Mr Benmoussa and Mr Draiss reiterated the message of the day: 'We will help you. If Madeleine's here, we will find her.'

En route to our visit to the Observatoire Nationale des Droits de l'Enfant, a Palace-sponsored child-welfare watchdog, a crowd of kids suddenly came into view. There must have been over a hundred of them, and they were all holding up posters bearing Madeleine's face with the words 'All Moroccan Children Are With You, Madeleine' above it and 'Madeleine: Back Home' underneath. Beaming, they chanted in unison: 'Madeleine! Madeleine! Madeleine!' This welcome was as unexpected as it was overwhelming, and we couldn't help but smile. In fact, I couldn't stop myself smiling and on this occasion, my tears were all happy ones. It was impossible not to be touched by their enthusiasm and their unspoiled beauty and innocence. If ever a reminder were needed of how special and important children are in this world, one second in the company of our new little friends would provide it.

From the Observatoire Nationale des Droits de l'Enfant, we learned that the heart of each Moroccan community is not the town hall or police station but the health centre. Accordingly, a new computer network system linking all the health centres in Morocco – including, crucially, those in rural areas – had been designed and was ready to be launched from their headquarters. A special webpage about

226

Madeleine had also been created to coincide with our visit to Rabat. Gerry and I were completely blown away to be invited to press the 'go live' button, activating not only Morocco's new network but with it the 'Madeleine page', thereby alerting all the health centres across the country to her disappearance and our need to find her.

> *A good day (if any can be without Madeleine). A positive and reassuring visit. In some ways we hope that Madeleine is here. I long for that day when I'll have my beautiful Madeleine back in my arms xx*

On our final morning, the lady who'd been interpreting for us arranged for us to meet the minister of Islamic affairs, who happened to be her father-in-law. I was keen to talk to an Islamic religious leader to seek the support and prayers of the Muslim community. The minister was an academic, senior cleric and an adviser to the King, and he seemed kind, genuine and receptive. We explained that we lived in Leicester, a multicultural city where many people of different faiths had been praying for Madeleine, and told him how important this was to us. I asked if he would urge the Muslim people here to pray for her, too, and for all missing children. He promised us that he would, adding that he was certain we would be reunited with our daughter.

Before leaving Morocco, we had a call from the British police attaché. He told us that by the time the CCTV pictures had been requested from the garage in Marrakesh where Mari Olli was convinced she'd seen Madeleine, all footage from before 14 May had been erased. Apparently, the local police had visited the garage soon after Mari's call and reported that there was no CCTV. However, they had looked only on the forecourt, failing to notice the camera in the shop. When the images were finally retrieved several days later, it was too late.

This was soul-destroying news. If this little girl was Madeleine, she could have been back with us by now. If she wasn't, we would at least have been able to eliminate this sighting from the investigation and put an end to our own hopes that it might lead somewhere. As it is, we still don't know whether that little girl was our daughter, and we may never know.

I was grateful to find there was a jet available to return us to Portugal. At Lisbon airport, Gerry and I said our good-byes to Clarence. He was going home to his family and the Media Monitoring Unit. He'd done a fantastic job over the previous three weeks (with everything we'd packed in, it felt like much longer than that), and what was important to us was that we knew Clarence cared deeply about getting Madeleine back and would continue to help us in any way he could. We couldn't have anticipated he'd be rejoining us as soon as he did, and we never thought for a minute that, five years down the line, he'd still be fighting Madeleine's corner alongside us.

In the meantime, we would be welcoming Justine McGuinness, who would be arriving as coordinator of the Find Madeleine campaign on 22 June: Madeleine's fiftieth day away from us.

Back in Praia da Luz, we were regaled with tales of twinny exploits from Auntie Anne and Uncle Michael, including the 'Let's paint the bedroom with Sudocrem' saga. It was good to know they'd had fun!

Our trips to these key cities had been hard going, but we were satisfied that they had boosted our campaign. Looking back on them now, however, we can't help but wonder whether many of the powerful figures we encountered were merely handing out platitudes. With the eyes of the world upon us, and anyone associated with us, their agreement to meet Gerry and me was perhaps designed more to forestall potential criticism from the international press than to benefit Madeleine. But we learned a great deal of lasting value from the NGOs and I have no doubt that their representatives, committed as they were to the plight of missing children, were genuinely motivated to help. And at the very least we had spread the word across Europe and north Africa, and that could, and still can, only improve our chances of finding Madeleine.

Keen to find out what progress, if any, there had been in the PJ investigation, two days later we were back in Portimão with Guilhermino Encarnação and Luís Neves. While we were there Neves took a phone call and suddenly became very animated. He was clearly worried and angry. The Dutch newspaper *De Telegraaf*, he told us, had revealed in an article that they'd received a letter from someone claiming to be Madeleine's abductor. The letter alleged that her body was buried in Odiáxere, about ten miles from Luz.

There had been plenty of crank calls and letters from all over Europe. The reason why this claim had been singled out by the newspaper as a story (not that there ever has to be a reason, or so it seems) was that the letter was apparently very similar to one received the year before regarding the location of the bodies of two young girls abducted in Belgium. They had been found later the same day, albeit fifteen kilometres away from the location given.

A hundred or so reporters had now gone up to Odiáxere to look for Madeleine's body. I might sound quite matter-of-fact about this now, but at the time I was beside myself, of course. It felt as if cold, hard reality was hitting me with a sickening thud. I remember leaving the room and locking myself in the toilet. It was probably the tiniest cubicle I've ever seen, which only intensified my suffocating fear. I pulled out my mobile phone and began to text six devout family members and friends (quietly, in my head, I thought of them as my 'prayer group'): 'Please pray for Madeleine.' I returned to the meeting room. Somebody texted back: 'Of course. Everything OK?' The lack of a response was probably enough of an answer.

Gerry was far more rational about this incident than I was, although I'm sure deep down he was just as scared and not as certain as he seemed. 'Kate, where is the credibility?' he tried to reassure me. 'This information has come from a newspaper acting irresponsibly!'

He was proved right, thankfully. The PJ were in contact with the Dutch journalists to compare the two letters, which were found to be quite different, and searches of the area later that day turned up nothing. Interestingly, two search-and-rescue soldiers who'd come out to Praia da Luz to lend a hand in May, completely of their own accord, phoned Sandy that evening. They assured him they'd scoured the area in question then and were confident there was nothing terrible to be found there. We'd met these guys the previous month and they were good, decent blokes. They won't know how much relief and comfort their call brought me that night.

All relationships have their ups and downs and our dealings with the PJ, though generally amiable enough, were no exception. On the evening of 17 June, the Portuguese police were quoted on Sky News as having stated that the crime scene at apartment 5A had been contaminated by us and our friends, and that as a consequence vital evidence had been lost. I was livid. First of all it was unfair: the preservation of the crime scene was the responsibility of the police and should have been overseen by an experienced officer. Second, it was inaccurate. The forensic department clearly stated (as would be confirmed in the PJ files released the following year) that significant contamination had resulted from police dogs being allowed into the room before they conducted their examination. Third, it was incredibly insensitive, implying as it did that we had destroyed evidence that could have helped to find our daughter. And that, especially, hurt badly.

The following morning, Gerry rang several people – Ricardo Paiva, British Consul Bill Henderson, Ambassador John Buck and DCS Bob Small – seeking some kind of explanation and redress for these comments from the PJ.

We were told that their spokesman, a chief inspector called Olegário de Sousa, was embarrassed and apologetic. A couple of days later he came along with Guilhermino Encarnação to our regular meeting, where he appeared suitably chastened and admitted that he'd fallen into a 'media trap'. We knew as well as anyone that it takes a while to become media savvy if you're not used to dealing with the press, and Sousa certainly wasn't. Media liaison was not a role that existed in the Portuguese police in normal circumstances, and he had been nominated as the PJ spokesperson for the case largely, I think, because he spoke good English.

Given the restrictions of the judicial secrecy law, the police usually had little reason to engage with the press, or not officially, at any rate. The unprecedented efforts of the PJ to accommodate the demands of the international media were perhaps partly responsible for the grumbling in the Portuguese press that we were being given 'special treatment'.

Alex Woolfall had advised us early on not to speak to any reporters who approached us directly. Since everyone wanted to speak to us it would only have resulted in us talking to the press constantly, saying the same things over and over again, and there was nothing to be gained from that. The British media, used to statements, briefings and press conferences, were familiar with working in this way, but it undoubtedly caused some consternation among their Portuguese counterparts, who operated on a much more informal basis. Over the summer, we also began to realize that elements within the Portuguese police routinely flouted their own law, and indeed maintained extremely close relationships with selected journalists.

At our next meeting with Neves and Encarnação, on 28 June, we tentatively raised the possibility of bringing in Danie Krugel, a South African ex-police officer who claimed to have combined DNA and satellite tracking technology to develop a device that could be used to locate missing persons.

I know this sounds mad, so let me rewind a little to explain. Danie's name, and his offer of help, had reached us via a variety of sources within the first few weeks of Madeleine's disappearance. At the time we were in too much turmoil to pay much attention to anything so esoteric, and in any case we had all our hopes pinned on the police investigation. Towards the end of May, a friend of Danie's arrived in Praia da Luz and virtually pleaded with me to take up his offer. She spoke of references from the South African police, for whom his machine had brought results, of its 80 per cent success rate and of the support of the South African minister for justice. Whether we were influenced by the distance this young mother had travelled just to talk to us, or whether we were simply plain desperate, I can't be sure – putting it in perspective today, I'd say it was the latter – but by now we were more receptive.

We were told all we needed to do was to provide samples of Madeleine's DNA. Desperation does strange things to people. We're scientists and we don't believe in hocus pocus or crackpot inventions. How on earth can a machine use a single hair to locate somebody anywhere in the world? It's impossible, surely. It makes no sense to us now and it didn't then. But we wanted so badly to find Madeleine that we didn't need to know how it worked. We even managed to turn a blind eye to the fact that Danie's 'matter orientation system' hadn't been formally tested by any independent and trustworthy authority. Danie sounded like a nice person (family man, 'fellow Christian'), and indeed he was. As the director of protection services and occupational health and safety at the Central University of Technology in Bloemfontein, he was professionally credible, and he was prepared to bring his machine over from South Africa to find Madeleine for us. I feel a heavy sadness now, though, at the memory of how close to the edge we were, and how vulnerable that made us.

I remember talking to Gerry and Sandy, trying to decide what to do. Even Sandy, who dismisses anything lacking logic or transparency as mumbo-jumbo, felt, as we did, that since the investigation appeared to have ground to a halt, it was worth trying anything. What else did we have? What harm could it do?

So, in the second week of June, we had confided in Auntie Janet and our friend Amanda back in Leicestershire and got them to go round to our house looking for hairs that could only be Madeleine's. They came up with five head hairs from the inside of a coat hood and a couple of eyelashes from her pillow and couriered the lot off to Danie in South Africa. They didn't question what we were doing: they, too, were just desperate for Madeleine to be home.

A week or so afterwards, Danie informed us that he had obtained 'signals' relating to Praia da Luz, but that he would need to come over in July and operate the machine in the Algarve to produce more accurate results and pinpoint Madeleine's location. This all seemed to make sense – or at least, more sense than trying to find her from Bloemfontein.

So here we were now, discussing all this with Luís Neves and Guilhermino Encarnação. Somewhat to our surprise,

234

they seemed quite amenable to giving it a go and agreed to smooth Danie's transfer through the airport (he had certain requirements to ensure the safety of his MOS machine) in a couple of weeks' time.

Another matter I raised that day was how significant they felt it was that Fiona, Rachael and Russell had all reported seeing Robert Murat outside our apartment on the night Madeleine had been taken. Luís suddenly got quite agitated. 'No, Kate!' he snapped. Our friends hadn't mentioned this in their statements, he said. Slightly thrown by this rather aggressive response, I insisted, a little nervously, that I was sure they had: not in their first statements, but in the ones they had given after Murat was named as an *arguido*, having recognized him straight away from the television news.

They had merely stated when and where they had seen this man and that he'd been offering his services as an interpreter. That was it: they hadn't voiced any suspicions that he was involved. I can't imagine why Neves seemed to want to brush my question aside. Perhaps it was simply because he didn't have an answer. I'm aware now that the PJ were struggling to move the Murat line of inquiry forward and they were probably feeling quite frustrated. Perhaps I just touched a raw nerve.

At our next meeting, Neves was to change tack and tell us that one of the Ocean Club managers, Sílvia Batista (the lady who had translated for us on 3 May), had also reported seeing Robert Murat outside our apartment that night.

There were so many unanswered questions going round and round my brain; so many days when all I wanted to do was pull the duvet over my head and for it all to go away.

13

THE TIDE TURNS

On Saturday 30 June, a piece entitled 'Pact of Silence', written by journalists Felícia Cabrita and Margarida Davim, appeared in a Portuguese newspaper. The criticism implied in the title was in itself interesting, given that this was a country where disregard for judicial secrecy carried the threat of a prison sentence. This was probably the first article openly to cast doubt on our version of the events of 3 May. It raised suspicions about us and our friends, about our characters and about our potential involvement in Madeleine's disappearance.

Several days before it was published, all of us – Fiona, David, Jane, Russell, Matt and Rachael, as well as Gerry and I – had been contacted on our mobile phones by a reporter. Everyone had given her short shrift, but it was clear that somebody had provided her not only with our mobile numbers, but with other personal information, too. She had addressed me as Kate Healy, and although this was the name by which I was always known before Madeleine's abduction, since then I'd only ever been referred to as Mrs McCann. She called Gerry 'Gerald', a name he never uses. She knew that Jane and Russell had recently moved to Devon.

It was obvious that this reporter had been given access to our statements, our passport details or some other official documentation. There were no prizes for guessing by whom. Evidently there was a leak within the Polícia Judiciária. We brought up this matter at our next meeting with Neves and Encarnação on 5 July. They agreed that, yes, there must be a leak from the PJ, but in spite of the endlessly cited judicial secrecy law, no internal inquiry was ever launched.

Since our series of campaign trips, it had become apparent that, with coverage having reached saturation point, the press were exploring different angles. Their appetite for the 'human-interest' aspect seemed insatiable. No longer was it about our lovely missing daughter: it was becoming the Kate and Gerry show. Our friend Jon Corner had predicted this very early on. After sitting in on an interview session with British journalists one day, he'd said to us, 'They're asking you about whether you still go running and what kind of trainers you wear, for God's sake. The longer this goes on, the worse it's going to get. It will all be about you, not Madeleine.'

We had made a strategic decision to signal to the media that we would be withdrawing from the spotlight. The face of the campaign had to be Madeleine's, not ours. We would continue to give interviews that were in her interests, of course, but otherwise, until there was an important development or event, we would be running the campaign more quietly and not commenting on everyday matters. There was no point in diluting the impact of the campaign by reporting on it constantly.

Much to our surprise, however, the press, and in particular the photographers, showed no sign of leaving Praia da Luz. This put us in a difficult position and led to some friction with Justine McGuinness, our new campaign manager. As we had very little to say, yet at the same time the papers still seemed to require a daily photograph of us, we were essentially appeasing the tabloids without generating any significant benefits for the campaign. It wasn't necessary to bombard the public day in, day out with pictures of us, and the presence of the photographers encouraged the journalists to stay, to write pieces to accompany the photographs, even though there was nothing much to be written. This was no doubt the background to a lot of the ludicrous tales that now appeared, embellished by quotes supposedly uttered by us or by 'sources close to the McCanns'. The lack of new fuel for the machine also meant that a lot of the knocking pieces springing up in the Portuguese press were promoted to the front pages in the UK throughout July and on into August.

After expressing our intention to remain in the background, we talked about how we might put the resources now at our disposal to good use in the longer term if the search for Madeleine continued to yield nothing. Our visits to Spain, Germany, the Netherlands and Morocco had given us a glimpse of the massive scale of the problems of child abduction, trafficking and exploitation, and we felt we must broaden the scope of our campaign to embrace all the victims of these terrible crimes. We were now aware of the need, for example, to set up coordinated and effective child rescue alerts across Europe. Given the huge support we had been given ourselves, we had a moral obligation to try to do something to make Europe a safer place for all children. If, God forbid, we couldn't help Madeleine, we were determined that some lasting good should come out of our nightmare.

The sexual exploitation of children in particular is shockingly rife worldwide. The victims of the billion-dollar child-pornography industry are becoming younger, too: approximately a third are under the age of six. A lot of what I'd learned made me feel sick. I was horrified, as a reasonably intelligent and well-informed person, and as a mother, by how little I knew of this. I felt as if I'd been living my life in a cocoon.

Another valuable source of information was Lady Catherine Meyer, the friend Cherie Blair had mentioned to me in her phone call. Catherine, the wife of the former British ambassador to the US, had set up PACT (Parents and Abducted Children Together) after her own two sons were abducted by her ex-husband. She has fought tirelessly ever since for a better international response to such crimes. I so admire her commitment to and passion for protecting children. She is feisty, determined, has a good sense of humour and is not afraid to say what she thinks. Such qualities are essential in this field, where there is so much red tape to be dealt with.

At the end of June, Gerry spoke to Ernie Allen, CEO of the National Center for Missing and Exploited Children (NCMEC) in the USA. This organization was established in 1984, thanks to the lobbying of Congress by John and Revé Walsh. When their six-year-old son Adam was abducted and found murdered in Florida in 1981, they had experienced the same kind of pain and frustration at inadequate responses that we were suffering now. Today the NCMEC offers a vast range of resources to law-enforcement agencies investigating cases of missing, abducted and exploited children, as well as training and education for people working in this field.

I came into the sitting room just as Gerry was finishing this hour-long phone call to find my husband almost radiant and brimming with optimism. He was already planning to fly out to Washington, DC at the earliest opportunity to find out more about the work of the NCMEC for himself. It wasn't just Ernie's positive attitude and encouragement that had lifted Gerry, but the numerous examples he had cited of missing children who had been found, sometimes years later. There really was hope. I hadn't seen Gerry looking so inspired in two months.

Although our lives were unpredictable and could never now be defined as normal, sometimes days would go by when we jogged along fairly evenly. But then we would be poleaxed by some bolt from the blue. Unfortunately, most of these shocks would be bad ones. The saddest were those delivered with the intention of causing harm.

There were frequent attempts to extort money from us, which were the reason for most of Detective Ricardo Paiva's visits to our apartment. One I remember from the last days of June was fairly typical. A Dutch man contacted the PJ on the email address given on their website, saying that he knew who had Madeleine and where she was. And asking for money, of course. At the instigation of the PJ, Gerry set up a separate email account to correspond with this guy, buying time for the police to track him down from the IP address he was using, passing incoming messages to the PJ and taking their advice on what to say in his replies. The man was emailing from an internet café, and within a few days, on 6 July, he was arrested in the Netherlands (having been under surveillance in a casino, if I remember rightly). Another couple, an Italian man and a Portuguese woman, had been picked up only the previous week for a separate extortion attempt. As they were already wanted by the police in France it was a mystery why they'd thought it a good idea to draw attention to themselves in this way.

Thankfully, though, there were some nice surprises, too, arising in particular from the kindness and friendship of some wonderful people now entering our lives.

At the beginning of July we received the following letter:

Dear McCanns,
I have a house in P da L, been ashamed of the intrusion to your lives by our media . . . and if you would care to come to lunch/dinner at any time before Wednesday next, do ring and let me know.
I cook decent meals.
Sincerely,
Clement Freud

I'm embarrassed to admit that Gerry and I thought this letter was a hoax; more embarrassing still, while we were vaguely aware of Sir Clement, we had to have our memories refreshed by Sandy and Justine before we could place him exactly. Mind you, he wore so many hats – humorist, MP, gourmet, gambler, press columnist, advertiser of dog food, radio and TV personality – that he was hard to pin down.

Gerry responded with a phone call and Sir Clement invited the seven of us there at that time – Gerry and myself with Sean and Amelie, plus Trisha, Sandy and Justine – to lunch the following day. He would be heading back to the UK a few hours later. Sir Clement was eighty-three by then, but his intellect was still razor-sharp (he was appearing on the demanding Radio 4 panel game *Just a Minute* right up to his death in 2009). I'm usually very intimidated by people with brains the size of planets, but Clement was incredibly warm, funny and instantly likeable. His opening words were 'Can I interest you in a strawberry vodka?' It was midday.

I hesitated for a split second, rapidly trying to work out if he was joking. His expression, as always, was deadpan. Not wanting to appear unsociable, I responded, 'Er, OK then. That would be nice.' Of course, Clement's remark about cooking decent meals was tongue-in-cheek: among his other accomplishments, he had trained as a chef and was for many years a food writer and restaurant critic. I can confirm that the lunch he prepared for us that day was bloody marvellous: watercress and egg salad followed by a chicken and mush-room risotto – the best risotto we've ever tasted before or since. Clement cheered us up with his lugubrious wit, and would continue to do so by email after his return to England.

There was another invitation a few days later, from the detective Ricardo Paiva and his wife, to dinner at their apart-ment in Lagoa Norte. We were pleased to accept. It was reassuring to have a close and amicable relationship with someone who was officially involved in our daughter's case, even if it wasn't perhaps the done thing to be socializing with one of the investigation team. It made us feel that Ricardo and his wife genuinely cared about us and, more importantly, about Madeleine. Sean and Amelie were very excited to meet their little boy – especially as he had lots of excitingly unfamiliar toys to share with them. Two other couples, neighbours of Ricardo's, also joined us.

As far as such a thing was possible in my cold new world, it was a good evening, though I found it hard to allow myself to really relax and enjoy it. Ricardo made us a great martini and his wife had prepared a fantastic meal. She and their friends spoke only a little English, but it was an improvement on our Portuguese.

Meanwhile, on 2 July, we had moved out of the Ocean Club and into a rented villa, the cheapest we could find that suited our requirements (Gerry was now on unpaid leave), in Parque Luz, about ten minutes' walk away. Apartment 4G was no longer available, and I think this perhaps prompted Mark Warner to try to ease us out. They had been good to us, but we had been with them for over two months by then and I can see that our presence must have been unsettling for their other guests. Like everyone – except for us, sadly – they had to move on. Sean and Amelie were still welcome at Toddler Club (and Mark Warner carried on allowing us to use their pool, too).

The move made sense for us as well. At the villa we had more privacy. We also rented a small flat at the Ocean Club for Justine. She had ended up doing a different job from the one she'd signed up for – media liaison in addition to campaign management – and was having to spend more time in Portugal than either we or she had anticipated. Trish and Sandy came with us, sleeping on a fold-down bed in the bedroom we were using as our office or, when other people came to stay, taking themselves off to Justine's apartment.

On Thursday 11 July, Fiona, Rachael and Russell were back in Portugal. The PJ wanted to 'clarify' their statements, evidently in relation to their sightings of Robert Murat, by holding an *acareação*, a 'confrontational interview', between the witnesses and the *arguido*.

This legal procedure involves bringing interviewees together effectively to argue the toss about the inconsistencies in their accounts, in front of an arbitrator, with a view to reaching a consensus. Russ, Rachael and Fiona had to sit in a semicircle with Murat and his lawyer, Francisco Pagarete – so close together, Russell recounted later, that his knee was virtually touching Murat's. They waited for a while because the police said Sílvia Batista would be joining them. For some reason she never did.

I'm sure this interviewing technique must have been incredibly uncomfortable and stressful for everyone. The statements given by Russell, Rachael and Fiona were read out in turn, in Portuguese, by the questioning officer, Paulo Ferreira, and then translated by an interpreter. Guilhermino Encarnação was also present. They were asked to confirm that their respective accounts were correct, which they all did. During the reading of each statement, they told us, Murat leaned forward, staring intensely at the person who had given it. His statement was then read out in Portuguese, which made it difficult for Fiona, Rachael or Russ to dispute it in any detail, and he was asked some questions, again in Portuguese. Many of these he was advised not to answer by Pagarete (as was his right as an *arguido*), and on one occasion he and his lawyer left the room altogether for a private conversation. The only responses given by Murat comprehensible to our friends were that he hadn't been outside our apartment on 3 May and that the three of them were lying. When we saw them afterwards they were noticeably incensed by Murat's manner during the *acareação*.

The next day Gerry left for London to attend the National Police Bravery Awards. We had been invited there by the *Sun*, who sponsored the event and wanted to give us a special award. We didn't feel comfortable with that. We hadn't performed some brave deed, we had merely responded to the disaster that had befallen us as any parent would. They told us that was fine: we didn't have to accept any tribute. All they wanted to do was support us. If we thought it would help, one or both of us could come along, whatever felt right. I was reluctant to leave the twins any more than was necessary so we decided that Gerry would go, and just say a few words to express our thanks to the police. He was pretty emotional, especially after a clip from the 'Don't You Forget About Me' film was shown, and so were quite a few of the police, apparently. They gave him a standing ovation. While he was in London he took the opportunity on the Friday to visit the CEOP headquarters, and spent a few hours there learning more about their work.

That weekend, the children and I flew out to the UK and

were joined by Gerry in Yorkshire. Michael and Anne-Marie had asked us to stand as godparents to their children. Katie and Patrick had never been baptized as babies, and I think the decision to do this now had perhaps been precipitated by what had happened to us. It had concentrated everyone's minds on how fragile life is, how it can be wrecked in an instant.

Naturally, we badly wanted to be at the baptism. I had not set foot in the UK since Madeleine's abduction and although for me this was an emotional journey, it was not the same as 'going home'. The press, however, were bound to see it that way, and we were worried they would turn up in force and spoil this family occasion. So, with the cooperation of the authorities in both countries, we kept it under the radar, and, thanks to the police, for once we managed to stay one step ahead of our media shadows, much to their annoyance when they eventually found out. Instead the church was patrolled by police – Skipton, Michael declared, had never seen so many – a rather more reassuring and less intrusive presence.

We flew back to Portugal early on the morning of Sunday 15 July – the day Danie Krugel, his team and his 'matter orientation system' arrived in Praia da Luz. He gave us some fairly vague information about the procedure and reaffirmed his machine's 80 per cent success rate. He wouldn't let us see any of the equipment because of the necessity to 'protect his trade secrets' while he awaited a patent.

No idea at all how it works. Seems ridiculous, but then no more than some of the psychic stuff we've already acted on and given

*time to. We have got <u>nothing</u> to lose and have said that we will
'leave no stone unturned'* . . .

In spite of the cynical tone of my diary entry, we were
actually both quite excited about the prospect of Danie's
work, though I think this was probably due more to the fact
that *something* was happening which might take the investigation forward than to absolute faith in his methods. It
might come to nothing, we knew that, but anything was
better than the sense of stagnation we felt was beginning to
seep in.

We still had plenty to do, whether it was coming up with
campaign ideas to complement the investigation or trying to
reply to the thousands of letters and emails we continued
to receive. And emerging from those gruelling early weeks,
we were able to devote more time to Sean and Amelie. We'd
been so destroyed, so consumed by our pain and fear, that we
felt our role as their parents had been compromised. We had
all been robbed of so much, including the twins. Not only
had they had their big sister snatched from them but we had
been absent, physically and psychologically.

In mid-July I found Amelie standing in our room, looking at a photo of Madeleine in a frame by my bedside. 'I miss
my sister,' she said, quite clearly. 'Where has my sister gone?'
I was caught completely unawares. I realized I'd underestimated both her grasp of the situation and the scope of
her vocabulary.

Maternal guilt often weighed heavily on my shoulders.
The twins needed our love. They needed *us*. The capacity to
love is limitless, I was often told, but I was so engulfed by

Madeleine that I worried I might not have enough love left over for Sean and Amelie. Something else to beat myself up about. And not only did they need us, we needed them. Their love and laughter was the best medicine we could have asked for and we'll be eternally grateful for that, and for them.

Wednesday 18 July. The start of a downward spiral for me. When I look back on our meeting with Neves and Encarnação that day I recognize it as a turning point: the beginning of what was to blow up into a whole new nightmare.

On the plus side, it could be said that we covered a lot of ground. But it was all incredibly deflating and some of it was downright stomach-churning. Once again the police shared details about Murat; once again they bemoaned the absence of hard evidence. My frustration with their lack of progress, combined with what they were actually telling us about him, whipped up a storm of fury in me that was completely out of character. It seems to me now as if for several months I was possessed by some demonic alien that infiltrated my thoughts and filled me with anger and hatred. I needed a face on which to pin all this rage, someone to blame. And although, as I now know, the PJ had no case against Murat, they handed him to me on a plate. Since they had insinuated throughout that he might be the person responsible for the unimaginable fear and pain suffered by our little girl, is it any wonder I felt as I did?

The meeting ended with a final body blow. Danie Krugel, on whom we had, irrationally, hung so much hope, had produced a report for the PJ based on his findings. His machine had recorded a 'static signal' from an area around the beach, close to or on the Rocha Negra cliff. Although this included villas, apartments and other buildings, the implication of the 'static signal' was that Madeleine was most likely to be dead and buried there.

I wasn't sure how much more I could take. Each piece of bad news, regardless of how real or plausible it was, invariably plunged me into despair. There would be endless tears, out-of-control hysteria and feverish sessions of prayer. And there would be several visits to 'my rocks' – a quiet part of the beach away from the promenade. As swimmers and sunbathers preferred the sandy stretches, this area, where the rocks reached down to the water, was usually deserted, and afforded me some shelter and privacy. I still go back there on my visits to Praia da Luz to be on my own. Here I would simply sob to a friend on the phone for hours on end, sometimes without articulating a single word. Today was one of those days. I could feel myself sinking lower and lower into a black and lonely place. What I didn't anticipate this time was just how long it would take me to climb out of it again.

There was one piece of good news. We heard that the UK's National Policing Improvements Agency, in conjunction with the Portuguese police, were to conduct a new ground search. We'd been trying to establish the exact scope of previous searches, and pressing for another one, for ages. Finally, on 20 July, the NPIA received a request from the PJ for search advisory assistance. Progress! In recent weeks the PJ had seemed more receptive to the ideas of the UK police, especially since the arrival of José de Freitas, a SOCA officer from England. As José, whose parents were from Madeira, was fluent in Portuguese, he had been able to forge a rather better working relationship with the local police than had been achieved previously, and the PJ seemed to have become more willing to share information.

Before the new search a comprehensive geological survey, from air, land and sea, would be carried out. We found out only later (much later) that the UK team had been instructed by the PJ to proceed on the basis that Madeleine had been killed and her body dumped. They would be using GPR (ground-penetrating radar) for detecting ground disturbance, devices for penetrating walls and specialist dogs. The police files reveal that the NPIA were willing to assist with searches based on other suppositions but this had to be at the PJ's request. Evidently there was no such request. No other theories were to be considered at this point, it seems.

This search, the second or maybe even the third over the same terrain, would encompass the land identified by Danie Krugel (it would later be extended to include both Robert Murat's villa and apartment 5A at the Ocean Club). Although we didn't, in our rational moments, set much store by his results, we were keen for this area to be checked just to make sure. And such a search didn't necessarily mean turning up a body; it could reveal vital clues. By now we were more than familiar with cases where evidence had been missed the first time round and discovered on further searches (in one instance the UK police had told us about, a wallet sitting in a bush). At this stage, I was also still giving some credence to the information we were receiving from psychics, some of whom were suggesting that we should scour nearby territory again. Whatever everyone else's reasons, we needed to be sure that everything had been done as meticulously and extensively as possible.

Day eighty came and went, and still no Madeleine. Eighty days was significant for me because that was how long the Belgian schoolgirl Sabine Dardenne had been kept captive by the evil rapist and murderer Marc Dutroux before being found and freed. I clung on to 'happy' endings like these but, needless to say, as the deadlines in my head passed I'd be knocked for six again. That same day, 22 July, the *Sunday Express* ran the headline: 'MADDY'S PARENTS TO FACE INQUIRY'. For 'neglect', according to the newspaper. By now we were no strangers to this line of attack, but it was still incredibly hurtful as it blamed us, indirectly, for Madeleine's abduction. We were not hurt so much by what people might or might not think of us but by the painful reminder that, however unwittingly, we'd given this predator an opportunity. We had not been there for Madeleine. And, as I've said before and will say again, our guilt over that is a heavy cross we will bear for the rest of our lives. As for the abductor, he must have been smiling smugly to himself and thinking, Keep blaming the parents. Just leave me out of it, hidden and anonymous, to carry on doing what I do – stealing children.

Had everyone forgotten about this man? Whoever he was, he was still out there.

14

WARNING SIRENS

If 18 July was the date I now identify as a turning point, the following Monday, 23 July, was the day when the warning sirens should have started to sound.

Gerry, accompanied by Justine, had flown out to Washington, DC, primarily to visit the National Center for Missing and Exploited Children in Alexandria, Virginia, a trip he'd been keen to make since establishing contact with the centre's CEO, Ernie Allen. Some other useful meetings and television interviews – including one for *America's Most Wanted*, hosted since 1988 by the campaigner for missing and abducted children John Walsh – had been arranged around it. He was also able to meet the attorney general, Alberto Gonzales, who undertook to offer US assistance, including the expertise of the FBI, to the Portuguese authorities.

That evening I phoned Ricardo Paiva to ask for his help with a couple of letters I needed to have translated. He sounded strange, distant; certainly not his usual self. He mentioned the forthcoming ground search, adding that

Encarnação wanted to talk to us before it began. I distinctly remember him saying, 'Our investigation will be changing direction.' Danie Krugel's report had given them a bit of a jolt, he told me.

I was surprised. Surely the police couldn't be placing too much faith in the findings of an unknown and untested magic machine? I began to worry that perhaps they had some more solid lead that supported Danie's theory. I hoped to God I was wrong.

The next day Bill Henderson rang to say that the PJ had deferred both the search and our regular 'updating' meeting with them until the following week. Both pieces of news depressed me. Why did everything seem to take so *long*? With hindsight it is clear to me something was going on in Portimão I would never at that time have anticipated.

In the evening, Ricardo and José de Freitas came over to our villa. Ricardo didn't say very much. José explained a little about the planning that was going into the search and talked about Danie Krugel's role and 'agenda'. He mentioned that the police had discussed Krugel with a professor in Belfast, who had described his machine as 'pseudo-science-fiction'. I'm assuming José meant the British police, who had, I imagine, relayed this assessment to the Portuguese. I'm not sure, however, whether the PJ had fully taken it on board. Logic, it seems, often flies out of the window when you're under pressure and desperate for a result. Any result.

At bedtime one evening while Gerry was in the States, Amelie said to me in a small voice, 'Daddy at work. Mummy not going to work. Mummy not going anywhere. Mummy stay here.' There was a gulp from Mummy.

Remembering now the uncertainty, unpredictability and chaos of our lives then, all the people coming and going, some of whom we knew and some of whom we didn't, brings home to me just how unsettling and frightening this whole experience might have been for Sean and Amelie, in spite of their resilience.

Gerry flew back to Portugal that Thursday. On Sunday 29 July, after twelve long weeks with us, Trisha and Sandy returned home to Scotland. They had been absolute towers of strength and we had relied on them for so much that it was hard not to feel somehow stripped of a protective layer and impossible not to cry (even for Gerry, whom Trish dubbed 'Tiny Tears' after an emotional goodbye!). They had put their own lives on hold for us for three whole months and their practical and emotional support was even more remarkable considering that they were dealing throughout with their own anguish at the loss of their niece and goddaughter.

On Monday we had what would turn out to be our last regular meeting with Neves and Encarnação, in every sense of the word. They talked to us about the search, which was due to start in two days' time, and, yet again, about Robert Murat. The following evening Ricardo was supposed to be calling at the villa to speak to us. At 10pm he phoned to say he couldn't make it but would see us the next day. He didn't.

Apart from finding little things like this slightly puzzling or exasperating, I hadn't sensed any profound change in the behaviour of the PJ, or in the direction their investigation was taking. Our attention was focused on the search, and on campaign plans we were making with Jon Corner, who was coming over to Praia da Luz to lend a hand. My mum, dad, Auntie Janet and Uncle Brian had also flown in for a visit. By 2 August, however, those sirens were wailing so loudly I cannot understand how I missed them. And yet I did.

That morning Gerry and I, along with Jon and a colleague, were preparing to drive to Huelva in Spain to put up posters of Madeleine. Jon was intending to do some filming and several of the British journalists were going to join us there, on the give-and-take principle: it would give them a story centred on Madeleine, rather than on us, and this in turn would publicize our efforts. As I was dropping Sean and Amelie off at Toddler Club, I had a phone call from Gerry. The police wanted to come over at 10am. Something to do with forensics, they'd said. Great timing. And forensics? What was that all about?

We'd never lied about anything – not to the police, not to the media, not to anyone else. But now we found ourselves in one of those tricky situations where we just didn't seem to have a choice. As it happened, Gerry had a mild stomach upset which we used as an excuse to postpone the trip. We didn't feel good about this at all, but even if the judicial secrecy law had not prevented us from giving the main reason, can you imagine what would have happened if we'd announced to the journalists heading for Huelva that the police were coming to do some forensic work in our villa? We were not to know our excuse would prove to be no more than a temporary holding measure. If we had, we wouldn't have bothered trying to keep the scurrilous headlines at bay.

My mum, dad, Brian and Janet set off for the town to get

out of the way before the police arrived. Ten o'clock came and went, as did lunchtime, then the afternoon. It was 5pm when they eventually showed up. They told us they wanted to shoot some video footage of our clothes and possessions. The forensics people would then take these away and return them the following day. They offered no explanation as to why they were doing this. Gerry and I just assumed it was on the suggestion of the British team, who had no doubt pointed out that it should have been done much earlier. We could kind of see the point: after all, the abductor could have brushed against some of our belongings and left traces of his DNA. Even at this late stage, it might be possible for some vital information to be retrieved. We were even quite pleased this was happening, that something was happening which might help find Madeleine.

Left with only the clothes we were wearing, we were all asked to leave the villa. It was early evening and we had to find somewhere to go with two tired and hungry toddlers in tow. When we were allowed back, we found four detectives in the house: José de Freitas, João Carlos, Ricardo Paiva and a woman called Carla. They went through the list of what had been removed. I was not only confused, I was devastated: as well as all of our clothes, they had taken my Bible (my friend Bridget's Bible, to be precise), Cuddle Cat and my diaries. Why had they taken my diaries? Obviously not for any forensic purpose: the abductor couldn't have been in contact with them because they hadn't existed until halfway through May. And the Bible had been lent to me by Bridget's husband Paddy a week after Madeleine's abduction. My journals were private and full of personal thoughts and messages to Madeleine. I felt violated.

All I remember is José saying that 'an anomaly' had appeared in the investigation. His tone suggested that we shouldn't worry, it was just something that needed to be ironed out. Whether this is what he intended to imply, or just my interpretation, I cannot say. When you are innocent, it doesn't occur to you that you could be considered in any other light. Whatever the case, difficult as it is to believe, I *still* didn't smell a rat.

We finally made it to Huelva the following morning, so all was not lost on that front – even if we did discover when we arrived that it was a public holiday. It didn't matter: the local people were so kind and obliging and we came back feeling that it had been a very productive trip.

The police returned our belongings to us later that day, thrown into big black bin bags,

. . . creased to hell. All a bit of a hassle. I hope it's worth it.

Worth it? Dear God, Kate.

We spent much of the weekend planning for the hundredth day since Madeleine's abduction, a milestone that would be reached on 11 August. A hundred seems such a small number now, the milestone distant and diminutive, but back then it felt like a lifetime. And that was to us: I couldn't bear to think how long it would feel to Madeleine. In addition to holding a church service for our daughter, in which we wanted to involve the local community, we were eager to do something for all missing children. With the help of Google and NCMEC, we were preparing to launch a

Don't You Forget About Me channel on YouTube. We also had quite a few media interviews lined up.

Meanwhile, the NPIA ground search continued. By Saturday it had reached Robert Murat's house. As Gerry and I left Justine's flat that afternoon, we noticed a mass of vehicles parked around Casa Liliana. It wasn't long before the place was swamped by journalists, photographers and satellite vans. We were not aware that the next day apartment 5A would be re-examined, though we did see some activity there when we drove past on the Sunday. If we had known, we'd have welcomed the news. The chances of anything being found there three months after the event seemed remote – apart from anything else, the apartment had been let again several times since Madeleine's disappearance – but it was another stone that should not remain unturned.

It was on Monday 6 August that the atmosphere changed. At the PJ's request, Gerry went off to meet them at a café in Portimão. They didn't need me, they said, so I stayed in the villa and busied myself looking after the children and doing some work. Gerry returned minus the car. While he'd been in the café, the police had impounded it for forensic testing and brought him back to Praia da Luz themselves. Again we assumed, at least initially, that this was a procedural measure recommended to the PJ by the British experts. Madeleine had been missing for over three weeks when we'd hired the car, but perhaps it still needed to be ruled out of the investigation.

That lunchtime, having collected the twins from Toddler Club, I was pushing them out of the Tapas reception entrance in the double buggy when we were suddenly ambushed by a horde of journalists and TV cameras. I felt completely exposed. I was confused, too: we hadn't been bothered too much by the press for a good few weeks and there had been a tacit agreement that Sean and Amelie would not be photographed. Something had changed. Cameras were clicking, Portuguese voices were firing questions at me and the mood was suddenly hostile. Ocean Club staff helped us back inside and away from mêlée. I realized I was shaking.

It emerged that there had been stories in some of the Portuguese papers that morning suggesting that Gerry was somehow involved in Madeleine's disappearance. Sniffer dogs had discovered traces of Madeleine's blood in apartment 5A, it was claimed. It was insinuated that she had died there and her body had been dumped in the sea.

The following day the press reported that a sample of 'blood' had been sent to the UK to see whether a DNA profile could be extracted from it. Understandably, we were surprised and concerned. We had seen no blood that night; neither, as far as we knew, had any been found by the police or the forensics team from Lisbon. Even if it was blood (and this was never proven), it could have come from any number of people who'd been in the apartment before or since Madeleine's abduction. It could even have come from the abductor. Just supposing it was Madeleine's: maybe she tripped over? Had a slight nosebleed? To infer from this that she was dead would be a preposterous leap. Yet it seemed it was this development – or to be precise, the interpretation put on it either by the Portuguese press or by whoever leaked it – that was responsible for the media hysteria in Praia da Luz.

We were given no information at all about what was going on but we were determined not to be derailed by the madness around us. We'd intended to take Sean and Amelie to Toddler Club the next morning as usual until Justine called to warn us of a media frenzy at the Ocean Club. We'd also discovered half a dozen photographers lurking outside our villa. We left as planned for the Belavista Hotel in Luz, where I was scheduled to be interviewed on BBC Radio 4's *Woman's Hour* via satellite radio. It produced the only light moment of the day: my cringe-worthy response when Jenni Murray asked me how Gerry and I managed to keep each other going. I embarked on a spiel about how we both had different strengths and weaknesses and elaborated by reeling off my husband's many talents and skills. Of course Jenni then wanted to know what mine were (this was *Woman's Hour*, after all). My mind went completely blank. 'Um . . . well . . . er . . . I do the cooking,' I managed eventually. Boy, do I know how to sell myself. One thing's for sure, whatever talents I may have, interview technique isn't one of them.

As soon as we'd finished with *Woman's Hour*, Gerry and I were approached by Steve Kingstone, a BBC journalist. He appeared genuinely worried. 'Do you know what they're saying? They're saying that you killed Madeleine.'

I'm not sure if there was anything in the world that could have been more offensive to us. We agreed there and then to do an interview with the BBC's Richard Bilton for pooled broadcast. Gerry, keeping his fury in check, was calm and very firm. 'If the police have evidence that Madeleine has come to any harm, then we as her parents have a right to be informed,' he said in that interview. 'If we have to go back to square one and start again, then let's do it.'

Wednesday 8 August. We had an early start to see off my mum, dad and Uncle Brian, who were flying home. As our car still hadn't been returned to us by the police we enlisted the help of a lovely taxi driver we'd got to know in recent weeks. Despite the crowd of photographers, we manoeuvred the children into the Ocean Club without incident before heading for the Tivoli Hotel in Lagos to be interviewed for the BBC's spiritually based magazine programme *Heaven and Earth*. Talking about our faith at that point, as we teetered on the edge of a new precipice, was a little surreal, but somehow, against the odds, while it was taking a battering we were both managing to cling on to it.

In my wobbly moments, I sometimes wondered whether religion was no more than a crutch to be leaned on when the going gets tough. Maybe it had been invented merely to maintain order in society, promoting compassion and justice and providing solace in the bad times. If so, that didn't make it a bad thing, just not what I'd been led to believe it was. 'Maybe religion is just for the weak,' I remember saying to Trish during one dark spell of doubt. 'Kate, do you think Auntie Janet is weak?' she replied. Janet has great faith in God, much deeper than mine. She is also one of the strongest people I know. Trisha didn't need to say any more.

Back at the villa, Justine phoned to tell us that Alex Woolfall had been in touch on behalf of Mark Warner. He was so sorry, but he had no choice but to ask us to stop using the Toddler Club. Apparently, several Ocean Club guests had complained about the media scrum outside the reception entrance and, of course, we were the reason it was there. I was so upset. The injustice of it all was starting to get to me. Poor Amelie and Sean. They were the ones who would suffer. We'd tried so hard to provide them with stability, to make sure they had other children to play with and lots of activity, and now even this was to be taken away from them.

My immediate reaction was to angrily blame these guests for their selfishness. But eventually I realized they were quite right to complain. Like us, they didn't want their children subjected to this frankly pretty frightening mob. No, it was the media who were at fault. As it turned out, Sean and Amelie were able to return before too long. We worked out a system whereby one of the nannies would meet us at the twenty-four-hour reception, away from the other parents and children, and take the twins on to the crèche from there.

João Carlos returned our car at lunchtime (albeit with a piece missing from the boot). He said that Neves and Encarnação were ready to see us later that afternoon. Thank goodness! Finally someone was going to explain to us exactly what was happening. João told us he would come and meet us at 3pm near the police station, to avoid the media – we wouldn't be going to the British Consulate this time. On our way to Portimão we dropped Auntie Janet, Sean and Amelie at the home of Susan and Haynes Hubbard.

If we'd wondered about the change of venue for our regular informal meeting, the reason for it soon became clear: this *wasn't* our regular informal meeting. We were taken to an upstairs room at the police station where we were greeted by Luís Neves and Guilhermino Encarnação. Our interpreter this time was a police officer, not Proconsul Angela Morado, as was usually the case. The whole demeanour of Neves and Encarnação was different. They looked serious and cold.

There had been a 'shift' in the investigation, they said. They had always been optimistic that Madeleine was alive, but now things had changed. Almost instantaneously I could feel my breathing pattern altering and that familiar constriction in my throat. Gerry asked if any evidence had come to light to suggest that Madeleine was dead but they wouldn't reply. There was a lot of frowning going on which, combined with the language barrier, made it less obvious that they weren't answering us. Gerry was then asked to leave the room. Now the sirens in my head were deafening. I was on my own and afraid. Please God, let my Madeleine be OK.

Tell us about that night, they said. Tell us everything that happened after the children went to bed. I gave them every detail I could remember, as I had before, but this time they responded by just staring at me and shaking their heads. I was reeling with confusion, disbelief and panic. What the hell was going on? Evidently not satisfied with my account, they pressed me. Was there anything else I wanted to add? Anything else unusual that had occurred that night?

Of course there wasn't. If there had been I would have told them on 3 May. I'd recounted absolutely everything and anything – more than they wanted or needed to know, probably, just in case some triviality I recalled might be significant. How could they think I would hold something back that might help my daughter? Why were they asking me this? *Why?*

Neves stated bluntly that they didn't believe my version of events. It 'didn't fit' with what they knew. Didn't fit? *What did they know?* I was sobbing now, well past the stage of silent tears and stifled sniffs. I began to wail hysterically, drawing breath in desperate gasps.

Why did I think Madeleine had been alive when she was taken from the apartment? they persisted. I explained between sobs that there had been nothing to suggest otherwise; no indication that she might have come to harm. Had I ever considered that she may be dead? Yes, of course. Early on that was all I thought, all the time: that some paedophile had grabbed her, abused her and later killed her. Then I'd begun to wonder if she was being held by pornographers, I told them, or had been taken for someone who wanted a child.

I was becoming more and more distressed and more and more scared. I wanted Gerry. Still they pushed me. They proposed that when I'd put Madeleine to bed that night, it wasn't actually the last time I'd seen her. But it was. *It was!* I felt I was being bullied, and I suppose I was. I assume these tactics were deliberate: knock her off balance by telling her that her daughter is dead and get her to confess. Because I was in no doubt now that they were trying to make me say I'd killed Madeleine or knew what had happened to her. I might be naive but I'm not stupid.

On and on it went. They tried to convince me I'd had a blackout – a 'loss of memory episode', I think they called it. My denials, answers and pleas fell on deaf ears. This was their theory and they wanted to shoehorn me into it, end of story. At last they seemed to decide that the interview was over. They told me I could ring them any time, day or night, to give them the information they were waiting for.

I was allowed to spend a couple of minutes with Gerry, but I don't think he was able to get much sense out of me. Then it was his turn to be interrogated. He managed to remain a little calmer than I had but he was still visibly upset and shaken afterwards. He gave the police his account of the events of 3 May and the reasons why he didn't believe Madeleine had been killed in the apartment. Through his tears he pleaded with the two men: 'Do you have evidence that Madeleine is dead? We're her parents. You have to tell us.'

'It's coming,' Neves told him. 'It's coming!'

Outside the room, I was praying – begging prayers. I was beginning to come unstuck. But if I thought the police had finished with me, I was mistaken. Before long I was ordered back into the room to join Gerry for round three.

Once again Gerry wanted to know if the case had now become a murder inquiry. The answer was indirect: 'You can probably guess that from our lack of response.' In a slightly threatening manner, Luís asked why I wasn't looking him straight in the eye. There was no reason, other than that I was incapable of looking at anyone properly: my own eyes were so swollen and sore that I was struggling to keep them from closing completely. Finally, Gerry tried to establish when – and if – we would be having another meeting with them. 'The next time we meet it will be across the table.' The message behind this rather Delphic statement was clear: there would be no more informal meetings.

Outside the police station we were surrounded by the press. There was no need to ask how they knew we were there. On our way back to Luz we had a call from Angela Morado, who had been informed by the police that her services would not be required at our meeting that afternoon. She'd naturally been concerned by this departure from the norm. Gerry spoke to her. I was too upset to talk to anybody.

We drove first to the Hubbards' to collect Sean, Amelie and my aunt. When we calmed down a little and told them what had happened, we were presented with several shocked faces. Susan suggested I went and had a bath as I was still pretty shaky. In her bathroom I leaned over the washbasin and peered into the mirror. My eyes were narrow slits in fat, purple lids. My blotchy face seemed to be ageing by the day. Where are you, Madeleine? What is happening? What's going to become of us all?

Gerry's brother and his family arrived from the UK a short while later. We had to ask them to get a taxi from the airport and then smuggle them through the side entrance of the villa in order to shield our young niece and nephew from the media. Not quite the welcome they'd been expecting. It was, inevitably, a difficult evening. Gerry made several phone calls in search of help and advice, and we spoke to Alan Pike, who was sympathetic, understanding and rational, as always.

We awoke the next morning feeling deprived of sleep and generally quite awful, but Gerry, at least, managed to kick into gear and get on the phone again. Once he'd talked to Angela Morado and the British Embassy in Lisbon, we took refuge in Nossa Senhora da Luz for fifteen minutes. That day and the next we had a host of interviews scheduled to mark the hundredth day since Madeleine was taken from us. My immediate instinct was to cancel them all. I was tired out and there were more pressing issues to be dealt with. But that would have broken one of our rules: keep your focus and don't let others push you off track.

We were doing these interviews for Madeleine. If ever there was an extra incentive to mobilize every remaining shred of strength, this was it. Gerry had not initially liked our search being described as a 'campaign'. Not only did it suggest a long-term quest but the military imagery grated. Yet here we were, one hundred days later, involved in skirmishes on several fronts. The term was beginning to seem more appropriate by the day.

The interviews were all taking place in a villa on the Meia Praia in Lagos. It was a terrible day: both the atmosphere and the line of questioning followed by the press were intensely antagonistic. Their focus, dictated by the behaviour of both the police and some sections of the media over the past few days, was very different from ours. We wanted to talk about one hundred days without Madeleine, the search, and the launch of 'Don't You Forget About Me' on YouTube; they wanted to talk about blood and dogs.

It's all a bit of a blur now, but I do remember one journalist persisting sceptically with a familiar thread: 'Why has Madeleine got all this attention? How have you managed to run this campaign when you have lost your daughter?'

Gerry and I both replied, 'Well, what would you do?'

'I don't know.'

'Come on, what would you do if this was your child? Would you do nothing?'

He didn't reply. We felt like two lone figures with catapults fighting an army.

What made it worse was our distress that all the time and effort we'd put into publicizing the hundred-day landmark and the plight of other missing children was being trampled underfoot. It was exasperating and the disrespect and injustice we felt on Madeleine's behalf were very hard to stomach.

Later, Angela and Cecilia Edwards, who was taking over from Bill Henderson as British consul, came over to the villa to discuss the recent problems with the media and the way we had been treated by the police. Alan Pike also flew out from the UK on a mercy mission. We were very grateful for the opportunity to reconnect with him face to face for a dose of his calm, considered advice. It all helped to strengthen our armour.

15

ONE HUNDRED DAYS

Saturday, 11 August 2007. Here we were. Day One Hundred: a day we'd hoped we'd never reach. There was a horrible, sad inevitability about it. It was a day when we would be buoyed up by loving kindness one minute and brought crashing down the next.

At 11am, Gerry and I walked down to the little church we loved so much, where Susan and Haynes Hubbard and Auntie Janet, with the help of many others, had organized a One Hundred Days of Hope service for Madeleine and missing children everywhere.

On this occasion we saw the massive media presence outside as a positive sign. They were not here today about blood and dogs, and it was important to us to show the world that we weren't giving up or giving in. The service was beautiful and uplifting. The church was full, with many Portuguese people among the congregation, which mattered very much to us. Haynes led the service. He is such a strong man, his trust in God unwavering, especially when the going gets tough. At one point during his sermon he made the point that it would be the easy option for everyone to turn away from Gerry and me right now. What we badly needed at this time, he declared, was their support.

Gerry and I both got up to say a few words. We were just so grateful that the local people had stood by us through these hundred long days. To know they were rooting for Madeleine, regardless of the nonsense with which they were being bombarded by the press, filled us with warmth and strength. If we could be stronger then so would the hope for Madeleine. We left Nossa Senhora da Luz to unexpected and rather overwhelming applause. As I wrote in my diary later:

I have no doubt the local Portuguese community are behind us. We were kissed to death again!

For Sean and Amelie, today was just another day. It wasn't always possible for us to paint on brave faces for them, but we did try. They were growing up before our eyes and we didn't want to inflict additional confusion, worry or sadness on them. After the service, we took them and the rest of our family group up to the Millennium area of the resort. The children loved splashing about in the pool there and even had a little knock-about on the tennis court. It melted my heart to watch them playing so happily, oblivious of the shattered lives around them.

Earlier in the day Gerry had called Ricardo Paiva. Olegário de Sousa had given a statement to the BBC regarding new 'evidence' that had emerged and indicating that Madeleine may be dead. He went on to say that family and friends were not suspects. We tried to explain to Ricardo that we desperately needed to know what was going on. The chaotic and upsetting events and rumours of recent days and the complete lack of real information were compounding our already unbearable agony. Rather to our surprise, Ricardo phoned later to say that he was on his way round to see us.

When he arrived, Ricardo explained this 'evidence' a little further. His tone was sombre as he told us about the two springer spaniels that had been brought out to Portugal by the British police to assist in the search. Keela, who could alert her handler to the tiniest trace of blood, had done so in apartment 5A. Eddie, a victim-recovery or 'cadaver' dog, trained to detect human remains, had indicated that somebody had died there. Test results on the samples taken from the flat were awaited from a forensics laboratory in the UK.

I trusted Ricardo back then but I struggled to understand how, never mind why, somebody could have killed Madeleine and removed her body within such a short time frame. It didn't make sense. And, like the business of the 'blood', this 'evidence of death' seemed tenuous in the extreme. The police appeared to be telling us, on the say-so of a dog, that someone had definitely died in apartment 5A and, since nobody else they knew of had passed away there, it must have been Madeleine. Supposing she had been killed – and we think this extremely unlikely – she must have been taken out of the apartment within minutes. Did they really believe that a dog could smell the 'odour of death' three months later from a body that had been removed so swiftly? They were adding two and two and coming up with ten.

But of course to me, as Madeleine's mother, it didn't have

to make sense at this point. The merest suggestion from Ricardo that it was even possible she had been killed in that flat was like a knife being twisted into my chest. My eyes, so tired of tears, succumbed to them yet again.

So Madeleine's dead? . . . Psychopath? Burglary gone wrong? I need her body before I can believe this. I just can't accept this. God, let them be wrong.

It's hard to imagine that anything could have brought a glimmer of light into that dark evening but a remark by Bill Kenwright, the chairman of Everton FC, made the world seem slightly less awful than it had a second before. Our family were watching television when the Premiership highlights came on. Not only were many of the players wearing Madeleine T-shirts and wristbands but Bill, when asked about the pressure facing clubs and managers at the start of the new season, replied that it was nothing compared with the pressure Gerry and I were under. Although we hadn't had any direct contact with Bill, we knew that he had supported the search for Madeleine from the start and had encouraged others to do so, too. The fact that he hadn't forgotten her and was still publicly showing his solidarity really touched us.

The following three weeks felt like an eternity. It was like being on some kind of endurance course run by sadists. The newspapers in both Portugal and the UK churned out endless damning pieces that were at best speculative and mostly complete fabrications. We were living in a luxury penthouse with a swimming pool! We drank fourteen bottles of wine on the night that Madeleine was abducted! A syringe containing a tranquillizer had been found in our apartment on the night! It was all so offensive and unjust. While selling papers and making money, these stories very effectively distorted the opinions of the readership, especially in Portugal, where our daughter needed help the most.

Cultural differences were open to misinterpretation. The fact that our children slept for ten or twelve hours a night, for example, was perceived by many people in Portugal as outlandish – if not, in the circumstances, downright suspicious. The Portuguese retain elements of the southern European lifestyle, which traditionally involves a longer break in the middle of the day than we are used to, and later nights. Proper, leisurely lunches, rather than a snatched sandwich, are not uncommon, followed in some places by naps for adults and kids alike, and even small children stay up for late-night meals with the grown-ups. It's a lovely way of life, but not one practised by many of us in more northerly climes.

Evidently it didn't matter to the newspaper editors whether there was any truth in these tales or not. Well, it mattered to Gerry and me and it mattered to our family and friends. Above all, it mattered for Madeleine. The media's constant refrain was that keeping Madeleine in the headlines could only be a good thing. I beg to differ.

Meanwhile, the police said nothing. In spite of our attempts to find out, we had no idea what was happening with the investigation. We knew they planned to interview us again, and we wanted to get this over with and clear up any

concerns they had. We didn't even know if anyone was looking for our daughter any more. I had just about been able to
cope when we had at least some information. This silence
was too much to bear.

15 August
The whole situation seems to be getting more unbelievable.
We've always said that whatever happens, we need to know the
truth. I never thought that would include the need for us to
have our names cleared. What is going on with people? Where
is the common sense?

Dear God. Please bless and protect our Madeleine wherever
she is. Please give us and our families the strength to get
through this. Please give the police the wisdom, intelligence
and honesty to solve this crime and find Madeleine.
Amen x

Life went on, of course. Relatives and friends came and went,
to be replaced by more relatives and friends, all of whom
continued to do a sterling job providing both emotional
support and practical help. We carried on giving interviews
when appropriate. We had no idea if this was helping or not
but we had to do something. We went to church, often
several times a day, for Masses, vigils, private prayer and
reflection. We made phone calls, wrote and replied to emails
and letters. We spent time with Sean and Amelie, playing
games, reading stories, watching movies and taking trips to
the beach, the zoo or a café. None of it was getting us anywhere.

17 August
Finding it hard to talk to anyone at the moment as I'm full of
so many negative emotions – anger, bitterness, frustration,
desperation . . . It doesn't make you a very nice person.

Gerry had been talking for some while now about us going home. He reasoned that we could achieve just as much there in terms of the campaign, probably more. He also felt that if we were back in Rothley the media attention would quieten down a bit, certainly in the Portuguese press, where the worst smears were originating. At home it would be much easier for our friends and relations to support us, and better for us all emotionally. Although the twins seemed quite happy, it had to be said that our life in Praia da Luz was quite artificial – not that life at home was going to be normal, by any stretch of the imagination – and they needed stability in the long term.

I appreciated all of this. The thought of some respite from the poisonous headlines was balm for the soul. It would be lovely for Sean and Amelie to be back in their own bedroom, playing in their own garden and going back to nursery to re-establish friendships. I realized that they needed to reconnect with home. It had recently emerged that they believed Madeleine was at our house in Rothley. Worried that the 'pyramid of information' they were building in their heads might not be structurally sound, Gerry rang the child psychologist David Trickey for advice. It broke my heart to hear Gerry explaining gently to the children afterwards that Madeleine wasn't there. Sean looked quite confused, and perhaps a bit scared, too, but they accepted it.

However, for many weeks I'd fought against the idea of going home. Even considering it was an enormous emotional and psychological mountain for me to climb. We had always said we would not leave without Madeleine, and I still felt that to do so would be to abandon her. In mid-July I had slowly started to come round to Gerry's way of thinking – we had to return some time, after all – but now, a month later, with matters taking a turn for the worse, there was even more reason to stay. If we didn't, it would feel as if we were caving in to the bullying tactics of the media and the PJ. We were beginning to suspect that there was an agenda to force us out of the country and take the pressure off the police. I had no intention of allowing that to happen.

It was a difficult dilemma. Before I could think about going, I had to be completely confident in my own mind that I would not be leaving Madeleine, that we were not capitulating to any such agenda and that we were not giving up.

19 August
Madeleine, sweetheart, it's not getting any easier at this end. I just have to hope that whoever is with you loves you too and is treating you kindly and fairly.

20 August
The news today suggests that they're going to arrest a 'new suspect' in the UK. It's likely to be more tabloid fabrication. There's so much shit that's been written, much of it outrageous. And coupled with the void of information from the police, who knows what's going on!

By this time, we felt as if we had been completely cut adrift. The police ignored us, we were up against a convoluted system neither of us really understood and the media juggernaut was now well and truly out of control. If we were going to have any chance of protecting ourselves, we needed somebody familiar with the system, a Portuguese lawyer, to represent our interests. Later that day, Gerry contacted Carlos Pinto de Abreu, a human-rights lawyer in Lisbon, who'd been recommended to us, and arranged for us to go and see him the following afternoon.

We left for Lisbon at lunchtime, with our kind and trustworthy taxi driver. At his office Carlos was joined by three colleagues and his wife, a doctor, who helped with interpretation where needed. We took them through as much as we could: the night of 3 May, our relationship with the police, the leaks to the media and the scandalous headlines. We felt better knowing that Carlos and his team would be able to advise us.

A bit upset on the way back . . . I had 'flashes' of Madeleine in my head being hurt, abused and screaming for us – but we weren't there. So awful.

We arrived in Praia da Luz late in the evening and discovered Sean and Amelie in our bed. They were quiet but still awake, which, I have to admit, secretly pleased me. I needed them with me. Thank God for Sean and Amelie.

On 23 August we did an interview with Telecinco, a Spanish TV channel, in Justine's flat. We had a pre-interview chat with the team about the topics we would be unable to talk about, such as the investigation, and areas we felt it was important to highlight to help our search.

The main reason why we couldn't discuss the investigation, obviously, was that we could say very little without breaking the judicial secrecy law. In any case, as we were now being kept in the dark, we didn't know much about it ourselves by this stage. Making public any details we had been told could jeopardize the investigation, not least by alerting the abductor. We were not prepared, either, to get into a debate about the continuing speculation and lies in the media.

It was stifling in the small flat. It was a hot August day, hotter still under the TV arc lights, and we were pretty uncomfortable before we even started. We readied ourselves for the interviewer's first question. It was about the investigation. And his second question? About the investigation. As was the third. Blood and dogs were mentioned again. It was as if the conversation we'd had a few minutes earlier had never taken place. After five or so of these unanswerable prompts, Gerry, who was suffering badly from the heat, removed his mike and left, visibly exasperated and upset. Giving the interviewer the benefit of the doubt – he was bound to push us for something new, I reasoned – I carried on, attempting patiently and politely to explain why my husband had reacted as he had.

In spite of having had my fingers burned so many times since Madeleine's abduction, I've always believed in trying to see the good in people, at least until they give you cause to do otherwise. Not everyone repays such faith. Telecinco aired our interview that weekend. Its main focus wasn't

Madeleine, or the search, or the campaign. Far too dull and 'samey', clearly. No, the whole piece was centred on their big scoop: Gerry 'storming off'. The papers gleefully reproduced stills of Madeleine's distressed father under headlines like 'GERRY CRACKS!' As our grannies used to say, you live and learn.

Meanwhile, Gerry had flown to Scotland to appear at the Edinburgh TV Festival. This had been arranged back in early June, when he had reasoned that if Madeleine was still missing by the time the date came round, press coverage would have died down and the event would present us with a good opportunity to remind people of the campaign. The fact that his interviewer would be Kirsty Wark, the highly respected *Newsnight* presenter, who had grown up a few miles down the road from him in Kilmarnock, had certainly influenced his decision to accept the invitation.

On the Friday, he was giving a telephone interview from Edinburgh to the *Daily Telegraph* when he was asked to comment on an article that had appeared that day on the front page of the Portuguese newspaper *Tal e Qual* under the headline: 'PJ BELIEVE PARENTS KILLED MADDIE'. I think this was probably the last straw for Gerry, and he completely lost it. I was equally gobsmacked. Initially my fury was directed not at the police but at the paper, for running such ridiculous, disgusting nonsense.

The basis of the Edinburgh Festival interview was the international impact of the Find Madeleine campaign and how it had been brought about. Now, of course, this serious discussion would be taking place amid a media firestorm. Gerry gave several additional interviews in Scotland, in which he appealed to journalists to report responsibly. For the most part, his pleas were ignored.

When I heard that my mum had got wind of the *Tal e Qual* story and the rumours it had prompted, I phoned her. She was so distraught she could hardly get a word out. I texted DCS Bob Small, saying how disappointed I was that the police were claiming Madeleine was dead, *without any evidence*, and how unsupported we had felt recently.

As our main liaison with the British police, Bob was not privy to the investigation details. This was for our protection, he told us, as sharing knowledge we would otherwise not have had could potentially compromise us. In the light of the volume of information being released into the public domain by police sources via the media, this seems farcical now. It did emerge, however, that Bob had concerns of his own. He explained that the British police regarded the use of sniffer dogs as intelligence rather than evidence, and he was perplexed at the apparent fixation of the PJ on the idea that Madeleine had died in the apartment. He told Gerry he thought they'd get a shock when the forensic results came back.

The next day Gerry rang Ken Jones, head of ACPO, the Association of Chief Police Officers. He, too, was beginning to despair of the investigation and the way it was being handled. It was good to know we weren't alone, and that we weren't going totally mad, but why wouldn't anyone speak out about this? Many people in top positions were saying the right things to us privately but it seemed nobody could – or would – do anything about it. If someone had stood up and said, 'Stop! This is all wrong!' things could have been very different.

Carlos Pinto de Abreu advised us to sue *Tal e Qual*. (We did begin proceedings, but shortly afterwards the paper went bust, we found ourselves with bigger problems and we decided not to pursue the matter through the Portuguese courts.) Sadly, although the paper's article was certainly ridiculous and disgusting, it was not, incredibly, nonsense. I'm not saying the police did believe we had killed Madeleine. I have never for one second thought that. What became clear to us, however, was that some faction within the PJ was indeed the source of the story. We can only assume that their objective was to make everyone else believe it, in order to 'solve' a case they were under immense pressure to conclude. What better way was there to achieve that than to harness the power of the media? So much for the law of judicial secrecy.

I hasten to add that I do not mean to tar all of the Portuguese police with the same brush. There were many officers who worked very hard on the case, certainly early on, and their efforts to get to the truth were being undermined by these disgraceful actions just as surely as ours were.

On Monday 27 August I had a call from Esther McVey, a Liverpool friend from my late teens, by then a television presenter and Conservative parliamentary candidate. Esther was on the board of Madeleine's Fund. She said she was scared by our current situation and uncomfortable with what she felt was a 'political shift'. For our own safety, and 'to protect Madeleine's good name' (I wasn't quite sure what she meant by that), she thought we ought to come home. It seemed I was being pressurized from all quarters and I didn't like it.

As it happened, however, the very same day we learned that we would need to vacate our villa by 11 September – news that put a different complexion on matters and forced Gerry and me to tackle this difficult and emotionally charged issue. We could have rented somewhere else in Praia da Luz, of course, but it would have been a lot of hassle for not much gain if we were intending to leave before long anyway. We had waited in vain for the police to call us back for interview. Finally, and very reluctantly, I agreed to set a date for our departure. Monday 10 September it would have to be. It was one of the toughest decisions I've ever had to take.

I knew, though, that I would be returning to Luz when I could, to reconnect with the last place I had seen Madeleine and to remind the authorities that I was not going to allow my daughter's disappearance to be forgotten. I could just imagine the police and the government rubbing their hands with glee at seeing the back of us at last and wrapping up the case with unseemly haste. I hoped to God I was wrong.

That Wednesday I began to sort out some of our belongings ahead of our return to Rothley, packing clothes we wouldn't need before we left and putting surplus toys into big bags for local orphanages. The villa was heaving with toys, teddies and games sent by kind-hearted members of the public, not only for Madeleine, but for the twins, too. We were so touched, and they had provided lots of entertainment, but we couldn't possibly keep them all.

The very idea of leaving Portugal without Madeleine made me feel sick. Who'd have thought, when the five of us had landed here in April, full of excitement, that only four of us would be going home? The reality of what we were doing was killing me.

A couple of days later I was going through the children's DVDs when I came across Madeleine's favourite: *Barbie: The Princess and the Pauper*. She loved that film, and she loved the two main characters, the princess and the poor village girl. If it was an Erika day, she'd say, 'Mummy, you pretend to be Anneliese and I'll be Erika.' The next day our roles would be swapped. I could see Madeleine now, with her pink princess blanket over her head, the corners pulled together under her chin like a headscarf, singing 'If I was a girl like you . . .'

Sean and Amelie were talking about Madeleine quite a lot by now. I wore a locket with a picture of Madeleine inside, and Amelie had taken to opening it. 'See Madeleine,' she'd say, or 'Night night, Madeleine!' And then she would give her a kiss.

Started to feel a bit 'funny' again. My fear for Madeleine is creeping back. It's so hard to block it. Sometimes I wonder if I should try and pretend that she never existed to make it easier, but I just can't.

Thursday 30 August was another milestone we could hardly bear to think about. It should have been Madeleine's big moment: her first day at school. She'd been so looking forward to this. She had talked about it excitedly, while in my mind's eye I had pictured her in class, having fun and making lots of new mates. Now all her friends would be starting without her.

It was an awful day. Every hour, I'd see her standing there in her new uniform, smiling at me. I cried, I prayed and I held my husband and children tightly. We could make things right for her. If only we could get her back we would work through anything and everything she'd endured. We would make sure that her life was as full and as happy as it should always have been.

Clement Freud returned to Praia da Luz on 31 August and called Gerry that day. 'Is it true, Gerry?' he said, without preamble.

'What's that, Clement?'

'That you're close to a breakdown and needing medication?'

Very funny.

'I have a lot of empathy with the *Express* though, you know,' he went on.

For a split second Gerry thought he was serious. 'Why's that?'

'Well, you see, we both suffer from poor circulation.'

Thank God for people like Clement who kept us smiling.

On the night of 1 September I dreamed about Madeleine for the first time in four months. I was astonished that this hadn't happened before. The workings of the mind are impossible to fathom. It was a good thing it hadn't, because it was such a dreadful experience – far more painful than anything that had occurred in real life since the night she was taken – I'm not sure I could have survived it in the early weeks.

We had a call from one of the girls at the children's

nursery school. 'Guess what?' she said. 'Madeleine's here! She's been here for a couple of days. She's fine.' We rushed to the nursery immediately. And sure enough, there was our Madeleine. She looked beautiful, just as I remembered her. I ran over to her, my face split by the widest smile, the tears running down my cheeks, and just held her and held her and held her. Although I was dreaming, *I could feel her*. It was as if parts of my body that had been hibernating for four months suddenly began to stir. I could sense the cold, dark days lifting as I luxuriated in warmth and light. And Madeleine *was holding me*, her little arms wrapped tightly round me, and it felt so good. I could smell her. I could feel her with every one of my senses as I soaked up this heavenly moment.

My Madeleine. I wanted to stay like this for ever.

And then I woke up.

Ice began to course through my body, driving out every endorphin and remnant of warmth. I didn't understand. What was happening? How could this be? *I could still feel her!* A heavy boot connected with my stomach and the ache in my chest was worse than I'd ever known it. I was struggling for breath, almost as if I were being strangled. Please God, don't let her go! Stay with me, Madeleine. Please stay with me. Don't go – stay with Mummy. Please, sweetheart, hold on. I love you so much.

I started to cry. The crying built into seismic sobs. An unearthly sound, like the howl of a wounded animal, was coming out of my mouth. The crushing pain in my chest intensified to the point where I thought I was going to die.

I'd been with her. And then she was gone. Again.

16

FANTASY LAND

The day after the dream had been a difficult one. That night I'd gone to bed with puffy eyes. I woke on the morning of Monday 3 September with puffier ones.

There was a phone call from Ricardo. He would be coming over later as he needed Gerry to sign some release forms so that the emails relating to the Dutch extortion attempt could be used as evidence in court.

Alan Pike was back in Praia da Luz today to see how we were coping with recent events and our preparations for returning to the UK the following Monday. We spent several hours talking about my recent low episodes and the support we were going to need at home. He reassured us that he would be keeping in touch with us and that we would continue to see him regularly. Gerry and I spoke of the craziness going on around us: the media speculation, the lies, and the change in the attitude and the behaviour of the police. At one point I remarked sardonically, 'They'll be hauling us in as suspects next!'

'Now you're wandering into fantasy land,' replied Alan.

At 4.30pm Ricardo arrived with a female colleague and the forms Gerry needed to complete. After his colleague left with the paperwork, Ricardo asked if we had any queries he could answer. 'Do you have any information for *us*?' I inquired.

He clarified with us the date of our planned departure back to the UK and told us that the PJ wanted to 'interrogate' me on Wednesday and Gerry on Thursday. We'd waited almost four weeks for these interviews and it was obvious they had been hastily arranged once Bob Small notified the PJ that we would be leaving the country. Otherwise, why now? As far as we knew, they didn't have the forensic results back yet.

We should bring our lawyer with us to the police station, Ricardo went on. Gerry smelled a rat. The law has changed now, but back then witnesses were not normally entitled to legal representation. 'Isn't it unusual for witnesses to be questioned with their lawyer present?' he asked. It was like pulling teeth, but these were teeth that would have been falling out very soon anyway. We were not going to be questioned as witnesses, Ricardo finally admitted. 'So what *will* our status be, then?' Gerry pressed him.

'It's called *arguido*.'

As if we'd never heard the word.

I dropped my head in my hands in utter disbelief. I began to shake and cry. I shouted at Ricardo, 'What are you doing? Why are you doing this? I can't believe what's going on! This is ridiculous. It's despicable.' I shook my head over and over again. 'This can't be happening. This just *cannot* be true!'

What kind of country was this? And while the PJ were going down this track, leading the media and public to believe we were responsible for our daughter's dis-appearance, *who was looking for Madeleine?*

I remember crying out in despair, 'What will our parents think? How will they cope with this? What are you trying to do? Destroy our family completely?' These were of course rhetorical questions, but they would subsequently be thrown back at me as some kind of proof of a guilty conscience. My remark about our parents in particular was perceived as strange and suspicious. To me it was a completely under-standable reaction. We love our parents and were greatly concerned about their health and emotional state. They had lost their granddaughter. They had seen their own son and daughter in extreme pain and distress and every aspect of our characters ripped to shreds in the newspapers. They'd been through so much already, and now this.

Trisha and Eileen were staying with us for what was intended to be our final week in Luz. Hearing the commotion from the next room, where they were playing with Sean and Amelie, they came running in demanding to know what was happening. Within seconds there were more tears and more shouts of dismay and disbelief. Once again things were going from bad to worse. Much worse.

Ricardo left, looking every inch the sheepish messenger boy he was. We were left with our minds whirling. My immediate worry was Amelie and Sean. If this farce con-tinued in the same vein, and we ended up being formally accused of doing something to Madeleine, people were going to start calling for the twins to be taken away from us. I could feel the panic building up inside me. Between sobs I blurted out my fears to Trisha and Eileen.

It's hard to describe their response, but if you picture two lionesses whose young are under threat for their lives it will give you the general idea. Remembering it now actually brings a little smile to my face. Hell hath no fury like two women from Glasgow.

'That *won't* happen! We won't allow it to happen! Nobody will get near them. They wouldn't stand a chance. Don't even think like that, Kate!' they growled, their eyes flashing with conviction. But I was still worried.

Our plans for the evening went out of the window. We cancelled an interview we were scheduled to give *Paris Match* and dinner with Clement Freud. Gerry rang DCS Bob Small, who was astounded by this latest development. He promised to make some phone calls. Bob was finally able to get hold of Luís Neves, who was reportedly out of the country. Luís claimed not to know anything about it.

We made several more frantic phone calls ourselves – including one to Alan Pike, to let him know that we were now entering fantasy land. After dinner with the family, Gerry and I got Sean and Amelie ready for bed together. We would do whatever it took to protect our precious family and make it whole again.

Sean was so gentle as I was lying with them tonight. He gave me two kisses on the lips and put his arms around me while Amelie was chat, chat chatting!

At 9.50pm, I rang Clement. 'Come on round,' he said. 'It'll be nice to see you. But you'll have to forgive my night-time attire.'

We found Clement watching a cookery programme, dressed, as promised, in his nightshirt. It was so ordinary and comforting, a bit like going to see your grandad after a horrible day at school. He gave me one of his looks and a giant glass of brandy, and managed to get a smile out of me with his greeting: 'So, Kate, which of the devout Catholic, alcoholic, depressed, nymphomaniac parts is correct?'

His response to our catalogue of horrors was merely to raise an eyebrow. Clement had this way of making everything seem a little less terrible. When he heard about the dogs, he remarked laconically, 'So what are they going to do? Put them on the stand? One bark for yes, two for no?' He was right, of course; it *was* ridiculous.

A couple of hours later, fortified by our brandies (it was my first-ever taste of the stuff), some useful snippets of advice and several amusing anecdotes, we left our friend feeling quite a bit better than we had when we'd arrived. The shock of that day, and of what we were now facing, on top of the trauma of Madeleine's absence, never left us for a second, but it was interludes like this that gave us just enough strength to carry on.

By the next morning photographers were appearing sporadically outside our villa. There were press hanging around outside the church and film crews prepared to chase us through the streets either on foot or in the car. It was irritating and wearying. Occasionally Justine would ask us to 'give' something to the photographers to appease them ('They're under a lot of pressure too') and we ended up reluctantly allowing them to snap us going into the church and sitting on the rocks. We could hardly have stopped them anyway, short of refusing to leave the villa, but we were not happy about it. This was all about us, not Madeleine, which was precisely what we'd been striving to avoid for two months or more.

Later we were invited to Susan and Haynes Hubbard's house. It was as relaxing and enjoyable an afternoon as was possible right then. Sean and Amelie splashed about in the paddling pool, built train tracks and played 'babies' with dolls. Susan prepared a delicious meal, initiating the twins into the delights of king prawns, which they've loved ever since (thanks, Susan!), and the children, including our two, made the pudding: a banana split for everyone. Boy, were Sean and Amelie proud of themselves.

Susan and Haynes were, and remain, such a great source of strength. Sometimes you wonder whether particular people are brought into your life at a particular time for a reason. It certainly seemed to me that the Hubbards were a gift from God. This afternoon was so ordinary, but that's precisely why it was so valuable to us. We longed for our life to be ordinary again. In the meantime, these fleeting intervals of normality, precious time among friends with Sean and Amelie, were the closest we could get to it. Perhaps they always would be.

These days are so painful and everything is tinged. How long can we go on living like this? There are days when I just want to 'fast forward' all of our lives so that they'll be over, with no more pain, and we'll all be together again.

Wednesday 5 September. Our 'interviews' with the PJ had been put back by a day because our lawyer, Carlos, was in court and unable to be present. Instead we filled the day with emails, phone calls and packing. We met up with Justine to discuss what steps needed to be taken to ensure that our return to Britain would be as quiet as possible. When Gerry and I went out for a run later we saw Justine again, hurriedly approaching us from the top of the hill. The *Evening Standard*'s front-page headline tonight, she informed us, was to be 'RESULTS BACK: ARRESTS IMMINENT'. That would certainly set the cat among the pigeons on the eve of our 'interrogation'. I might sound flippant now, but at the time this was no joke, believe me. Since the police had not deigned to inform us, we had no idea whether the results of the forensic tests in the UK really were back, let alone what, if anything, they revealed.

Gerry and I talked at some length about the PJ's strategy, or our perception of it: namely, to put us under such extreme pressure, with the help of leaks to their contacts in the media, that if we were guilty (or even if we weren't) we'd crack. And the pressure on us was indeed immense. We were both used to working under high stress – with critically ill patients, for example – but this was different. This was a situation over which we had no control whatsoever.

We still harboured a faint hope that in the end the PJ would not declare us *arguidos*. Maybe our readiness to stay in Portugal to address any questions that remained would have thwarted their attempts to cast us in a bad light in the court of public opinion? Maybe the interview on 8 August, when they'd clearly tried to get me to confess, had been their best shot at getting us to crack and, since that hadn't worked, they would now change tack? There again, they hadn't eased up on the pressure, and fresh lies were appearing in the media every day. As I say, it was a faint hope.

I got myself ready for the following day – clothes out, shower, hair wash, even a DIY leg wax. It sounds daft now but I knew that it would help if I felt confident and good about myself. And how exactly are you supposed to prepare for being interrogated in a foreign language about the abduction of your child? All I could do was to tell the police the truth – again – and hope that was what they were actually interested in.

> Dear God, first and foremost please bless and protect dear Madeleine. Please help to return her to us as soon as you can. Give us as a family the strength to get through this ordeal. Thank you.

The Algarvian wind was wild and menacing overnight, howling eerily, sweeping around the walls of the villa and battering the shutters backwards and forwards. Not surprisingly, it was a restless and unsettling night and we were all awake at four in the morning. Gerry and I got up at 8am to find a posse of Portuguese journalists and cameramen camped outside our villa. You'd have thought we'd have been used to this by now, but we never got used to it. And today, especially, we felt hounded and trapped.

I was due at the police station in Portimão at 2pm. We followed our regular morning routine, taking Sean and Amelie to Toddler Club via the Ocean Club's twenty-four-hour reception. Then we walked down to Nossa Senhora da Luz for half an hour of private prayer, with the press pack still in pursuit. At least once we were in the church and had closed the doors, calm descended instantly and we were able to concentrate on what we were there for. We prayed fervently for Madeleine, for strength and for justice.

We stayed on for the Anglican service at 9.30am, led as usual by Haynes. He and the rest of the worshippers present that morning wrapped us in kindness and support. We thanked them and urged them not to lose sight of what was important – Madeleine – and to keep her in their thoughts and prayers.

Gerry phoned my mum to explain what was happening, and what was likely to happen, including the probability that we would be made *arguidos*. Of course, she was extremely upset. I know how helpless our parents must have felt at home and how it must have compounded their fears and their frustration.

Strangely, I was feeling OK. I think by now I'd switched on to autopilot and an inner strength and calmness I hadn't expected to find had begun to take over. My instinct to protect my child was more powerful than my fear and I could see very clearly what needed to be done. Even thinking about it several years later, that sensation returns. My recollections of that day are almost clinical. And I suppose the situation was so extreme, so nonsensical, that my brain struggled to register it as real. I had somehow floated out of my body and was watching events unfold as though they were happening to somebody else.

At 1.15pm Gerry drove me to the police station in Portimão. Trish came along for moral support. There were hordes of people outside the police station. As well as the ever-present journalists, photographers and film crews there was, perhaps more disconcertingly, a crowd of local on-lookers. Justine, in a vivid blue dress, was trying, with some difficulty, to keep them all under control. Gerry gave me a kiss and a whispered 'Love you' and I headed for the door with Trisha at my side. Immediately my path was blocked by jostling bodies and camera lenses. Unless they wanted a mother on a mission colliding with them, they would have to move, and sure enough, they all frantically shuffled back-wards as I reached them, standing on each other's toes, tripping over one another and falling down. I just kept walking.

Carlos Pinto de Abreu and his assistant, Sofia, were wait-ing for me inside. Carlos told me he'd already had a long discussion with Luís Neves. It wasn't looking good, he said. Not an encouraging start.

At 2.30pm, half an hour after the interview had been due to begin, Ricardo Paiva appeared, handed me a list of interpreters and instructed me to pick one. Not only was it exasperating that this hadn't been sorted out in advance, it also seemed pointless to ask me to make the choice. What difference did it make? I didn't know any of them. I opted for the first name on the list. If nothing else, she was local to Portimão and I didn't want to have to wait hours for one of the others to arrive from Lisbon or wherever.

Accompanied by Carlos, Sofia and the interpreter – who turned out to be a lady in her sixties or thereabouts, originally from Mozambique – I finally went in for my interview at 2.55pm. There were three PJ officers in the room. João Carlos and Ricardo Paiva were joined by Paulo

Ferreira, a man I'd never met before. João Carlos asked most of the questions, all of which I answered in as much detail as I could. He started with the Tuesday night of our holiday week, moving on to the Wednesday and then the terrible Thursday. At one point early on, something was read out from my initial statement, given on 4 May. It wasn't quite accurate and I explained to the officer that the original meaning seemed to have been lost slightly in translation.

To my astonishment, the interpreter became quite angry and suddenly interrupted, 'What are you saying? That we interpreters can't do our job? The interpreter will only have translated what you told her!' I was staggered. Quite apart from the fact that in this instance she was wrong – this definitely wasn't what I'd said – surely an interpreter is there to interpret, not to interfere in the process? My trust in her took a dive.

At 5pm, we had a fifteen-minute break, which I spent standing in the corridor outside the interrogation room. Carlos came over and told me not to be so definite in some of my answers. He was referring, apparently, to a couple of claims by witnesses put to me by the questioning officer: allegations that they had seen Gerry or me doing this or that. As these claims were untrue, I had said so. I couldn't understand why, as long as I was certain a statement was wrong, I shouldn't refute it. Although Carlos's stance bothered me, I tried to take his guidance on board. But it did rather undermine my confidence.

When the interview resumed, the atmosphere still seemed quite amenable. I didn't feel intimidated or threatened and I remained eager to give the police as many details as I could, especially as I was aware that a lot of what I had to tell them should have been sought in the immediate hours and days after Madeleine's disappearance. The more information there was available to the police, I reasoned, the more complete the jigsaw would be and the greater the chance of us finding Madeleine.

We stopped again at 7.50pm, supposedly for five minutes. I was getting tired by now and hoping it would all be finished fairly soon. No such luck. Those five minutes stretched into two and a quarter hours. Carlos had disappeared into a meeting with several of the PJ officers and I was starting to feel upset and frustrated. It had been a long day and I just wanted to be back at the villa with my family. Trisha had been patiently waiting all this time too, sitting in the reception area in a fug of cigarette smoke.

Meanwhile, in Praia da Luz, Gerry was becoming increasingly worried. I heard later that he'd twice come back to Portimão in the hope of collecting Trisha and me. At midnight he was sent home. Our lawyer would bring us back, he was told.

At last Carlos reappeared. He was shaking his head and looked anxious. I had no idea what had been going on but it was rapidly becoming clear that things were not as straightforward as I'd hoped.

It was 12.40am by the time the interview – and the attendant rigmarole of having it translated into Portuguese and then read back to me in English by the interpreter – was over. I was told I would have to return at ten o'clock in the morning. Outside the room, Paulo Ferreira stopped me in the corridor and said in a portentous tone, 'You must go back now and listen very carefully to your lawyer. He has something important to say to you.'

I left the station with Trish, Carlos and Sofia a little after 1am. The lateness of the hour had not deterred the hundreds of cameramen and spectators waiting to gawp at me as I emerged, exhausted, from the main door to the now familiar rapid clicking and whirring of the cameras, squinting into the dark against the incandescent flashbulbs. Was this real? Was this actually my life? Carlos gave a statement to the crowd. It was in Portuguese, so I cannot tell you what he said, except that my status remained that of witness.

As we pulled away in Carlos's car, I remember catching the eye of a young British photographer we'd got to know over the previous few months. Like the rest, he'd been desperately trying to get a few 'good' pictures of me climbing into the car. 'Just doing his job . . .' He held my gaze for an uncomfortable few seconds before suddenly lowering his eyes to the ground. His body language signalled shame and embarrassment. He was a nice lad.

Back at the villa, Carlos informed me, as Ferreira had indicated, that he needed to speak to Gerry and me in private. We sat down in the sitting room with Carlos, and Sofia, Eileen and Trisha left us to it. Carlos still looked very concerned. There was a great deal we needed to discuss, he told us. He reiterated that the situation was not good. The PJ had a lot of 'evidence' against us, and I was certain to be made an *arguida* in the morning.

First he cited video footage the police had shot of the reactions of the blood and cadaver dogs in apartment 5A and also around our hire car. I would be shown this on my return to the police station, he said. Presumably repeating what he had been told by the PJ, he explained how samples from both these sites had revealed Madeleine's blood and one of them indicated a 15 out of 19 match with her DNA.

I was totally perplexed. Although this news, if true, seemed to add weight to the possibility that Madeleine had at the very least been physically harmed, unusually I didn't dwell too much on the frightening implications. I can only assume this was because what we were being told didn't make sense. If, as the PJ alleged, Madeleine's blood was in the boot of our car, which we had not rented until 27 May, how on earth had it got there? Did this mean someone had planted it? I could see no other explanation. The police theory, it seemed, was that we had hidden Madeleine's body, then moved it later, in the car, and buried it elsewhere.

Next came the matter of a crumpled page the police said they had discovered in my borrowed Bible. It seemed this was felt to be highly significant because the passage on that page, in II Samuel 12, dealt with the death of a child. I knew nothing about any pages being crumpled, let alone in which part of the Bible. The fact that I had asked to see a priest on the night of Madeleine's disappearance was also seen as evidence of guilt. *What?* I was beginning to find my credulity stretched to breaking point. 'Don't people in Portugal talk to priests in times of need?' I asked Carlos. Apparently not. They only called for a priest when they wanted their sins to be forgiven. Good grief. This was definitely not the faith with which I was familiar.

A witness claimed to have seen Gerry and me carrying a big black bag and acting suspiciously. This was absolute nonsense, but 'evidence' of this kind came down to one person's word against another's. And it appeared that, as far as the PJ were concerned, our word counted for little.

'If you were Portuguese,' Carlos said with an air of resignation, 'this would be enough to put you in prison.'

The only conclusion I could draw was that we'd been framed, though this seemed completely implausible. Faced with something like this, way beyond the sphere of your experience, it is natural to dismiss it as impossible, but that doesn't mean it is. When I thought about all that had happened so far, maybe anything was possible. In any event, it seemed we'd underestimated the magnitude of the fight we had on our hands. Even our own lawyer appeared to think, based on what he'd been told, that the police had a good case against us. I could see by this time that Gerry was starting to crack.

Then came the best bit. Carlos announced what the police had proposed. If we, or rather I, admitted that Madeleine had died in an accident in the apartment, and confessed to having hidden and disposed of her body, the sentence I'd receive would be much more lenient: only two years, he said, as opposed to what I'd be looking at if I ended up being charged with homicide.

Pardon? I really wasn't sure if I could possibly have heard him correctly. My incredulity turned to rage. How dare they suggest I lie? How dare they expect me to live with such a charge against my name? And even more importantly, did they really expect me to confess to a crime they had made up, to falsely claim to the whole world that my daughter was dead, when the result would be that *the whole world stopped looking for her*? This police tactic might have worked successfully in the past but it certainly wasn't going to work with me. Over my dead body. 'You need to think about it,' Carlos insisted. 'It would only be one of you. Gerry could go back to work.'

I was speechless.

The incentive to accept this 'offer' seemed to be that if we didn't agree to it, the authorities could or would go after us for murder, and if we were found guilty, we might both receive life sentences. Was this what it came down to? Confess to this lesser charge or risk something much worse?

Gerry was distraught now. He was on his knees, sobbing, his head hung low. 'We're finished. Our life is over,' he kept saying over and over again. The realization that we were at the mercy of an incomprehensible criminal justice system had hit him hard. It was excruciating to see him like this. I love him so much and he is usually so strong. I was very conscious that my response was different. Maybe I should have been on my knees, too. Why wasn't I crying? Was my behaviour making me look cold or guilty? Again, my only explanation is that it was beyond comprehension. I might as well have been a character in a soap opera. Any time now the director would call 'Cut!' and this scene would be over. Even today, I struggle to believe it actually took place.

There was a phrase Carlos must have used about twenty times: 'This is the point of no return.' I could feel myself shaking. He was a man with three daughters of his own. 'Do you want me to *lie*? What would you do, Carlos? If one of your daughters was missing, and this happened to you, what would you do? Would you confess to a crime you hadn't committed, knowing full well it would mean everyone would stop searching for her?'

'I'd consider it, yes.'

Heaven help us. My confidence in Carlos was evaporating almost as quickly as my faith in Portuguese justice. I couldn't tell if he believed us, which, given that his job was to defend us, was a major worry, to put it mildly. Even if he did, I was no longer sure he had the backbone to stand up for us.

It was one thing to make us aware of the PJ's proposal, and perhaps Carlos was duty bound to do that; it was quite another, however, to suggest we accept it. I was horrified, and told him so in no uncertain terms.

My anger and ferocious maternal instinct began to permeate Gerry's despair. He was regaining his composure, his powers of reason and his fighting spirit.

'They've got nothing!' he fired at Carlos. He began pointing out the many flaws in the PJ's 'evidence' and the complete absence of any logic. 'This should be your job, not ours!' he said. He asked Carlos whether he felt he was up to the job. Carlos thought so. Did he need assistance? Not at the moment, but he would if the case came to trial.

Trisha and Eileen, disturbed by the noise, appeared from their room. Keeping a lid on my anger for long enough to enable me to communicate clearly, I brought them up to speed. Within seconds there were three raging lionesses pacing the villa.

Recognizing the need to switch into crisis-management mode, we calmed each other down. Gerry and I made it very clear to Trisha and Eileen that if we didn't return from the police station the next day, they should take the children out of the country as soon as possible.

It must have been close to 4am when Carlos and Sofia left, saying they would see me at the police station later that morning. On her way out, Sofia came over and gave me a hug. She told me she believed in us, that she was 'with' us, and tried to allay my concerns about Carlos. I should trust him, she said. He was 'very good'. It was a relief to know that somebody in Portugal was on our side.

Gerry and I just looked at each other, not knowing quite what to do or what was to become of us. We'd experienced many periods of despair since our beloved daughter had been taken away, but this one would take some beating. Our lives, our family, our whole future hung in the balance. We couldn't just go to bed. We had to do something. Despite the time, Gerry rang Bob Small and, in a voice laced with panic, explained what was going on. Bob was shocked. He wasn't aware of any forensic results, he told us, and certainly none suggesting what had just been shared with us. He tried his best to reassure Gerry. 'Just tell them the truth. It'll be OK,' he insisted. Perhaps he was trying to convince himself.

It was almost 5am when we finally got to bed. Extra prayers tonight.

Madeleine, sweetheart, please don't forget how much we all love you. We will keep fighting, darling, and we will keep searching for you. Hang in there, Madeleine.

17

ARGUIDOS

Friday 7 September. After a measly two hours' sleep we got up and braced ourselves for the day ahead. I remained calm. For a good couple of hours we were on the phone, calling family and friends to make them aware of the situation and to give them the green light to voice their outrage and despair if they wanted to. Nobody needed a second invitation. They'd all been struggling to contain their concerns for a long time.

Justine arrived to help. While Gerry talked again to Bob Small, she was ringing selected newspaper editors in the UK. We knew only too well how we would be portrayed in Portugal that morning, and Justine wanted to give the British media a broad outline of what was really going on so that they wouldn't resort to simply repeating whatever wild nonsense the Portuguese press decided to publish.

It was time to go. I vividly remember standing quietly for a few minutes in the sitting room. There were several thoughts scrolling through my mind. There's going to be a riot when news of all this reaches people back in the UK . . .

There's no way our government will stand for this. (Four months down the line and still so naive!) The PJ can beat me up and throw me in a prison cell but I will not lie . . . I will do everything I can to help Madeleine and to preserve our family . . . I know the truth and God knows the truth. Nothing else matters. It'll be OK.

I was still in control and I felt strong.

Justine was going to drive me to Portimão. Gerry would be following us there that afternoon for his own inter-rogation. I told Justine we needed to stop at the Ocean Club on the way. Amid the chaos of that morning, I'd discovered, too late, that Trisha had decided to take the twins to Toddler Club to save us an extra job. It was, of course, the right thing to do from a practical point of view, but I'd missed their departure and I needed to see them and hold them before I left Praia da Luz. After all, I had no idea whether I'd be coming back. I knew this would make us late, but given the hours and hours I'd spent to date waiting in that bloody police station, I didn't really care. The children were in the play area next to the Tapas restaurant. I went over and hugged and kissed them. Embracing them tightly, I told them, 'I love you.' Please God I'd be back doing the same thing that evening.

Justine and I made our way over to Portimão in her little car. In spite of the gravity of what lay ahead I had to stifle a smile as we pootled along, alternating between second and third gear with the occasional kangaroo jump thrown in for good measure. The journey seemed to take for ever. Just when it seemed the whole situation couldn't get any more surreal, before turning the corner to the police station, Justine stopped the car, took her lipstick out of her bag and, looking into the rear-view mirror, began to reapply it.

The street leading to the police station was once again lined by huge crowds of press and onlookers. I was suddenly boosted by a surge of adrenaline (must've been my Scouse fighting genes kicking in). I got out of the car and walked calmly towards the entrance, my head held high. I felt strangely invincible. There was some jeering from the locals as I passed by, apparently, but I didn't hear it. The police were not looking for Madeleine, I reminded myself. They hadn't been looking for my baby for weeks. The mere thought of that incensed me. There was no way I was going to let her down, too.

Justine remained outside to give a statement to the media. By this stage, they knew as well as I did that I was about to be declared an *arguida*. Carlos, Sofia, my interpreter and Cecilia Edwards, the British consul, were waiting for me inside. Carlos appeared ever so slightly more positive this morning. My interpreter, too, seemed warmer today.

I wasn't taken to the interrogation room until 11.50am, so my late arrival made no difference, as I'd been pretty sure it wouldn't: I was getting used to the PJ's concept of time. The same people were present as the day before. Today Carlos had advised me not to answer any of the questions put to me. He explained that this was my right as an *arguida* and it was the safest option: any responses I gave might un-intentionally implicate me in some way. He knew the system better than I ever would, so it struck me as prudent to accept his guidance. Since I was unable to comprehend how any-thing I'd said already could have led me to this point, I wasn't about to try to get through to the police again now.

As anticipated, my interrogation began with João Carlos explaining that my status from this moment on had been changed from witness to *arguida*. He ran through the rights and obligations this conferred on me. I sat there quietly, trying to compose myself despite the anger bubbling below the surface. *They haven't been looking for Madeleine* . . . Then they started. What had I seen and heard after entering apartment 5A at 10pm on 3 May 2007? Who called the police? At what time? Who contacted the media? It's actually quite difficult not to answer when someone asks you a question. The natural reaction is to reply, out of politeness if nothing else. And of course the urge to say what I thought about some of their vile and ridiculous insinuations was hard to suppress. On the other hand, I was very weary and at least repeating 'No comment' didn't involve engaging my brain. It certainly speeded up the translation process. With luck it would mean these proceedings wouldn't drag on any longer than they had to.

Ricardo Paiva played a more prominent role in the interrogation this time, which did nothing to maintain my equilibrium. This was the man who had invited us to his home for dinner. Our children had played with his son. 'The twins were restless in the UK so you sedated them?' he was saying. 'In the UK you were trying to give Madeleine to a family member? You get stressed and frustrated with the kids?' I knew exactly where this line of questioning was going and, as much as it riled me, I refused to rise to it.

If I'm honest, I'd been quite nervous about seeing the videos of the dogs. I had no idea what to expect, although I was quite sure something couldn't be quite right about the results they had apparently produced. We knew from Bob Small that the responses of specialist dogs were, or ought to be, classed as intelligence, not evidence, but in my head I'd built up these film clips into the most damning 'evidence' imaginable; the 'I rest my case, Your Honour' finale. Now Ricardo was giving me his spiel about the dogs. 'These dogs have a 100 per cent success rate,' he said, waving an A4 document in front of me. 'Two hundred cases and they've never failed. We have gone to the best laboratory in the world using *low-copy* DNA techniques.' His emphasis suggested this was the gold standard. I just stared at him, unable to hide my contempt. What did *he* know about low-copy DNA? I was so tempted to ask him to elaborate. These dogs had never been used in Portugal before, and he knew little more about them, either, than I did.

Ricardo started the video player. I saw the dogs going into apartment 5A, one at a time, with the handler, PC Martin Grime (then of the South Yorkshire police, later self-employed). Each dog ran around the apartment, jumping over beds, into the wardrobe and generally having a good sniff. At one point, the handler directed the dogs to a spot behind the couch in the sitting room, close to the curtains. He called the dogs over to him to investigate this particular site. The dogs ultimately 'alerted'. I felt myself starting to relax a little. This was not what I would call an exact science.

In footage of the apartment next door to ours, one of the dogs began to root in the corner of a room near a piece of furniture. PC Grime summoned the dog and they left the flat.

The film show continued. Now we were in an underground garage where eight or so cars were parked, including our rented Renault Scenic. It was hard to miss: the windows were plastered with pictures of Madeleine. In medicine we would call this an 'unblinded' study, one that is susceptible to bias. One of the dogs ran straight past our car, nose in the air, heading towards the next vehicle. The handler stopped next to the Renault and called the dog. It obeyed, returning to him, but then ran off again. Staying by the car, PC Grime instructed the dog to come back several times and directed it to certain parts of the vehicle before it eventually supplied an alert by barking.

Each time a dog gave a signal, Ricardo would pause the video and inform me that blood had been found in this site and that the DNA from the sample matched Madeleine's. He would stare at me intently and ask me to explain this. These were the only times I didn't respond with a 'No comment.' Instead I said I couldn't explain it, but neither could he. I remember feeling such disdain for Ricardo at this point. What was he *doing*? I thought. Just following orders? Under my breath, I found myself whispering, 'Fucking tosser, fucking tosser.' This quiet chant somehow kept me strong, kept me in control. This man did not deserve my respect. 'Fucking tosser . . .'

When researching the validity of sniffer-dog evidence later that month, Gerry would discover that false alerts can be attributable to the conscious or unconscious signals of the handler. From what I saw of the dogs' responses, this certainly seemed to me to be what was happening here. We would later learn that in his written report, PC Grime had

309

emphasized that such alerts cannot be relied upon without corroborating evidence.

Towards the end of my interrogation, I walked over to Ricardo and asked why he'd asked us over to dinner that night. Had it been a strategic invitation? He looked a little uncomfortable. 'Like everyone else, we trusted you,' he said. Good God in heaven. I think if anyone was justified in having problems trusting others, it was Gerry and me, not the PJ.

As I walked out of the interview room at 3.15pm, Gerry was on his way to Portimão for his interrogation. I wasn't allowed to see him but I had been able to speak to him on the phone. Carlos told me it looked as if we could be up in court on Monday. For the moment I would not be permitted to leave the country. This news didn't affect me as badly as might have been expected. Nothing that happened surprised me any more. Every new twist was as bizarre as the last and I just couldn't believe in any of it. Besides, I wasn't sure if I'd even get out of the police station, let alone home. In the end that dispensation, at least, was granted, and I was allowed to leave. As I walked out of the door there was the inevitable noise and shouting and a fresh plethora of photographs, this time of 'Kate the *arguida*'. I was very tired and desperate to see my children, who had been taken by Trisha to Susan Hubbard's house. Justine drove me there, tailed all the way by the Portuguese press.

As I squeezed my beautiful babies tightly, pressing my nose against them to inhale their sweet scent, not wanting to let them go, a sense of wellbeing and warmth swept over me. This was what was important. This was why we needed to keep battling: our family; our children. I sat down, cup of tea in hand, in the bosom of my family and friends and listened to the tales of the day from Amelie and Sean. It was as though I had momentarily been transported in a Tardis to another much nicer world where everything was happy and innocent. It was lovely while it lasted.

I took the twins back to our besieged villa at 6.30pm and rang Alan Pike to talk through the day's events and let him know that I was OK. Reinforcements arrived in the shape of Sandy and Michael. It was reassuring to have another couple of men around. The phones were red hot again. Many relatives and friends had expressed through the media at home their concern and disgust at the way Gerry and I were being treated. Phil had gone as far as mentioning the 'deal' put to us indirectly by the PJ. Gerry was uneasy about that being made public (though this might have been because he was inside the police station at the time). I had no qualms. It had happened, it was the truth and it was outrageous. The PJ responded by saying, 'We don't do deals.' Not officially, maybe, but from where we were standing it was certainly a deal, and a thoroughly reprehensible one at that.

After dinner, a lot of chat and some much-needed down time, I went to bed. Kate McCann, the *arguida*; Madeleine's mum, the *arguida*. Publicly suspected of killing my precious daughter or at least of disposing of her body. The mere idea made me want to vomit. The world was not only cruel, it was mad. This scenario would be considered too far-fetched even as a plot for a movie, surely. I was burning with the injustice of it all and my heart broke that bit more for my little girl.

Gerry wasn't back from his interrogation until 1.30am.

Like me, he was officially declared an *arguido* at the start of the proceedings. His intention had been to take Carlos's advice, as I had done, and refuse to answer any questions. But when the first question – along the lines of 'Did you dispose of your daughter's body?' – was put to him for the third time, incensed by its sheer absurdity and offensiveness and by the way the interviewing officer was goading him, he simply couldn't stop himself. In these conditions, his reaction was perfectly understandable, but unfortunately our inconsistent responses to interrogation led to me being portrayed as 'difficult' or even 'guilty' in certain sections of the media and, of course, by the nutters who pour forth bile on the internet. However, I suppose this was a minor problem in the grand scheme of things.

Like me, Gerry had been relieved by the inadequacies revealed by the sniffer-dog video, dismissing it as 'the most subjective piece of intelligence-gathering imaginable'. Ricardo had told him, too, that they had recovered Madeleine's DNA from inside the hire car, using the 'best forensic scientists in the world'. When Gerry asked to see the DNA report, Ricardo became quite flustered, waving PC Grime's document in the air and saying, 'It is the dogs that are important!'

At that point Gerry began to feel a lot better. He realized that no one could have planted forensic evidence to implicate us because – despite what we had been led to believe by the PJ and the newspaper headlines – there *wasn't* any such evidence. They had no proof that Madeleine was dead. All they actually had was the signal of a dog trying to please its instructor in an apartment from which

Madeleine had been taken three months earlier. As we now know, the chemicals believed to create the 'odour of death', putrescence and cadaverine, last no longer than thirty days. There were no decaying body parts for the dog to find. It was simply wrong.

It would be eleven months before we learned the truth from the released PJ files: the full report from the UK Forensic Science Service, sent to them *before* they interrogated us, had concluded that the DNA results were 'too complex for meaningful interpretation'.

There was no evidence whatsoever that Madeleine was dead. The search had to go on.

On the drive home from the police station it had become clear to Gerry that Carlos believed charges were likely and that we might have to stay in Portugal. The preparation of a case like this could take years. If the charge was murder, rather than the lesser crime of hiding a body, we might even be remanded in custody for all that time. Given the lack of evidence, it was impossible to understand how such charges could be brought, but if you'd told us a few weeks earlier that we were going to be declared *arguidos* we wouldn't have believed that, either. The prospect of being separated from Sean and Amelie, holed up in jail unable to prepare our defence properly, was terrifying. Gerry was seriously considering sneaking us into a car and driving us all across the border to Spain. It would have been crazy. The whole world would have thought we were guilty, and maybe that was what the police were hoping we'd do.

Most people find it hard to comprehend how innocent people can confess to crimes they haven't committed. Gerry and I don't. Not now. The monumental psychological duress we were under can easily lead to bad, irrational decision-making. Thankfully, we resisted the urge to flee. When we left Portugal, it would be with the blessing of the PJ and our heads held high.

Saturday 8 September. We were on tenterhooks all day, waiting to hear whether we would be allowed to go home. Rachael had found a couple of criminal lawyers in London she was sure could help us. Michael Caplan and Angus McBride of Kingsley Napley had worked on several high-profile cases, including the Pinochet extradition proceedings and the Stevens inquiry. Gerry gave them a call. They discussed Madeleine's case in detail, what had happened so far and how Kingsley Napley might be able to assist us. Meanwhile, we tried to rein in family and friends from speaking any further to the press. Enough had been said and we were very conscious that we – and Madeleine – were at the mercy of the Portuguese judicial system. Being overly critical at this delicate point could, and probably would, work against us all.

Late that afternoon, we were notified by Liz Dow, the British consul in Lisbon, that Luís Neves and Guilhermino Encarnação had declared us 'free' to leave the country whenever we wished. Thank you, God.

On the advice of the lawyers, we decided to get out as soon as possible. We would go the next day rather than leaving it until Monday. Then it was all hands on deck to pack everything up and clear the villa. Michael volunteered to stay on for a couple of days to organize the cleaning, hand back the keys and arrange for our remaining belongings to be shipped home by a removal company.

In view of the immovable wall of journalists, cameramen and film crews that remained outside the villa all day, Gerry and I felt it would be prudent to stay on the premises. The rest of the family, using the side entrance, took Amelie and Sean for some lunch and a swim. Although we had a lot to do, there was one arrangement I had been particularly eager to keep: an ecumenical feast-day service at Nossa Senhora da Luz that evening. The little church and its wonderful community had been so important to us since Madeleine's abduction and celebrating its feast day meant a great deal to me. I badly wanted to be there, for Madeleine, and of course to say my goodbyes and express my heartfelt thanks to all our friends and supporters in the parish, especially a small and faithful group of elderly Portuguese ladies. We knew, though, that if we went the media circus would overshadow and spoil everybody else's celebrations. I was deeply disappointed to have to miss it.

We heard from Clarence that evening. Before long Justine would be moving on to pursue her political career and we'd always hoped he would be able to return as our family spokesperson. The government, however, had other ideas. They forbade him from any further involvement with us because of our *arguido* status. Clarence was very upset, as were we. This was the first sign we had of doors starting to close on us because of this unwarranted stigma. We felt that our government had abandoned us. It hadn't occurred to me that they wouldn't protect us and I berated myself, once again, for my naivety. I knew the situation was bad but I still didn't fully appreciate just how detrimental the recent turn of events would be to us and to Madeleine.

With the family around there was always the odd funny moment to alleviate the tension and keep us sane. That last evening, Gerry's mum was sitting outside on the patio giving it lots of granny chat (which our granny does exceptionally well) when we suddenly spotted a big, furry boom microphone hovering over the patio wall. Whether it was Eileen's colourful outburst on finally noticing this fluffy intruder, or the thought that anyone would need a boom microphone around Granny McCann (she's quite loud), we all collapsed into fits of belly-aching laughter.

Some time after midnight, Justine notified the media that we would be returning to the UK early the next morning. We'd rather not have done this but as we knew they would get wind of our departure anyway, telling them a short while in advance seemed to give us the best chance of managing the situation and trying to minimize the almighty scramble that would ensue when they found out.

The next morning we packed our last bits and pieces and said a tearful farewell to Susan Hubbard before rousing Sean and Amelie. Their bedtime had got later and later in recent months – I think they were becoming Portuguese by this stage! – and they were still very sleepy, but once they were properly awake and heard they were going on a plane they were very excited.

I had never expected to be leaving Portugal under these circumstances. It was incomprehensible to be going home as a family of four – something that still sends shivers down my spine – and to be going in this way, under a cloud of suspicion, was almost more than we could stand.

Of course, many sections of the press would suggest we were running away, but as I've recounted, the decision had been made several weeks earlier. All we were doing was leaving a day earlier than originally planned. Our situation here was untenable. We were trapped within four walls, surrounded by hostility, and not only did this restrict what we were able to do for Madeleine, it was no kind of environment for our other two children, either. I resented being pushed out of the country, as I saw it, but ultimately we had to do what was right and fair for Sean and Amelie and what would best equip us to help Madeleine.

By 6am the media were stationed outside in their droves. An hour later we left the villa and Praia da Luz, Gerry driving the children and me in our hire car while a local British friend kindly took the rest of the family. The heaviness of our hearts almost took second place to sheer terror on that journey. We were chased the whole way, mainly by the Portuguese and Spanish press, who tailgated us dangerously. There were torsos hanging out of sun-roofs, huge video cameras balancing on shoulders and heavily laden motorbikes brushing the sides of our car as they skimmed past. A helicopter hovered overhead. It was utter madness, and extremely frightening for the children as well as for us. An image of Princess Diana flashed through my mind. It was easy to see now how her tragic death had come about.

Gerry's foot kept pressing down harder on the accelerator as he instinctively tried to put a safe distance between us and the car that was practically touching our bumper. I urged him to slow down. The most important thing was to stay in control and to try to blank out the craziness all around us. It didn't matter how quickly we got there. It didn't matter if we were pursued all the way to the airport. It did matter that we stayed alive. I'd said so many prayers over the last four months but I'd never anticipated having to beg the Lord to protect us on the A22.

Although the friend driving our relatives behind us was in slightly less jeopardy, they too were getting a taste of the motorway mayhem. 'Jesus!' Granny McCann memorably remarked. 'It's like the Wacky Races!'

Mercifully, we all arrived at the airport in one piece. There we said goodbye to Eileen and Sandy, who were flying home to Glasgow, and Michael, who was taking our hire car back to Praia da Luz. On hearing about the interpretation of the forensic results, the lawyers at Kingsley Napley thought it wise to hold on to it for the time being. Trisha was coming to Rothley with us. At the risk of repeating myself, I can't imagine how we'd have coped without the help of our wonderful family.

Needless to say, once Justine had informed the media of our return, every journalist in town, it seemed, had tried to book a seat on our flight and a fair few of them had succeeded. By the time we were strapped into our seats, I was beyond caring. The majority of them respected our need to be left alone. Only one or two were unable to resist the temptation to ask that inane question, 'How are you both feeling?'

So how *were* we feeling? Full of a confusing mixture of

relief, disbelief, oppressive sadness, piercing guilt and pain. The sadness, guilt and pain were dominant. We were going home without Madeleine. I was leaving her behind. *I'm her mother and I'm leaving her behind.* My heart ached as it was torn away from my last geographical link with my little girl.

When we touched down in the Midlands, I couldn't hold back the tears any longer, even though I could see how they were worrying Amelie. We were home at last; home without Madeleine. Soon we would be walking into our house, the house we'd only ever lived in with Madeleine. My chest hurt, my throat felt swollen and my head began to spin. Gerry put his arm round me. I glanced up to see the strain on his face and his red, watery eyes. He was being so strong but I knew he was dying inside.

Slowly and solemnly, we came down the steps from the aeroplane, Gerry with a sleeping Sean resting against his chest and me with Amelie, tired but awake, on my hip. What did the future hold for our family now?

On reaching the tarmac, Gerry gave a short statement to the waiting reporters and film crews. He was breaking, his voice tight as he fought the persistent urge to bawl.

. . . While we are returning to the UK, it does not mean we are giving up our search for Madeleine. As parents, we cannot give up on our daughter until we know what has happened. We have to keep doing everything we can to find her.

Kate and I wish to thank once again all those who have supported us over the past days, weeks and months. But we would like to ask for our privacy to be respected now that we have returned home.

Our return is with the full agreement of the Portuguese authorities and police. Portuguese law prohibits us from commenting further on the police investigation.

Despite there being so much we wish to say we are unable to do so, except to say this: we played no part in the disappearance of our lovely daughter, Madeleine.

A Special Branch officer drove us to Rothley. As we got closer and closer to our village, memories of so many happy times began to fill my mind, interrupted constantly by chilling reminders of the hard reality of our existence now. At last we pulled into our cul-de-sac and the media throng assembled there sprang into action. I hadn't seen our house since we'd left for our holiday, full of excitement, that April morning. We lifted our sleeping babies out of the car, took a few deep breaths and headed towards the front door. My Uncle Brian, Auntie Janet and our friend Amanda were already there, waiting to let us in and welcome us home. I cuddled them all, needing to be held tightly, and then I cried and cried and cried.

A short while later, I went upstairs and opened the door to Madeleine's bedroom. I needed to do this. I needed to feel her close. I didn't go in, I just let my eyes wander round the shocking-pink walls and up to the stars on her ceiling, over her teddies and dolls, and then to her bed and her pillow. I could almost see her there, lying on her side in a foetal position, her little head resting gently on the pillow with her fine, blonde hair spread out artlessly behind. 'Lie with me, Mummy.'

As for Sean and Amelie, it was as if they had never been

away. Within seconds they were running around the play-room, making us pretend cups of tea, pushing their teddies and Noddy about in buggies and rushing out into the garden to whizz down the slide.

For us, it was straight down to business. Michael Caplan and Angus McBride arrived that afternoon for a thorough discussion of our situation. Our family's future looked bleak and we needed help. When they left three and a half hours later we felt more positive, confident that we now had the right people to guide us through this mess.

In the evening the phone was ringing off the hook and there were a few visitors, too, mainly members of our family coming round to give us a hug.

Being back in our house wasn't as bad, or even as sad, as I'd feared. In fact it was quite comforting. Perhaps just having our own familiar bits and pieces around us relieved some of the stress. Perhaps it was the knowledge that Sean and Amelie were happy to be where they belonged. Or perhaps it was that the whole house was full of reminders of Madeleine. Maybe it was a combination of all these con-solations. Whatever the case, when we climbed into bed shortly before midnight, life felt momentarily tolerable. And we still had our hope.

This wasn't over yet.

18

THE FIGHTBACK BEGINS

We woke up that Monday morning with a daunting task ahead of us. Declared *arguidos*, labelled as suspects in the press and consequently considered by many to be guilty of *something*, we needed to clear our names, comprehensively and quickly, before we could continue the search for Madeleine on any effective level. While suspicions remained among the authorities and the public that we had somehow been involved in our daughter's disappearance, fewer people were going to be looking for her. To have to devote our time and physical and emotional resources to this extra battle, while Madeleine was still out there somewhere, was galling in the extreme.

The media coverage was absolutely huge, driven, it seemed, by the 'ultimate twist': the parents who were conducting an international campaign now rumoured to be suspected of hiding their own daughter's body. It was despicable given that the basis for the stories was simply untrue. And yet we could see how it was happening: the Portuguese press were publishing information from police sources, which was picked up by all the other newspapers, and the fact that we had been made *arguidos* appeared to justify it. The damage being done was immense. We felt as if we had no control over anything. It was like 3 and 4 May all over again.

We, like Robert Murat, would remain *arguidos* until or unless somebody was charged or the case was closed. Although a new penal code imposed an eight-month deadline on inquiries, the police or the prosecutor could apply for extensions as they felt necessary. It meant we could be facing this frenzied speculation for a long time to come.

Over the next few weeks our days would be filled with phone calls, emails and meetings, interspersed with hours holed up in the study in front of computer screens, researching and gathering information. We worked sixteen-hour days and frequently fell into bed at 2am. We rarely left the house, except for meetings and the occasional trip to the park with the children, or to squeeze in a short, head-clearing run or spirit-boosting visit to the local church. Potty-training Sean and Amelie was probably the nearest we got to a break. There were many difficult decisions to be made that compounded our pain and worry. Any action we chose to take had to be looked at from every angle. Would people understand why we were doing it and support it, or would it be presented negatively in the media and bring us even more detractors?

The issues we needed to deal with most urgently were protecting our children and ensuring the safety of our family, preparing our defence with our lawyers and trying to stop lies being published in the press.

One of the first things we did was to ring our GP. We

wanted to make contact with the social services to pre-empt any interest they might be obliged to take in us. In the light of the headlines and our *arguido* status, we realized there would be pressure on the authorities to assess the welfare of the twins. It all seemed so crazy and unfair, but we had to confront it head on. Our doctor came round that Monday morning and we talked things through with him.

Wild stories were appearing in the papers about my 'fragile' mental state, my 'inability to cope' with my 'hyper-active' children, eating disorders and sedatives. All complete bullshit, yet not once had our GP been contacted for any information about us. The police had not sought access to our medical notes and nobody had ever asked him if we were well and healthy, what kind of people we were, whether he'd ever had any concerns about us or our parenting skills or if we were on any medication.

Three days later we had a meeting with a social services manager and a local child-protection officer. They went through various formalities with us and, while they took care to keep everything on a totally professional footing, I could tell they felt uncomfortable about having to subject us to this sort of scrutiny. But we'd resigned ourselves to it. We'd expected it, accepted it and we had nothing to hide.

The local police also visited us within the first twenty-four hours, primarily to advise us on security. Our home was fitted with sensor alarms. If anyone broke in, these would alert the police station, rather than go off in the house, enabling officers to be at our door within minutes. We were also given personal alarms to carry with us at all times. My dad and a friend secured another two feet of trellis to the fence surrounding our garden, providing a twelve-foot barrier against potential intruders, including the photographers who were already snooping at the back. Blinds were quickly put up at all of our windows for a modicum of privacy. A week or so later, Control Risks sent a technical expert to check our phone lines and rooms for any bugging devices. If we had wondered back in May whether we'd entered a whole new world, we were now certain we had.

The press settled themselves outside our house for a couple of days before agreeing to retreat to the end of the cul-de-sac. There they were to remain, in varying numbers, for three months. Somewhere there must be a whole library of exciting photographs of me driving in and out of our road. I can only imagine how annoying the media presence was for our neighbours, but they put up with it stoically and showed us nothing but kindness and support.

Once again our family, friends and neighbours came to our rescue, shopping, cooking, cleaning, washing and iron-ing, opening mail, entertaining the children and providing a shoulder to cry on and many a hug. As they had been in Portugal, Sean and Amelie were blissfully untroubled by this semi-organized disorder and I thanked my lucky stars for that. They played inside and outside, upstairs and down-stairs, leaving a trail of toys and laughter in their wake. But the frustrating necessity to shore up our defences not only distracted us from the search for Madeleine, it also robbed us of time with the twins.

We tried to set aside periods of the day to take them for a swim or watch a DVD with them, but these weren't nearly as frequent as we'd have liked. Perhaps not surprisingly, they were both a little unsettled at night for a while, often padding through to our bedroom in the small hours. We didn't put up much resistance to their efforts to clamber into our bed. It was nice to have them with us, even if it had to be at ridiculous o'clock.

On Tuesday 11 September we had an 8am conference call with Michael Caplan, Angus McBride and Justine. It was decided that Justine and Angus would visit the editors of the main tabloid newspapers and Angus would explain to them that there was absolutely no evidence to support our involvement in Madeleine's disappearance.

Angus and Justine's action seemed to make next to no difference and tales of blood and dogs, provided by the usual unnamed 'sources close to the investigation', continued to appear, augmented by talk of supposed 'clumps of hair'. There were erroneous reports of a '100 per cent match' between samples taken from the vehicle and Madeleine's DNA. Even if this had been true (which it turned out it wasn't), it was perfectly feasible that Madeleine's DNA could have been in the car for entirely innocent reasons, on clothes, toys and other items that belonged to her.

Since there was no match, the most likely explanation for the presence of particular DNA sequences in the car – and certainly a far more rational one than a dead body having been there three weeks after her disappearance – was that the DNA was mine, Gerry's, Sean's or Amelie's. Since Madeleine inherited her DNA from Gerry and me (as have the twins) she possesses strands common to us all.

But I guess that didn't make for quite so good a story.

Yet judging by the continuing flood of touching and encouraging letters, flowers and gifts, many of the general public, in the UK and Ireland, at least, saw through the lies and speculation. I cannot overemphasize how important this show of solidarity was to us. It was a source of strength and hope and it helped us to keep going through the toughest of times.

Having no knowledge at this point of what had or had not been found by the forensic tests commissioned by the PJ, we wanted to conduct our own, independent examination. Michael and Angus suggested that we arrange for a full forensic screen to be performed on the Renault Scenic hire car, which had been left with a friend in Praia da Luz.

Later that Tuesday Angus flew out to Lisbon for a meeting with Carlos Pinto de Abreu to try to clarify our legal position in Portugal. Meanwhile, Bob Small paid us a call. We were pleased to see him: he is one of the good guys. While he always remained completely professional, we knew that he cared about us, about Madeleine and about justice. You'd have thought you could expect this of all police officers and people in authority, but our experience had taught us otherwise. Compassionate though Bob was, he was still unable to answer many of our questions ('Constrained by my position . . .'), which was upsetting and exasperating.

Very frustrating. You wonder, if the shit really hits the fan (as if it hadn't already!) who will actually put their necks out and stand up for us?

I embarked on a detailed chronological account of all our movements from 3 May to 7 September, when we were declared *arguidos*. I had kept a record of a lot of this information in my journals, but there were still gaps in the first three weeks, before I started to keep my diary. I phoned all the friends and family who had come out to Praia da Luz during this period, as well as everyone with whom we had been in close contact at home, and asked them to go over everything they recalled, too, to corroborate my own memories, pinpoint dates and times and fill in any blanks. I also contacted Foreign Office officials and consular staff to confirm details of all our meetings with them. It was imperative that my report was as thorough and complete as possible.

I worked on this almost solidly for the next three weeks. Gerry has always scoffed at my perfectionist tendencies and attention to detail, but he was scoffing no longer! My journals were so comprehensive, covering everything down to the most insignificant and boring incidents you can imagine, that by the time I had finished I was able to account for what we did and where we were at virtually any given time over the whole four months. I would have put Sherlock Holmes out of a job, if I say so myself.

Although I was satisfied with what I'd achieved, it was a travesty I'd had to produce it at all. Since 4 May, practically every step we'd taken outside our Mark Warner apartment or the villa had been followed on television by the entire world. How could we possibly have secretly hidden our daughter's body, in such a safe place that it hadn't been discovered, and then removed it (if our hiding place was that good, I wonder why would we have bothered), transported it in our Renault Scenic (which we hadn't hired until 27 May) and buried her elsewhere – all without our media stalkers ever noticing a thing? It simply wasn't feasible.

Yet this was what was being insinuated. It was hard to understand how anyone could take this theory seriously. The secrecy surrounding the case can't have helped. Perhaps people thought the PJ had a stack of other more damning evidence they weren't yet revealing. They hadn't.

No wonder by the time I went to bed at night I often felt close to exploding with exasperation.

> *Gerry's had a few tough days and was upset earlier on today. He seems very stressed although it's not surprising . . . Who'd have thought our lives would have ended up like this? What have we done to deserve all this? Immoral, inhumane, a total injustice. I don't know how the Portuguese police can sleep at night.*
>
> *Madeleine, nobody here, especially me and Daddy, is going to stop looking for you. We will do EVERYTHING to find you, sweetheart. May God, Mary and the Angels protect you until that time. Love you. Miss you. xxxxx*

By this time Gerry was deep into his next task: researching the validity of responses produced by blood and cadaver dogs. Along the way he spoke to several experts, and in the coming weeks we would learn a lot about the subject. This is what one US lawyer had to say about the objectivity and success rate of this procedure:

The most critical question relating to the use of the dog alerts as evidence is how likely is the dog's alert to be correct. In this regard, the only testing of these handler and dog teams recorded an abysmal performance. Here 'the basis' for the possible past presence of human remains is that there is a 20 or 40 per cent chance that a dog's 'alert' was correct. In other words, with respect to residual odour, the dog-handler teams performed significantly worse than if the handlers had simply flipped a coin to speculate as to the presence of residual odour at each location.

> State of Wisconsin v. Zapata, 2006 CF 1996 –
> defendant supplemental memorandum

These tests, it should be noted, were performed within twelve hours of body parts being removed from the testing area. Just imagine much how worse the results would be after three months.

Almost all erroneous alerts originate not from the dog but from the handler's misinterpretation of the dog's signals. A false alert can result from the handler's conscious or unconscious signals given by them to lead a dog where the handler suspects evidence to be located. We are mindful that less than scrupulously neutral procedures which create at least the possibility of unconscious 'cueing' may well jeopardize the reliability of dog sniffs.

> United States v. Trayer, 898 F. 2d 805.809 (CADC 1990)

On Wednesday 12 September, Gerry was contacted by Edward Smethurst, a commercial lawyer. He represented a businessman called Brian Kennedy (not to be confused with my uncle Brian Kennedy), a successful entrepreneur who owned various companies, including Everest Windows and Sale Sharks Rugby Club. Brian, he told Gerry, had, like many people, been following the unfolding drama of Madeleine's disappearance since 3 May. Now, seeing things going from bad to worse, he had decided he could no longer stand idly by and watch. He wanted to step in and help us financially and in any other way he could. A meeting with Edward and Brian was arranged for that Friday at the Kingsley Napley offices in London.

On Friday morning, Angus McBride kindly drove to Rothley to pick us up and take us down to London. Brian Kennedy and Edward Smethurst joined us in a meeting room shortly before midday. Brian was much younger than I was expecting, very relaxed and personable. He told us a little about himself. Originally from Edinburgh and married with five children, he was wealthy, obviously, but a self-made man: he had started out as a window cleaner. Then he asked me to give him an account of what had happened on the evening of 3 May. I talked for a couple of minutes before he stopped me. 'OK, that's enough. I've always believed you. I just wanted to hear it from you. That's fine.'

We discussed the immediate problems facing us: our *arguido* status, the need for legal assistance, the media coverage and the public-relations difficulties associated with that. Brian's contributions were full of passion and sincerity and what he said next will stay with me for ever. 'OK. First of all we need to deal with all this stuff and get it out of the way. Then we need to concentrate on the most important thing:

finding your daughter.' I wanted to cry. Well, actually, I did cry. Here was somebody, at long last, who could see through all this rubbish and the damage it was doing. Here was somebody who wasn't turning his back on us because it was the easiest or 'safest' thing to do. And most importantly, here was somebody who was able and willing to help us find Madeleine. We had a chance. Madeleine had a chance. I resisted the urge to run around the table and throw my arms around him. Instead I stammered out my gratitude. 'Thank you, Brian, thank you. Thank you so much. Thank you. Thank you.' My heart was doing mini leaps for the first time in months.

Discussions between ourselves, Brian and Ed, our lawyers and representatives from Control Risks continued through the afternoon. We left feeling weary but upbeat, and as we said our farewells, Brian got his hug.

Everyone had agreed that it would be a great help to have Clarence Mitchell back on board to take care of media liaison, communications and public relations. We knew he was keen to rejoin us in spite of the government's edict. Within three days, Clarence had resigned from the Civil Service and was back in the fold, his salary generously taken care of by Brian. Being Clarence, he rolled up his sleeves and got started immediately. We were absolutely delighted – as, incidentally, were the many little old ladies who wrote to tell us that they were sleeping much better since the return of 'that nice Mr Mitchell'.

Once the twins had settled back where they belonged, they began to feel Madeleine's absence from our home and family more keenly. A week after our return, Amelie jumped into bed with me at two o'clock in the morning. 'Where's Madeleine gone, Mummy?' Trying not to crumble, I explained to her gently that Madeleine was still missing and that although we hadn't found her yet, we were all still looking. She asked me the same question when she woke up again five hours later.

The children had been away from their nursery school for four and a half months and we decided it was probably time they went back. We were prepared for it to take them a few mornings to get used to nursery again. What we hadn't bargained for was the emotional impact it would have on Gerry and me. Madeleine had started at this nursery at eighteen months and had still been going there when we left for Portugal. It was awash with memories. We knew the staff really well and we knew how fond they were of Madeleine. The first morning was very tough, and there were many wet eyes around the building.

After lunch, I went to collect Amelie and Sean. As we were getting into the car, Sean asked, 'Where's Madeleine?' Then he answered his own question. 'She's round there.'

He was pointing to an annexe called the Coach House where the older children were based, the place where he remembered Madeleine going each morning. I recalled how the twins used to stop at the window on the half-landing of the main building, which overlooked the play area outside the Coach House. 'There's Magalin!' they would say in their toddler babble. 'There's Magalin!' Their doting big sister would wave up at them, bringing beaming smiles to their little faces. God, it hurt. For the rest of that day, I would hear Seany wandering around the house telling anybody within earshot, 'We can't find Madeleine.'

Everywhere I went with the twins, the associations with Madeleine brought back memories that increased the agony. In the park I could still picture her coming down the slide. At the swimming pool, there she was in her little yellow swimming cap, waving to me as I watched proudly through the window. But gradually I began to force myself to go on little expeditions that I knew would make Amelie and Sean happy. I took them back to Stonehurst Farm – 'our farm'. I could see Madeleine feeding the sheep. I could see her talking to the donkeys. I could see her swinging on the rope in the hay barn. I could hear her giggling and I wanted to giggle with her. Farmer John was coming towards us across the farmyard, shouting, 'Tractor ride in five minutes!' Then he spotted me, and his eyes filled with sorrow. He quickened his stride in our direction and threw his strong farmer's arms around me. He didn't say anything. He didn't need to. I knew big-hearted John felt my pain and my yearning for our little Madeleine ('with three Es') to come home.

On Thursday 20 September, Gerry and I travelled to London again to meet no fewer than five lawyers. Just five months earlier I would never have imagined even knowing that many lawyers, let alone needing to call upon their services. Gathered in the Kingsley Napley offices were Michael Caplan and Angus McBride, our UK criminal lawyers; Edward Smethurst, Brian Kennedy's lawyer; Carlos Pinto de Abreu, our Portuguese criminal lawyer; and Rogério Alves, another Portuguese lawyer.

Brian had suggested bringing in Rogério because he felt

we needed additional legal support in Portugal. Gerry and I spent some time on our own with him in another room, basically to get to know him a little, and vice versa, and to familiarize him with our perspective on matters. My first impressions were of a rather talkative man, but much of what Rogério said made a great deal of sense, even if the 'uncomfortable truths' he needed to spell out to us didn't make for easy listening. He asked about our relationship with Carlos and listened as we explained our concerns, which related mainly to Carlos's behaviour and attitude during the *arguido* interview period.

We rejoined the others an hour later, discussed our strategy, decided upon a plan and worked out who would be doing what. It was agreed that Rogério would join the legal team. He and Carlos knew each other well and were a good combination: Carlos was a details man while Rogério, who was president of the Portuguese Bar, had a high profile in Portugal and a good working relationship with the media. Between them, it was felt, we would have all the angles covered. Rogério would represent me in Portugal while Carlos continued to act for Gerry. We would petition the prosecutor, asking to be informed of the evidence against us. At the same time we would put forward our own catalogue of information, which would include my detailed account of our movements from May to September 2007, a record of all our trips in the hire car and Gerry's research into the reliability (or otherwise) of blood and cadaver dogs.

The meticulous record of events in my journals enabled us to account for every journey we made in the Renault Scenic, taking us to within a few kilometres of the much-publicized 'unexplained mystery mileage of the McCanns' hire car' which, of course, was not a mystery at all.

We would also supply a list of all the witnesses we believed should have been interviewed before we were made *arguidos*. It was an extensive list, but everyone on it was an obvious candidate. I'm sure the man or woman in the street would take it for granted that it was necessary, if not crucial, for the police to talk to all these people in the course of investigating any potential suspect, so it shouldn't have been beyond the wit of experienced officers to have done so. It was straightforward common sense, not rocket science.

Our GP I've already mentioned. Also included were the staff at the children's nursery at home, who spent a great deal of time with them and witnessed our interaction with them on a regular basis; Trisha and Sandy, Madeleine's aunt and uncle and godparents, who came out to Portugal on 5 May and lived with us for the next three months; Alan Pike, the trauma psychologist who had talked to us for hour upon hour; not forgetting Fiona, David, Russell, Jane, Matt, Rachael and Dianne, none of whom was ever re-interviewed before the police decided to declare us *arguidos*. And the list went on. Trisha and Sandy's testimony would, you'd have thought, been particularly relevant to the hypothesis that we had 'stored' Madeleine's body, since they were with us the whole time. But then, perhaps the PJ were never looking for evidence that supported our innocence.

We got to spend some nice time with Sean and Amelie this evening – baths together and Wallace and Gromit. *They are both so lovely, loving and delightful. It breaks my heart*

*thinking about what fun our three children would be having
together now. They had such a close and beautiful relationship.*

All the preparatory work was now being put into action.
Brian Kennedy arranged for Jane Tanner to see an FBI-
accredited forensic sketch artist to try to create an image of
the man she saw carrying a child on 3 May. A forensic team
had been sent over to Praia da Luz to carry out the full
examination of the Renault Scenic. And on 24 September, a
forensic scientist from Control Risks came to take samples of
hair from Sean, Amelie and myself.

On the night Madeleine was taken, you may remember,
Gerry and I had been very concerned that Sean and Amelie
had hardly moved in their cots, let alone woken up, despite
the commotion in the apartment. Since Madeleine was
snatched apparently without making a sound, we had always
suspected that all three children might have been sedated by
the abductor. We mentioned this to the police that night and
several more times in the following weeks, but no testing of
urine, blood or hair, which could have revealed the presence
of drugs, had ever been done. Apparently, hair grows at a rate
of approximately 1cm per month, so it was possible that hair
samples taken even four months later could provide us with
additional information. It was worth a shot, at least. I asked
for samples of my own hair to be taken as well simply
because I was fed up with the constant insinuations that I
took tranquillizers, sleeping pills or any medication, for that
matter.

The process seemed to take ages and we all lost loads of
hair. I couldn't believe they had to take so much. The

scientist cut chunks of it from Sean and Amelie's heads while they were sleeping. I cried as I heard the scissors in their baby-blond hair. I felt angry that the children had to go through this further insult. As for me, I looked as if I had alopecia. Though I cursed the abductor and the PJ, I had bigger things to worry about.

All the hair samples produced negative results. While this didn't totally exclude the possibility that the children had been sedated, especially given the time that had elapsed, it meant nobody else (including the PJ and the media) could prove otherwise. It also confirmed that I didn't 'abuse' sedative medication. It is sad that we had to go to such lengths to demonstrate this; sadder still that such tests weren't carried out at the time.

While Gerry and I laboured away, hour after hour, at our desks, the media onslaught continued unabated.

THE McCANNS ARE LYING
IF A BODY ISN'T FOUND, THE McCANNS WILL ESCAPE
BRITISH POLICE SAY MADELEINE DIED IN THE APARTMENT
NEW DNA LINKS TO KATE
FSS CONFIRMS PARENTS SEDATED THEIR CHILDREN
GERRY IS NOT MADELEINE'S BIOLOGICAL FATHER

By now you might think I'd have become immune to these headlines, but they still shocked me.

KATE'S ALCOHOL-FUELLED UNIVERSITY DAYS

OK, so maybe there was the odd one with a grain of truth in it, but they were few and far between.

Angus McBride paid a second round of visits to newspaper editors, this time with Clarence. Michael Caplan had written to the chief constable of Leicestershire police asking him to intervene. On 17 September, the chief constable wrote to newspapers and broadcasters urging restraint, to little effect. On 8 October he sent a further letter, again making it clear that much of the media coverage simply had no foundation and that rumour appeared to have taken precedence over due diligence.

It was the nights that were the worst. Not only did lying awake in the dark take me straight back to the most awful night of all, but my brain, finally free of the preoccupations of the day, would wander unbidden down black and terrifying avenues. I struggled constantly to think nice thoughts and drift off to sleep, but the demons had me in their grip and would torture me mercilessly with images too frightening and painful to share. Where is my Madeleine? Please, God, do something!

After Madeleine was taken from us, my sexual desire plummeted to zero. Our sex life is not something I would normally be inclined to share and yet it is such an integral part of most marriages that it doesn't feel right not to acknowledge this. I'm sure other couples who have been through traumatic experiences will have suffered similarly and perhaps it will reassure them to know that they are not alone. To those fortunate enough not to have encountered such heartache, I hope it gives an insight into just how deep the wounds go.

MADELEINE

Apart from our general state of shock and distress, and the fact that I couldn't concentrate on anything but Madeleine, there were two continuing reasons for this, I believe. The first was my inability to permit myself any pleasure, whether it was reading a book or making love with my husband. The second stemmed from the revulsion stirred up by my fear that Madeleine had suffered the worst fate we could imagine: falling into the hands of a paedophile. When she was first stolen, paedophiles were all we could think about, and it made us sick, ate away at us.

The idea of a monster like this touching my daughter, stroking her, defiling her perfect little body, just killed me, over and over again. It didn't make any difference that this might not be the explanation for Madeleine's abduction (and, please God, it isn't); the fact that it was a possibility was enough to prevent me from shutting it out of my mind. Tortured as I was by these nauseating images, it's probably not surprising that even the thought of sex repulsed me.

I would lie in bed, hating the person who had done this to us; the person who had taken away our little girl and terrified her; the person who had caused these additional problems for me and the man I loved. I *hated* him. I wanted to kill him. I wanted to inflict the maximum pain possible on him for heaping all this misery on my family. I was angry and bitter and I wanted it all to go away. I wanted my old life back.

I worried about Gerry and me. I worried that if I couldn't get our sex life back on track our whole relationship would break down. I know there is more to a relationship than sex, but it is still an important element. It was vital that we stayed

340

together and stayed strong for our family. Gerry was incredibly understanding and supportive. He never made me feel guilty, he never pushed me and he never got sulky. In fact, sometimes he would apologize to *me*. Invariably, he would put a big, reassuring arm around me and tell me that he loved me and not to worry.

I was determined not to be beaten by this, not simply to capitulate and accept it as just one of the unfortunate side-effects of this tragedy. Gerry and I talked about it a little, but mostly I analysed the problem privately in my head. I also discussed it with Alan Pike, who assured me that, like my ability to relax or enjoy a meal, it would gradually return and that I shouldn't fret about it too much. But I did. I even considered seeking specialist help. Deep down, though, I knew there were only two solutions: bringing Madeleine back or conquering my mental block. Since the first was not within my control, it was up to me to try to train my mind and my thought processes. So that is what I applied myself to doing.

In the small hours, any sleep we got was still often interrupted by the children. I welcomed their soothing presence. It didn't always make for the most comfortable night, however. Sometimes, by the time dawn came, it took me a moment to figure out who was where.

> *Seany arrived in the early hours of the morning and positioned himself towards the middle of our bed, with me and Gerry then squeezed together on one side. Amelie appeared several hours later by which time Sean had gone back to his own bed, although he did return later. I knew we should have got a Superking!*

Another morning I awoke to find myself sandwiched between Sean and Amelie with Gerry lying across the bottom of the bed. Cosy.

Every time I found one or both of the children in our bed in the morning, I'd feel an immediate pang of pain and guilt. For a few weeks around the end of 2006 and the beginning of 2007, Madeleine had gone through a phase of coming through to our room before morning. We'd generally been very disciplined about taking her straight back to her own bed. I'd helped her make a reward chart, still pinned on the kitchen wall today, on which we'd stuck a star for every night she stayed tucked up. When she'd earned enough stars she'd be allowed a special treat. (The PJ had seemed strangely interested in this chart when questioning me. Regardless of my explanation that it was about rewarding good behaviour, they'd insisted on referring to it as a 'punishment chart'.) How I longed now to be able to lift up the duvet and feel Madeleine climbing in next to me. She'd never have to go back to her room again.

On the whole my faith remained strong, aside from the occasional wobble of despair. I went to church to talk privately to God, and amid the hours of toil in the study I'd make brief forays upstairs to say a novena to this saint or that saint.

> *Dear God. Please help us to find Madeleine. Please let the person(s) who has her stay calm. Please let them be treating her well. Please give them a way out. Please strengthen my faith and trust in you. Stay with us Lord. Amen.*

On 25 September, we heard that a little blonde girl resembling Madeleine had been spotted with a group of Moroccan peasants. We received a photograph, taken by a Spanish tourist, in which the child was being carried on a woman's back. Although she did look like Madeleine, our first reaction was that she appeared to be too young. The picture was too grainy for us to be absolutely sure. Her hair was also parted on the wrong side of her head. But she did seem to stand out as possibly not belonging to this group. She was so fair and they were dark-haired and dark-skinned.

Needless to say, a contingent of the press pack had already jumped on planes to Morocco to try to track down 'Madeleine'. In the meantime, CEOP were using special IT techniques to improve the resolution of the photograph, and then facial-recognition software to try to establish whether or not the child could be Madeleine. Brian Kennedy called us later that evening to ask if we would like him to fly out to Morocco to find out for certain. We weren't sure if this was either necessary or wise, but at the same time, of course, we were desperate to know. So off Brian went in his plane to northern Morocco.

Once again, we tried to remain calm and detached. With our rational heads on, we were fairly sure this wasn't Madeleine, so it was pointless getting our hopes up. But it wasn't a high-quality photograph . . . And what if she hadn't grown that much because she hadn't had enough to eat, or for some other environmental reason? Her parting could easily have been changed. Couldn't it?

The following day we learned that the little girl was not Madeleine. In spite of her fair colouring, she was the daughter of the woman carrying her in the picture. It didn't seem to matter how good we thought we were at keeping our emotions in check, news like this always brought us crashing down.

On 2 October, the national director of the Polícia Judiciária, Alípio Ribeiro, removed from our case a detective named Gonçalo Amaral, the coordinator of the investigation into Madeleine's disappearance. Until then I'd barely heard of Sr Amaral. In the five months he held this job I never met him. Gerry did only once, very briefly. The reason for his removal, it was said, was that he had made controversial remarks about the involvement of the British authorities in the investigation. By the following summer, we would be hearing a lot more from the mystifying Sr Amaral.

Early that month Ribeiro also made a statement commenting on the continuing headlines in the press. He said that many were speculative or contained false inform-ation, adding that the police were still considering several other scenarios, not just the theory that Madeleine had been killed. Four months later, Ribeiro would remark in an inter-view that the PJ's decision to make us *arguidos* had been 'too hasty'.

Finally, we thought, someone in authority was showing common sense and decency. But it seems these sentiments were not shared by everyone in Portugal. By May 2008, Sr Ribeiro was no longer in his post.

19

ACTION ON THREE FRONTS

By October, with the battle to clear our names under way, we were able to concentrate properly on our top priority: finding Madeleine. Since the very beginning, various friends had proposed hiring private investigators. So far, beyond following up the odd piece of information outside Portugal, we had not gone down this road. Apart from the legal complications and the potential for interference with the official investigation, we had been reassured that, after a shaky start, the police were doing everything that could be done. Although we had been devastated by the slow response in the first twenty-four hours, and by the initial lack of communication with the police, once the investigation had got going, with the involvement of the British authorities and the cooperation of the UK police, our confidence in it had grown. The media attention also kept up the pressure on the authorities in both countries to do more.

Until the summer, we had believed that our best hope of Madeleine being found lay with the police. We needed to believe that. However, as the months rolled by, our faith in them had rapidly declined, hitting rock-bottom in August. Once we were declared *arguidos*, it became frighteningly clear to us that they were no longer looking for Madeleine. What they were looking for now, it seemed, was a conviction. Feeling more desperate for Madeleine now than at any time since that first night, we had no option but to launch our own investigation. But if it wasn't for all the help we have been given by Brian Kennedy, I'm not sure how, or even if, any search would have resumed. It doesn't bear thinking about.

We knew nothing about private investigators. As I've said, my only concept of private eyes came from freewheeling-detective-cracks-the-case-again shows on the telly, and I imagine the same went for most of the friends who'd suggested them. We pictured a smart, intuitive lone operator, scornful of authority, who somehow always manages to see what everyone else has missed and never fails to get his man.

Of course, the real world is very different. Not that I'm saying real-life private detectives are not smart and intuitive, but most of those we've come across operate within companies, ranging from large international firms to smaller 'in-house' teams, and most of their work is not quite as simple as it appears on the TV. A lot of it is conducted on behalf of corporate businesses rather than individuals, and probably involves more time on the phone or at the computer than jumping around tailing suspicious characters or physically searching for clues. Private investigators are constrained by many limitations. Unlike the police, they have no authority to question anyone who does not wish to speak to them, they are not legally allowed to search property without the owner's consent and they do not generally have the same access as the police to resources like criminal records or car registration databases.

Venturing into unfamiliar territory of any sort is never easy, and exploring the field of private investigation has been a total minefield for us. We were approached by many firms and individuals in several countries, all claiming to have the relevant expertise. Where do you start? How do you choose? Who do you trust?

Over the course of four years, we've employed several different investigation teams of various sizes and structures. While each of these teams has been working on the case we have continued to review our progress and explore new strategies and options. When we have taken on a new firm or person it is not necessarily because we have been dissatisfied with the work of the existing or previous team. It is simply that lines of inquiry can hit a brick wall, and it is difficult for investigators to maintain the same level of motivation over a long period if results are not forthcoming. Different people have different ideas and often someone with something extra to bring to the search will come along. When it seems the investigation has stalled or needs a fresh impetus, we have responded by changing or adding to the team to keep the search moving forward. It must be said, though, that the time and energy it takes to brief a new team is immense. Just bringing them up to speed is an exhausting and emotional process.

Our first investigators, the Spanish company Método 3, began working for us in October. With private investigations technically illegal in Portugal, we felt the closest we could get would be a firm from somewhere on the Iberian Peninsula, which would have the advantage of familiarity with local systems, culture and geography and the best network of contacts in the region. M3 also had links to the Spanish police, who, in turn, had good connections with the Portuguese police.

We assembled all the source material we could for the investigators, passing on my detailed chronology of events and the research we were compiling, making endless lists of potential witnesses – some of whom we knew the police had interviewed, many more we suspected they had not – and reported sightings of little girls who could have been Madeleine. As a result of the huge publicity the case had been given, the police and press had been overwhelmed by such reports from the outset. Sometimes 'Madeleine' has been seen in different countries, thousands of miles apart, on the same day. These tip-offs needed to be sifted and any credible information followed up.

We have no doubt that M3 made significant strides, but unfortunately, in mid-December, one of their senior investigators gave an overly optimistic interview to the media. He implied that the team were close to finding Madeleine and declared that he hoped she would be home by Christmas. Gerry and I did not pay much heed to these bullish assertions. While we believed they'd been made in an attempt to cast the search in a positive light, we knew that such public declarations would not be helpful. Credibility is so important. That glitch apart, M3 worked very hard for us and, just for the record, their fees were very low: most of the money they were paid was for verified expenses. Although we went on to employ new teams, we maintain good relations with M3 today. We had the sense that they genuinely cared about Madeleine's fate, something that, sadly, we have found we cannot take for granted.

We had one particularly bad experience with a man named Kevin Halligen (or Richard, as we knew him). Halligen was the CEO of a private-investigation firm called Oakley International which was hired by Madeleine's Fund for six months from the end of March 2008. Oakley's proposal and overall strategy were streets ahead of all the others we'd considered and the company came highly recommended. As the sums of money involved were pretty hefty, we agreed that our contract with them would be split into three phases with a break clause at the end of each phase. This gave us an opportunity to terminate the contract at any of these points if we wished to do so without incurring financial penalties. An independent consultant was also employed by the fund to liaise with Oakley and oversee the work they were doing.

The first and second phases of the contract ran fairly smoothly. Oakley had put in place systems to gather, collate, prioritize and follow up the information coming in as a result of appeals Gerry and I made around the first anniversary of Madeleine's abduction. There is little doubt that at that stage progress was being made.

During the third phase, however, we began to have concerns. Feedback appeared to be less forthcoming and contact with certain members of the Oakley team dropped off. At first we couldn't be sure whether this was a manifestation of the inevitable waning motivation I've mentioned or of a more troubling problem. Rumours about Halligen prompted us to make inquiries before we decided whether or not we should extend our contract with Oakley. To cut a long story short, we chose not to do so. The termination of the contract, in September 2008, was quite acrimonious, and unfortunately, that was not the end of it.

Several months later, one of the investigators sub-contracted by Oakley contacted us to demand payment for his services. We had already settled Oakley's bill for this work months before, but apparently the company had not paid him. He was not the only one. Over time several more unpaid subcontractors came to light. We were upset that, although a lot of hard work had been done on Madeleine's behalf, it seemed money provided by her fund might not ever have reached the people who had earned it.

In November 2009 we heard that Halligen had been arrest-ed on suspicion of fraud after a discrepancy in a hotel bill. At the time of writing, he is on remand in Belmarsh prison, fighting extradition to the USA in connection with money-laundering and wire-fraud charges, all of which he denies.

For the most part, though, our experiences with in-dependent investigators have been good. In October 2008, we set up a small team, spearheaded by a former police officer, over time adding a wider circle of strategy advisers and specialists to call upon as required. This tried and trusted system has enabled us to recruit the best-qualified people available to handle particular tasks as they arise, and we have made encouraging progress with it.

As we got our first investigation team up and running in the autumn of 2007, Gerry returned to work at Glenfield

Hospital on a part-time basis from November (full-time from January 2008), while I stayed at home with the children. Apart from the fact that no salaries had been coming in for four months, he had to go back for the sake of his own sanity. His driving role in our campaign was severely restricted by our *arguido* status and the obstacles it placed in our path. Gerry is passionate about his work, he needed to keep busy and focusing on different projects helped him to cope. If it is a generalization that men compartmentalize their lives, it's certainly true of Gerry. Almost every evening, after the kids are in bed, he is at his computer or on the phone meeting the demands of his other job: continuing the campaign to find Madeleine.

I'm sure Gerry's approach is healthier, but I reacted differently. With Madeleine constantly in my head, trying to return to my old life would have felt to me as if I were some-how pushing her to one side, and I simply couldn't do it. It has been essential that Madeleine, and the rest of my family, remain my priority and I wanted to be around more for Sean and Amelie than would have been possible had I returned to general practice. I wonder, too, if I'd actually be able to cope with it now. All GPs have a handful of patients who present with comparatively trivial problems. In view of what I've been through, and am going through still, I'd be concerned I wouldn't have quite the sympathetic ear I once possessed. And I'm sure some of my patients would undoubtedly find it awkward dealing with me, too.

On a practical level, there has been too much to do in any case, especially more recently. Although I have been blessed with plenty of willing helpers, even handling the mail is virtually a full-time job, and some projects, such as analysing the PJ files once they were released to us, have involved months of work.

We were dreading our first Christmas without Madeleine. As winter approached, the prospect of this usually joyous occasion only deepened the ever-present sense of loss. One morning in November, Amelie talked incessantly about her sister on the way to nursery. 'Madeleine's getting a big teddy bear for Christmas,' she was saying as we arrived. By this time, I was quite tearful. It always warms my heart to hear Sean and Amelie chatting about Madeleine but it was the mention of Christmas that tipped me over the edge. I had a few words and a few hugs with a couple of the girls who looked after the twins, then pulled myself together and got on with the rest of the day.

That night I headed to bed relatively early. It had been a tough day emotionally and I was very tired. Stupidly, I switched on the television to catch the news headlines and caught a review of the next morning's papers. Within seconds I was confronted by Madeleine's face on the front page of a tabloid beneath a headline screaming, 'SHE'S DEAD'.

I got little sleep after that. I thought I would never be able to stop crying. The pain was crippling.

Early in December, Amelie said to me, 'Mummy, Madeleine's coming.'

'When?' I asked.

'Santa's going to give her a big cuddle then bring her to Mummy.'

Above: the steps leading down from Apartment 5A to Rua Dr Francisco Gentil Martins.

Below: an aerial view of the Ocean Club Waterside Gardens, showing the Tapas restaurant (A) and our apartment (B).

I feel a strong bond with Praia da Luz – the place I last saw Madeleine. **Above**: the church of Nossa Senhora da Luz; **below**: the Rocha Negra, pictured early one morning on my mobile phone from 'my rocks' on the beach.

Clockwise, from left: praying at the shrine at Fátima. The lovely children of Rabat, Morocco, touched our hearts. Meeting the Pope: a very important day – for us and especially for Madeleine. Wherever she is, I know that God is with her.

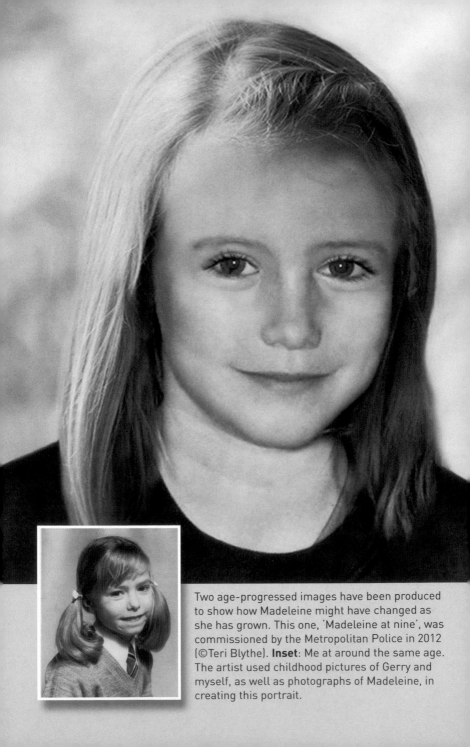

Two age-progressed images have been produced to show how Madeleine might have changed as she has grown. This one, 'Madeleine at nine', was commissioned by the Metropolitan Police in 2012 (©Teri Blythe). **Inset**: Me at around the same age. The artist used childhood pictures of Gerry and myself, as well as photographs of Madeleine, in creating this portrait.

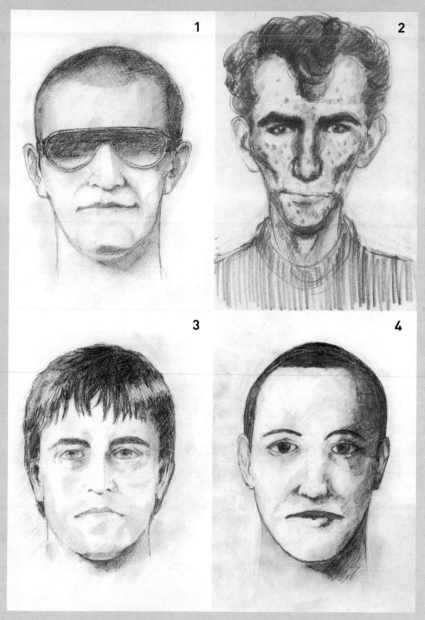

Several witnesses reported seeing men behaving suspiciously around the Ocean Club in the days leading up to Madeleine's abduction (full details are given in the **Key Sightings** section on page 370). The witnesses helped to produce images of these men, who have yet to be identified.

Artist's impressions of the man and child seen by Jane Tanner on the evening of 3 May 2007, around the time Madeleine was taken. This man was crossing the junction of Rua Dr Agostinho da Silva and Rua Dr Francisco Gentil Martins, which runs alongside apartment 5A. He has never been traced. Did you see him? Was it you, or someone you know?

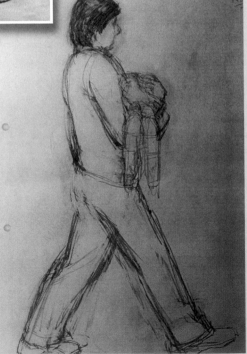

We couldn't have faced Christmas on our own. We spent it quietly at Anne and Michael's in Yorkshire with my mum and dad, and then went up to see Gerry's family in Scotland for a few days. In Glasgow I slept on an airbed with Amelie because Sean wanted a 'proper bed' – not the most comfortable of arrangements! 'Girls together,' said Amelie. 'Mummy, Amelie and Madeleine. I'll save this place here for Madeleine.'

We had hoped that the judicial secrecy restrictions would be lifted early in 2008, giving us access to the police files and with it the freedom to speak. It was not to be. The police asked for a three-month extension because of the 'unusual complexity' of the case. The president of the Portuguese Order of Lawyers, António Marinho Pinto, apparently took another view. He was later to be quoted as saying, 'There are strong reasons to fear that judicial secrecy is being used to conceal the fact that the police have gone down a blind alley and don't have a way out.'

On Tuesday 8 January – 250 days since Madeleine's abduction – there were more appalling headlines. 'IT WAS HER BLOOD IN PARENTS' HIRE CAR.' The emphasis was clearly designed to present this completely false assertion as incontrovertible fact. As we tried desperately to keep the public looking for our child, elements of the press, it seemed, were hell bent on telling the world not to bother, because she was definitely dead. This was our daughter they were writing about. How could these people be so heartless?

Happy New Year.

These terrible headlines never lost their power to cause us profound distress. The worst culprits were the *Daily Express* and, to a slightly lesser extent, the London *Evening Standard*. The previous year, after one of the outrageous fantasies claiming that we had tranquillized our children, we had got in touch with Adam Tudor at Carter-Ruck, and begun to explore the possibility of taking legal action. As we did not want to make enemies of the major media organizations, we decided to keep this as an absolute last resort. We had relied on them in the past to get our message out to the public and we knew we would need their assistance again in the future, but this was fast becoming the only option left to us.

Now, in the space of a couple of weeks in January, the *Express* published three completely untrue stories, which basically rehashed yet again coverage dating back to September 2007, when we had been made *arguidos*. It was the last straw. We had tried every avenue and felt if we didn't do something these fabrications, as well as discrediting our efforts to find our daughter, were going to follow us for the rest of our lives. We had a meeting with Adam Tudor, who was extremely helpful and went through the pros and cons of legal action in considerable detail. Adam and his partners agreed to take on the case on a no-win, no-fee basis and that certainly made our decision a lot easier. The thought of having to spend potentially hundreds of thousands of pounds to get justice would have been a major deterrent.

It took a couple of months of legal to-ing and fro-ing, but the Express Group finally conceded that their stories were untrue. They agreed to acknowledge this in the High Court, and on the front pages of both the *Express* and the *Daily Star*, stating that they had agreed to pay £550,000 into Madeleine's Fund to aid the continuing search.

Although this sum was much higher than we had anticipated and would have been ready to accept, we had been told
that if the case went to court we could expect substantially
more and, potentially, 'exemplary' damages – a departure
from the principle that the purpose of awarding damages is
to compensate the plaintiff rather than punish the
defendant. In other words, the Express Group could have
been additionally penalized not only for causing us harm,
but for doing so for purely commercial motives.

But for Gerry and me, the money was very much a
secondary matter (though, of course, hitting the Express
Group in the pocket would underline the seriousness of the
offence and serve as a warning to others to think twice before
running similar material). All we really wanted was for these
articles to stop, and for the Express Group to admit they
were not true. The corrosive effects of their stream of lies
(over a hundred articles were cited in our action) about both
the search for Madeleine and us were immeasurable, and we
would much rather none of it had ever been printed in the
first place.

With freedom of the press comes a moral responsibility to
behave with integrity. Publishing untruthful allegations
harms lives. Sometimes the harm is irreversible, regardless of
apologies and financial compensation. As a family, we only
barely managed to survive and I am sure that, without the
support of the general public, friends, family and those who
came directly to our aid, like Brian Kennedy, Edward
Smethurst, Richard Branson and Stephen Winyard, who
were prepared to stand up for us in our darkest hour, we
probably wouldn't have done.

When our action against the Express Group was con-cluded, we also issued a formal complaint against Associated Newspapers, and particularly the London *Evening Standard*, which at that stage they owned. After a rather protracted series of negotiations we came to an agreement involving financial compensation and a front-page apology in the *Standard*. We could probably have successfully sued all the national newspapers in the UK but we didn't want to spend time and energy on long wars of attrition like these. Besides, we had achieved our aim. The press were now well aware that we would take action if they continued to print these fictions about us and Madeleine, and as a result coverage in the UK did improve at last. With hindsight, we probably should have done this earlier, but by the time we finally did so, we were prepared to go the distance. It's just a shame we had to do it at all, and if the media had listened to us, to Angus, Justine, Clarence and to the chief constable of Leicestershire police, it could have been avoided.

In the wake of our libel action against the Express Group, the seven friends who were on holiday with us in Portugal also filed formal complaints against the company. They settled out of court, for a total of £375,000, which was also paid directly into Madeleine's Fund.

Robert Murat, too, had his problems with the media. He received £600,000 in damages and apologies from four newspaper groups, and, later, further substantial damages and another apology from Sky Television, for numerous false claims published about him.

Adam Tudor and his colleague Isabel Hudson continue to do a vast amount of work for us, without payment, most of it quietly, behind the scenes. They have given us invaluable advice, for example, in our attempts to deal with the widespread defamatory material circulating on the internet. We have taken action against one or two websites, but it has proved almost impossible to get this stuff removed from some of them, particularly those hosted in the USA. Friends flag up some of the worst offenders for us, but in the end it comes down to picking your battles. You could spend your whole life doing nothing but trying to shut down crank websites with little prospect of success.

That January, we also began our campaign for the introduction of coordinated child rescue alert systems (CRAs) within Europe. We knew to our cost that the response to child abductions can often be haphazard and disorganized and we'd seen on our European visits how widely procedures varied. Given the ease with which anyone – including abductors and child traffickers – could now move from country to country, there was an urgent need not only for properly functioning national systems, but for a cooperative policy that allowed for the launch of cross-border alerts when appropriate. A lot of groundwork had already been done to develop, improve and unify CRAs by the European Commission, with the help of Missing Children Europe and individual NGOs, but we hoped that our involvement, and the publicity it would bring, might help speed up the process.

It had always been part of our plan for the future of the Find Madeleine campaign to use our resources, and the attention focused on us, to try to save other children and their families from the same nightmare. As a result of the unprecedented publicity surrounding our case, Madeleine's image had become almost iconic, the face that represented all missing children. Her plight had brought the whole issue into the spotlight, greatly increasing public awareness. That was something positive in itself. We realized that while the appetite for news of her remained high, we should capitalize on the platform it gave us to help other missing and exploited children.

Until Madeleine was taken, I'd been aware of only a few child abduction and murder cases. Horrific though they were, they seemed such a rare occurrence, and of course, you never dream anything like this will happen to your family. As we learned more, and discovered the massive scale of the problem, we were appalled. Sickened and perplexed at first by how little I had known, I was only now beginning to realize that such ignorance was widespread. In general these crimes are so poorly publicized, probably because they are so low on the political agendas of too many countries, that public awareness, too, is low.

It is difficult to be precise about the number of children who go missing each year, primarily because there is no standardized method for collecting, recording and categorizing data within Europe, or even nationally. Some countries have no recording system at all. For every high-profile case like ours, there are many others that go unreported by the media.

In the UK alone, in 2009–10, more than 200,000 reports of missing children and teenagers were received by the police. This figure encompasses a wide range of cases, of course, including runaways and juveniles absconding from care homes (who make up the great majority of this number), as well as parental and family abductions, and the most serious but thankfully by far the smallest group: stranger abductions (or 'stereotypical kidnappings', as they are known in the US).

An average of more than 600 child abductions a year has been recorded since 2004–5 in England and Wales. The real figure, however, is likely to be much higher. A significant number of family abductions (which, according to several official sources, are, worryingly, on the increase) are not actually reported, and other cases may be omitted from the statistics – for example, those that do not meet the legal definition of child abduction. It is important to note, too, that abductions leading to more serious crimes, such as sexual abuse or homicide, will not be recorded as abductions but as the more serious crime. Not all attempted abductions will necessarily be recorded, either, depending on the procedures of various police forces, which can also distort the true picture.

What is not in doubt is that the available statistics underestimate the scale of the problem. Child abductions and attempted abductions are not isolated incidents and occur in *every* country. Authorities and governments who suggest otherwise are likely to be hiding the truth.

Having your child stolen is the most terrible ordeal imaginable. As a parent, you need to know that all that can be done is being done – and as quickly and thoroughly as possible. The gold standard in child rescue alert systems is the USA's AMBER Alert, an acronym for America's Missing:

Broadcast Emergency Response and named for Amber Hagerman, a nine-year-old girl abducted, raped and murdered in Texas in 1996.

Gerry had been hugely impressed by what he had learned about the AMBER Alert system on his visit to the States the previous year. It is a voluntary partnership between law-enforcement agencies, broadcasters, transport companies and the wireless industry to activate an urgent bulletin in the gravest child-abduction cases. It is important that it is reserved for the most serious situations (defined by a set of criteria), to avoid the airwaves being constantly inundated by false alarms that might dilute the attention and response of the public. The goal of an AMBER Alert is to instantly galvanize the assistance of the entire community. Its raison d'être is simple: time is the enemy in the search for an abducted child. It was clear to Gerry and me that if such a procedure had been in use in Portugal, Madeleine might have been swiftly tracked down. It breaks our hearts just thinking about it.

In 2001, the NCMEC launched a campaign to promote the programme, originally a local initiative in Texas, across the country. An AMBER Alert training kit, video and manual for law-enforcement agencies and broadcasters were produced and distributed nationwide. At the time there were only twenty-seven AMBER systems in operation; now there are over 120, and it continues to grow and evolve. As well as dramatically improving the speed and success rate of the recovery of abducted children – by January 2012, 554 as a direct result of an AMBER Alert activation – it has been found to deter some abductors, who may release a child on hearing of an AMBER Alert bulletin.

In 2003 the USA established a nationwide AMBER Alert system, which is coordinated by the assistant attorney general. Key to the success of this programme is that it is driven by the government. Countries in Europe need similar leadership.

I think it would be fair to say that Europe is at least twenty years behind the US in dealing with this issue. At the time of Madeleine's abduction only two of the twenty-seven countries in the European Union had a national child rescue alert system in place: France and Belgium. A scheme in Greece was launched soon afterwards. In Britain, Sussex had been the first police force to introduce such a programme, in 2002, followed by Surrey and Hampshire, and by 2005 every force in England and Wales operated a CRA. However, they were rarely, if ever, used and were not 'joined up' across the country. National coordination of CRAs is essential, and for this reason it is vital that the implementation of these systems is spearheaded by government.

In February 2008 Gerry and I travelled to Brussels to meet the team at Missing Children Europe, the umbrella organization for twenty-one NGOs in fifteen EU states, each battling child abduction and sexual exploitation in their own country. I use the word 'team' loosely: we were taken aback to discover that MCE then consisted of just two and a half staff. I asked Delphine Moralis, the deputy secretary general, why there seemed to be such resistance in European countries to developing CRAs. She put it down to a lack of understanding about what these involve and how they work. Stressing the importance of cross-border alerts, she cited a recent case of a child abducted in northern France. The French child rescue alert, the Alerte Enlèvement, was launched, but the weakness here was that while people hundreds of miles away in the south of the country received the alert, absurdly, the Belgians, less than an hour away from where the abduction had occurred, knew nothing about it.

Although it was an informative day, we left feeling very demoralized. It was obvious that there was little movement within Europe in terms of protecting children from abduction and exploitation, and what was happening was happening painfully slowly because of the bureaucracy involved. There also seemed to be a sense of resignation about all this: 'Yes, it's frustrating, but what can we do?' I felt utterly exasperated.

Why aren't all EU countries rushing to develop CRAs? I kept asking myself. Why aren't governments financing such projects? Tackling child abduction and sexual crimes against children seemed very far down their action lists. Was their thinking that it would be wisest to keep the problem quiet so as not to panic the population? That people need to believe we are a modern society and our countries are safe? That children don't vote? That counter-terrorism measures and fighting gang crime bring greater plaudits? Lack of financial incentive? Or simply that missing children are just that: missing. Out of sight and out of mind.

On our return, we enlisted the help of one of the UK's top human-rights lawyers, Geoffrey Robertson, QC. He kindly produced a written declaration we could take to the European Parliament to try to push to the top of the political agenda the need for a unified child rescue alert across the continent.

In March, Gerry and I watched a documentary about Caroline Dickinson, a thirteen-year-old British girl who was sexually assaulted and murdered in her bed in a youth hostel dormitory on a school trip to France in 1996. The perpetrator of this appalling crime, Francisco Javier Arce Montes, was finally caught, years later, thanks to an observant US immigration official. This itinerant sexual deviant had been assaulting young girls all over Europe for twenty years before killing Caroline. Despite having been convicted and jailed several times, on his release Montes was able to carry on committing similar crimes and evading capture simply by moving from region to region and from one country to another. If ever there was an argument for a European sex offenders register (or even a national one in those states that don't have it), surely this is it.

1 March

Unbelievable! I feel so angry with Europe and this so called European 'Union'! We need to start demanding. We need information: everyone who was in Praia da Luz for a start. All DNA, especially unidentified DNA, and subsequent testing of people in the area. We need information regarding similar offences. How we go about it, I don't know but it's time to start brain-storming again.

I was struck by how common it is for such crimes to be repeated over and over again by the same people. If Madeleine's abductor was a sex offender or a child trafficker, for example, the chances are that he would have offended before. I cast my mind back to what the British consul had told me in the police station in Portimão that first day about the reports there had been of intruders getting into bed with children. I needed to know more about this.

I got in touch with the retired British consul for the Algarve. He told me that he used to have regular monthly meetings with British tour operators along the coast in Albufeira, at which crime was invariably one of the topics covered. At one of these meetings in August 2006 he had been informed by the tour operators of the spate of incidents I'd heard about the day after Madeleine was taken, in which an intruder had got into holiday apartments at night, climbed into children's beds and subjected them to various forms and degrees of molestation. It seemed the attacker would often lock the door to the parents' bedroom before assaulting the child. In one case, the paedophile had put on some of the father's aftershave in an attempt to soothe or deceive the child.

It was believed that this offender (or offenders) watched for patterns and routines in a family's behaviour, established 'weaknesses' in the security of their apartment and determined in advance where parents and children slept. Cold shivers ran down my spine as it hit home that this might have applied to us. The British tour operators had been keen for this information to remain confidential (and you don't have to be a genius to work out why that might be). I pressed the former British consul on what happened afterwards. Had there been an investigation? Had anybody been convicted? He wasn't sure but thought that an immigrant construction worker had been arrested and released pending trial, which was likely to take place some years down the line. Unbelievable.

In spite of some of the terrible discoveries I was making as I learned more of the stories and statistics relating to missing and exploited children, it wasn't all bad news. Gradually, my outlook was growing more positive and I was beginning to get past my early certainty that Madeleine must have been taken by a paedophile and murdered. I was coming to realize that didn't have to be the answer. Meeting Ernie Allen and the people at NCMEC played a big part in helping me along this road.

Gerry and I flew to Washington, DC to visit NCMEC at the end of March. Ever since his first trip there, Gerry had been keen for me to go, too, and see for myself the work they were doing. It didn't take me long to understand why. Ernie's support was not only encouraging, it was based on solid facts and figures. In the States, research shows that around 56 per cent of children abducted by strangers are recovered alive. 'Don't let people tell you that there is no hope,' he said. 'There are a host of scenarios under which your child could be alive. You have to keep battling for her.' We felt even more convinced that Madeleine was out there somewhere and, if such a thing were possible, our determination to find her was even greater.

Everybody at the centre was fantastic: warm, helpful and upbeat. The American can-do approach to life ('Let's focus on solutions, not problems') makes anything seem possible, or at least, absolutely worth trying. Such optimism and energy go a long way towards motivating people. They certainly motivated Gerry and me. The obstacles to the implementation of an AMBER Alert-type scheme across Europe suddenly seemed more surmountable than they had in recent weeks, the future brighter.

The following day we were able to see Jeff Sedgwick, then assistant attorney general and national AMBER Alert co-ordinator. While in Washington we were also fortunate to have the opportunity to meet Ed Smart, the father of Elizabeth Smart, who was abducted from her bedroom in Salt Lake City in the early hours of 5 June 2002, aged fourteen. She was found alive nine months later, less than twenty miles from her home, with her abductors. Ed was lovely. We talked about the role and success of AMBER Alert and the need for a similar system in Europe. He emphasized how important it was to keep Madeleine's face in the public consciousness. Later we talked about Elizabeth and the difficulties the family had faced amid the joy of their reunion. It was a very emotional morning.

Just over a year after chatting to her dad, we got to meet Elizabeth herself. She had been in London and came up to Rothley to spend a Saturday afternoon with the four of us. When I went to meet her at the railway station I was excited but a little nervous, too. What would she be like? What would we talk about? I wasn't even sure I'd recognize her: the only pictures I'd seen were of a younger Elizabeth. I needn't have worried. I spotted her straight away and found her warm, kind, intelligent and humorous. Over lunch we talked about many things, including her life now and the forth-coming trial of her abductors. Sean and Amelie even persuaded her to join them for a painting session. What perhaps stood out most to us was how amazingly well-adjusted Elizabeth is. A real survivor, body and soul. I hope with all my heart that the same is true of our Madeleine.

On 10 April 2008 we went back to Brussels, this time to the European Parliament, to present our declaration to the MEPs and petition them to help with the establishment of a coordinated CRA. For the declaration to be formally adopted, over 50 per cent of the 785 MEPs would need to sign it. The media presence at the press conference that followed was impressive. We were told there hadn't been such a turn-out since Prince Charles and the Dalai Lama had appeared at the parliament. It was a good sign, we thought, for the future of children all over Europe.

Our day, though, was to finish with a nasty twist. You'll recall that, back in October, we had supplied the Portuguese public prosecutor with a list of people from whom we felt statements should have been taken. In response the Portuguese police had decided to come to Leicester to be present while the British police interviewed Fiona, Dave, Russ, Jane, Matt, Rachael and Dianne, as well as many other individuals whose testimony had never been sought. The questions to be asked were those Gerry and I had suggested to the prosecutor (obvious and pertinent ones, I hasten to add), with a few additions from the PJ.

It just so happened that the PJ's trip to the UK coincided with our visit to Brussels. While we were finishing lunch, Clarence had a phone call from a Spanish journalist who told him that he'd been given what appeared to be witness statements made by Gerry and me to the Portuguese police.

The part of my statement in which he was interested was Madeleine's comment to us on the morning of the day she disappeared: 'Why didn't you come when Sean and I cried last night?' I don't think I need to remind anyone how I have been tortured by this question since the moment Madeleine was taken from us. My reason for having shared it with the police was plain: it was potentially highly significant.

As Clarence relayed his conversation with the journalist, I could feel my anger and frustration building. Not again! How many of these leaks would we have to bear before this whole nightmare was over? Needless to say, before long Clarence was besieged by calls from the media, all of them asking about this 'breaking story'. We could see what was going to happen. The news of our efforts in Brussels would be spiked and replaced by 'MADELEINE LEFT ALONE TO CRY' or whatever attention-grabbing headline took the fancy of the sub-editors.

I don't remember many occasions when I've been as angry as I was that day. The Portuguese police – both those currently and previously involved in the inquiry – had had our statements for eleven and a half months. How had this information come to be released – completely illegally, I might add, at the risk of sounding like a cracked record – today of all days, when Gerry and I were in Brussels trying to do something positive for child protection? The effect it would have was obvious: it would discredit Gerry and me and detract from what we were trying to achieve. We were gutted.

If you think I'm being paranoid, think on this. In a meeting seven weeks after Madeleine was taken, Guilhermino

Encarnação had tried to reassure us that the PJ were not trying to portray us in a negative light. 'If we really wanted to do that,' he said, 'we'd release the comment Madeleine made to you on the day she disappeared.' Bingo.

As we'd feared, the day's McCann story changed and the media ran with the leaks from our statements.

We were determined not to let our frustration at this injustice get to us. On our return from Brussels, we started to lobby all of the 785 MEPs, urging them to sign the declaration. Just adding your name to a bit of paper sounds so easy, but it does require the signatory to make the time and effort to attend the official signing in person. We are all afflicted by apathy at times, and that goes for politicians too – maybe even more than for the rest of us. And so we pushed – along with friends, family, supporters, the charity Missing People, Missing Children Europe, Catherine Meyer and the five MEPs who had sponsored our declaration – making the journey to the European Parliament in Strasbourg that June to give the campaign, and the MEPs, one final nudge. By September we'd achieved our goal. We had 418 MEPs' names on our declaration and it was formally adopted as a resolution by the European Parliament.

We were relieved and delighted. We knew that this was no more than one small step in achieving our aim, but it had been a shot in the arm of the frustratingly slow bureaucratic process and brought child abduction to the forefront of the minds of those who were actually able to do something about it. Let's hope it stays there.

20

THE GOOD, THE BAD AND
THE MAD

At 1am on Wednesday, 27 February 2008, Gerry and I were woken suddenly from our sleep. The room appeared to be shaking and a photograph of Madeleine toppled over on my chest of drawers. We were terrified. Our immediate thought was that somebody was trying to kill us. Maybe a bomb had gone off, or perhaps a gang was trying to break into our house. Gerry got out of bed and went to check on Sean and Amelie before having a good look around, inside and out. I prayed for our safety.

With the occasional death threat turning up in our morning mail, it is perhaps not surprising that our first instinct was to think we were being attacked. When we began to calm down, we realized that in all probability it had been an earth tremor. I started to cry as we hugged each other, fear and then relief giving way to a deep sadness at what our life had become.

As we waited for the Portuguese judicial procedure to run its course, we felt completely out on a limb. Since August, when the PJ had begun to turn against us, we had been very disappointed with the attitude of the British authorities. Contact with us reduced to a trickle and little, if any information was shared with us. After we were made *arguidos* the situation deteriorated further. The UK police would argue that their hands were tied: the Portuguese might have perceived any 'interference' as an attempt to undermine their primacy in the investigation, which would have had implications not only for the current inquiry but also for any future international cooperation. We were aware of the frustrating constraints of this delicate relationship, but to us, it just felt like a betrayal.

The most difficult thing for us has been that we know the British police considered aspects of the investigation to be substandard and we honestly don't think they believed we were involved in Madeleine's disappearance. Comments made to us privately by several officers (including the most senior ones) confirmed this, but did nothing to prevent us from feeling we'd been hung out to dry when radio silence was maintained in public.

It is exasperating, too, that while we know the UK police are well aware of the selective leaks to the media, and what they seem designed to achieve, they still insist they have a cooperative relationship with the PJ. These leaks have included confidential statements taken by officers in Britain and supplied to the Portuguese police – and in some cases, the breaching of that confidence has caused immense damage to people other than ourselves.

It all makes this 'cooperation' look very one-sided. By declining to speak out about this kind of behaviour, which wouldn't be tolerated in our country, they are conveying the impression of a tacit acceptance of it, even agreement with it.

In the spring of 2008 – almost a year after Madeleine was last seen – the PJ decided they wanted to conduct a re-enactment in Praia da Luz of the night of 3 May 2007. The participants required were Gerry, me, Fiona, Dave, Jane, Russ, Rachael, Matt, Dianne and Jes Wilkins, to whom Gerry chatted in the street that night just after his last glimpse of Madeleine. They weren't interested in using actors or stand-ins. So either everyone agreed or the reconstruction wouldn't go ahead.

Our understanding was that as *arguidos*, Gerry and I were obliged to attend. The other witnesses received reasonably friendly emails from the PJ, via the British police, inviting them to take part. They were a bit baffled and replied requesting more details about the purpose of this belated re-enactment. It seemed it would not be filmed, or at any rate, not for information-gathering through public broadcast. Our friends had watched, with increasing horror, what had happened to us. If they were suspicious that the PJ might be trying to use them to somehow strengthen a flimsy case against us, or even to implicate one of them, it would be understandable. There were worries, too, about the likeli-hood of a media furore blowing up around the whole thing, especially as the proposed dates had already been leaked to the newspapers. The biggest concern, though, for all the witnesses approached, was how a re-enactment of the kind the PJ were proposing could actually help to find Madeleine. This question remained unanswered.

At that point the tone of the correspondence grew more brusque and what had seemed to be a request began to sound more like a summons. Some people decided they wanted to take legal advice before agreeing to anything. In the end there was no quorum and the plan was abandoned.

Meanwhile, the distressing landmarks kept coming. In May we faced the unthinkable: the first anniversary of Madeleine's abduction. In the preceding days we gave a plethora of media interviews, and on 30 April an ITV documentary in which we participated was screened. Our aim was to relaunch the search for our daughter by appealing to the public directly for as much information as possible about her disappearance, including reports that had already been made to the authorities. As the UK police were simply passing on all leads they received to the PJ without sharing anything with us or our independent investigators – which, sadly, remains the case today – there were huge gaps in the puzzle we were desperate to fill. A dedicated phone line had been set up for this purpose, which people could call anonymously and confidentially.

As for the day itself, the prospect was so awful we didn't know what we would want to do. My inclination was just to stay quietly in the house with Gerry, Sean and Amelie. Gerry, on the other hand, felt the need to be with other people. Johnny, Trish, Sandy and Michael were going to represent us in Praia da Luz at a service of hope for Madeleine at Nossa Senhora da Luz. At home there was to be a service in Rothley at the Parish Church of St Mary and St John, and a Mass at Our Lady of the Annunciation in Liverpool, where Gerry and I were married. In the end we attended both. Afterwards I was glad we did. It was a day for private anguish but probably not one on which we should have been on our own.

We asked all those who wished to remember Madeleine, and missing children everywhere, to light a candle and say a prayer at 9.15pm. All over Britain and beyond candles and lanterns were lit and torches shone heavenwards. Everton FC illuminated the night sky with their floodlights and Chinese lanterns were released in Rothley. The Archbishop of York, Dr John Sentamu, wrote a special prayer for Madeleine and urged everyone to redouble their efforts to pray for her safe return.

9 May

Sean and Amelie have been a huge source of comfort to me. I have no idea how I could carry on if they weren't here. How parents who have lost an only child continue, I do not know. Seany is a big soft 'Mummy's boy' which is nice. He is very gentle and generally just lovely. Amelie is a real character but so sensitive and 'in tune' . . . She often says how much she likes you, Madeleine, 'my sister', and what she's going to give you of hers when you're back. I heard her saying a prayer for you today, too.

Monday, 12 May 2008 was Madeleine's fifth birthday. If I'd known on her fourth birthday that she wouldn't be back with us for this one, either, I'm sure I'd have gone under. There is something to be said for living one day at a time. As we've continued to do since, we had a tea party at home, with balloons, cake, cards and presents, attended by family and friends and Madeleine's best buddy, Sofia, whose birthday she shares. The presents go into Madeleine's room to await her return. Her pink bedroom remains exactly as it was when she left it, but it's a lot busier now. There are gifts people have sent – from teddy bears to rosary beads – and photographs and pictures Sean and Amelie have drawn for her pinned on the walls. She also has a keepsake box in which the twins leave little things for her: the last sweet in their packet, a new drawing, sometimes just a leaf that has taken their fancy! Everyone sits in there from time to time to feel close to her. The children sometimes borrow toys to play with for a while but they always return them for Madeleine.

The month of May, as well as Christmastime, always sees a surge of mail. There were periods in the first year when we had to go to the post office day after day to collect several crates of letters. The volume we have received over the past four years is absolutely staggering – and we still get a bundle almost every day. Thank God for the friends and relatives who help us with it. We sort the post into boxes labelled 'Information/for follow-up', 'Well-wishers', 'Psychics/Dowsers/Visions', 'Nasty' and 'Nutty'. The 'Well-wishers' box is always by far the fullest, I'm glad to say. The 'Nasty' pile has never been huge, and it is rare nowadays for that box to be needed. The nonsensical letters destined for the 'Nutty' box, though, have arrived fairly consistently.

We have seen the best and the worst of mankind in our postbag as well as in our lives in general. Although we have experienced behaviour and attitudes so offensive and cruel that we would never have believed they existed, the goodness that lies within the vast majority of people has shone through it all.

The swell of solidarity from the general public in the immediate aftermath of Madeleine's abduction was beyond anything that we could have ever imagined. Back in the UK, our parents, too, were kept afloat by a big cushion of love and support. I believe it saved us all from the abyss. When Gerry and I were made *arguidos* and castigated daily in the media, many people, not surprisingly, didn't know what to think. A section of public opinion, especially in Portugal, certainly turned against us, though outside Portugal this contingent was not as big as the media suggested. We continued to receive hundreds of letters every week, most of them reassuring, and plenty of them criticizing the press and expressing their abhorrence of the conduct of the authorities towards us. So although many doors had been slammed in our faces, we never felt we were entirely on our own.

From children we've had prayers they've composed themselves or pictures they've drawn for Madeleine. We've had handwritten letters from people in their eighties and nineties which have touched us deeply. I feel honoured that these elderly people, with their wisdom and long experience of the vagaries of life, have taken the time to share their thoughts and good wishes with us. Mums have written, dads have written, people from all walks of life from all around the world. Before our lives changed in the way they did, I don't think I'd ever considered writing to somebody I didn't know in their hour of need. Having discovered how uplifting the encouraging words of a stranger can be, I have done this myself now on several occasions.

In the earliest days people sent or brought teddy bears to Rothley, which friends tied in their hundreds to the railings round the war memorial in the middle of the village. They stayed there for weeks and weeks, in the sun, wind and rain, all waiting for Madeleine to return. As autumn faded and still she wasn't home, my aunt removed them and parents from Bishop Ellis and Rothley primary schools kindly took them home and washed and dried them. The regional director of the charity Samaritan's Purse/Operation Christmas Child then arranged for the toys to be taken over to orphans in Belarus in time for Christmas. We were sent a little stack of photographs of these gorgeous children receiving Madeleine's bears. The joy on their faces at having a single teddy of their own brought us to tears.

Unbeknown to us at the time, shortly after Madeleine went missing, a group called Helping to Find Madeleine was formed, made up primarily of working mums (and a few dads) from around the world who badly wanted to help. I was completely bowled over when I heard about everything they were doing for our campaign. Such commitment and effort from complete strangers takes the breath away. And yet there have been so many people like this, supporters who print and distribute posters, organize cake sales to raise money for the fund, produce handmade books full of lovely messages and prayers and send the most thoughtful gifts for Madeleine.

We've had people put money for the fund in our hands on trains, in car parks and in the supermarket; cabbies who tell us to donate our fare. Such warmth and compassion is another trigger for tears. Amelie and Sean began to learn about 'happy tears' at a very early stage of their lives and they look a little less puzzled these days when faced with a mother who is smiling and crying at the same time. 'Are they happy tears, Mummy?' they ask anxiously.

'Yes, sweetheart.'

'Oh, that's OK, then.'

Gestures of solidarity never fail to lift our spirits and our hearts. Take the lorry driver who recognized us in a traffic jam on the M6 one day, pulled up alongside us, tooted his horn, showed us his Madeleine wristband through the window and gave us a fingers-crossed sign. He probably didn't have the first idea how much that meant to us.

This grass-roots support firmly underpins the higher-profile help we have been so fortunate to receive from those in a position to bring funds and influence to our search for Madeleine. We cannot begin to express our thanks to the wealthy and successful people who have come to our aid and showed the courage to stand by us when many others ran a mile. Just because someone has the wherewithal to help financially or publicize our cause, it doesn't mean they are obliged to do so, and they could very easily have chosen not to. We know, for example, that friends and business associates of Brian Kennedy tried to discourage him from getting involved with us, 'just in case', but neither his generosity and passion nor his faith and trust in us have ever faltered.

The involvement of some of our well-known backers has been criticized – 'Why is one child receiving all this attention and support when there are so many others needing help?' Why? Well, these people are human beings and their hearts have been touched. Most of them are parents or grand-parents themselves, they care about children and they have been shocked by how Gerry and I have been treated.

We are just immensely grateful for any assistance we

receive, no matter who gives it, no matter what it entails, no matter how big or how small. It all helps us. It all helps Madeleine.

So for every baddy there are a thousand goodies; probably many more. And then there are those it is impossible to be sure about – the folk whose correspondence goes into the 'Nutty' box. We must assume that most of these letters, though not necessarily all of them, are sent by people suffering from mental illness, and I don't want to make light of their problems. Indeed, it is concerning, if our mail is anything to go by, how many vulnerable individuals there seem to be out there with psychiatric conditions that remain either undiagnosed or inadequately treated.

Mental illness is a difficult thing to understand. It's not like a broken leg or blocked artery, where the condition and solution are obvious. Gerry and I have a little personal and professional experience of it, and during the six months I worked in psychiatry I found it heartbreaking as well as quite fascinating. To see someone you know as a warm, interesting and intelligent person when well and stable admitted to the ward in an uninhibited, distant and dishevelled state is very upsetting, and I can only begin to imagine how difficult it must be for partners, families and, of course, for the patients themselves, who must be so frightened and frustrated.

Over the last five years we have been contacted by various people evidently afflicted by conditions such as schizophrenia and bipolar disease (manic depression). Some of them appear to have become fixated on Madeleine and her plight. Paranoid delusions, delusions of 'reference' (when random events convey a special meaning to the sufferer) and 'racing thoughts' (where the mind uncontrollably brings up random thoughts and switches between them rapidly, whether or not they are related to each other) have come into play. All of these symptoms can be extremely sad, disabling and potentially dangerous for the person experiencing them.

Within days of Madeleine's disappearance, several people with major psychiatric problems made their way over to Praia da Luz and somehow managed to get to see Gerry and me. In spite of the state we were in, we found it hard to ignore anybody who was trying to help, even if what they were telling us was complete nonsense. Some of them were very persistent: they would track us down again and again, wielding their piles of papers full of totally illogical 'facts', figures and symbols. It was draining and at times a little scary.

On our return to the UK we had a number of such callers turn up on our doorstep, along with assorted psychics and visionaries. Sometimes I would open the door and immediately wish I hadn't: the behaviour of psychiatric patients can be unpredictable and with Sean and Amelie following me every time I answered the doorbell I felt very vulnerable and anxious. One day Gerry, in what I can only assume was a moment of weakness, let the self-appointed 'Lord's Helper' into the house. He was a tall, elderly gentleman sporting a wooden crucifix the size of Kansas around his neck. I stared at Gerry in disbelief and soon decided it would be wise to take Sean and Amelie out to the park. Thankfully, the Lord's Helper proved to be totally harmless, even if he was not on the same planet as us that day.

Gerry and I were, I suppose, fortunate to have been surrounded all our lives by good and loving people whose outlook on life and respect for others was similar to our own. But maybe this background only magnified our shock when we were first faced with the small but vociferous group who wished us ill. We had never come across people like this before and it is perhaps the fact that they are so rare that amplifies their voices. But their words and actions are generally less comprehensible than those of the psychiatric cases.

When criticism surfaced shortly after Madeleine was taken it was hard to bear. Nobody likes to be criticized, but this was kicking us when we were down. Then the criticism began to turn nasty. We received letters spitting venom like 'Your daughter will be getting tortured and it's all because of you,' or 'Your daughter's six feet under. Shame on you.' And those were the restrained ones. Other letter-writers took a warped pleasure, it seemed, in going into lurid detail which I couldn't bring myself to repeat here about what might have happened to Madeleine 'because of you'. Having to cope with this on top of our raw pain almost pushed us over the edge. We simply couldn't understand why anyone would want to inflict more agony on us. These people were actually taking the trouble to sit down and write this filth, to spend money on a stamp and take their poison-pen letters to the postbox. Did this make them feel better? Needless to say, after Gerry and I were declared *arguidos* the abuse escalated. We had mail delivered to our house addressed

'Child Killer Kate McCann' and 'The Lying Bastards'.

The internet has provided individuals like this with a largely unregulated opportunity to set up websites and forums and blogs where they can share their bile and hate with other faceless, anonymous lowlife, all locked away in their bedrooms talking to each other online. In the early days this upset me tremendously, but gradually I grew a protective shell. I learned to ignore it and then to pity these people. To have so little compassion or understanding and so much malice in your heart must surely make you one hell of an unhappy soul. And the capacity to devote so much time to a hate campaign (for some it seems to be practically a full-time occupation) speaks of an empty and friendless life. Thankfully, these sad specimens are not as numerous as they might appear to be. Many of them post messages on websites under a host of different names in an attempt to make the 'anti-McCann lobby' look greater than it is.

As well as those who prefer to hide behind computer screens there are the publicity-seekers, like one group set up by a man who has had the gall to use our daughter's name in the title of his nasty little organization. He and his cohorts prey on vulnerable families who have experienced tragedy. We are not the first to be targeted and, sadly, we probably won't be the last.

In practice, this bunch have been more of a nuisance than anything else. The only time their activities have seriously distressed me was when they leafleted our village just before Sean and Amelie were due to start primary school. Early that evening a local lady knocked on our door, quite upset. She handed me the offensive pamphlet that had been pushed through her letterbox. Apparently, this had been delivered to all the houses in Rothley except ours and handed out in the village during the day. My visitor told me she was disgusted by it. She hadn't wanted to worry me by bringing it round, but she 'couldn't bear the injustice'.

This incident grieved me more than I would have expected. Up to that point, this man's activities had always been confined to the internet and therefore, presumably, to like-minded individuals. Now he was spreading them in the community and, worse still, in *our* community. I knew most of the villagers were behind us, but there was always the possibility that a few people might be influenced and I feared that any unpleasant gossip might poison the atmosphere at the twins' new school and create problems for them at this crucial time. How *could* someone do this to two four-year-olds?

I did log a complaint with the Leicestershire police but, as seems to be the case with so many of these things, there was apparently little they could do.

So we took legal action against him, as a result of which he undertook not to repeat his allegations and was obliged to pay the court fee of £400. It hasn't made a great deal of difference. He is still going around insinuating that we were involved in Madeleine's disappearance, only now he is just being slightly more careful about how he says it.

Others have caused us distress, misdirected our investigation and wasted our time and funds by falsely claiming to know where Madeleine is. Although we have trained ourselves not to get our hopes up, there will always be that tiny voice in your head saying, 'Maybe this time . . .' But these days, when this 'information' amounts to nothing or is exposed as a hoax or extortion attempt, the emotional swings and the final crash are less severe than they used to be.

Hoaxes of one kind or another have run into the hundreds, probably thousands now. Some of these people are just after publicity; others have sought money. Although by and large the police are adept at dealing with this kind of crime, it still hinders our search. In deciding whether to promote the reward on offer for Madeleine's safe return, we have always had to weigh the inherent risk of attracting greedy criminals against the possibility of luring out of the woodwork somebody who really knows something. We now take the view that anyone with genuine information will be aware of the reward. If they want it, I'm sure they'll find a way of getting in touch.

It has been far more upsetting and damaging, frankly, to find ourselves let down by people in positions of trust, the very people who ought to be acting in Madeleine's best interests. Unfortunately, there have been a few of them. Another revelation that appalled us was the existence of individuals whose lives seem to be governed by how they can turn any situation to their own advantage. If their personal agenda is not their prime focus, it is never far behind. They might even be helping, or at least seeming to help, but all the time they are calculating what's in it for them. There are journalists and 'criminologists' I could name whose interest in Madeleine has far less to do with recovering an abducted child than with profiting from her misfortune. They continue to offer their services and 'expertise' to promote themselves and make money, often muddying the waters in the process.

You wonder what drives some of these people. Avarice? The need to feel important? Or perhaps something lacking in their lives? Perhaps they are just consumed by a sense of worthlessness and hatred. Maybe some human beings are just born that way.

Thank God for the nice 'quiet majority', as they often describe themselves, though they haven't been quiet to us. They have helped to keep our faith in humanity alive and confirmed to me that my innocent, pre-May 2007 view of the world was not so wide of the mark: most human beings *are* inherently good.

21

CLOSING THE CASE

As the summer of 2008 approached, the investigation into Madeleine's abduction remained classified and Gerry and I remained *arguidos*. It was like trying to lead our lives in purgatory. At some point – who knew when? – the PJ were going to have to hand their evidence to the prosecutor for examination and he would decide whether to file charges against us, order the PJ to continue the investigation or 'archive' the case, which would mean it would stay on file but all active inquiries would cease. In the meantime, fuelled by the customary leaks, speculation in the press about what would happen when rumbled on.

At the end of June, Gerry and I made the difficult decision to take a break. It did not feel right at all to go on holiday without Madeleine, but fourteen unbelievably harrowing and stressful months had passed since she was taken and we were running on empty. We owed it to Sean and Amelie, and we owed it to Madeleine to be physically and mentally fit to go on looking for her. We needed peace and quiet, and to be as far away as we could from the clamour in Europe. So we

386

opted to go and visit Auntie Norah in Vancouver. Clarence told the press firmly that the timing and destination would not be disclosed.

Canada was the perfect choice. We all spent five days of our holiday in a cabin on a remote lake in rural British Columbia. It was an idyllic place, surrounded by forest, tranquil and unspoiled, with nobody there but us – and possibly a few bears and moose. Of course, there were tough moments. The solitude emphasized the yawning gap in our family, but that is with us always, wherever we are. Sean and Amelie absolutely loved their adventure and it was wonderful for Gerry and me to be able to spend so much time together with the children.

Perhaps it was too much to expect our trip to remain completely secret. One night, back in Vancouver, Gerry was woken by a phone call from a DC Johnson of the Leicestershire police, wanting to fax us some information. Gerry told him that we didn't have access to a fax machine and suggested emailing us at our usual address. DC Johnson said it wasn't that important, he could drop it off when we were back, and asked when we were leaving. Gerry told him and we went back to sleep.

Mysteriously, on our arrival at Vancouver airport on 10 July for our flight home, we found a reporter and photographer waiting for us. There were four more at Heathrow. When Gerry phoned Leicestershire police to speak to DC Johnson, they were puzzled. They said they had no information for us, knew nothing about the phone call and had no DC Johnson working for them. Stitched up again. Still, at least the newspapers got their photographs!

While we were away, there was a hearing in the High Court relating to an application we had made on Madeleine's behalf for access to all the information held by Leicestershire police relating to her case. As nobody else was now searching for her, we wanted our own investigators to have the chance to check this material for any relevant leads. Naively, I'd thought a court order would be seen by the police, who were always telling us their hands were tied, as a way of helping us without upsetting their Portuguese counterparts. If they were required by law to pass us this information, surely the PJ would need to accept that? I couldn't have been more wrong. The UK authorities fought our application tooth and nail. I was shocked by the force of their opposition and the lengths to which they seemed prepared to go to deny us this access in these circumstances.

The British police had their reasons, of course, among them the investigative primacy they were obliged to concede to the Portuguese and the concern that being in possession of information otherwise known only to the police and the perpetrator might compromise Gerry and me, since at this point we were still *arguidos*. All of this the assistant chief constable for Leicestershire made clear in a statement written for the court. He had come out to Portugal shortly after Madeleine's abduction and had seen us at our most grief-stricken, and yet he felt able to comment of Gerry and me in this statement: 'While one or both of them may be innocent, there is no clear evidence that eliminates them from involvement in Madeleine's disappearance.' We were completely staggered. No evidence to eliminate us? Whether or not it was his intention, that line stuck in our heads as 'guilty until proven innocent'.

Given the extreme opposition we faced, we realized this was a battle we weren't going to win. Reluctantly, we made a tactical decision to accept a smaller amount of information. Having to withdraw was quite galling, especially as the eighty-one items disclosed to us included trivial details that our family had passed on to the police in the first place.

Meanwhile, in Portugal, Gonçalo Amaral, removed as co-ordinator of the investigation in October 2007, reared his head again. On 30 June he retired from the police force altogether. His reason for doing so was, he said, to regain his 'freedom of speech'. Nine months after his removal from the investigation, Amaral's association with it appeared to have increased remarkably. As speculation about the closure of the case mounted, he, along with several of his ex-PJ friends, began to appear in newspapers and on television. His purpose appeared to be to convince the Portuguese nation that Madeleine was dead. He had, he said, written a book about the case that would be published very soon.

On Monday 21 July, the Portuguese attorney general's office announced that the investigation of Madeleine's disappearance was to be archived, pending further evidence. The case files were to be released and the *arguido* status of Gerry, myself and Robert Murat was to be lifted. There was no evidence to suggest that Madeleine had come to serious harm and no evidence to implicate Gerry, me or Robert Murat in what had happened to her.

Gerry and I received no official notification of this from

the Portuguese authorities. I heard the news at about 4.30pm from a French news agency via Sky News and BBC News 24. It did not come as a great surprise as both the day of the announcement and its content had been pre-empted by the newspapers on Friday and we had been tripping over photographers and news crews at the end of our road all day.

It may sound odd, but in some ways we were glad the investigation had been closed. As I've said, we were far from convinced that there was any real investigation taking place anyway, so to have it officially brought to an end didn't feel like as big a loss as might have been expected. While the PJ had continued to supply the usual response – 'The official investigation continues. All credible lines of inquiry will be pursued' – we had been receiving messages from concerned people who had tried to pass on information to the police, only to be told, 'The child is dead.' Now that this 'investigation' had concluded, reports could be channelled directly to our own team, which would give them, we hoped, more to go on. It was certainly better than nothing.

As for the dropping of our *arguido* status, it was hardly a cause for celebration. All it meant was that, after eleven months of being pilloried, we were back where we started. Madeleine was still missing and we still had to find her. All the same, it was a relief, of course. In spite of my disgust with the whole business, I could appreciate that not being an *arguida* was preferable to being an *arguida* and that Gerry and I were in a better position than we had been the day before. It was also a public acknowledgement that the Portuguese authorities had nothing to implicate us in Madeleine's disappearance, just as we'd always insisted. And we hoped that some of the doors that had been closed to us since September 2007 would now reopen.

With the inquiry closed, our Portuguese lawyers, Carlos Pinto de Abreu and Rogério Alves, were allowed to consult the case files, and wasted no time in doing so – although the DVD containing the files took ten days to reach them. Given that leaks had become such an epidemic by this time, it will astonish nobody to learn that the prosecutor's fifty-seven-page summary of the PJ's final report had been on a Portuguese website since the day after the news broke.

Amaral and his chums had evidently been poised to take full advantage of the long-awaited lifting of judicial secrecy. Now they really went to town: we had staged a kidnap, or Madeleine had died in our holiday apartment and we had hidden her body; we had influenced the British police and organized our campaign to mislead investigators into searching for a living child, and so on and so forth. No longer gagged by the law, Amaral was talking more and more openly to journalists and turning up on television chat shows. A friend in the Algarve kept us updated on his activities. It was unpleasant and distressing to hear what he was saying, but we had to know what Madeleine was up against in Portugal. And it was incessant. With the best will in the world, it is hard for anyone to absorb this stuff day in, day out and remain completely objective, especially when it is never challenged or balanced by an alternative viewpoint.

It is impossible to convey, particularly to people outside Portugal who were not aware of Amaral's behaviour, just how difficult this smear campaign was both to withstand and to counter. And we desperately needed to counter it: we have always believed that the information that can lead us to our daughter is likely to come from Portugal. This is where the crime was committed, after all. Blackening our names was one thing, but if people there were taken in by Amaral's theories, they were going to think there was no point in looking for Madeleine, or in passing on any information that might be relevant. We are quite sure that Amaral's posturing has reduced our chances of finding her.

Why on earth would a former police officer want to convince the world that a missing child was dead – with no evidence whatsoever to support his claim? The only conclusion we could draw was that he was attempting to justify his actions while in charge of the investigation and at the same time promoting his forthcoming book to cash in on our misfortune. It just beggars belief.

I spent many days in tears, sobbing at the injustice being done to Madeleine by the very people who should have been helping her. There were times when I felt so incensed by the conduct of Amaral and his friends I thought I simply wouldn't get through the pain and anger. It was utterly frustrating that there didn't seem to be anybody in Portugal prepared to stand up against this man. Surely there were intelligent and knowledgeable people in positions of authority who could see through these offensive allegations. Why were they all staying quiet? Was it because it wasn't their problem? Were they scared to speak out? Perhaps Amaral had tapped into some kind of national subconscious desire for this to all just go away. The country was already reeling from a child-abuse scandal involving Casa Pia, a state-run institution for orphans and other disadvantaged children (when this finally came to court in 2010, six men, including a TV presenter and a former UNESCO ambassador, would be convicted) – the first such case ever to be tried in Portugal. Perhaps it was more convenient and less troubling to lay Madeleine's disappearance at the door of her foreign parents, put an end to the matter and move on. Who knows?

On 24 July 2008, three days after the inquiry was closed, Gonçalo Amaral launched his book about our daughter's disappearance. For this to have been possible, confidential information relating to the investigation would have to have been passed to his publishers, and any number of people involved in the production of the book, well in advance of the lifting of judicial secrecy. Needless to say, it repeated his theories, dressed up with fabrication and speculation. What it failed to include was any evidence – something one would expect to be rather important to a police officer – or any detail that didn't suit his story.

Dear God. I'm finding it really difficult to believe you're there at the moment. The more our suffering and pain continues and the more we are tested, the more I find myself doubting your presence, which is really scary. Without you, we have nothing; certainly nothing more than a slight chance so it's almost impossible to give up on you. Please God, if you can't bring Madeleine back imminently, please give us a sign, something positive.

Gerry and I talked about taking legal action against Gonçalo Amaral but we had concerns about the time and effort this would involve. We did not want to be diverted from our own investigation just as we had put the restrictions of the case behind us and we feared that any resolution through the Portuguese courts would take too long. For the moment we hoped the fuss would die down and Amaral would let up.

While struggling to cope with all this, I had a task of Herculean proportions facing me: combing through the 5,000 or so pages of documentation contained in the case files that had been presented to the prosecutor and received by our lawyers on 31 July.

We were pleasantly surprised by the prosecutor's conclusions and by how emphatic he was about the lack of any evidence to suggest either that Madeleine was dead or that we were involved in her disappearance. For several months we'd been concerned that if the case was closed, it might be closed in a way that left a dark cloud of suspicion hanging over us, so this came as a big relief. Initially, though, I was a little sceptical as to how much use the PJ's files were likely to be to us, bearing in mind that latterly, at least, the principal focus of their inquiry seemed to have been Gerry and me.

Four days later, the files were released to the media. DVDs containing our names, dates of birth, addresses, phone numbers, passport details, and those of our friends, relations, Mark Warner staff, witnesses and potential suspects, were being dished out to any journalist who asked for a copy. All those months we'd spent begging for scraps of information about what might have befallen our daughter and now here was the whole lot being distributed to every Tom, Dick and Harry. There is a big difference between what is in the public interest and what is of interest to the public, and surely when it comes to the dissemination of official police records it is the former that should prevail. It meant we had to seek advice on preventing identity theft and other fraud.

Naturally the media were going to be scouring the files for 'juicy' stories and angles, without a thought for the consequences for people who had tried to help the investigation. Now potentially valuable witnesses who had spoken to the police in confidence would be losing their anonymity. Gerry and I knew only too well the enormous strain this imposes on such victims and their families. Few people are equipped to deal with it. It had been our intention to go through the files with our investigation team and extract any information relevant to furthering our search. But now, with the media devouring it and rushing out to beard key witnesses, many others would be frightened off. It was crazy, and yet another blow to our chances of finding Madeleine.

We were splashed over the papers once again, of course, the tone swinging from the negative (the dogs, Kate refusing to answer questions) to the more supportive (criticism of the PJ for overplaying the DNA evidence). But exposure of a few of the injustices perpetrated on Gerry and me didn't outweigh the damage done.

In the meantime, I set to work on the files. Scrutinizing them would in the end take up six months of my life, and it would be a painful as well as time-consuming labour.

The 5,000-odd pages were divided into volumes and annexes, which seemed very disjointed. Usually the information was presented chronologically rather than separated according to subject matter. As a result, pieces of data relating to a certain line of inquiry or suspect were scattered throughout the files in different sections. The majority of the material was in Portuguese, so one of our first jobs was to find a company to translate it into English. Ultimately, the entire file would be translated, at a cost to Madeleine's Fund of almost £100,000, but initially Gerry and I spent hours scanning through it to prioritize the sections we wanted most urgently. Then I began on the few sections that were in English, primarily statements from British witnesses or information forwarded to the PJ by the Leicestershire police.

> *9 August*
> *Feeling a bit unsettled and agitated this evening. Going through the files brings back the emotion, desperation and uncertainty. At the same time, I have a slight flicker of hope that maybe something will emerge soon – but I'm just too scared to go there.*

Inevitably, I spent a great deal of time bringing together bits of related data in order to get a clearer picture of what they actually represented. But I waded through the documents doggedly. It was essential that I did. I don't believe anybody else would have examined them in such microscopic detail, or with the same determination or motivation, as Gerry and I. How could they? They were not Madeleine's parents.

One of the most concerning and upsetting pieces of information to emerge quite early was the record of sexual crimes against children in the Algarve. This discovery made me feel physically sick. I read of five cases of British children on holiday being sexually abused in their beds while their parents slept in another room. In three further incidents, children encountered an intruder in their bedrooms, who was presumably disturbed before he had the chance to carry out an assault. I guessed these were the reports that Bill Henderson, the British consul at the time of Madeleine's abduction, had told me about.

These incidents had occurred within an hour's drive of Praia da Luz over the three years prior to Madeleine's disappearance. The PJ had never mentioned any of them to us. In fact, I gathered from the files, some of them hadn't even been recorded by the authorities at the time they were reported (evidently, they were not considered to be actual crimes). So they might never have been brought to light if the parents of these children hadn't been brave enough to come forward to the British police after Madeleine was taken and relive their nightmares. They did so in the belief that there could be a link between what had happened to their children and what had happened to her.

It broke my heart to read the terrible accounts of these devastated parents and the experiences of their poor children. Unbelievably (or maybe not, by this time), there was a familiar thread running through them all. The parents had called the police; they hadn't felt that the crime was taken seriously, by the police or by their tour operators; statements were often not taken; DNA and fingerprint evidence was frequently not sought. In most instances there was no sign of a break-in. I cried for hours after reading a letter of complaint from one mother to the GNR regarding the sexual abuse of her daughter and the lack of proper attention paid to it by the authorities. The final line in particular has haunted me ever since:

> It is difficult to see with this lack of investigation or interest how a profile of this man can be built up. It did not appear to us that there was any great incentive or determination to find the offender and bring him to justice . . . Furthermore, it could all have been so much worse . . . indeed this man could go on to do much worse to another child if he's not stopped now.

Six months later, our beloved Madeleine was grabbed from her bed.

Of course, none of these children was abducted and these crimes may be completely unrelated to what happened to Madeleine. We do not know who has taken our daughter and for what purpose. What these cases do demonstrate, however, is that British tourists in holiday accommodation were being targeted. At the very least, the possibility of a link between these incidents and Madeleine's disappearance should have been investigated.

It is so hard not to scream from the rooftops about how these crimes appear to have been brushed under the carpet. The authorities have known of them for a long time and yet the perpetrators, as far as the families are aware, remain free. But we can't shout about them. Children are involved and they need to be protected. We are extremely grateful, however, to their parents for having the courage and compassion to share their experiences with us to try to help us find our daughter.

These atrocious offences occur all around the world, of course, not just in Portugal. But if individual countries do not acknowledge and deal with them thoroughly, they will multiply. Unless these criminals are tracked down and punished, and measures are put in place to stop them, not only will they continue to offend but others will flock to what they see as an easier milieu for their activities, eager to take advantage of weaker laws and laxer attitudes.

Combing through the files, I despaired. It was only now that I became aware of just how cursory some of the police work had been. Vital questions had not been asked, alibis not verified, lines of inquiry left dangling or, at best, not adequately documented. There is no doubt that the police were overwhelmed, both by having to deal with a crime of this nature under such scrutiny and by the sheer volume of information pouring in. The systems and resources they needed simply weren't there. I felt some sympathy with them over the challenges they faced, and it was clear that Paulo Rebelo, who replaced Gonçalo Amaral as coordinator of the investigation, had tried to make up for some of the initial inadequacies by checking back for anything that had been overlooked. But the discovery of each missed opportunity was another twist of the knife in my chest.

It was here I found the receptionist's note in the Ocean Club staff message book explaining that we wanted to book the Tapas restaurant for the rest of the week because we were leaving our children alone in our apartments. I was dismayed. This was a glaring green light to a child-taker –

and yet no mention is made of it in the files until December 2007. *December 2007!* Seven months after Madeleine's abduction! I could only conclude that its relevance had not been appreciated by the police.

Door-to-door inquiries appeared to have been delayed and haphazard. If nobody was at home, too bad: as far as I could tell they didn't get a second visit. Many of the witness statements looked extremely vague and brief, crying out for what seemed blindingly obvious and essential questions to be asked and answered. Those made by the Ocean Club staff in particular were very sketchy, even allowing for the fact that almost 130 employees were interviewed in the space of just a few days. We have discovered since that there were staff who were not interviewed at all.

Night after night, I read of depraved individuals, British paedophiles, Portuguese paedophiles, Spanish, Dutch and German paedophiles, and of the horrific crimes they'd committed. The police went to visit some of them, looked around their apartments and recorded merely, 'No sign of the minor.' Was that enough to eliminate these vile characters from the inquiry? If more had been done, there was certainly nothing in the files about it. No description, no photograph, no alibi, no DNA. Just 'No sign of the minor.'

27 August
A late night. Depressing reading. So many child molesters! Dear God, please don't let this have been what's happened to Madeleine. Please, God.

It's difficult not to criticize, and I know I'm a bit of a

perfectionist, but honest to God, when your child has been stolen, surely you are entitled to expect more than this. Much more.

It was unsettling to realize, from some of the statements in the files, how people can be completely wrong in their recall, opinions and feelings, and yet so utterly convinced they are right that what they tell themselves becomes hardened in their minds as fact. A member of staff based at the Millennium restaurant, for example, stated how she saw us there every morning having breakfast with the children. She described in detail what a nice family we were and what a lovely relationship we had with Madeleine. Very kind of her to say so – but we weren't there. We had breakfast in the Millennium restaurant only once, on our first morning in Praia da Luz, along with all of our friends. As I read these statements, it became slightly less baffling to me that Robert Murat and the witnesses who said they saw him on the night Madeleine was taken could all be so certain of their conflicting recollections.

One of the reasons I was so staggered when we were made *arguidos* was that I knew there was nothing to implicate us. And yet now I was finding testimony from witnesses claiming they had seen us in places where we hadn't been or doing things we'd never done. Some of these inaccurate reports weren't particularly harmful but others could have been. On top of these 'facts', notes had been taken of various suspicions. Not surprisingly, all of these accounts seem to have been given *after* we were declared *arguidos*. Once we were presumed to be complicit in Madeleine's fate, people apparently began to 'remember' actions or events that might support that theory. One witness reported having seen Gerry in Lagos on 7 May, on his mobile phone, saying to some-body, 'Don't hurt Madeleine.' At the time we were both in Praia da Luz surrounded by media, police and embassy officials – as, of course, Gerry's phone records showed.

Working through each volume and appendix, I made notes and produced a summary of each section, outlining areas where I felt further digging was needed and comment-ing on whether or not I felt this was achievable, given the limitations imposed on our independent investigators. At regular intervals Gerry and I met up with Brian Kennedy to discuss progress and set ourselves action points. Despite my initial scepticism of the likely usefulness of the files, and my frustration and despair at what I was finding there, having access to all this information *did* help us with our own search. For a start, it provided us with the names and contact details of potential witnesses we would otherwise have known nothing about. It gave us something to work with to move our investigation forward.

It was good to have confirmation that none of the local searches, and particularly the properly planned and executed search finally carried out in August 2007, had turned up any evidence to support the theory that Madeleine had been killed and her body dumped nearby. We'd been told very early on that the majority of child sex offenders who kill their victims dispose of the body within a few kilometres of the abduction site. This fact, together with the absence of any sign of Madeleine in the vicinity of Praia da Luz, increased the chances that she had been removed from the area and in many ways gave us more hope that she was alive.

It was only through having the police files that we learned of several key sightings of a suspicious individual or individuals near our apartment in the days and hours around Madeleine's abduction. As chilling as some of the accounts were to read, I appreciated that knowing about them gave us the opportunity, at last, to develop these leads.

In addition to the man and child seen by Jane Tanner at about 9.15pm on the evening Madeleine was taken, and the similar sighting forty-five minutes later by the family from Ireland, there were six reports from four independent witnesses of a 'suspicious' male noticed around the Ocean Club. He was described either as watching our apartment or generally acting oddly, or both. Details of all eight sightings are given at the end of this book (corresponding artists' sketches can be found in the illustrations).

The police did not appear to feel that Jane's sighting in Rua Dr Agostinho da Silva and the man and child reported by the Irish holidaymakers in Rua da Escola Primária were related. They seem to have concluded that these were in all likelihood two different men carrying two different children (if, they implied, these two men actually existed at all). The only reason for their scepticism appeared to be an unexplained time lapse between the two sightings. They didn't dovetail perfectly. To me the similarities seem far more significant than any discrepancy in timing.

Every time I read these independent statements in the files (and neither could have been influenced by the other, remember – Jane's description had not been released to the public before the Irish witnesses made their statements), I am staggered by how alike they are, almost identical in parts.

As a lawyer once said to me, apropos another matter, 'One coincidence, two coincidences – maybe they're still co-incidences. Any more than that and it stops being coincidence.'

Who knows why there was a forty-five-minute gap between the two sightings, or where this man might have been in between? I long ago stopped trying to come up with answers because I don't think I need to. If the child was Madeleine – and in five years, no father has ever come forward to say it was him and his daughter – why would we assume he would be behaving normally or logically? There is nothing normal about stealing a little girl from her bed, so why should his subsequent actions be predictable? The abductor would hardly have been expecting to see Jane walk-ing towards him as he escaped, let alone have anticipated that Gerry would be standing talking round the corner. Whatever plan was in his mind, he might well have been forced by these near misses to change it pretty quickly.

Naturally, I was interested to see what 'evidence' the PJ files contained against the first *arguido*, Robert Murat. I was aware of our friends' accounts of having seen him near our apartment on 3 May and Luís Neves and Guilhermino Encarnação had, of course, fed us negative 'information' about him for almost two months. But our own bitter experience of the PJ's way of working had taught me that I needed to take that with a pinch of salt. I tried to clear my mind of all these possible influences and remain as objective as possible as I explored the files in more depth.

I read Murat's statements and the statements of others concerning him. I read the transcripts of his phone calls, intercepted by the police. I recognized details we had been told (I even found the Casanova newspaper clipping the police had described to us), but I could see now that the PJ had put their own spin on these to present them as suspicious – in much the same way as they had cited Bridget's Bible as an indication that I had something to hide. I came across nothing that could be classified as hard evidence against Murat.

As was to be expected, for the most part, the later volumes of the files were devoted to Gerry and me. I still despair at the lengths to which certain elements of the PJ were prepared to go to try to unearth some sort of evidence to use against us. On the night Madeleine went missing, Russell, anxious to get posters produced and out there quickly, asked me for my camera, so that he could use the photographs of Madeleine stored on it. The PJ appear to have been determined to prove we'd brought these posters on holiday with us from Britain. They sent them to a forensics lab for analysis, asking for information on how old they were and how they had been printed and cut. Having established that Kodak paper had been used, they contacted a Kodak representative to find out where this paper could have been bought. I was so exasperated to read all this. There was a much easier, more obvious way of confirming how and where these posters were produced. They could have just asked. As it was, it took them until April 2008 to verify that the posters had been run off, on the night of the abduction, by Amy Tierney, the Mark Warner duty manager, using her own Kodak paper and her own Kodak printer.

We knew the police didn't have any evidence against us, of

course – if they had, we'd have been in jail. We certainly wouldn't have been allowed to leave the country. This was confirmed by the reports in the police files from Mark Harrison, the British NPIA search expert, Martin Grime, the blood and cadaver dog handler, and John Lowe from the Forensic Science Service in Birmingham.

Mark Harrison, on the results produced by the sniffer dogs, concluded: 'It must be stated, any such indications without physical evidence to support them cannot have any evidential value, being unconfirmed indications. Additionally, I consider no inference can be drawn as to whether a human cadaver has previously been in any location without other supporting physical evidence.'

Martin Grime: 'No evidential or intelligence reliability can be made from these alerts unless it can be confirmed with corroborating evidence. The dog alert indications *must* be corroborated to establish their findings as evidence.'

John Lowe: 'Low copy number (LCN) DNA profiling is highly sensitive; it is not possible to attribute a DNA profile to a particular body fluid.' In other words, it is not possible to determine whether DNA has originated from sputum or blood.

On the matter of the DNA sample retrieved from our hire car, Mr Lowe continued:

A complex LCN DNA result which appeared to have originated from at least three people was obtained (but there could be up to five contributors). There are 37 components in total [Madeleine's DNA profile is made up of 19 different components]. The individual components in Madeleine's profile are not unique to her; it is the specific combination of 19 components that make her profile unique above all others. Elements of Madeleine's profile are also present within the profiles of many of the scientists here in Birmingham, myself included. It's important to stress that 50 per cent of Madeleine's profile will be shared with each parent. It is not possible in a mixture of more than two people [as was this specimen from the car] to determine or evaluate which specific DNA components pair with each other. Namely we cannot separate the components out into 3 individual DNA profiles. In my opinion therefore this result is too complex for meaningful interpretation/inclusion.

As I stated earlier, even if Madeleine's DNA had been identified in any of the samples from the apartment or the car, there were perfectly legitimate reasons for it to have been there. As it was, her DNA was *not* identified in any of these samples. The test results were all described by the scientists as 'incomplete' or 'too complex for meaningful inter-pretation'. And still all those stories about Madeleine's blood and 100 per cent DNA matches were deliberately fed to the media and thence to the whole world.

All of this information had been given to the PJ before they interrogated us in September 2007. Yet they chose to ignore it and declared us *arguidos* regardless.

22

STANDING UP FOR THE TRUTH

The weekend of 13 and 14 September 2008 was not one of our best. On the Saturday I was bothered by a persistent caller (dubbed by Sean and Amelie 'the man with the poorly head'), whose initially erratic behaviour ultimately became terrifying when he jumped over the fence into our back garden and tried to get into the house through the patio doors. His last act before being carted off by the local constabulary was to throw one of my large ceramic plant pots through the windscreen of my cousin Anne-Marie's car, parked in our drive.

As if that wasn't enough for one weekend, on my way back from church the next day I received a text from one of the staff at the children's nursery, sympathizing with me about the appearance of entries from my diary in the paper and hoping I was OK.

My diary? *What?*

Welcome to our world.

She was right. Transcripts of my diary for May to July 2007 had been splashed across five pages of the *News of the World* and I'd known nothing whatsoever about it. The familiar heavy sensation in my chest returned and I started to cry. Surely they couldn't do this?

The coverage was presented in a sympathetic way – in fact, some friends and family assumed the diary had been published with my blessing – but that was hardly the point. Anyone with any decency understands that a diary is private and very personal to whoever wrote it. And as everyone knew, May to July 2007 had been an extremely traumatic period for me.

It didn't take me long to figure out what had happened. After taking away my journals in August 2007, the PJ had had them translated into Portuguese. To my horror, back in July excerpts had already been published in a pro-Amaral newspaper in Portugal – just three days after the launch of the former officer's offensive book. Now that version had been sold or given to the *News of the World* and translated back into English. I knew only too well from my interviews with the PJ how words and meanings could get lost in translation, and it was obvious this was what had occurred here.

'I was really upset' had become 'I was fed up', 'I never felt that relaxed' became 'I'd never felt so relaxed', and so on. Most of it, though, consisted of my thoughts and messages from the heart to Madeleine. I felt as though I'd been mentally raped.

Two days later, I discovered from the PJ files that on 27 June 2008 an investigating judge, Pedro Frias, had ordered the destruction of all copies of my diary, on the basis that it was not of interest to the investigation, it was a personal document and its use would be a violation of the person to whom it belonged. Why, then, had this order not been complied with? And who had given this material to the media? We had a pretty good idea.

17 September 2008

I feel like climbing into a hole and staying there. Sometimes it just feels like we are getting tested beyond all limits . . . Yet again I've been feeling today that the only way this can stop, justice prevail and all be well again, is if Madeleine is returned to us. I am clinging to my hope that the good God I have always believed in exists and that somehow and at some point, He will bring Madeleine back to us.

After several unpleasant days of phone calls between lawyers, the *News of the World* agreed to make financial restitution. Sadly, there was no other way I could be compensated – the damage had been done. It was especially disappointing given that this was the paper that had put together and promoted the reward package back in May 2007, but we had to seek redress as a deterrent. Unfortunately, though, it seems too many newspaper editors view this as an occupational hazard.

Towards the end of October I contacted Ernie Allen in the US to ask if the NCMEC team there would be willing to produce an age-progressed image of Madeleine. It was clear that a lot of people were still picturing her as a child of not quite four. It was hardly surprising, considering Gerry and I found it difficult ourselves not to cling to the Madeleine we knew. Despite the fact that almost a year and a half had gone by we were still receiving photographs of blonde toddlers from concerned members of the public asking, 'Could this be Madeleine?' We needed to remind everyone that the little girl we were looking for had grown.

A forensic artist named Glenn, who was very patient and understanding, took on the task of producing an image of Madeleine as she might look at six, which was the age she would be by the time his portrait had been finalized and released. He worked with photographs and sophisticated computer software, even seeking advice from a forensic anthropologist to achieve as close a likeness as possible.

The first picture of 'Madeleine, aged six' arrived without warning via email in mid-December. I was devastated. Caught unawares, I could not stop crying. It just wasn't how I'd imagined my daughter would look. It brought home to me how much time had passed and smacked me in the face with the cruel realization that I didn't actually know what my little girl was like any more.

As it turned out, this wasn't the finished article, just a rough draft. I dried my eyes and, over the coming weeks, with the help of many more photographs of Madeleine, pictures of Gerry and myself at the same age and a lot of feedback and suggested amendments from me, we arrived at an acceptable or 'close enough' resemblance. I was anxious about appearing to be too critical but Glenn was at pains to reassure me that my comments were vital to him. I was the expert, he told me. The viewing public was very forgiving and the human brain had an amazing ability to 'fill in the blanks'. 'As artists, we can feel quite disappointed when a recovered child doesn't quite resemble our age-progressed image,' he said. 'But what we think matters little. It's what the witness thinks that matters most.' The image is an investigative tool, not a true likeness, and in the end, it isn't important how faithful it is to the real child as long as it achieves its aim.

When I look at the final picture of 'Madeleine, aged six', I still can't really see her as our Madeleine. This little girl looks a bit too American and, though she is pretty, if I'm really honest, I think Madeleine is prettier. Maternal bias again.

As 2008 drew to a close, Gonçalo Amaral was still parading his unsavoury theories around Portugal and beyond. By the autumn it had become clear that he was not going to go away. We were beginning to realize that the harm being done to our search for Madeleine, especially in Portugal, was outweighing our reluctance to be distracted from it. We needed to put a stop to this serious damage. We had already spoken to our legal team on several occasions about taking action and knew that the only way of assessing our chances of success would be to seek advice from a Portuguese libel lawyer.

We had first talked on the phone to Isabel Duarte on 28 November. She was very understanding and sounded nice. By this point we felt as though we had been condemned by an entire country, so to receive sympathy from someone in Portugal was like stepping into a welcoming warm bath. Six weeks later, Gerry went to Lisbon to meet her. Although we were still resisting the temptation to sue, her parting shot left a lasting impression on him. 'Don't forget! *That man* said you buried your daughter on the beach!'

On Monday, 7 April 2009, we discovered that a

pro-Amaral article had appeared in *Público*, one of the most respectable newspapers in Portugal. Since it had, in the main, steered clear of the Madeleine 'story' and was well regarded by the country's opinion-formers, this was a worrying development.

By coincidence, that weekend Gerry and a couple of our holiday friends had been in Praia da Luz, where significant events and sightings potentially related to Madeleine's disappearance were being reconstructed, using actors, and filmed for a Channel 4 documentary we were working on (at last – a re-enactment people would see). I had stayed at home with Sean and Amelie – there was no need for me to put myself through this. I desperately wanted to return to the village when the time was right, but we did not feel we could go there as a couple until we could do so safely and quietly, without our visit turning into a media-fest and causing yet more disruption. As it was, the press, suddenly forgetting that the world was in economic crisis, were claiming that disgruntled workers blamed us for redundancies at the Ocean Club and the downturn in the local economy in general, and made much of Gerry being 'heckled' in Praia da Luz. In fact, maybe two people in a good-sized crowd shouted something at him. Those holding pictures of Madeleine, which they pressed to their hearts to show their support, didn't warrant a mention.

For his next trick, Amaral produced a 'documentary' based on his book, which was screened in Portugal on 13 April. A friend in Luz who phoned to tell us about it the next day was very upset, describing it as 'awful'.

I've always been considered quite a gentle person but

these attacks stirred up terrible emotions in me. It was as if my whole body was trying to scream but a tightly screwed-on lid was preventing the scream from escaping. Instead I was just howling internally. My punch bag certainly came in handy at times. Amaral's documentary was the last straw. On 20 April we took the decision with Isabel Duarte to sue him.

While she did the preparatory work, we were off to the States again – to appear on Oprah Winfrey's talk show. We had been asked if we'd consider being interviewed by Oprah not long after Madeleine was abducted but we'd had a lot on our plates then and there was no particular objective it would have served. This time we had our age-progressed image to publicize, and the global reach of Oprah's massively popular show would give us a fantastic opportunity to stamp this on the worldwide public consciousness.

It wasn't until we arrived in Chicago that it really hit me what a huge deal this interview was for our search for Madeleine. Oprah has more than once been described as the most influential woman in the world. Certainly when she speaks, as they say across the Atlantic, America listens. I was overcome by nerves.

Getting ready for the interview on the day was an event in itself. A choice of clothes and shoes had been brought to our hotel for me. Later that morning we were taken over to the Harpo Studios and introduced to Oprah's team. I had my make-up and hair done by two lovely ladies (if only I could look like that every day!). Just before we were due to go on, Oprah dropped in to see us. She came across as smart, strong and warm, and I was completely in awe of her. While she wanted to show what we as a family had had to endure, her main intention, she said, was to emphasize that Madeleine was nearly six, still missing – and *alive*. We were so grateful we wanted to hug her. In fact I'm sure we did hug her.

The show was recorded live in front of a studio audience. My nervousness intensified, partly because of the enormity of it all, and partly because I knew how important this was for Madeleine. I was emotional, too, especially when I looked at the screens on the set displaying rolling images of our Madeleine smiling back at us. Oprah was as good as her word. She did not dwell too long on 'human-interest' topics, concentrating instead on areas she knew would promote our search. And, of course, we launched the age-progressed picture of Madeleine which, thanks to the team at NCMEC and to Oprah, would now be seen by millions.

On Madeleine's sixth birthday, 12 May 2009, I met Isabel Duarte for the first time. I'd been reluctant to spend this emotional day in a meeting but our options were limited and, as Gerry pointed out, maybe this was exactly what we ought to be doing on Madeleine's birthday. I was very impressed by Isabel. She was a pocket dynamo: tiny and attractive but immensely feisty, strong, intelligent and compassionate. You could see the desire for justice burning brightly in her.

Isabel suggested that first of all we should apply for an injunction against Amaral's book and the DVD of his documentary with the aim of preventing the distribution and further repetition of his damaging theories. The next phase would be to sue Amaral for libel. It was an inspiring meeting and I will never forget Isabel's words to me as she leaned across the table, looking me straight in the eye: 'Today is a very important day for your daughter.'

Later the same month, Amaral was given an eighteen-month suspended prison sentence in connection with a case in which three of his officers were accused of torture. The mother and uncle of another missing child – eight-year-old Joana Cipriano, who had disappeared in 2004 from a village seven miles from Praia da Luz – had been imprisoned for her murder, although no body has ever been found. They claimed they had been tortured into confessing (the police maintained that Sra Cipriano had fallen down the stairs). The officers concerned were cleared but the jury found that Amaral had falsified statements relating to the torture case. His conviction was upheld in the Supreme Court in March 2011. Joana's mother is still in jail.

Falsifying statements? It was difficult to understand why anyone would believe the theories of a police officer found guilty of such malpractice. While coordinating the investigation into Madeleine's disappearance, Amaral had been an *arguido*. How on earth had he come to be put in charge of an inquiry into the disappearance of another missing child?

On 22 May I had a phone call from our lead investigator. He warned me that a British tabloid would be running a piece the following day about a convicted paedophile called Raymond Hewlett, who had been staying in Tavira on the Algarve in May 2007. The proximity of Tavira to Praia da Luz and the fact that this man was a paedophile ticked all the boxes for the redtop papers, and they jumped on the story. All of a sudden, Hewlett was cast as the man who could have taken Madeleine.

We were exasperated. We now knew that there had been

hundreds of paedophiles on the Algarve at that time and if, God forbid, one of them had been involved, Hewlett seemed a less likely candidate than a lot of others. He was in his sixties, for a start, much older than the man seen by Jane and other witnesses. But to the press that was irrelevant. They had a name and a photograph and they were off.

We were desperate for somebody to investigate Hewlett, not because we thought he had anything to do with taking Madeleine but because we wanted to eliminate him from the inquiry and quickly put an end to the media speculation. But the UK authorities told us they couldn't help. ('It's a Portuguese investigation . . .')

My main worry was that Hewlett, who had terminal throat cancer, would die before anyone took an official statement from him. Then the media would take the line that it was probably him, Madeleine was dead, game over, and we would be left with an uphill struggle to prevent this theory from becoming established. All the hard work we'd done recently to motivate the public to believe in our search again, and to undo the harm being done by Gonçalo Amaral, would be ruined. Sometimes it seemed as if we spent as much time trying to clear the path for our investigation as we did actually investigating. I wasn't sure I had the strength for another battle. It was so frustrating.

Sure enough, the tabloid interest in Hewlett raged on until July. In the meantime, he was questioned in connection with a case dating back to 1975, but not by Leicestershire or Portuguese officers. He also spoke to the tabloids, but refused to see our investigators unless we paid him to do so. He died a few months later.

* * *

On 27 August we learned that an American girl called Jaycee Lee Dugard, abducted in the USA at the age of eleven, had been found *eighteen years* after her disappearance. She had been taken by a sex offender and his wife and kept in an outbuilding in their garden. During this time she had borne her kidnapper two daughters. We listened to this news with very mixed emotions. Of course it was fantastic that Jaycee had been found and reunited with her family, but the appalling circumstances of her captivity and the suffering they had all endured for so long, the precious years cruelly stolen, were heartbreaking.

As the hours went by, however, our feelings changed as we realized how much the joy of this reunion, even after those eighteen horrific years, would outweigh the tragedy for Jaycee and her family. Their experience underlines how children can be hidden for many years and still found alive. This was a positive day not only for Jaycee, but for Madeleine and all missing children, wherever they are. We have always said that no matter how long it takes us to find Madeleine, and whatever she has had to endure, we will get her through it. We just desperately need to be given that chance. None of us must give up on these children.

In the meantime, we had been caught up in the byzantine workings of the Portuguese legal system. To date there have already been six separate decisions made on our request for an injunction, entailing four separate court hearings. The injunction against Amaral's book and DVD was initially rejected on the basis that any damage had already been done (decision 1). Isabel appealed on our behalf, as we strongly believed that damage was *still* being done, both to the search for Madeleine and to our family's human rights. The Appeal Court agreed that our case should be reconsidered (decision 2) and on 3 September 2009 four of our witnesses went to court to testify. Five days later the judge granted the injunction and ordered that Sr Amaral's theories must no longer be repeated (decision 3). He and his publishers would be required to ensure that all unsold copies of his book were removed from shops and warehouses across Europe and deposited with Isabel Duarte or face daily fines. As expected, Amaral in turn appealed against this decision.

Amaral's appeal was heard in December in Lisbon, over five days that ended up being spread over three consecutive months. Gerry and I felt it was important, essential even, for us to attend to represent Madeleine. She needed somebody there for her. She was the victim in this, not Gonçalo Amaral. I also needed to see the whites of Sr Amaral's eyes. We flew out to Portugal on 10 December.

> Not sure how I feel about seeing Mr Amaral – for the first time ever, I hasten to add! I know I'm not scared but that man has caused us so much upset and anger because of how he has treated my beautiful Madeleine and the search to find her. He deserves to be miserable and feel fear.

We were warned of the threat of a demonstration against us outside the courtroom, and our Portuguese advisers, worried about our welfare and negative publicity, felt it might be a good idea if we stayed away after all. But if we backed out, the bullies would have won. We'd come here for

Madeleine, and we had no intention of letting her down. Besides, we couldn't think of anything anyone could do to us or say about us that would be worse than what we'd already suffered. In the event, this 'demonstration' consisted of two middle-aged women, friends of Gonçalo Amaral.

And so it was that on 11 December 2009 I first laid eyes on Sr Gonçalo Amaral. It was also the first time he had laid eyes on me. It is extraordinary that he could have said and written so many awful things about a person he had never met. He had obviously spruced himself up in recent months. The moustache, gold chain and bulging tummy familiar to me from unflattering newspaper photographs were nowhere to be seen. Now he was sporting a smart haircut, nice suit and hat, and – an intriguing touch – a diamond earring. I wasn't afraid, but I admit that my heart beat a little harder and I clutched my wooden holding cross tightly as he walked past, flanked by his entourage. Here was the person who had been entrusted with finding our little girl and who had failed her – not simply by being unable to find her when he was in charge, but by then speaking out in a way that in effect hindered other people, ourselves included, from finding her.

I couldn't stop staring at him. It was as if I were trying to look inside his head. If the intensity of a stare could penetrate bone, I'm sure I would have managed it. What made this man tick? How did he rationalize his behaviour? How did he manage to sleep at night?

The other person we got to see that morning was Luís Neves, looking slightly dishevelled and a bit older (we all did, I'm sure). I'd badly wanted to look this man in the eye, too, since the day I was made *arguida*. The last time we'd spoken he'd accused me of refusing to do so. Today the tables were turned. However hard I fixed my gaze on him, he would not look at me. We had liked and trusted him, but it felt as if he'd turned his back on us. I'd believed he was stronger than that. I'd thought he was one of the good guys. I was disappointed in him and disappointed in myself, too, for putting my faith in him.

The trial was adjourned until the following month. Amaral's lawyer's secretary had suspected swine flu, and that meant Amaral's lawyer had to be 'quarantined' too, we were told. Still, we had come for Madeleine's sake, we had been there, and that felt important. We had already decided that we'd take this opportunity to visit Praia da Luz, so all was not lost.

I had promised my daughter and myself that I would return to Luz, and it had taken a long while for me to be able to do so both safely and in peace. In the middle of winter the village was tranquil. Gerry and I were able to seek solace at Nossa Senhora da Luz, I spent time at my rocks on the beach and we caught up with friends. To this day I still return quietly to Luz from time to time to feel Madeleine close to me.

We were back in Lisbon on 11 January 2010. For some reason I couldn't put my finger on, I was more anxious about the proceedings this time. But Isabel is a match for anyone, and I was reassured to have her on our side. In the corridor outside the courtroom, there was something about the way Amaral's cronies greeted him, with much sycophantic back-slapping, that made me distinctly uncomfortable.

The prosecutor in our case, José de Magalhães e Menezes,

gave an objective account, reiterating that there was no evidence either that Madeleine was dead or that Gerry and I were involved. A little while later, up popped Ricardo Paiva, who surprised me by remaining quite calm, even if he did contradict himself during his testimony. Paiva said he believed Gonçalo Amaral's assertion that Madeleine was dead and that Gerry and I had staged a kidnap.

The most disturbing thing about this is that it is Paiva who, to this day, receives any information about Madeleine coming in to the Portuguese police. If this is what he believes, we have a real concern that he may not be considering such information objectively.

During a break in the proceedings, I was going down the big stone staircase to the ladies' as Gonçalo Amaral was coming up. Thoughts of what I ought to say or do to him flashed through my mind but I stayed strong and passed him without comment, our shoulders briefly coming within a foot of each other.

By the time the court session ended nine hours later, I was relieved in more ways than one. Skinny bums aren't made for wooden benches. The press were poised outside like vultures. Gerry and I had decided not to say anything to them, on the basis that it would be best not to interfere with the legal proceedings in any way. In retrospect, it was the wrong decision. Amaral and his followers showed no such restraint, spouting off unopposed, with the result that the reporting of the case that night and the next day was extremely one-sided.

The following morning, Gerry gave a few pertinent statements to the media assembled outside the court in an attempt to redress the balance of their coverage of the previous day's proceedings. I had to laugh when I saw the front-page headline for the next day's *Daily Express*: the arrestingly original 'McCANN FURY'. I've lost count of the times I've been driving along, seen that headline on a newsagent's board and wondered to myself what we were furious about now. I suppose it just fits the page nicely.

Gerry had to leave towards the end of the second day because of work commitments, and Fiona kindly agreed to fly out and join me. The first two days had highlighted the injustices heaped on Madeleine, provoking a lot of anger, exasperation and hurt, and Gerry was worried about leaving me to face more of the same on my own. I'm sure I'd have been fine, but it was good to have Fiona there. We had hoped 13 January would be the last day of the trial but it was adjourned again, this time until February. The journey home was a difficult one. As soon as Fiona and I sat down on the plane, everything hit me full in the face: Madeleine, who she is, what I miss; the pain, the injustice, our life. I started to cry and couldn't stop. I was just exhausted by it all.

The final session of the injunction trial took place on 10 February 2010. I travelled to Portugal on my own to meet Gerry, who was flying in from a work trip to the Netherlands, at Lisbon airport. On the plane I sat next to a nice gentleman from Porto, and we spent a lot of the flight talking. After all that has happened and everything that has been said, Gerry and I worry about what ordinary people in Portugal, people like us, think of us and whether they believe what they read in the papers. We completely understand that they are proud of their country and want to trust their police force. Everybody needs to feel safe. I've wished so often I could plead with them face to face: 'Don't believe what has been written about us; please don't listen to gossip and reckless speculation. We are good people and we love our children dearly. Please give us a chance and help us find our daughter.'

As this kind, intelligent and humorous man chatted away to me on the plane, I felt a huge sense of relief. Maybe there were others like him who cared about what had happened to Madeleine and to our family. Maybe others could also see the injustices. 'I wish you well and I hope you succeed to-morrow,' he said as we disembarked. 'Good luck!'

In the course of the appeal trial we heard from repre-sentatives of Amaral's publishers, the producers of his documentary and the TV channel that had aired it. A university professor of criminology and several PJ officers were also called. The two final witnesses the following morn-ing were the general manager of the documentary production company and a journalist from *Correio da Manhã*, a pro-Amaral tabloid that gave house room to his claims on a regular basis.

After lunch, we returned to the courtroom for the summing-up of each of the lawyers. This was a horrible experience and one which, stupidly, I wasn't prepared for. The summaries of the defence appeared to be focused more on attacking Gerry and me personally than on what we were actually here to resolve: the damage wreaked by Amaral's book and DVD. Amaral's lawyer also seemed intent on turn-ing it into a UK-versus-Portugal battle, suggesting that we acted as if we owned their country. Clearly the defence were trying to incite the Portuguese people and keep public opinion on their side. It was ridiculous and unfair.

I was totally drained by the time we boarded the plane and, unusually, fell asleep within minutes of taking my seat. We arrived back in Rothley just before 2am. It was good to be home.

I love you, Madeleine. We will keep fighting, regardless of how many battles we have to face. Please God, good will overcome this evil. Love you, honeypie. We all do – so much. xxxxx

On 18 February, after an unsettling morning of waiting, we received the judge's decision. We had won. Amaral's appeal was rejected (decision 4) and the injunction against his book and DVD stood. Thank goodness for some sanity and thank goodness for Isabel.

On 1 March, we heard from a Portuguese friend that Amaral had been interviewed on television by Miguel Sousa Tavares, a celebrated journalist and writer. Our friend was delighted. Finally, an interviewer had asked Amaral the questions crying out to be asked of him for two and a half years. The interview was apparently quite aggressive, and Tavares had given Amaral a rough ride, but the points made were all pertinent and justified. It had been a long time coming. If only there were more people brave enough to challenge individuals like this.

Devastatingly, however, by the autumn everything had flipped again. On 19 October 2010, we were hit with a bolt from the blue. Clarence was told by a *Sun* reporter that yet another decision from the Appeal Court had reversed the injunction and lifted the ban on the sale of Amaral's book and DVD (decision 5). We hadn't even been aware that another judgement was about to be made, and neither was our lawyer. This broadside just came from nowhere. How many appeals was Amaral going to be allowed? How could other judges come along and overturn a decision made by three courts before them?

The latest verdict was that Amaral's poisonous allegations did not damage our investigation in any way and nor did they affect our human rights. Common sense tells us otherwise. How could spreading the word that a child is dead *not* damage the search for her? There was more waffle about the injunction contradicting the constitution of Portugal and undermining democracy by prohibiting free speech. Does this mean that a person could go out and start accusing their next-door neighbour of being a serial killer? As I understand freedom of speech, it does not equate to freedom to slander and libel someone with impunity.

It was impossible to comprehend. I felt utterly beaten. In a sixth decision in 2011, our appeal against the reversal of the injunction was rejected. We are at a loss to understand why, but we struggle on. At the time of writing, we are preparing to return to court in Portugal for our libel case against Amaral to be heard.

We were still reeling from this when along came Wikileaks. At the end of 2010, the *Guardian* published details selected from thousands of sensitive diplomatic cables leaked by the controversial whistle-blowing Wikileaks website. Among them was one of two messages that concerned Madeleine. It was a note of a meeting on 21 September 2007 – two weeks after Gerry and I were named as *arguidos* – between Alex Ellis, the British ambassador in Portugal, and Alfred Hoffman Jr, the outgoing US ambassador, in which Ellis tells Hoffman that the British police 'developed the current evidence against Madeleine's parents'.

The cable was three years old and what it contained didn't amount to much, either. It related to the British police sniffer dogs that barked in our holiday apartment and near our car. In the sense that this work was carried out by the UK police, then yes, their actions did lead to us being declared *arguidos* by the PJ, but the British officers did not actually develop evidence as such, because there was no evidence to develop.

So this was old news: we didn't pay it much attention and in the UK it created no more than a ripple for a day or so. To our dismay, however, the Portuguese press, galvanized by Gonçalo Amaral, lapped it up. Off he went on another round of the interview circuit – he even held a press conference on the matter – seizing this opportunity to air his allegations once again. It was absolutely soul-destroying.

What probably galls me the most about Amaral's interviews is the way he presents himself as a person who, perhaps above all others, really wants to find Madeleine and get to the bottom of her fate. I cannot begin to express how much this outrages me. His conduct in relation to the search for our daughter has led us to believe otherwise. There is nobody in the world more desperate than Gerry and me to find our daughter and to discover the truth – the whole truth – about what happened to her. What does he think has been the focus of our existence since 3 May 2007?

At that point it was almost two and a half years since the prosecutor had closed the file and removed our *arguido* status. How many more times will we have these disgraceful slurs thrown at us? How many more times will they be pushed down the throats of the Portuguese public?

Gonçalo Amaral has been convicted of falsifying statements and has coordinated investigations into the disappearance of two little girls, neither of whom has been found. Why is this man being allowed a platform from which to peddle his absurd and offensive ideas? They say what goes around comes around. For Madeleine's sake, I certainly hope so.

23

ADAPTING TO OUR NEW LIFE

On 4 May 2007, I became Kate McCann. According to my passport, driving licence and bank account I was Kate Healy. I hadn't kept my maiden name for any particular reason – it was just who I was and who I'd always been. But when Madeleine was taken, the press automatically referred to me as Kate McCann, and Kate McCann I have been ever since. Overnight our old life had gone and I'd become a different person.

So, it seemed, had our daughter. Madeleine would be the first person to correct anyone who makes the mistake of shortening her name. 'I'm not Maddie, I'm Madeleine!' And quite right, too. It's often done inadvertently, or in a good-natured attempt to sound more familiar and friendly, but the press know what her name is and yet to this day they insist on calling her Maddie or Maddy. I find it quite disrespectful. Unfortunately it's what happens when your name is too long to suit their headlines – and there have been plenty of those.

We have all changed from the people we were. Gerry's family miss their fun and gregarious 'baby' brother. What they have now is a much more serious sibling who is always busy and usually exhausted. I'm certainly not as laid-back as I was. I have less time for niceties and, sadly, I've become more cynical – though not without justification, I hope. I am wearier and I know a little spark that used to be within me is missing. There have been positive changes, too, though. We rarely grumble about little inconveniences or disappointments any more: we know how unimportant they are in the grand scheme of things. We recognize how we have been blessed by so much goodness and kindness and we certainly appreciate just how precious life is.

I don't think there can be a single aspect of our old life that has not been altered or influenced in some way by Madeleine's abduction. I look back now and wonder how on earth we have made it this far. If it weren't for the solid relationship between Gerry and me, I'm not sure we would have done. Before our world was shattered, my dad commented to me more than once how lucky Gerry and I were to have found each other. Most couples, he told me, don't have what you have. I can't speak for other marriages but I do feel lucky, especially given what has happened to us, that we have such mutual love and respect. The fact that we're still together and still doing OK is in itself quite an achievement (as the column writers and psychologists keep reminding us). The statistics show that most marriages subjected to such traumatic experiences break down.

It would be a lie to claim that everything has been plain sailing. No relationship, however strong, can emerge unscathed from what is probably the most painful and terrifying ordeal any parent could suffer. Inevitably, we sometimes reach certain stages, or go through phases, at different times and find different ways of coping with our anguish. Gerry was functioning much sooner than I was. I felt a tinge of resentment that he was managing to operate and I wasn't; sometimes I found it almost offensive, as if somehow he wasn't grieving enough. On other days I would feel I was a failure for not being capable of doing as much for Madeleine as he was. It was equally difficult for Gerry. He needed my help and support and I was so consumed by my own grief that I simply couldn't give *anything*.

When I finally reached the next rung of the 'coping ladder', I could see that my husband's ability to drag himself up from the hell into which we'd been catapulted was a godsend. Without it, the campaign to find Madeleine would never have got going in the way it did.

Gerry has tried, quite successfully, to compartmentalize his life, his thoughts and his focus. I have no doubt this ensures a more efficient and less stressful existence, but I can't do it. Madeleine is there in my head all the time. Either I am consciously thinking about her or some reflex brings her into my mind, whatever I am talking about or doing. This doesn't make me a more loving or caring parent. I think it's just that fathers and mothers are different; that carrying and bringing a child into the world possibly creates a uniquely visceral connection. All the same, I know being this preoccupied and consumed isn't helpful, either to her or to me.

The awful sense of Madeleine's fear I once experienced every waking hour has, however, eased a little. What remains is a lasting awareness of the terror she would've felt in the disorientating moment she first opened her eyes to find herself with a stranger. I cannot imagine this will ever fade completely.

It was a long time before I was able to allow myself to take any real pleasure in anything. I couldn't watch television, read a book, listen to music or follow the football, as I might have done to relax in my old life. I couldn't go to the cinema or out for a meal. I couldn't browse in shops. Madeleine was in my thoughts when I woke up in the morning and as I battled to fall asleep at night. I couldn't even sit down unless it was for a purpose, to eat or to work at the computer. How could I possibly take pleasure in anything without my daughter?

It was partly the feeling that I had to be doing something to help Madeleine every moment of every day, partly that so much of what I used to love reminded me of the life we should still have been leading and now made me sad. Sometimes the most innocuous and unexpected triggers can set me off: the smell of newly mown grass, or a song I associate with happier days. The hymn 'On Eagle's Wings', which Gerry and I chose for our wedding, gets me every time. It was over two years before I could bring myself to play music again. In the end it was the thought of how unfair it would be to deny Sean and Amelie, who loved singing, something I'd loved, too, that got me over that hurdle.

Gerry, meanwhile, was able to switch off from time to time and I'm sure that was a great help to him. I felt guilty for his sake that I couldn't do the same. He was desperate to share his moments of relaxation with me, to have his old Kate back, even if only briefly. He would suggest doing something nice – and I would cry.

Despite his inner strength, determination and capability, Gerry has his own down days, of course. He's been such a rock through so many long and testing times that when he crumbles, it is all the more concerning. There's something particularly distressing about seeing a strong man reduced to a heap, crying like a baby. Especially when he is the most important man in your life. I remember finding him on the couch one day, with Sean and Amelie sitting on either side of him, watching TV. When he looked up at me there were tears rolling down his face. I glanced at the screen to see what they were watching. It was *Doctor Who*: Madeleine and Gerry's favourite episode.

At times it has taken Gerry everything he's got to fight for his own survival and there's just been nothing left to give me. Occasionally, when I've been as low as it's possible to be, or afraid I was losing control completely, I've longed for a chance to talk it through, or even just to feel Gerry's arm around my shoulder, but he simply hasn't had the strength. He knows or fears that if he allows himself to be sucked into my despair, he might be brought crashing down, too. I understand this awful predicament only too well because I've experienced it myself with other relatives when I've been struggling. It sounds selfish and it feels selfish, too. But our lives remain precarious and sometimes it is all you can do to keep your own head above water, let alone anyone else's.

Fortunately, Gerry's worst days don't usually coincide with mine and for the most part we've been able to buoy each other up. We also know it is essential that we somehow make time for each other if we are to keep communicating, avoid growing apart and escape becoming another marital breakdown statistic. I say 'somehow' because since 2007 our life has been hideously busy as well as traumatic. The relentless workload of the search for Madeleine, organizing and participating in fund-raising events, Gerry's full-time job and the general demands of family life have left us with little space for anything else.

I took a cognitive approach to getting our sexual relationship back on track, concentrating hard on what Gerry means to me, as a husband and as a friend; on the love we have for each other and the three beautiful children we created together; on our unity as a couple and as a family of five. It seems to have worked. If my mind ever starts to wander down dark alleys, I fight against that, focusing on what I have that is good and important. And I tell myself that I cannot, and will not, allow this evil person to destroy anything else in our life.

I'm sure Alan Pike was right and it helped that I was gradually, *very* gradually, able to allow myself some pleasure and relaxation in general. Whether this was just a matter of time I don't know: it certainly took well over a year. I remember very clearly the first brief moment of peace I experienced. It was on our first holiday since Madeleine's abduction in the summer of 2008, in that wonderful isolated cabin in British Columbia. Gerry and I had been for a run together through the forest and returned to find that Auntie Norah had prepared a fabulous lunch for us. After we ate I went for a long soak in the bath, taking a glass of red wine with me. I lay back, completely immersing my head and letting the burning hot water wash over my face. My mind was at rest, my body calm ... and suddenly I felt the weight of our life lift temporarily. It was fleeting, but it was good.

Just acknowledging this slow personal 'improvement', however, brings a wave of guilt over me. My life is weighed down by guilt: guilt for what happened to Madeleine, guilt at surviving this whole horror, guilt that our family, especially Sean and Amelie, have had to experience any of it, guilt for not being quite the person or wife I once was and guilt about taking even five minutes for myself. Perhaps being a mother and a Catholic is a double whammy when it comes to guilt. It is certainly a heavy load to carry around with you. It preys on your conscience and when you weaken it can pull you down.

That said, the knowledge that I am a stronger and more able woman now than I was a couple of years ago helps me to shake off a little of that guilt: I recognize that this is a positive development, for me, for Gerry, for Sean and Amelie, and for Madeleine.

4 December 2010

We went to the Leicestershire and Rutland Irish Golf Society dinner dance last night [the proceeds were being donated to Madeleine's Fund]. *It was a really good 'do' – lovely people and great music. We definitely felt 'safe' and most importantly, among friends. Gerry and I danced for a large part of the evening. We hadn't danced since Madeleine was taken. We actually enjoyed it. It felt a little strange but I wasn't consumed with guilt as is often the case in these situations. Gerry looked really happy, almost glowing. It felt good to share some smiles and laughter with my lovely husband.*

Our pain might be the most acute, but our whole family, as well as our closest friends, suffer it to some degree, too, every day. Fiona, Dave, Russell, Jane, Rachael, Matt and Dianne live with the additional trauma of having been with us when the abduction took place. So many people miss Madeleine – their granddaughter, sibling, niece, cousin, godchild and friend – and of course they worry about Gerry and me. We all have our own needs and cannot always deal with each other's. This has been very hard for us – especially given the incredible support our family and friends have been throughout the last four years.

Several of my friends have had their own problems in recent times: events that in our old life we would have classed as pretty major. 'It's nothing compared to what you're going through,' they say, sounding almost guilty for even mentioning their difficulties. But deaths in the family, marital breakdown, and cancer are not 'nothing'. We appreciate that knowing somebody else is going through something worse doesn't lessen your own pain. Having a child abducted would be way up there in any hierarchy of human ordeals, but it would be nonsensical and unfair to try to measure anyone else's tragedies against such a yardstick. We have tried to support our friends as best we can, but sometimes our depleted reserves of time and strength have prevented us from doing as much as we would have wanted.

I own up that my expectations of others have sometimes been too high. Early on, friends and relatives were there for us constantly, devoting their time and resources to anything that might help find Madeleine. Inevitably, as time moves on, motivation wanes, priorities change and people have their own lives to lead. This is only natural. But while I understand that, at times it makes me sad that anyone else is capable of switching off when Madeleine is still missing. And I suppose I envy them their freedom to do so. However, I don't have the slightest doubt that if ever we ask friends or relations to do something for us, or need them with us, they will be there like a shot. Compared with other families who've suffered equally horrific events, in this we have been fortunate indeed.

Alan Pike warned us that we would lose some good friends as a result of our tragedy. On the plus side, new people would come into our lives, and we might un-expectedly grow closer to friends who had previously been more peripheral. He was 100 per cent right. Some relation-ships have drifted for reasons which haven't always been apparent. As upsetting and surprising as this has been, we've learned to accept that it's not unusual in such circumstances, and there is every chance these friendships might be rekindled in the future. From the start it was difficult to talk to anyone who hadn't been intimately involved with what happened. It felt as if they didn't really understand or, in some cases, simply had no concept of what our life was like now and, perhaps just because we were so exhausted, we struggled to reconnect with them.

Certain reactions to our situation have been hard to deal with (though they can be interesting from an anthropo-logical point of view!). For some people it seems too painful to bear. It's as if they are almost pretending Madeleine's abduction never happened. Perhaps by not mentioning it, or even acknowledging it, they are trying to reassure themselves that the world is still a good and safe place. While this is difficult for us to handle, living as we do with our pain every single day, we realize that everyone has their own way of coping with their feelings. It doesn't mean they don't have them. In the case of those we know less well, we understand that sometimes people just don't know what to say. For Gerry and me it feels easier, and right, to talk about Madeleine and we are relieved when others do so, too. We cannot behave as if she doesn't exist.

One of the big changes in our life has been the loss of our anonymity – something I'd always taken for granted, as I suppose most people do. It had never occurred to me just how far-reaching the consequences would be. As Kate Healy, I could do what I liked, when I liked, talk to whoever I wanted to talk to, behave naturally without feeling I was being judged by those around me. Suddenly, in the cruellest of circumstances, people the world over recognized us and were au fait with all kinds of personal details about us.

Cynics will argue that we 'courted' the media (God, how I detest that expression). If by this they mean that we enlisted their help to spread the word that our daughter had been stolen and we were desperate to find her, then we hold our hands up. Every decision we have made in the last five years, and every encounter with the press, has been undertaken in Madeleine's interests, not in ours. What would these critics have done if it was their child? Hidden away and hoped for the best? What would *you* do?

What we have always needed, and still need, is the help of the public to track Madeleine down, and we believed, and were advised, that this was the best way of reaching them.

Our relationship with the media remains finely balanced and uneasy. We are dependent on them to keep Madeleine in people's minds and to publicize requests for information related to any new developments in our investigation. At the same time, engaging with them is like riding a tiger. Thankfully, we no longer need to call upon Clarence's skills round the clock but he still steps in and rolls up his sleeves when required. As for their attitude to us nowadays, we typically see a flip-flopping approach, in both the UK and Portugal. One day they will report our public appearances reasonably soberly and factually, the next they will be finding fault. And the day after that the anti-McCann commentators, the ones who criticize everything we do, will wade in, harking back to how we left the children unattended, or opining that we should go away and give up.

As a direct consequence of becoming known (I can't bring myself to use the word 'famous'), I am now very self-conscious in public places. Some people will come up to me and wish me well, others just stand and stare, or nudge their companions and whisper, 'Look, there's Kate McCann,' whereupon five heads will swivel towards me. I've seen shop assistants run over to tell their colleagues, and three more heads pop up behind a counter. I am left wondering, What are they thinking? Do they believe what has been in the newspapers? I've never been that interested in shopping, but these days I find it even more of a trial. When I have to do it, I fly in and out as quickly as possible.

On one of my first expeditions after our return from Portugal, I went to collect a *Jungle Book* DVD I'd ordered for the children. As soon as I stepped out of the car I began to feel very anxious. I didn't want anyone to see me but the arcade was busy. I hurried inside the store, looking down at the floor to avoid any eye contact. Waiting in a queue at the till, I fought an urge to run out of the shop. It was all taking too long, I felt exposed and the tears were welling up. Served at last, I was rushing out of the arcade clutching my DVD when somebody grabbed my arm. It was a former colleague. I burst out crying and she hugged me tightly as people manoeuvred their way round us. 'Kate, you look so scared,' she said. 'Hold your head up. You have *nothing* to feel bad about.'

I worried that if people saw me smile or laugh, they'd think it inappropriate. After all, I thought it inappropriate myself. I worried that if they noticed me out and about they'd be saying, 'How could she? I just couldn't if it were me.' I even worried about silly things like shoppers spotting me buying groceries in Marks and Spencer or Sainsbury's and frowning on me for not going somewhere cheaper like Aldi and putting the pennies saved into Madeleine's Fund. None of this seemed silly to me at the time, though. It really bothered me.

There were several occasions when I was out with Sean and Amelie and one or other of them would have a tantrum. They were toddlers, they were doing what every toddler does, but I was afraid that people would judge my children and the way I dealt with their behaviour. Would they think the twins were unhappy or traumatized, or scared of me? That there were problems in our family? What would they tell their friends? As a result, I was unsure of how I should react. In my old life there would probably have been a few stern words, or I would simply have pretended to ignore my screaming child in the hope that if I appeared to be taking no notice he or she would soon calm down. Now, though, with everyone watching me, I didn't feel I could speak firmly to them in public, let alone raise my voice. I usually found myself trying *ever* so hard to reason with them, or gently asking them *ever* so nicely to please stop.

Sean and Amelie resumed their swimming lessons a few months after our return from Portugal. While Amelie, like her big sister, was very keen, Sean was not up for it at all. He clung to me, bawling, as I tried to encourage him to go into the pool with the instructor and the other children. What should I do? Go for the easy option and take him out with me? He'd learn to swim one day – it didn't have to be now. Or leave him with the instructor, despite his tears and heartrending cries of 'I want my mummy'? It was horrible. I was aware of all the other parents observing this spectacle through the poolside window. Would they think badly of me for leaving my son there crying? 'She's a hard one, that Kate McCann . . .' In the end, I looked pleadingly at the instructor and asked her, 'What do you think I should do?'

'Hand him to me and walk away. He'll be fine,' she said confidently. I'm sure she was right, though it wasn't much fun having to watch my little Seany, all red-faced, blotchy and sobbing, through the glass. But after a few more challenging lessons, we got there. He loves swimming now and is very good at it, thanks to the good sense of his instructor.

The attention of strangers isn't all bad, of course. Sometimes those who take the trouble to write to us apologize for their familiarity: 'We just feel as if we know you.' No apology necessary. It is their warmth and support that has sustained us, even if it does seem a little odd sometimes that people about whom we know nothing know so much about us. It is heartening and comforting when shoppers come up to me in the supermarket and say, 'How are you, Kate? We're all behind you.'

There is a fine line between sympathetic interest and intrusion, and it's a very hard one to define. We often have callers at the house who want to pass on information, usually psychics or mediums (somebody who'd had a vision turned up on our doorstep on Christmas Day 2010, while we were in the middle of our Christmas dinner, and I'm afraid received rather short shrift from Gerry!). We've had total strangers knock on the door and say, 'Hello! We were just passing and thought we'd drop by to see how you are.' These people are kind and well meaning, and their sentiments are very much appreciated, but some of their actions can be a little disconcerting. As I say, the line is difficult to define, and any forays across it, given that they are so well intentioned, even more difficult to criticize.

I feel much more vulnerable than I did five years ago, particularly as a parent. I remember the worries I had about Madeleine when she was small, many of them irrational. What if a wasp flew into her mouth and stung her and her throat swelled up? What if a passing dog suddenly jumped up and mauled her? I'd never, ever considered the possibility that a man might steal my baby from her bed. Since that night my anxieties for Sean and Amelie have escalated. I've worried more about accidents, illness and, not surprisingly, about whom they are in contact with.

I've worried about the future, about the children going off to university and perhaps being keen to travel, as I was. I don't want them to go. I want to hang on to them and keep them close and safe. I've spoken to Alan Pike about my fears, both the rational and the irrational ones, and I give myself little pep talks: 'You must be strong. You have to let them experience life. Most children make it to adulthood without any major mishaps or tragedies. As long as you're there to support them, they'll be OK.'

As advised by the experts, we've tried always to be open with Sean and Amelie and to answer all their questions truthfully as they arise. When Amelie, at about three and a half, became preoccupied with the idea that Madeleine might have run away, we explained the abduction to the children in the simplest and least frightening way we could. It wasn't right to take things that belonged to somebody else, we reminded them, but this was what had happened to Madeleine. She hadn't run away: somebody wanted her and had taken her from us. The twins understood that this was wrong, and that it had brought us sadness, but they dealt with this new knowledge in a very matter-of-fact way: a naughty man had stolen their sister and now what we must do was find her. As they grow up, we continue to respond to everything they ask us carefully but honestly.

To my great relief, I can say, hand on heart, that today Sean and Amelie are incredibly happy children, remarkably well adjusted, well rounded and emotionally in tune. We are so proud of them. A great deal of credit is undoubtedly due to the family and friends who surrounded them with love and warmth in Portugal and have continued to do so back at home. In years to come, I am sure they will find some solace in the fact that their mum and dad did everything in their power to find their big sister. Of course, we continue to hope that their greatest solace will be the safe return of Madeleine to our family.

I am often asked, 'Has your faith been tested? Do you get angry with God?' There have been many times when I've felt God has deserted me or that He has let Madeleine down. I've occasionally doubted His existence altogether. And yes, I've been angry with Him. I've shouted out loud and on occasion I've hit things (I'm afraid even the church pews have had the odd thumping!).

I do not blame God for Madeleine's abduction. The abductor is responsible for that. What I do wrestle with, though, is the inexplicable fact that despite so many prayers, almost total global awareness and a vast amount of hard work, we *still* do not have an answer. My aunt quotes a saying: 'Pray as if everything depends on God. Work as if everything depends on you,' and I truly believe this is what we've done.

I've never in my life prayed for anything or anyone so much, or in so many different ways. Thousands of other people, maybe millions, have prayed. So if Madeleine is alive, why hasn't God brought her back to us? If she is not, surely He could lead us to the truth and put a stop to the terrible anguish of not knowing? What do we have to do, how long do we have to wait, until He tells us something? *Anything?*

I've found it hard, too, to understand the further awful experiences that have come our way. How can so much suffering and injustice be heaped upon one family? It is said that God only gives you a cross He knows you can bear. Well, I'm afraid this cross has been far too heavy for far too long.

For now, though, at least, my anger towards God seems to have subsided. I believe in Him and I still feel His presence. There have been, and still are, many blessings in our life in which I see the hand of God. I cannot fully explain them otherwise. In spite of my scientific background and relatively analytical mind, Darwin's theories and chance just don't cover it for me. If I still cannot understand why events have happened as they have, and I sometimes end up having serious words with God about His slow progress, for the most part I try my best to accept that it is not for me to question His plan. Maybe I just need to be patient and trust Him.

There is one thing of which I am confident: I believe wherever Madeleine is, God is with her. And during my calmer moments, I also believe that in God's time, we'll get there. A couple of years ago I was saying a prayer for Madeleine with the twins and remarked that it had been a long time since we'd seen her. 'No, Mummy,' said Amelie. 'It's just a teeny-weeny time.' She was right, of course: a few years is a drop in the ocean compared to a lifetime.

Gerry has certainly struggled over the last couple of years with his faith. While he still believes in God, he is no longer convinced of the power of prayer. In his words, 'If prayer worked, we would've had Madeleine back a long time ago.' He's also mentioned to me, on more than one occasion, that nowhere in Christ's teachings does it say you'll reap your reward on this earth. Gerry has always believed that everyone possesses God-given talents which we should use to the best of our ability, he recognizes the benefits of the church community and he continues to insist that something good has to come out of this whole experience.

To a certain extent it already has, in the sense that Madeleine's case has greatly increased public awareness of the whole issue of missing, abducted and exploited children. We have tried to support various organizations working on behalf of these children – including Missing People, PACT, Missing Children Europe and the NPIA. On Wednesday, 27 January 2010, we marked our daughter's thousandth day away from us with Still Missing, Still Missed: An Evening for Madeleine, a gala dinner from which half the proceeds, amounting to £45,000, went to Madeleine's Fund and the other half to Missing People and Missing Children Europe. It is vital that this huge worldwide problem is tackled and that other children and parents are saved from suffering what our family has had to suffer.

In the wake of our 2008 campaign calling for a coordinated Europe-wide child alert rescue system, the European Parliament dedicated one million euros to fund projects aimed at developing interconnecting child rescue alerts. Two of the grants went to schemes designed to strengthen cross-border compatibility and coordination. Since then, I am pleased to say that significant progress has been made. According to the European Commission, which allocates the funds, ten EU member states (Belgium, France, Greece, UK, Netherlands, Luxembourg, Portugal, Germany, Italy and Romania) now have CRAs in place. The UK's new nationally coordinated child rescue alert was launched on International Missing Children's Day, 25 May, 2010.

There is, of course, still some way to go. Given the economic downturn, it is likely to be years before every one of the twenty-seven EU member states has in place a functioning CRA with appropriate cross-border facilities. However, provided national governments demonstrate the will to protect our children, and acknowledge their moral obligation to do so, with the ongoing support of the European Commission, this goal *can* be reached.

In the meantime, the search for Madeleine goes on. Sean and Amelie often talk about how their sister might escape, how we could rescue her and what they would do to the 'naughty man' who stole her. Once they suggested, 'Maybe we should tell the police that Madeleine is missing and ask them to help us, too.' Quite.

After the autumn of 2007 our connection with Leicestershire police dwindled and that made me sad. Their officers worked so hard on Madeleine's behalf and we know they'll rejoice if and when we find her. The Leicestershire force continued to take the line that they would pass on any relevant information to the Portuguese authorities. While this was all that was legally expected of them, we'd hoped for much more. They had been placed in a difficult position, we acknowledge that, but we had not been prepared to accept the platitude that work in Portimão was still ongoing when we knew this was not the case. Of course, every police force in the UK, and many beyond, has assisted in the search for Madeleine and for this we are extremely thankful. We are particularly grateful to Jim Gamble and the team at CEOP for the initiatives they developed with us to help keep Madeleine's abduction in the forefront of the public consciousness.

But a harsh fact remains. After the case was closed in July 2008, no police force anywhere was actively investigating what happened to Madeleine. We were the only people looking for her.

Never having experienced any sort of cross-jurisdiction investigation, it is difficult for us to understand why, especially within Europe, a more joined-up approach, drawing on the best expertise available, is not taken in cases of missing children. We have been told that this happens in crimes involving drugs, money-laundering and terrorism, where the primacy of the country in which the crime has been committed seems to be less of an issue. Surely the disappearance of a child merits the same attention from governments?

It was simply unacceptable for the authorities to decide no more could be done to find Madeleine when no comprehensive review of the case had been undertaken. Our daughter deserved better. All missing children and their families deserve better. There were still many stones to be turned and a review remained an unturned boulder.

By 2011, we were still pressing the British and Portuguese governments to do more, or at least something. A year after our initial request for a review of Madeleine's case, Alan Johnson, the second home secretary we met, had commissioned CEOP to undertake a 'scoping' exercise – basically to establish whether they felt a review may be of benefit. Their report was delivered to the Home Office in March 2010. Although we have never seen it (we were told this was not possible because it was 'sensitive'), it has been widely described as highlighting some deficiencies in the investigation and hence areas that warrant further attention.

We met the current home secretary, Theresa May, and wrote to her several times. Still no further forward, and in the dark as to whether the British government had even broached the matter with the Portuguese authorities, in November 2010 we started a petition to lobby the two governments to conduct an independent review. We were at a loss to comprehend why such a commonly used procedure wasn't an obvious option and why our request had gone unanswered.

An independent investigative review is standard procedure in most major inquiries that remain unsolved, let alone the highest-profile missing-child case in Europe. A process of this type can help to identify areas for further exploration and new avenues yet to be pursued. Cases can remain unsolved simply because two pieces of the jigsaw have not been linked. Sometimes it's hard to see the wood for the trees, and fresh eyes can often pick up some vital nugget that may have been overlooked by investigators grafting away on a case day in, day out. Who knows what might be revealed?

Who is the man Jane Tanner saw carrying a child, very probably Madeleine, away from our holiday apartment? Who is the man seen watching the apartment in the days before? Five years later he, or they, remain to be identified. 'Clear the ground under your feet' is a maxim the police like to quote. Had this been done? Had all those in the vicinity of the Ocean Club that spring, especially those with knowledge of our movements, been eliminated on solid grounds? Not according to what we'd read in the police files. For a start, there were still people who had not been interviewed. Nor had everyone's description been taken or their movements accounted for. An investigative review was our best chance of answering these questions.

While awaiting a response from the government we carried on doing everything we could to find Madeleine and explored ways in which we might pursue disclosure of all information held by the authorities in relation to her disappearance in the event that our appeal for a review fell on deaf ears. Our own search has significant limitations. Crucially, we do not have access to all of the reports that have come in to the inquiry. The Portuguese authorities possess a great deal of material that was not included in the police file released into the public domain. The British police, too, hold information we do not have. In the absence of any other active investigation, the more information we could acquire, the more complete the picture would be and the stronger our chances of finding our daughter. Surely it was in Madeleine's best interests that we and our team were given access to records that were otherwise just sitting there gathering dust?

It may be suggested that in criticizing individuals and organizations involved in the investigation we are merely seeking someone to blame because Madeleine hasn't been found. This isn't true. If we had allowed ourselves to be consumed by bitterness, we wouldn't have survived this far. What's done is done, and we are not interested in looking for scapegoats but in focusing on areas of the investigation that may yet yield results and taking our search for our daughter onwards. There are lessons to be learned for the future, in terms of both the handling of crimes against children and the treatment we have received from the authorities and the media, and if some good can come out of our experience, it is that the mistakes made will not be repeated.

And, critically, let's not forget that the perpetrator of this monstrous crime remains at large. This person who stole a little girl out of her bed and away from her family has been anonymous for far too long. If nothing more is done, he will continue to hide in the shadows, evading justice, and will be free to strike again.

People ask why we go on and the answer is that we still have hope – real hope. Madeleine is still alive until someone proves otherwise. And as we know, there is no evidence whatsoever to suggest she has come to any harm, other than as a result of being separated from her family.

Occasionally, in my mind's eye, I see Madeleine being looked after by someone else. As painful as it is to countenance the idea of her having spent longer with a stranger than she spent with us, to picture somebody other than us loving her and enjoying the precious years of her childhood that we should be enjoying, it is the best scenario I can envisage. I just want her to be well and happy.

There are many examples of abducted children being recovered years later. One of the most recent to hit the news, in China in February 2011, was that of six-year-old Peng Wenle, taken at three years of age, whose father had combed the country in search of him, putting up posters and pleading with local police for help. With the assistance of a campaign on the internet and the Chinese version of Twitter, Peng

Wenle was discovered begging on the streets. In January 2011, Carlina White, stolen from a hospital in Harlem, New York, as a baby in 1987, was reunited with her family after twenty-three years. She had been brought up by her female kidnapper and, suspicious of her history, had turned to the NCMEC for help. Shawn Hornbeck was abducted at the age of ten and recovered four years later. Crystal Anzaldi was found seven years after being snatched at fourteen months old. Steven Stayner, kidnapped at seven, escaped from his abductor seven years later. Jaycee Lee Dugard spent eighteen years with hers. How many more children are out there waiting to be found?

Bolstered by this hope, we have moved forward. We have grown stronger and adapted to our new life. But our daughter is still missing and our family will never be complete without her. We love her beyond words. We will *never* give up on her. We will not allow our story to end here.

EPILOGUE

This book was first published in the UK and Ireland on 12 May 2011 – Madeleine's eighth birthday. Within a year, editions had also been released in Portugal, the Netherlands, Brazil, Germany, Spain, Hungary, Sweden and Finland. Sales have been phenomenal and we are extremely grateful to everyone around the world who has bought and read it. Not only has a significant sum of money been raised to enable us to continue our search for Madeleine, the boost to public awareness of our daughter's plight must surely increase our chances of finding her: more eyes and ears, more discussion, more prompting and maybe, who knows, some pricking of consciences.

It was inevitable that publishing the book would expose our family to a fresh wave of intense press attention. Initially, I was adamant that I did not want it to be serialized by any newspaper, and especially not by a tabloid. It made no difference to me that such a deal would increase the book's profits and the share of those rewards going to Madeleine's Fund. Given how we and, more importantly, Madeleine had been treated by much of the British media, I just didn't want anything more to do with them. And I couldn't bring myself to entertain the prospect of seeing my innermost thoughts taken out of context and splattered all over a redtop. They seemed too precious for that and, I felt, deserved a little more respect than they might be accorded. So for some months I rebuffed all approaches. Yet this wasn't about me, it was about Madeleine, and I knew I must not cut off my nose to spite my face. In an ideal world, there would be no serialization. But of course, in an ideal world, there would have been no book, either. Madeleine would still be with us, where she belongs, and we would be an ordinary family of five of no interest to anyone in the wider world.

It wasn't until Gerry suggested that perhaps we could seek a different, broader kind of arrangement, in which the serialization of the book was combined with some specific backing for our campaign, that I opened my mind a little further to the idea. In the spring of 2011, we met a team from News International to hear what they had to offer. They were prepared to spearhead a drive to re-energize the search for Madeleine and to mobilize their readers to support our appeal to the British government for a review of the investigation into her disappearance – something we'd been calling for since 2008. It was this particular undertaking that persuaded me to agree to serialization in the *Sun* and the *Sunday Times* in the week leading up to the launch of the book. It was a trade-off – and there have been more than a few of those over the last five years – but, we hoped, a very important one for Madeleine.

It was a nerve-wracking week but thankfully the daily

coverage was helping to re-engage hearts and minds in the UK, and the response of other newspapers, too, was as positive and supportive as we could have hoped for.

With so many people and the weight of the media behind us, on Madeleine's birthday, the day the book was released, the *Sun* printed an open letter from Gerry and me to the prime minister, David Cameron, pleading with him to consider a review of her case. We hadn't wanted to challenge him so publicly, but we'd gone through the official channels, again and again, to no avail. We couldn't see any alternative now. It was this way or we might as well give up.

While Susan Hubbard, over from Portugal to look after Sean and Amelie, took charge of Madeleine's birthday party for Gerry and me in Rothley, our gift to our daughter was a marathon day of intensive interviews and press conferences in London. Back at our hotel that evening, Clarence received word that Gerry should expect a call from David Cameron's private secretary. Incredibly, it seemed the prime minister might already have agreed to a review. We hadn't expected a response to the open letter for several days at least, if we got one at all. We hardly dared hope this was true until several conversations with various government officials confirmed that a review was to be conducted by the Metropolitan Police. Oh my God! *Finally* help was coming. Happy birthday, Madeleine. Other than hearing that she had been found, there could have been no news sweeter to my ears. We were so grateful.

In spite of the government's long silence, it seemed that, unbeknown to us, work must have been going on in the background, including discussions with the Met. When the official announcement was made that night, we were swamped by calls, text messages and emails from delighted family and friends. The relief was immense.

By the next morning, the critics had already reared their heads, clouding the first ray of hope we'd had in ages. There were complaints that the Met had been 'ordered' to conduct a review and their independence was being compromised; that a disproportionate sum of money was being spent on revisiting the case of one missing child; that Mr Cameron was bowing to pressure from Rupert Murdoch's media empire. We were subsequently told that the PM had put in a *request* to the Met, which had reacted positively, and it appears that the funds are coming from central government and not out of the police budget. And it's fair to say that all politicians respond to media pressure and attention, whatever its source. For three whole years, we, with the assistance of kind donors, had been battling for our daughter and funding the *only* search there had been for her, and yet a small but vocal bunch of detractors seemed to think this vital helping hand was not appropriate. But if there's anything we've learned over the last five years, it's that you will never please everyone, regardless of what it is you're trying to do.

We were more preoccupied by the many questions swimming round our heads. Did the Portuguese authorities know about this decision? Would they cooperate? Would they cooperate *fully*? We were so pleased when the Metropolitan Police team assigned to the review (a squad of thirty, including officers and administrative staff) got cracking straight away. They were in touch with us within a few days and the following week we met several of them at Scotland Yard.

Almost immediately Gerry and I felt confident, reassured and hopeful. We know the review will be a long haul and results won't appear overnight. We know the 'golden nugget' may not be among the data accumulated thus far. But what we are sure of is that this process, whether it takes months or years, will bring us closer to attaining our goal. And possibly even all the way there.

To date, the Met officers have gathered together as much of the information that came into the original inquiry as they can. They've met the previous teams from Leicestershire police force and other UK law-enforcement agencies, several police units in Portugal and Spain and our own independent current and past private investigators. All of the information handed over is being put on to a specialized searchable database for the first time ever. This will undoubtedly make the review easier and more fruitful. The Met have also commissioned a new age-progressed image, reproduced in the picture section of this book, showing how Madeleine might look today.

Perhaps the most encouraging aspect for Gerry and me so far is how good the communication has been. We are regularly updated and while we don't expect the Met to share everything with us, at least we know that *something* is happening. That may sound fundamental but it's a marked and welcome change from what went before. From the moment I heard the news of this major step forward for Madeleine, a positive feeling had begun to spread inside me and it has remained with me ever since.

In the meantime, our search continues, as does our work to raise awareness for various charities and organizations concerned with missing people and their families as well as for the campaign to find Madeleine. We try to put our experience to good use when we can by sharing it in ways that might help others enduring similar heartache. In October 2011, for example, Gerry and I were invited to talk to counsellors and other professionals at the annual conference of CHUMS, the Child Bereavement, Trauma and Emotional Wellbeing Service, which helps children, young people and their parents or carers. In conversation with David Trickey, the child psychologist who advised us after Madeleine's abduction, we answered their questions about how we've supported Sean and Amelie and how we've coped ourselves.

In June I gave evidence at the UK's first-ever parliamentary inquiry into the rights of the families of missing people. I was joined by two other mums, Nicki Durbin and Sarah Godwin, whose sons, Luke and Quentin respectively, have been missing since they were teenagers. The inquiry, run through the All-Party Parliamentary Group for Runaway and Missing Children and Adults and led by APPG chair Ann Coffey MP, followed twelve months of campaigning by the charity Missing People for improvements to the support available to such families.

As things stood, if your house were burgled you would automatically be offered various forms of support. But if your child went missing, you might get nothing. It seems inconceivable that so little was being done for the victims of what I'm sure most parents would agree is a far more devastating event. In addition families need to know that everything possible is being done to find their missing loved one and to be spared the pain of unnecessary financial and legal red tape.

The inquiry heard evidence from a range of public, private and voluntary-sector organizations as well as from the families of missing people. While only one of the four sessions was directly relevant to our situation, it was enlightening and extremely disturbing to learn from others of the bureaucratic struggles they faced following the disappearance of an adult son or daughter or other relative. The distress caused in already agonizing circumstances by matters such as guardianship, presumption of death, the cross-matching of missing persons reports with unidentified bodies and managing and resolving a missing person's practical affairs is something I'm sure most people, myself included, hadn't appreciated.

In response to the inquiry's recommendations, the government launched its Missing Children and Adults Strategy in December 2011 – a bit of a landmark event in the field of missing people. The strategy aims to reduce the number of individuals who go missing, to protect those who do in their absence and to give their families access to the level of support already available to victims of crime.

The damage still being caused to our own search for our daughter by irresponsible, untruthful media reporting has been brought home to us on our recent visits to other countries. While we were in Amsterdam to publicize the Dutch edition of this book, a taxi driver, having established the purpose of our visit, remarked: 'Oh yes, I remember. You were the parents accused of killing your daughter! What happened after that?' Clearly that was where the story had ended in the Netherlands, and in probably every other country outside the UK and Portugal.

In Spain, during a live television interview, we were confronted by a film that could only be described as propaganda. Just before going on air, we had been shown the Spanish script, quickly translated for us by the interpreter, but by then, of course, we were in a difficult position. We were tempted to abandon the interview, but we knew what kind of message that would send out. We had no real choice other than to go ahead and try to put the record straight. So we sat in stunned silence, our hearts pounding fiercely, as selectively edited and apparently damning images gathered from media and Portuguese police file footage were displayed on a big screen for us, the studio audience and countless viewers at home to see: barking cadaver dogs; books, documents and medicines taken from the villa we'd rented in Praia da Luz; a clip from an interview with the ubiquitous Gonçalo Amaral.

The commentary presented these 'exhibits' as fact – as evidence of guilt. One of the books was a novel Gerry had taken to Portugal as holiday reading, *The Interpretation of Murder* – a bestselling historical crime thriller inspired by a visit made to New York by Sigmund Freud in 1909 – presumably singled out for no other reason than its sinister title. And the tablets shown were actually my father's Parkinson's disease medication, as was confirmed by the patient's name on the packets, conveniently out of shot, and not, as the voice-over suggested, sedatives that we had administered to our children. The Portuguese police knew this, and so would the producers of the programme, had they properly read the book they were supposed to be interviewing us about. Our treatment at the hands of the media is a central strand of our story and yet here we were, once again, forced to explain the facts and defend ourselves – live on television and via an interpreter. By now I've run out of superlatives to adequately express my shock and disgust at this abhorrent behaviour.

At home, public anger at the appalling ethics and standards of the press boiled over in the summer with the revelation that the mobile phone voicemail of thirteen-year-old Milly Dowler, abducted and murdered in 2002, had been hacked into by the *News of the World*. Phone hacking was nothing new – the *News of the World* had been investigated several years earlier when the phones of celebrities, politicians and members of the royal family had been illegally accessed, resulting in two convictions. Despite past assurances that the skulduggery had been limited to one 'rogue' journalist, numerous other potential victims were now emerging, many of them, like us, ordinary people catapulted into the public eye by personal tragedy, and as the huge scale of the phone hacking became clear, the whole country was, at last, moved to outrage. Given our experiences, it hardly came as a shock to us. There followed allegations of police bribery and cronyism between the Murdoch media empire and politicians, lawsuits, resignations, sackings and arrests. In the fall-out, Murdoch's takeover bid for BSkyB was withdrawn and the *News of the World*, abandoned by its advertisers, was closed down. But we very much doubt that such nefarious practices have been confined to one tabloid newspaper.

Top News International executives were summoned to appear before Parliament's Culture, Media and Sport Committee and the government set up a public inquiry under Lord Justice Leveson to further investigate the scandal. Gerry and I were invited to apply to assist the inquiry as 'core participants'. Knowing how useful our testimony could be, we decided we had a moral obligation to do so. While there is no evidence to suggest that our own phones were hacked, we have certainly suffered greatly from invasion of our privacy and defamation at the hands of the press. We had a lot to share and hoped that by contributing we might help to prevent others from being subjected to similar treatment.

After a meeting with David Sherbourne, the barrister representing the core participant victims, and preparing our witness statement, we appeared before Lord Leveson on 23 November to relate our experiences to him, to Robert Jay, the examining QC, and to all those present in court. At first we were both nervous and shaky (yes, even Gerry!) but the questioning was sensitive and sympathetic and the judge seemed sharp and very supportive. We gave evidence for the best part of two hours, concentrating primarily on the libellous headlines and reports that had appeared on a daily basis for months on end in many of the British papers. Going through them all again for the inquiry filled me with renewed disbelief. Some of them were so outlandish they might have seemed almost comical in less awful circumstances. As it was, the passage of time provided no fresh perspective. I was no nearer to understanding how these journalists and editors could be allowed to print such dreadful, untrue stories, or how they could sleep at night. I still wondered whether they had cultivated the ability to detach themselves from what they were publishing, or, worse, whether they simply didn't care.

The other area of interest was the diary that had been taken from me by the Portuguese police, without my knowledge or consent, back in August 2007, and which, to my horror and distress and again without my knowledge or consent, found its way into the pages of the *News of the World* a year later. Lord Leveson, like most normal, considerate individuals, I suppose, found this shocking and vowed to find out who was responsible for the buying and selling – something I've been very keen to establish myself.

We fervently hope that lessons will be learned and that real change will be brought about as a result of the Leveson inquiry. Clearly self-regulation has not worked. We recognize that balancing press freedom with privacy is difficult, but we'd like to see the activities of the media overseen by a properly independent body, with the help of effective deterrents and sanctions. Individual journalists should be accountable for what they write. In medicine, healthcare professionals have to take responsibility for their actions and repeat offenders are struck off to prevent them from ruining more lives. Why should journalism be any different?

At the time of writing, it has been five years since we last saw our daughter. She will now be nine years old. It is scary how time marches on. Madeleine has been in my head and my heart every minute of every day of those five years. As the weeks roll by, the months roll by, sometimes, as I'm swept along by life, I start to think about little Madeleine, as she was, and about what's happened, and then BOOM, it hits me – that uncomfortable, restless sensation, that heavy ache in my chest, the constriction in my throat. If ever I begin to worry that maybe I'm 'getting used' to life as it is now, I can guarantee that unmistakable feeling will be just around the corner, waiting to ambush me.

I hold on to the fact that we, and the search, are in a better position than we have been in a long while. We have a lot to be grateful for and good reason to be hopeful. A police review of Madeleine's case is underway, and we didn't have that a year ago. Our own capable and experienced team remains on standby, ready to respond if and when it is needed. And we still have immense support from people all over the world. The hundreds and hundreds of cards, Masses, gifts and flowers that came our way again on our fifth Christmas without Madeleine are testament to that.

In December Amelie asked me: 'Are we going to have a good Christmas, Mummy?'

'Yes, we are.'

'Even without Madeleine?'

'Yes, Amelie, we're still going to have a really good Christmas.'

And we did. Gerry and I were able to embrace the festivities and ensure that at the very least, Sean and Amelie had a Christmas full of fun and love. My New Year's resolution for 2012 was not only to remain positive, but to try to be *more* positive. It is a tremendous help to know that at last those stones are being turned.

One day I want to be able to write a closing chapter to this book. Until then, please don't give up on Madeleine.

If you have any information which may be related to her disappearance, please share it with us. We need you. Please contact: Metropolitan Police Service, Homicide and Serious

Crime Command – Operation Grange and/or the Find Madeleine team via www.findmadeleine.com, or call 0044 (0)845 838 4699.

Alternatively, speak to a religious leader in your community.

If you know what has happened to Madeleine or where she is now, for her sake and ours, please open your heart and let us know. It is *never* too late to do the right thing.

KEY SIGHTINGS

Five years on, as we strive to piece together the puzzle of what happened to Madeleine, many questions remain unanswered and several people who may be able to help us have yet to be identified.

The following sightings are still of great interest to us. Explaining them is very important to our continuing investigation, if only to eliminate the individuals concerned from our inquiry. Artists' impressions and sketches based on the descriptions given by witnesses can be found on the final two pages of the illustration section of this book.

SIGHTINGS ONE AND TWO

Witness One: Jane Tanner
Witness Two: Holidaymaker from Ireland

These two crucial sightings of a man carrying a child in the street, made around the time of Madeleine's abduction on the night of 3 May 2007, have been discussed in detail in this book.

The description of the man seen by Jane Tanner was eventually made public three weeks after Madeleine's disappearance and an artist's impression commissioned by our own investigative team was released in October 2007. Yet to this day no man has come forward to identify himself as the father, relative or family friend of the child in either case.

Although the police appear to have considered these sightings to be unrelated on the basis of the forty-five-minute gap between them, the similarities speak for themselves.

Artist's impressions of the man seen by Jane Tanner are reproduced on the last page of illustrations.

	Witness One sighting	Witness Two sighting
Date and time of sighting	3 May 2007; 9.15pm approximately	3 May 2007; 10pm approximately
Location	Rua Dr Agostinho da Silva, Praia da Luz	Rua da Escola Primária, Praia da Luz
Age of man	35–40	34–35
Height of man	About 5ft 10ins/1.78m (recorded incorrectly in statement as 1.7m)	1.75–1.8m (5ft 9ins–5ft 10ins)
Hair	Thick, dark, slightly longer at back of neck	Short, brown
Clothing	Beige or gold trousers wide and straight, chino-style; dark jacket	Cream or beige trousers; classic cut

Other	Carrying child across arms at front of chest; child's head to the left of man's chest	Carrying child over arms with child's head towards left shoulder
	Walking hurriedly	Did not carry child in a comfortable way
	Not felt to be a tourist because of the clothing worn	Not felt to be a tourist because of the clothing worn
Age of child	Young child, not a baby; assumed to be female because of clothing	Approximately four years; female; medium-blonde hair; pale skin, typically British
Clothing of child	Pale pink and/or white pyjamas with floral pattern	Light-coloured pyjamas
Other	Barefoot	Witness unsure (family members say child was barefoot)
	No blanket or covering	No blanket or covering

SIGHTINGS THREE TO EIGHT

It was only from the police files, to which we were given access in August 2008, fifteen months after Madeleine's abduction, that we learned of six sightings by four independent witnesses in the five days prior to her disappearance. A 'suspicious' male had been noticed watching our apartment and/or acting oddly nearby. In three of these reports a man was seen standing by the small car park directly opposite the entrance to the Ocean Club's swimming pool and Tapas restaurant (Ocean Club Waterside Gardens) on Rua Dr Francisco Gentil Martins. In two accounts, a 'suspicious' man was observed on the access path between the Ocean Club apartments (which include apartment 5A) and the pool and Tapas restaurant area.

Witness Three

This witness is a young girl whose grandparents used to own apartment 5A. As this flat is familiar and of interest to her, her report is very precise and credible. She saw the same individual watching our apartment closely on two separate days. On Monday, 30 April 2007, at around 8am, she noticed a man standing on the narrow access path running between the apartments and the pool and Tapas restaurant area. He was leaning with his palms against the wall surrounding the garden area of apartment 5A and looking up at the veranda.

On Wednesday, 2 May 2007, the witness saw the same man near the car park opposite the entrance to the pool and Tapas restaurant area on Rua Dr Gentil Martins. He appeared to be just standing there and watching apartment 5A.

Description: Caucasian male; light-skinned; 1.8m (5ft 11ins) tall; slim build; aged 30–35; short cropped hair, thought to be light in colour. He had spots and was 'ugly, disgusting even'.

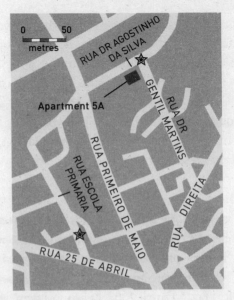

⭐ indicates the locations of the sightings described in this section.

Clothing: Thin, black leather jacket; light T-shirt; jeans with belt; trainers; dark, thick-framed sunglasses.
Portrait: Sketch number 1 on the penultimate page of pictures.

Witness Four

On Sunday, 29 April 2007, between 8 and 9am, this witness noticed a man loitering on Rua do Ramelhete whose appearance unnerved her. Three days later, in mid-afternoon on Wednesday 2 May, the witness saw the same man on Rua Dr Gentil Martins, on the opposite side of the road to apartment 5A, near the car park across from the entrance to the Ocean Club's pool and Tapas restaurant area. The witness said that the man was standing still and looking over in the direction of apartment 5A.

Description: Male of Portuguese appearance; approximately 5ft 10ins (1.78m) tall; slim build; 'very ugly – pitted skin with a large nose'.
Clothing: Casual; jeans.
Portrait: Sketch number 2 on the penultimate page of pictures.

Witness Five

This witness was walking down Rua Dr Francisco Gentil Martins with his partner around lunchtime on either Wednesday 2 May or Thursday 3 May 2007. They passed a man who was standing by the wall near the car park opposite the entrance to the Ocean Club's swimming pool and Tapas restaurant. The witness followed the man's line of sight and reported that he was 'staring fixedly' at an area close to our apartment block, where a white van was parked.

Description: Caucasian male with dark skin; assumed to be Portuguese and not a tourist; aged 25–35; 1.7–1.75m (5ft 7ins–5ft 9ins) tall; medium build; short, thick, dark hair reaching collar-level at the back.
Clothing: Plain light-coloured T-shirt.
Portrait: Sketch number 3 on the penultimate page of pictures.

Witness Six

On 3 May 2007, this witness was standing on the veranda of a first-floor apartment in the same block as 5A, overlooking the pool and Tapas restaurant area. Some time between 4pm and 5pm, she noticed a man coming out through one of the little gates leading from the terraces of the ground-floor apartments to the access path. His behaviour struck the witness as suspicious: he appeared to be trying to close the gate quietly, using both hands, and very slowly and deliberately checking in both directions before walking to the end of the pathway and on to Rua Dr Gentil Martins. The witness thought this was the first gate along the pathway from the road. If her recollection is correct, it was the gate to apartment 5B, where our friends Matt and Rachael were staying. That afternoon, Rachael, Matt and their daughter were on the beach at Praia da Luz with the rest of our friends. They were away from the Ocean Club complex from before 3pm until 6pm.

Description: Caucasian male; fair-skinned, assumed not to be Portuguese; aged 30–40; medium height; medium–slim build; very fair, cropped hair.
Clothing: Pale T-shirt.
Portrait: Sketch number 4 on the penultimate page of pictures.

In terms of both timing and location, these reports are highly relevant to the investigation into Madeleine's abduction. While the individual concerned may not be the same in all cases, there are certainly common characteristics to suggest that some of these sightings, if not all, could be related.

We believe that identifying these individuals could bring us much closer to finding Madeleine.

If you can help, please contact Metropolitan Police Service, Homicide and Serious Crime Command – Operation Grange and/or the Find Madeleine Team via www.findmadeleine.com, or call 0044(0)845 838 4699.

MISSING, ABDUCTED AND EXPLOITED CHILDREN: DID YOU KNOW?

The available statistics on missing, abducted and exploited children, nationally and worldwide, are patchy and incomplete. This is a problem readily acknowledged by those working in the field and it tells its own story. Without more extensive research and comprehensive figures, it is very difficult to identify and implement the necessary measures to safeguard children.

Although the situation is improving in some countries, there is still a long way to go. Many of the statistics below relate to findings in the UK and the USA. This does not mean that crimes against children are more prevalent in these countries, simply that these are among the countries where most research has been undertaken, leading to a better understanding of the issues. In fact, if anything, these countries are likely to become, or may already be, safer for children as a result.

There is a great deal the figures don't tell us and many

474

come with caveats, but I hope the examples recorded here will at least provide an indication of the scale of crimes affecting children, and of the success of properly functioning child rescue alert systems.

Missing Children

More than 200,000 reports of missing children and teenagers were received by UK Police during the year 2009–10.

NPIA Missing Persons: Data & Analysis 2009–10

Approximately three-quarters of missing persons return or are located within twenty-four hours of their disappearance.

NPIA 2010

In the USA, one in seven missing children is found as a direct result of somebody simply recognizing their face on a poster or flyer and notifying law enforcement. 97 per cent are located using a variety of efforts in addition to photograph distribution.

NCMEC

Abductions

An average of 600 cases per year of child abduction, or attempted abduction, have been recorded in England and Wales for the period 2005–6 to 2009–10.

UK Home Office Crime Statistics

The majority of completed child abductions are parental/family abductions, with 16 per cent involving abduction by a stranger.

G. Newiss and L. Fairbrother: Child Abduction: Understanding Police Recorded Crime Statistics, Findings paper 225 (Home Office, London, 2004)

The majority of abducted children are not taken to be killed, and murder in these circumstances is a rare event: an estimated 100 incidents occur in the USA each year. Of those victims who are murdered, over 70 per cent are dead within the first three hours.

> Katherine M. Brown, Robert D. Keppel, Joseph G. Weis and Marvin E. Skeen: *Case Management for Missing Children Homicide Investigation* (Office of the Attorney General and US Department of Justice, Olympia, Washington, May 2006)

There are approximately 115 cases of 'stereotypical' (stranger) kidnapping per year in the USA. 40 per cent of these victims are killed, 4 per cent not found and 56 per cent recovered alive.

> Andrea J. Sedlak, David Finkelhor, Heather Hammer and Dana J. Schultz: *NISMART 2 – National Estimates of Missing Children: An Overview* (US Department of Justice, October 2002)

In the US, by January 2012, 554 abducted children had been safely recovered as a direct result of an AMBER Alert activation since the programme's inception.

> NCMEC

For the period 2005–9, in those cases where an AMBER Alert had been activated, 79 per cent of children were recovered within 72 hours.

> NCMEC

By May 2011, Alerte Enlèvement, the child alert rescue system in France, had been launched ten times (for eleven children – one alert involved two children) since its inception in February 2006. Ten of these children were found alive.

In Greece, between May 2007 and May 2011, AMBER Alert Hellas had been activated fifteen times, for sixteen children, and thirteen of these children were recovered alive.

Child exploitation

Sex offenders are among the most consistent re-offenders and travel around to avoid conviction. Only three of the twenty-seven EU member states have functioning sex-offender registers – UK, Ireland and France.

In 2000 and 2001, of the arrests made in the US in connection with possession of images of child abuse, 39 per cent of the images involved children between the ages of three and five. 19 per cent involved children under three.

NCMEC

The World Health Organisation estimates that 150 million girls and 73 million boys under eighteen experienced forced sexual intercourse or other forms of sexual violence during 2002.

Office of the United Nations High Commissioner for Human Rights (http://www2.ohchr.org/english/bodies/crc/study.htm)

Mexico's social service agency reports that there are more than 16,000 children engaged in prostitution. Tourist destinations are among the areas with the highest number.

UNICEF
(http://www.unicef.org/protection/index_exploitation.html)

In Lithuania, 20 to 50 per cent of prostitutes are believed to be minors. It is known that some are as young as eleven. Children from children's homes, some aged ten to twelve years old, have been used to make pornographic films.

UNICEF

(http://www.unicef.org/protection/index_exploitation.html)

The Inhope 2007 Global Internet Trend Report states that during the last quarter of 2006, the number of 'processed reports about child pornography' stood at approximately 9,600 per month.

In 2001, the CyberTipline operated by NCMEC had received more than 24,400 reports of child pornography. By the beginning of 2006, that number had climbed to more than 340,000 and by 2010 to over 990,000.

The Internet Watch Foundation reports that many children seen being sexually abused in images broadcast on the internet are very young. Many are subjected to severe levels of abuse.

72 per cent of the victims appear to be between the ages of birth and ten. 23 per cent are six years old or under. 3 per cent are two or under.

44 per cent of images depict the rape or torture of the child.

IWF Annual and Charity report 2009

European hotline number for Missing Children: 116 000
International Missing Children's Day: 25 May

ACKNOWLEDGEMENTS

Writing this book has been emotional and exhausting. I hope and pray it helps us to find Madeleine and to uncover the truth.

Despite my 'stubbornness' (I still prefer to call it determination) and finishing ability, I'm not sure I would have had enough energy to complete it if it hadn't been for the invaluable help and support I've had along the way. In fact, I doubt it very much.

My editor, Caroline North, has been incredibly understanding, patient and perceptive. I'm aware that her role has involved a bit of a crash course in learning about our life since Madeleine was taken from us – possibly not the most pleasant experience. In spite of that, Caroline has worked tirelessly to guide and encourage me through the process and thankfully we've also managed to share quite a few laughs along the way. I am confident our friendship will not end here.

It was evident to Gerry and me on our first encounter with Bill Scott-Kerr, Sally Gaminara, Janine Giovanni and

Alison Barrow from Transworld that they immediately saw the bigger picture. This wasn't just about raising money for Madeleine's Fund, it was about finding her. And they genuinely wanted to help. The effort they have put into this campaign is confirmation of that. I don't think we could have asked for more from a publisher.

We originally met Neil Blair, then of the Christopher Little Literary Agency, in early 2008. At that stage, I couldn't have entertained the idea of writing a book. It didn't feel right and I simply wasn't strong enough. Once I did make the decision to share our story, I knew exactly where to take it. The warmth and professionalism shown from the start by Neil, and by Christopher Little, have made the whole experience much more bearable.

Our family and friends have continued to be a wonderful support and have rallied to our aid on numerous occasions, allowing me to lock myself away for long periods at my computer to get the job done. Maybe I'll actually get to have a cuppa and a conversation with them now.

Not only had I never expected to get to know so many lawyers, I didn't expect to like quite so many of them. Ed Smethurst, Adam Tudor, Isabel Hudson and Isabel Duarte in particular have laboured faithfully out of the goodness of their hearts, on Madeleine's behalf and ours, regardless of the day or the hour. Their priceless expertise and commitment has extended to the completion of this book. Cláudia Nogueira, formerly of LIFT Consulting, has also been a vital source of knowledge and advice and a very good friend.

There are two special people who have not been mentioned by name in these pages, but whose support and companionship have been unfailing. One is our lovely Portuguese friend from Luz. She has helped us in countless ways, including with this book, since we first met her on 11 August 2007: the hundredth day since Madeleine was taken from us. I will not name her as I'd hate to draw unnecessary intrusion into her life but I want to pay tribute here to her kindness and courage. It will never be forgotten. *Beijinhos, a minha amiga.*

And Emma Loach. Emma is one of the most selfless people I have ever come across and her input on so many levels has been invaluable. She played a significant role in our campaign for a child rescue alert system across Europe and in 2009 worked with us to produce a filmed re-construction of the events surrounding Madeleine's abduction. She has also responded willingly to my many queries and requests for an opinion on my writing. Even more importantly, she has helped me through the darkest and most unfathomable times over the four years I have known her. Our friendship is precious to me and I thank God that she walked into our life.

Although she is an integral part of my story, I couldn't overlook acknowledging my dear friend Fiona. She has been at my side since Madeleine was taken. While coping with her own grief, she has kept me afloat with her love, encouragement and strength-restoring hugs, as well as providing endless practical help. Gerry and I considered Fi and Dave special friends before 3 May 2007. Now we understand just how special they are.

Many of the people who have helped our family and our search for Madeleine over the last five years appear in this story. There are many more who do not, but we are no less indebted to them. I could have written a whole book about the thousands and thousands of others, in the UK, in Portugal and around the world, whose assistance and empathy have meant so much to us. I hope I have managed to convey in these pages the positive effect of such kindness and inspiration on both Gerry and me, and on our efforts to find Madeleine, along with our eternal gratitude. Indirectly, these people have all contributed to this book, too, by playing their part in buoying up my wellbeing and resilience.

Finally, I would like to thank my husband, Gerry – for his love, support and companionship. We've been in this together throughout and always will be. And, of course, dear Amelie and Sean, my amazing little rocks.

PICTURE CREDITS

Every effort has been made to trace copyright holders and to obtain their permission for the use of copyright material both inside the book and on the cover. The publisher apologizes for any errors or omissions and would be grateful to be notified of any corrections that should be incorporated in future reprints or editions.

INDEX

INDEX

Madeleine McCann was abducted in Praia da Luz, Portugal on Thursday, 3 May 2007. Kate and Gerry McCann established 'Madeleine's Fund: Leaving No Stone Unturned' in response to the many generous donations that started to flood in from the general public who were wanting to help the search for their daughter in some way. As there had been no police force in the world actively looking for Madeleine since July 2008, the fund enabled a small team of committed and experienced people to investigate Madeleine's disappearance. It continues to support the search and also runs awareness campaigns in several countries, to ensure the public know that Madeleine is still missing, and to encourage them to remain vigilant.

Once Madeleine is found, the fund will be used to assist searches for other missing children worldwide.

'It is a sad fact that for over three and half years not a single police force was looking for Madeleine. The launch of Kate's book with the support of the British public has re-energized the search – the Metropolitan police are now carrying out an investigative review of Madeleine's case following a request from the prime minister. This is a major step forward for us and Madeleine. Our daughter and whoever took her are still out there. Someone knows where. We still need your help to find them.'

Gerry McCann, April 2012